Valuation and Valuation Planning for Closely Held Businesses

Frank M. Burke, Jr.

Certified Public Accountant
Partner—Peat, Marwick, Mitchell & Co.

Prentice-Hall, Inc.
Englewood Cliffs, N.J.

Prentice-Hall International, Inc., *London*
Prentice-Hall of Australia, Pty. Ltd., *Sydney*
Prentice-Hall of Canada, Ltd., *Toronto*
Prentice-Hall of India Private Ltd., *New Delhi*
Prentice-Hall of Japan, Inc., *Tokyo*
Prentice-Hall of Southeast Asia Pte., Ltd., *Singapore*
Whitehall Books, Ltd., *Wellington, New Zealand*

© 1981, by

PRENTICE-HALL, INC.
Englewood Cliffs, N. J.

Library of Congress Cataloging in Publication Data

Burke, Frank M
  Valuation and valuation planning for closely
held businesses.

  Bibliography: p.
  Includes index.
  1. Close corporations — Valuation — United
States. 2. Close corporations — Taxation —
United States. I. Title.
KF6491.B87   343.7306'7   80-24585
ISBN 0-13-940007-9

Printed in the United States of America

Dedication

To Tyler, Todd, and Caroline

About the Author

Frank M. Burke, Jr., has been associated with the Dallas office of Peat, Marwick, Mitchell & Co. for more than two decades. He is Chairman of the Energy and Natural Resources Practice and a member of the firm's Board of Directors. In addition, he serves as the firm's Liaison Tax Partner for Energy. Prior to assuming his present post, Mr. Burke was Partner-in-Charge of Peat, Marwick, Mitchell's Dallas office's Tax Department for seven years.

Mr. Burke is a co-author of two books, *Income Taxation of Natural Resources* and *Federal Income Taxes—Research and Planning*, both published by Prentice-Hall, and he has written numerous articles for financial, legal, and accounting journals.

A member of the American Institute of Certified Public Accountants, the author has served on the Division of Taxation's Subcommittee on Statements of Responsibilities in Tax Practice. He is a member of the Texas Society of Certified Public Accountants and has been affiliated with several universities. He holds an M.B.A. Degree from Texas Tech University and a J.D. Degree from Southern Methodist University.

What This Guide Will Do for Closely Held Businesses

One of the most perplexing and difficult tasks in the life of a closely held business is determination of the value of such business or an interest in such business. Because of the complexity of today's business environment, it has become increasingly necessary to know the value of a business interest at different stages in the life of the enterprise. Such valuation may be needed internally when considering means of expanding or contracting business operations, or externally to meet the needs (whether tax or otherwise) of an owner. Additionally, valuation of a closely held business is needed to deal effectively with certain day-to-day problems of operating a business, e.g. value for borrowing purposes, value for insurance purposes, and the like. While the focus of this book will be on valuations for federal income and transfer (gift and estate) tax purposes, the principles developed herein should be equally applicable in other situations requiring the determination of the fair market value of a closely held business or interest therein.

Most valuation publications deal solely with valuing stock of closely held corporations. Equally important, however, is valuation of interests in other forms of closely held businesses, including sole proprietorships, partnerships, joint ventures, associations, and other noncorporate entities. This book will address valuation not only of closely held stock but also of other types of business interests. Many of the factors, methods, and techniques used in valuing closely held corporate stock apply with equal weight to valuation of other closely held business interests. However, little judicial precedent is available to assist in valuing noncorporate interests. As a consequence, guidance must be sought from stock valuation cases to overcome this problem. Accordingly, the bulk of the material in this book will deal with valuing a closely held corporation or an interest therein. Where appropriate, the utility of such material in valuing other closely held business interests will be mentioned.

Valuation of a closely held business is speculative. Consistently, a disparity will exist between the Internal Revenue Service and a taxpayer when a closely held business is valued for tax purposes. The cornerstone of the Internal Revenue Service's position when valuing closely held businesses is found in a 1959 Revenue Ruling. This ruling, still valid today, has been refined and expanded upon by the courts over the years. This book synthesizes those interpretations and presents an up-to-date analysis of the state of the art of valuing closely held businesses. Additionally, this book includes 20 practical, hypothetical cases that depict various steps and considerations in the valuation process. These cases are designed to assist the reader in applying the principles proffered to practical aspects of a valuation endeavor.

This book will guide anyone desiring to value a closely held business through the valuation process in the following ways:

- Chapter 1 provides an overview of fair market value as it applies to a closely held business. This understanding is basic to determining a defensible value of a closely held business.

- Chapter 2 examines valuation concepts as expressed in authoritative Internal Revenue Service guidelines. This discussion gives the reader an idea as to factors relied upon by the Internal Revenue Service in determining the value of a closely held business.

- Chapter 3 analyzes broad environmental considerations to be examined and considered at the onset of a valuation endeavor. These factors chart the course of the valuation process.

- Chapter 4 pinpoints approaches to valuation depending upon how a company is categorized by the Internal Revenue Service. Generally, a business to be valued will fall into one of two categories. Categorization of a business can significantly affect the valuation process.

- Chapter 5 deals with the impact a representative sale or exchange of a different closely held ownership interest within the same company will have on the valuation of a closely held business interest.

- Chapter 6 evaluates the common practice of utilization of comparable companies in the valuation process. Comparable companies generally consist of publicly traded corporations that have a readily determinable value. The use of this practice can weigh heavily on justifying a value before the Internal Revenue Service.

- Chapter 7 examines in detail the role of intrinsic factors in the valuation process. These factors relate to a value determination based upon attributes unique to the company to be valued.

- Chapter 8 shows how to determine the significance of the interest to be valued to the destiny of a business. Ability to control the destiny of the business can result in a higher value.

- Chapter 9 examines discount factors that apply in almost all situations. These discounts are recognized by the Internal Revenue Service and the courts.

- Chapter 10 analyzes the weight given to expert testimony by the courts and presents questions that can be asked of experts to substantiate and establish a value.

- Chapter 11 spells out the valuation approach to be utilized for preferred stock of a closely held corporation. The unique rules and guidelines that apply to valuation of preferred stock will be reviewed.

- Chapter 12 describes special situations unique to the business to be valued. These circumstances are usually beyond the general control of the entity or its owners. Examples of unique situations will be illustrated and their impact on value explored.

- Chapter 13 shows how, by planning ahead, the valuation process can be less of a burden. Additionally, transfer and income taxes can be avoided. This chapter discusses overall considerations in implementing valuation planning techniques.

- Chapter 14 describes how the value of ownership rights in a closely held business can be "frozen" by using various value freezing techniques. Utilization of these methods not only avoids a complicated value determination at a later date, but is also effective in minimizing tax incidence.

- Chapter 15 shows how, by shifting ownership rights within a closely held business framework, transfer taxes can be significantly diminished. Also, the closely held status of the business can be preserved. These positive aspects of shifting ownership will aid any closely held business owner in achieving his or her goal of less taxes and continuation of the family business.

The appendices that follow the chapters contain a reprint of excerpts from the Internal Revenue Service's *Appeals Officer Valuation Training Program* coursebook. This manual illustrates the Service's approach to valuing a closely held business. This manual is very beneficial in understanding the approach, method, and conclusions the Internal Revenue Service utilizes in valuation situations. Comprehensive examples are included in the manual.

The appendices also contain important Internal Revenue Service promulgations in the valuation area. Additionally, significant valuation cases are summarized. A checklist, as well as a list of sources to consult, is also given to assist the reader in specific valuation endeavors.

Frank M. Burke, Jr.

Acknowledgments

Without the valuable assistance of William R. Allbright, who spent substantially all of his first year in public accounting bringing together information from our files and preparing the final draft of the text, the timely completion of this book would not have been possible.

Mark L. Starcher also assisted in the completion of the book after Mr. Allbright entered law school.

The technical review by my partner, B. A. Parker, and the overall review of the proposed content by my partner, J. S. Smith, were invaluable aids to the planning, preparation, and completion of this book.

In addition, all of us who participated in the preparation of the book would like to acknowledge the patient assistance of LeAnn S. Thieme in typing the many drafts necessary to complete the manuscript.

Contents

Contents   **17**

Valuing a Closely Held Business for Maximum Benefit

FAIR MARKET VALUE

On many occasions and for various reasons, federal and state courts have been confronted with the difficult task of determining the fair market value of a closely held business or an interest therein. In recent years, much of such litigation has involved federal income and transfer (gift and estate) tax matters. These cases will be the primary sources of authority for the principles developed in this book. Nevertheless, such principles should be equally applicable in other areas when valuing closely held businesses or interests therein.

When valuing closely held businesses for purposes of federal transfer or income taxation, as in other valuation situations, the goal of the parties is to determine the proper fair market value. Fair market value has been defined by the courts as "the price at which property would change hands in a transaction between a willing buyer and a willing seller, neither being under compulsion to buy nor sell and both being reasonably informed as to all relevant facts."[1] This definition is well accepted in the area of federal taxation.[2]

The courts have also used this same general definition in other areas which require the determination of fair market value. In *Olson* v. *United States*,[3] the Supreme Court was confronted with the question of just compensation in a condemnation award. The Court held that such award should be equal to the fair market value of the property taken. This value was determined by the Court as "the amount (that) in all probability would have been arrived at by fair negotiations between an owner willing to sell and a purchaser desiring to buy."[4]

State courts have frequently applied the federal tax definition of fair market value in the valuation of property for ad valorem tax purposes, when the tax base is the fair market value of such property, or a proportion thereof.[5]

Based upon the foregoing, it appears that a common thread runs through the judicial interpretations of the term "fair market value" in various tax areas. The similarity in the approaches to valuation is not mere chance. There is strong evidence that the courts intend for the principles of valuation to be applied uniformly across the broad spectrum of valuation controversies, rather than inconsistently between the various areas.

Inherent in the definition of fair market value is the willing buyer-willing seller concept. Obviously, the best indicator of such concept is the open market where buyers and sellers communicate with one another and where exchanges take place. A lack of such a market for closely held business interests compels the need for a valuation process.

The Internal Revenue Code of 1954[6] treats fair market value in various sections throughout the Code.[7] It is interesting to note, however, that under the Income Tax Regulations it is stated that "fair market value of property is a question of fact, but only in rare and extraordinary cases will property be considered to have no fair market value."[8] As will be seen in the following chapters, the determination of fair market value is truly a factual determination having no absolute rules or guidelines. Each case includes a multiplicity of factors, the composition of which is unlike that in any other case.

DEFINITIONS—CLOSELY HELD BUSINESS INTEREST

As was stated in the introduction, the term "closely held business" is generally thought of as including primarily closely held corporations. However, the term also includes partnerships, sole proprietorships, joint ventures, associations, and other noncorporate entities. These ownership forms are usually represented by intangible instruments which allow the right of participation in the operation of a closely held business. These intangible instruments may be shares of stock in a closely held corporation, a partnership agreement if the business is a partnership,[9] or they may be nothing more than a permit or license to do business if a sole proprietorship. In the case of closely held corporations, a value is attached to the individual shares of stock. The collective values of the corporation's shares generally represent the value of the entity. With respect to valuing other types of business entities, imaginary shares can be created based on percentages of ownership, and then a value would be attached to the nonexistent shares. Again, the aggregate of the values of such nonexistent shares should generally equal the value of the entity. Obviously, many factors will cause the value of an individual owner's interest to be increased or decreased because of discounts or premiums. Accordingly, care should be taken to eliminate such discounts or premiums before including the value of each interest in the aggregate value of the entire entity.

The litigation and administrative pronouncements dealing with closely held corporate stock valuation make the term "closely held corporation" worthy of closer examination. If the attributes of a closely held corporation are understood, application of these attributes to other closely held business interests becomes clear. "Closely held corporation" has been defined as "a corporation with few shareholders whose stock is rarely traded and unlisted on any exchange."[10] It has also been defined by the Internal Revenue Service as "a corporation whose market quotations are either unavailable or of such scarcity that they do not reflect the fair market value."[11] Further, it has been defined as "a corporation . . . the shares of which are owned by a relatively limited number of stockholders. Often the entire stock issue is held by one family."[12] A business entity operating in other than a corporate form would similarly be classified as "closely held" if owned by a small group of persons.

CLOSELY HELD BUSINESS FAIR MARKET VALUE

The remainder of this book will be devoted to connecting the term "fair market value" with the closely held business concept. This approach will be based on tax planning concepts that benefit the owner when a valuation undertaking becomes necessary. The techniques discussed in this book will be blended with the principles and practice utilized by the Internal Revenue Service in valuing closely held businesses.

Three primary valuation premises surface once a basic understanding of valuation factors is obtained. First, representative sales or exchanges of other ownership interests within the business to be valued provide a good benchmark in determining the value of an interest within that same entity. Second, publicly traded corporate stock quotes provide a parallel value figure for a closely held business if the public company is reasonably similar to the business, or an interest therein, that is to be valued. Third, intrinsic factors inherent in each business to be valued provide excellent indicators of the overall value of a particular business. Once the three methods mentioned above are understood, an examination of discounts and premiums applicable to a specific interest to be valued will be discussed.

Additionally, the utilization of experts in substantiating a value will be addressed. Preferred stock considerations, as well as special situations in the valuation process, will round out the valuation approach portion of the text. It is at this point that the most important aspect of the valuation process will come into play.

The last three chapters will be devoted to analyzing and examining various planning methods available within a closely held business that 1) facilitate a valuation undertaking when it becomes necessary in the future, and 2) reduce transfer (gift and estate) and income taxes. A brief overview will initially be given to set the stage for the value planning that is available. Next, techniques that achieve a value freeze so that the value 1) will not vary with changes in the business environment over time in the hands of a designated owner, 2) will increase in the hands of a party that can absorb the value increase, and 3) can be readily determined at any particular point in time, will be examined. This discussion will center around restrictive agreements, recapitalizations (both corporate and partnership), and formation of a personal holding company for federal income tax purposes. Finally, the value planning discussion will focus on methods available to a closely held business that shift ownership rights, with a minimum of transfer tax, to a younger family member. These tools operate to preserve the closely held status of the business and are effective in reducing transfer taxes, both during life and at death. The techniques that will be discussed include gift programs, installment sales, trusts, and annuities. Although many of the methods discussed in the final chapters are appropriately considered to be sophisticated estate planning techniques, their place in valuation planning within a closely held business is quite necessary in reducing potential tax burdens.

NOTES FOR CHAPTER 1

1. O'Malley v. Ames, 197 F.2d 256, 257 (8th Cir. 1952). See also Gordon, *What is Fair Market Value?*, 8 Tax Law Rev. 35 (1952).

2. See, for example, Estate of Fitts v. Commissioner, 237 F.2d 729, 731 (8th Cir. 1956); Estate of Singer v. Shaughnessy, 198 F.2d 178, 181 (2nd Cir. 1952); and Reg. Sec. 20.2031-1(b), where the definition of fair market value is given for estate purposes. See also Hamm v. Commissioner, 325 F.2d 934, 937 (8th Cir. 1963), cert. denied 377 U.S. 993 (1964), quoting O'Malley v. Ames, note 1 supra. The definition is also given under Gift Tax Reg. Sec. 25.2512-1 relating to valuation of gifts, and Income Tax Reg. Sec. 1.170A-1(c)(2) as applied to charitable contributions. As applied to partnership operation and partner taxable income, see Helvering v. Walbridge, 70 F.2d 683 (2nd Cir. 1934), cert. denied, 293 U.S. 594 (1934). The term has also been used for determination of appropriateness of taxes imposed upon gains made from the sale of burial space. Montrose Cemetery v. Commissioner, 105 F.2d 238 (7th Cir. 1939). In United States v. Parker, 376 F.2d 402, 408 (5th Cir. 1967), the Court stated "(v)alue is not a strange or alien concept in tax law, and we have held that 'There is no distinction, for most purposes***, in the meaning of fair market value as used in an estate tax case and one involving income tax' Champion v. Commissioner, 303 F.2d 887, 892–893(sic) (5th Cir. 1962)." Palmer v. Commissioner, 523 F.2d 1308 (8th Cir. 1975) applied the definition of fair market value in determination of the inflated value of donated stock. See also Bankers Trust Company v. United States, 518 F.2d 1210 (Ct. Cl. 1975), cert. denied 424 U.S. 966 (1976), citing Jack Daniel Distillery v. United States, 379 F.2d 569 (Ct. Cl. 1967).

3. 292 U.S. 246 (1934).

4. Ibid. at 247.

5. Ozette R. Co. v. Grays Harbor County, 133 P.2d 983 (1943); Glen Alden Coal Co. v. Schuylkill County Commissioners, 27 A.2d 239 (1942); State ex rel. Hennessey v. City of Milwaukee, 6 N.W.2d 718 (1943).

6. All subsequent references to "Section" or "Sections" hereinafter refer to a Section or Sections of the Internal Revenue Code (as amended), unless otherwise indicated.

7. The term "fair market value" is used 173 times in the Code.

8. Reg. Sec. 1.1001(a).

9. Or may have partnership attributes even though no formal agreement exists. See Larson v. Commissioner, 66 T.C. 159 (1976).

10. F. Hodge O'Neal, *Close Corporations: Law and Practice,* Vol. 1, Chapter 1, p. 2, Section 1.03.

11. Rev. Rul. 59–60, 1959-1 C.B. 237, Section 1.

12. Ibid., Section 2.

Successful Tax Valuation Approaches

ALTERNATIVE VALUATION CONCEPTS

In the realm of valuation concepts, there are several overall pervasive alternatives which may be utilized depending upon the facts and circumstances of the particular situation. Different theories may apply in different factual situations. Further, a combination of theories may apply in a given situation to arrive at an overall value.

One commonly cited theory is based on the premise that the entity should be valued as if it were completely liquidated on the date of valuation.[1] Similarly, some theorists believe that an entity should be valued as if a third party purchased the company on the valuation date and immediately sold the assets.[2] Another theory is that the entity should be valued as an operating business at an amount equal to the going concern value. The difference between the going concern value and the liquidating value represents the value of the organization versus the value of the assets.[3] Some experts feel that a closely held business should be valued through comparisons with similar publicly held corporations.[4] Finally, some valuation theorists espouse the replacement cost theory under which there is an entrance value attached to the company representing the cost of creating the entity in the present market.[5]

All of these theories are utilized in one form or another in the valuation process. As indicated above, the facts will, in the end, dictate the proper theory or combination of theories to be utilized in each case. Accordingly, there is no one "proper" valuation theory to be applied in all instances.

REVENUE RULINGS

The Internal Revenue Service has issued several Revenue Rulings which provide guidance in valuation cases. These Revenue Rulings have shown a narrowing and refining of the Service's position as to valuation techniques and approaches. These rulings provide an excellent set of general standards which can be utilized in most valuation situations, whether for tax purposes or otherwise.

Revenue Ruling 54–77[6] was the Service's initial attempt to formulate a general outline of approaches, methods, and factors to be used in valuing the closely held corporation. Revenue Ruling 54–77 was subsequently superseded by Revenue Ruling 59–60,[7] which is the present authoritative ruling on the subject (see full text in Appendix B). Revenue Ruling 59–60 gives an outline of approach methods and factors for valuing shares of closely held corporate stock for transfer tax purposes. Revenue Ruling 65–192[8] made Revenue Ruling 59–60 applicable for income and other tax purposes. Revenue Ruling 65–192 also expanded Revenue Ruling 59–60 and made it apply to problems involving determination of fair market value of business interests of any type, including partnerships, proprietorships, and the like, and of intangible assets for all other tax purposes.[9] This ruling provides the connecting link for application of Revenue Ruling 59–60 to other closely held business interests. The Service realized that the factors used in valuing closely held corporations can, many times, be used to value other closely held business interests.

REVENUE RULING 59–60

As was stated earlier, Revenue Ruling 59–60 is the primary tax authority for valuing the stock of closely held business interests. Revenue Ruling 59–60 sets forth the premise that valuation is a question of fact dependent upon the circumstances. Since valuation is a prophesy into the future, it is an exercise of judgment and all available financial data and relevant factors need to be taken into consideration.[10] The specific value factors that Revenue Ruling 59–60 sets forth are as follows:

(a) the nature of the business and the history of the enterprise from its inception;

(b) the economic outlook in general and the condition and outlook of the specific industry in particular;

(c) the book value of the stock and the financial condition of the business;

(d) the earning capacity of the company;

(e) the dividend-paying capacity;

(f) whether or not the enterprise has goodwill or other intangible value;

(g) sales of stock and the size of the block of stock to be valued; and

(h) the market price of stocks of corporations engaged in the same or a similar line of business having their stock actively traded in a free and open market, either on an exchange or over-the-counter.[11]

The above represents an excellent listing of relevant valuation factors. Further, Revenue Ruling 59–60 represents a clear and concise statement of the relevant issues in valuing closely held business interests. It has drawn together significant factors and standards that 1) valuation experts have used over the years, 2) investors have used in making investment decisions, and 3) courts have relied on in deciding particular values. It is, however, merely a framework on which to build when valuing a closely held entity. A significant amount of judgment is still utilized in the valuation process.

The following chapters will expand on the basic factors of Revenue Ruling 59–60 and show exactly how a value is determined for an interest in a closely held business. Treatment and development of these factors by the courts will also be shown as will other influential matters to consider when determining values.

NOTES FOR CHAPTER 2

1. Weston and Brigham, *Managerial Finance*, 5th ed., 1975, p. 537.

2. Bosland, *Valuation Theories and Decisions of the Securities Exchange Commission,* Simmons-Boardman Publishing Company, New York, 1964, pp. 1–2.

3. Weston, note 1 supra.

4. Rustigan, Lentz, and Olsen, *Problems in Valuing Stock of a Close Corporation: A Panel Discussion,* N.Y.U. 1965 Fed. Tax. Inst. 1261.

5. Bosland, note 2 supra.

6. 1954-1 C.B. 187.

7. 1959-1 C.B. 237. (See Appendix B.)

8. 1965-2 C.B. 259. (See Appendix B.)

9. Revenue Ruling 65–193, 1965-2 C.B. 370 (see Appendix B) subsequently deleted an ambiguous portion of Revenue Ruling 59–60 dealing with the valuation of intangibles. Revenue Ruling 68–609, 1968-2 C.B. 327 (see Appendix B) stated that the usage of a formula approach (capitalization of anticipated earnings in excess of return on tangible assets) for determination of fair market value of intangible assets should not be used if there is better evidence available from which the value of intangibles can be determined.

10. Rev. Rul. 59–60, 1959-1 C.B. 237, Sec. 3.

11. Ibid.

3

Initial Valuation Factors to Consider

Before dealing with the more specific factors used in the valuation process, the peripheral considerations or factors having a bearing on the business to be valued must be considered. These peripheral factors pertain not only to the economic environment of the business, but also to the entity as a functioning body within such environment. The nature of the business, as well as its history, must be examined prior to a comprehensive study of the factors unique to the enterprise. This chapter will discuss considerations having underlying implications in any valuation endeavor.

NATURE OF THE BUSINESS

The nature of the business should be one of the first facts considered in the valuation process. The valuation of a business entity must be based upon the characteristics of the enterprise within its specific industry. For example, the valuation of a real estate company would require collection of information regarding the value of the property held by the company, the number and type of property leases held, comparative share of the market in commercial and/or residential property, the competitive climate of the real estate market where the property is held, and the overall economic environment in general and in the company's location specifically. On the other hand, the valuation of a magazine company would require data such as the number of subscriptions, advertising market and circulation strata both for the company and for the industry, and various other factors affecting the publication industry. The products or services offered by the business should be considered, as well as its operating and/or investment assets. The capital structure, physical facilities, and management quality should also be given consideration when valuing the business.[1] Microeconomic considerations in relation to the business being valued should be ascertained and analyzed. A broadly based understanding of the business increases the effectiveness of a value given to an entity or an interest therein.

HISTORY OF THE ENTERPRISE

Valuation of an entity should consider the growth and development of a business over the years prior to the valuation date. The volume of business, acquisitions or mergers, and development of processes or products are all important influences on the value of an enterprise. The history of the company "will show its past stability or instability, its growth or lack of growth, the diversity or lack of diversity of its operations, and other facts needed to form an opinion of the degree of risk involved in the business."[2]

A list of shareholders or owners and their proportionate interest in the business should be collected. The constructive ownership relationships by, between, or among owners should be determined so that the effect thereof on the valuation of various interests can be ascertained.[3] The objective is to be well-informed about the subject company and its past, present, and future capabilities. By examining the road the entity has traveled, one can better understand its course for the future. This understanding allows a stop along such road for valuation purposes to be dealt with effectively.

ECONOMIC ENVIRONMENT

The economic environment in which the entity operates must also be given proper consideration. Both the national economy and the economy of the industry in which the entity operates should be examined to determine the overall impact on valuation. Basic economic theories, such as supply and demand, prove that excessive profits due to the uniqueness of a product will increase the competition in such market. This could have a significant bearing upon the valuation of a business otherwise appearing to have a high value. Realistic and practical considerations command that a macroeconomic viewpoint be used for periods prior to and subsequent to the valuation date. Ignoring past and future economic considerations makes a meaningful valuation impossible.[4]

In narrowing the peripheral factors, an industry survey will show the relative position of the closely held business in its industry. A detailed analysis of the industry will lend substantial authoritative support to the ultimate value. Commercial publications, such as *Moody's Manual of Investments, Standard and Poor's Industry Surveys, The Wall Street Journal, Barron's Weekly,* and the like, should be freely consulted. Likewise, the United States Department of Commerce industry studies and studies by nonprofit organizations, such as Harvard Business School, provide an excellent source of information pertaining to economic and industry characteristics.

STATE STATUTORY GUIDANCE

State statutes and administrative authority may provide substantive guidance in the valuation direction of a closely held business. Particularly, statutes pertaining to the formation and operation of closely held corporations may enumerate criteria that will determine, inter alia, what constitutes a majority or minority interest.[5] State statutes may also contain standards frequently used for various state valuation needs.[6] Likewise, state taxing authorities may have directives pertaining to the valuation of closely held business interests.

NOTES FOR CHAPTER 3

1. Rev. Rul. 59–60, 1959-1 C.B. 237, Sec. 4.02(a).

2. Ibid.

3. Ibid., Sections 267 and 318.

4. In Estate of Wolfe v. Commissioner, 1954 P-H TC Memo ¶54,023, the prospects of a future beneficial zoning change affected the value of a tract of real estate. In Estate of Kimball v. Commissioner, 1946 P-H TC Memo ¶46,268, the unforeseeable length of time that abnormally high war profits would continue lowered the value of a manufacturing corporation.

5. See, for example, Florida—Fla. Stats. Ann. Sections 608.70–608.77; Delaware—Del. Code Ann. Tit. 8, Sections 341–356; Maryland—Md. Ann. Code Art. 23, Sections 100–111; Pennsylvania—Pa. Stats. Ann. Tit. 8, Subchapter XIV; New York—N.Y. Bus. Corp. Law Section 616 et seq.; Maine—Maine Bus. Corp. Act. Me. Rev. Stats. Ann., Tit. 13-A, Section 102(5) (1973); Texas—Tex. Bus. Corp. Act Art. 230-1 et seq. (1974 Supp.); Michigan—Mich. Bus. Corp. Act, MSA Section 21.200 (101 et seq.).

6. See Note, *Legal Standards of Fairness of Merger Terms Under Delaware Law*, 2 Delaware J. of Corp. L. (1977); Note, *Valuation of Dissenters' Stock Under Appraisal Statutes*, 79 Harvard L. Rev. 1453 (1966); and Lyons and Whitman, *Valuing Closely Held Corporations*, Business Lawyer, Vol. 33, July 1978, p. 2213.

4

Operating Company
vs. Holding Company:
Two Different Approaches

For valuation purposes, closely held businesses can generally be classified into two broad types: 1) an operating company, or 2) a holding company. The first of these types, the operating company, is an entity which is engaged in the manufacturing of products, the providing of services, or otherwise engaged in the active conduct of a business. The second classification, the holding or investment company, is an entity normally considered to be engaged in the passive retention and collection of assets. A holding company usually has the principal function of holding title to real estate, securities, or other assets generally for a small group of owners for the purpose of earning income therefrom.[1]

Techniques and methods used for valuing these two types of entities vary considerably. Section 5 of Revenue Ruling 59–60[2] specifies that primary consideration should be accorded to earnings when valuing the stocks of operating companies. Conversely, the greatest weight should be given to the value of the underlying assets when valuing the stock of a holding or investment company. The courts generally agree with this overall approach. The courts also recognize, however, that it is erroneous to rely exclusively on one valuation criterion to the exclusion of other relevant criteria.[3] Accordingly, some peculiar factual situations may require the use of valuation techniques contrary to the general rules.

OPERATING COMPANY STATUS

In most well-established operating companies, liquidation of the company's assets is a highly unlikely event. The continuance of the enterprise into the indefinite future is clearly indicated when 1) a company displays steady growth patterns and its activities have expanded over the years, 2) the business has a niche in the industry in which it operates, and 3) the company has far-reaching plans and substantial commitments for future operations. In a 1934 Supreme Court case, the Court indicated that to give liquidation value more than token weight in the valuation of a vigorous operating company is mere speculation. The Court stated that an event such as complete liquidation, while within the realm of possibility, is not reasonably probable and should be excluded from valuation consideration. To do otherwise allows for conjecture to become a guide for the ascertainment of value, a thing condemned in business transactions.[4] The theory espoused by the Supreme Court in 1934 is equally sound in today's valuation endeavors but has been somewhat mitigated when dealing with majority interest holders. The differentiation between what constitutes a majority interest and a minority interest is discussed in Chapter 8 of this book. Suffice it to say at this point that a majority interest holder would have the power to liquidate the closely held business, whereas a minority holder would not.

There may be instances in valuing an operating company where the valuation will involve a block of stock, or a percentage of ownership, which has the power to completely liquidate the business and obtain the assets. A district court was confronted with this controversy involving the estate tax valuation of a 95 percent interest in a corporation which owned a motel and a restaurant. The district court determined that valuation should take into account the liquidation value of the business since the economic conditions surrounding the valuation date would have permitted the corporation to easily liquidate. An incremental increase in value greater than that which otherwise would have been used for an operating company was made to reflect this power to liquidate.[5] The facts of the case dictated heavy reliance on liquidating value even though the company was considered to be an operating company.

Clearly, when a minority interest which has no power to liquidate the entity is being considered, the value of underlying assets of the entity is of little consequence. Accordingly, the general rule when valuing a minority interest holder in an operating company is that the company's earnings power will be given primary consideration and liquidation values generally should not be given significant weight. When dealing with the valuation of a majority interest in an operating company, if the facts at the valuation date indicate that liquidation was in fact a possibility and that the controlling block would consider such action, then liquidation value should also be considered but should not be controlling unless liquidation is actually contemplated.

Techniques and methods that will frequently be used when valuing an operating company involve the intrinsic factors, as specified in Chapter 7 of this text. Likewise, comparative corporate analysis (see Chapter 6) may be utilized. *Case One—Hutch Corporation* provides a simple determination of value of a minority interest holder when the company to be valued is an operating company.

CASE ONE

Valuation of an Operating Company

HUTCH CORPORATION

Facts

Miss Pako owns 100 shares in Hutch Corporation by virtue of a gift made to her from Mr. Hutch several years ago. Hutch Corporation (HC) is a closely held corporation engaging in the production and sale of various home renovation fixtures (i.e., ready-built bookshelves, lights, doors, cabinets, etc.). Mr. Hutch has contracted to sell his business to Dixon Renovations, Inc. Mr. Hutch and Dixon's Board of Directors agreed that HC will be valued as of July 31, 1981, under an intrinsic valuation method (see Chapter 7) giving significant weight to the earnings potential of HC. Mr. Hutch desires to compute the value per share of HC so that he can inform Miss Pako of the value of her minority interest.

HC's financial statements, in pertinent part, reveal the following information:

Total number of shares issued, outstanding (9900 held by Mr. Hutch and 100 held by Miss Pako)	10,000
Annual dividends per share	$ 3
Total assets	$ 776,500
Total liabilities	$ 400,000
Stockholders' equity	$ 376,500
Average weighted net income after tax over last five years	$ 45,000

Comparable corporate analysis (explained in Chapter 6 of this book) reveals the following ratios for comparable publicly traded corporations:

Price-earnings ratio	9:1
Dividend yield	12%

Mr. Hutch and Dixon's board members are in agreement that earnings should be weighted 50 percent, dividend capacity 25 percent, and book value 25 percent. No other discounts or premiums are to apply to the value determined under the agreed intrinsic valuation method.

Value

The determination of the value of each share of stock would be as follows:

I. Earnings

(a) Earnings per share	$ 4.50	
(b) Comparable price-earnings ratio	× 9	
(c) Adjusted "earnings per share" value of single share	$ 40.50	
(d) Weight attributed to earnings	50%	
(e) Share value attributed to earnings		$ 20.25

II. Dividends

(a) Annual dividend per share	$ 3.00	
(b) Comparative dividend yield	12%	
(c) Adjusted "dividend" value of single share	$ 25.00	
(d) Weight attributed to dividends	.25	
(e) Share value attributed to dividends		6.25

III. Book Value

(a) Book value* per share	$ 37.65	
(b) Weight attributed to book value	.25	
(c) Share value attributed to book value		9.41
Total intrinsic value per share		$ 35.91

* ($776,500 — $400,000 = $376,500 ÷ 10,000 = $37.65)

Analysis

The value determined in this fact situation represents an agreed value deemed to be adequate to compensate the owner for his interest. Other factors obviously need to be considered in other situations.

HOLDING COMPANY STATUS

The primary consideration when valuing a holding or investment company is the fair market value of the underlying assets of the entity to be valued. A holding or investment company is generally characterized as a company that does not engage in an active business. The courts recognize the general valuation premise that the value of the underlying assets is demonstrative of the value of a holding or investment company. In *William Hamm*,[6] the Tax Court was faced with establishing the value of a closely held company which 1) held and managed real properties, 2) held the stock of subsidiaries and interests in oil and gas properties, and 3) received rents, dividends, and other income from other investments. The court held that a determination of the value of the stock based solely on consideration of its current earnings failed to give adequate effect to the value of properties held by the corporation. This basic rationale is followed in the majority of holding or investment company valuations.

Early cases dealing with the valuation of holding companies discredited heavy reliance on the underlying asset value. In a 1936 case, the Third Circuit determined that the valuation method used by the Internal Revenue Service and the Board of Tax Appeals, which was based solely on the value of the underlying assets, was arbitrary since the method gave no consideration to the earnings and dividend capacity of the stock of the investment company.[7] A 1939 Delaware District Court decision agreed with the Third Circuit when it ruled that the valuation of the stock of an investment company based entirely on the value of the underlying assets was erroneous. The court in that case determined the value of the stock primarily by capitalizing earnings.[8] The recent trend, however, gives primary attention to the value of the underlying assets.[9]

The determination of value of a holding company involves computation of the net asset value by using fair market value amounts versus historical cost data. It is necessary to make adjustments to the financial statements of a closely held business to give effect to current values. The justification for the usage of fair market value of the underlying assets is that the investing public applies the necessary weight to earnings and dividends of the underlying assets which have a ready market.

Case Two — Key Investment Corporation provides a simplified example of the necessary steps to determine the value of a closely held investment type corporation.

CASE TWO

Holding Company

KEY INVESTMENT CORPORATION

Facts

Mr. Key is the single shareholder (15,000 shares outstanding) in Key Investment Corporation (KIC), a holding company set up by Mr. Key for his own personal tax benefit. Mr. Key is concerned that his personal term life insurance is inadequate to cover his potential transfer tax liability in the event of his untimely death. Mr. Key desires to keep his estate intact for the benefit of his family members.

Also, Mr. Key is considering setting up trusts for his children and wants to know the value of each share of KIC in order to determine a range of shares to place into trust. The assets of KIC are as follows:

	Cost	Fair market value
Parker Company stock	$ 120,000	$ 200,000
Kaiser Oil Limited partnership	35,000	40,000
Reed Manufacturing Corporation stock	75,000	110,000
Ronald municipal bond	8,000	10,000
Donald County property	102,000	90,000
	$ 340,000	$ 450,000

Value

Since the investments have been adjusted to reflect the fair market value, the adjusted net asset value would be:

Fair value of assets	$ 450,000
Divided by shares outstanding	÷ 15,000
Value per share	$ 30

Analysis

Due to the nature of the investments held by the corporation, a discount is generally applied to reflect the corporate layer of insulation which reduces the outright marketability of such assets by Mr. Key. (See Chapter 14 for a discussion of personal holding companies and their role in the valuation process.) Although the $30 value may be discounted, if the assets are projected to increase in value during the period of insurance coverage these factors may be counterbalancing. It may be to Mr. Key's advantage to insure himself for the full fair market value of the investments. His trust considerations can now be analyzed using the $30 per share value discounted as appropriate for the fact that the assets are held in corporate solution and further discounted for the minority status of the shares which would be transferred into trust (assuming, of course, that control is not transferred). See Chapter 8 for a discussion of valuation of minority interests.

COMBINED OPERATING AND HOLDING COMPANIES

As indicated above, once a business is classified in either of the two categories of entities (operating or holding), substantial authority exists to guide the taxpayer in establishing fair market value of a closely held business interest. However, in some cases controversies may exist as to the true character of the entity or as to what factor primarily accords value to the business, where the entity is an operating company owning valuable assets or is a holding company in control of operating companies. In the former situation, it appears that when the ownership interest in an operating company which holds substantial investment assets must be valued, the courts usually consider the operations separately from the investments.[10] This also applies, to some degree, to the later situation. However, the holding company status will generally act as a discount to a value computed under the earnings (or intrinsic) method.[11] This concept is elaborated on in Chapter 14. Valuation of a diverse closely held business is discussed in more detail in Chapter 12, which deals with special situations.

NOTES FOR CHAPTER 4

1. See Note, *The Estate and Gift Tax Valuation of Closely Held Holding Company Stock,* 50 Va. L. Rev. 337 (1964).

2. 1959-1 C.B. 237.

3. Schlegel v. United States, 71 F. Supp. 495 (D.C. N.Y. 1947), aff'd 164 F.2d 276 (2nd Cir. 1947); Cochran v. Commissioner, 1948 P-H TC Memo. ¶48,094.

4. Olson v. United States, 292 U.S. 246 (1934).

5. Wallace v. United States, 31 AFTR 2d 73-1395 (S.D. W. Va. 1973).

6. 1961 P-H TC Memo¶61,347.

7. Laird v. Commissioner, 85 F.2d 598 (3rd Cir. 1936).

8. Du Pont v. Deputy, 26 F. Supp. 773 (D.C. Del. 1939).

9. Richardson v. Commissioner, 151 F.2d 102 (2nd Cir. 1945), cert. denied 326 U.S. 796 (1945).

10. Estate of Hayes v. Commissioner, 1973 P-H TC Memo ¶73,236; Schlegel v. United States, note 3 supra; Gallun v. Commissioner, 1974 P-H TC Memo¶74,284.

11. This is reflected in the form of a lack of marketability discount. Chapter 9, infra. See Whittemore v. Fitzpatrick, 127 F. Supp. 710 (Conn. 1954), and Commissioner v. Hirshon Trust, 213 F.2d 523 (2nd Cir. 1954), cert. denied, 348 U.S. 861 (1955).

5

Use of Representative Sales
or Exchanges

One of the first items to consider when valuing a closely held business interest is whether or not a comparable bona fide sales transaction has taken place and whether such transaction is representative of the fair market value of the interest to be valued. Even though control may be closely held, there may exist some type of "market" activity for the ownership rights in a closely held business. On occasion, a truly comparable sale will exist which minimizes or eliminates the need for the entire theoretical valuation process. The courts, however, look carefully at value contentions relying on single or multiple sales of similar closely held interests at or around the valuation date.

An examination of the case law in which representative sales have been used in the valuation process provides little conclusive guidance. Over 20 years ago, the general attitude was that "(i)n determining the value of unlisted stocks, actual sales made in reasonable amounts at arm's length, in the normal course of business, within a reasonable time before or after the basic date, is the best criterion of market value."[1] More recently, the courts have appeared to take a paradoxical attitude. If a contemporaneous sale exists, the courts view such sale with disdain, seeking (and usually finding) a flaw. On the other hand, if no representative sale exists, the courts have been quick to wish for one upon which to rely. This inconsistency may, in part, be attributed to the lack of any easily defined criteria for evaluating comparable sales, thereby substantiating the premise that "(a) determination of fair market value, being a question of fact, will depend upon the circumstances in each case."[2]

41

During the initial examination of the entity to be valued, it should be determined if:

(1) there is any indication that a contemporaneous sale occurred;

(2) such transaction, if any, was at arm's length; and

(3) the parties to such transaction had full knowledge of the conditions surrounding the transaction.

If such questions are answered in the affirmative, then the appraiser has a good value basis upon which to build. Even if all of the above three elements are not present, a starting point for the valuation process has been established.

SALE BEFORE OR AFTER THE VALUATION DATE

The market in which sales occur before or after the valuation date must be examined. Such market should generally be free from abnormal influences or pressures and be truly representative of a willing buyer and willing seller negotiating for a sales price at arm's length.[3]

In *Estate of Lillian May Schroeder,*[4] the Tax Court took an extreme position when it ruled that a sale of the subject stock several months after the valuation date was the sole indicator of the fair market value on such value date. The court rejected the government's valuation, which was computed by taking the value of actively traded securities held by the subject investment company, adding a value for certain patent rights, deducting outstanding liabilities, and dividing by the number of outstanding shares. The Tax Court held that the actual sale was more representative of what a willing buyer would pay to a willing seller than other available factors. Along similar lines, a sale of stock 11 months prior to the valuation date and a sale 15 months after the valuation date were held to be indicative of the fair market value.[5] Also, the sale of stock three months before the valuation date was held by the Tax Court to be significant enough to be a fair approximation of the fair market value on the valuation date.[6]

The general rule for use in representative sales is that the closer the sale is to the valuation date, the greater the weight the sale will receive. The amount of weight a representative sale will receive depends largely upon the change in the financial condition of the subject company during the intervening period between the valuation date and the representative sales date.[7] Sales over two years from the valuation date have been held comparable in instances where there was no material change in the financial condition of the company.[8]

Case Three—Slickerson Corporation parallels the fact situation confronted by the Tax Court in *Estate of Lillian May Schroeder.* In that case, the court determined that a sale of stock several months after the value date was the fair market value of the stock to be valued.

CASE THREE

Sale of Stock After Valuation Date

SLICKERSON CORPORATION

Facts

Omar Sprivens held 750 shares (out of 10,000 shares of capital stock out-standing) of the Slickerson Corporation (SC) at the time of his death on February 15, 1981. All of the stock is closely held and is not listed on any securities exchange or traded in the over-the-counter market. SC derives its income from royalties on patents, interest, dividends, and gains on sales of securities listed on the New York Stock Exchange. Pertinent financial information is as follows:

Fair market value of securities held in portfolio	$ 625,000
Patents at cost, less depreciation	$ 50,000
Outstanding liabilities	$ 200,000

The only sale of shares of the capital stock of SC in the past ten years was the sale by an estate of 100 shares to Travis Shelty, the company's president, for $25 per share. It is necessary to determine the value of the 750 shares owned by Omar Sprivens in SC as of February 15, 1981, for estate tax purposes.

Value

Contended by taxpayer	$ 25
Contended by government	$ 50
Determined by the Tax Court	$ 25

The Commissioner contended that the value for estate purposes of the 750 shares is $50 per share. The Commissioner valued the patents at $75,000. The $50 per share figure is computed as follows:

Fair market value of portfolio	$ 625,000
Fair market value of patents	75,000
Outstanding liabilities	(200,000)
Value attributed to Owner's Equity	$ 500,000
Shares outstanding	÷ 10,000
Value per share	$ 50

The Commissioner's value represented a liquidating value under ideal circumstances and without costs. It is not representative of the fair market value. Under the similar facts in *Schroeder,* the fair market value of the shares was held to be $25 with the court observing that: ". . . we think this (representative sales) figure more nearly represents what a willing buyer would pay a willing seller than the figure determined by the (Internal Revenue Service)."*

Analysis

In most instances, the value determined by a representative sale will provide a base upon which the ultimate value figure will be built. It is rare when a sale before or after the valuation is the exact indicator of the value needed. All factors must be considered, and such additional factors will affect the impact of the representative sale on the ultimate value.

---

*Estate of Lillian May Schroeder v. Commissioner, 13 T.C. 259, 263 (1949).

SIZE OF THE REPRESENTATIVE SALE

Obviously, the closer the representative sale size (shares of stock, percentage interest, etc.) is to the interest to be valued, the more credible is the representative sale value. The Tax Court has held, in *Estate of Vandenhoeck*,[9] that sales of small lots of stock in an inactive market are not indicative of fair market value of a larger block. On a comparative basis, if the size of the interest sold is within a reasonable range of the size of the interest to be valued, and the market conditions have remained substantially the same, then a representative sale should provide the needed indication of value, provided the original sale was a bona fide sale. Those sales not being truly representative of an arm's length transaction would require analysis under the following section.

NON-ARM'S LENGTH—PRIVATE TRANSACTIONS

Sales of business interests among family members subsequent or prior to the valuation date have a lesser bearing on the determination of fair market value than do other representative sales.[10] The preferential treatment generally given family members in intrafamily transactions creates a non-arm's length implication even though the substance of a bona fide sale may be present. The implication that a "donative" intention is involved in many intrafamily transactions has been recognized by the courts.[11]

Surprisingly enough, sales of business interests between or among so-called "corporate insiders" before or after the valuation date may be considered fairly reliable for determination of a relevant value range. The reasoning is that insiders generally 1) are well-informed of the true status of the entity, 2) have a better understanding of the worth of the business, and 3) have negotiated in a "willing seller-willing buyer" environment. The sales price of the interest sold when corporate insiders are involved must, however, be closely examined to make sure no additional consideration is involved (e.g., performance of services or other forms of disguised payments). Sales between insiders of business interests as exact measures of fair market value have been met with varied approval by the courts. One case held that insider sales were true indicators of the fair market value needed. (See *Case Four—Estate of E. W. Hunt.*[12]) Other cases have given insider sales little specific weight in pinpointing a value.[13]

A representative sale may receive more weight if the Internal Revenue Service has accepted (or failed to contest) the value used in such sale. If, for instance, shares were sold wherein the taxpayer had significant long-term capital gains, and such gains were not contested or disallowed upon audit of the taxpayer's return, then the value has withstood Internal Revenue Service scrutiny. The courts have recognized that this prior consideration is of probative value in the solution of the valuation problem.[14]

CASE FOUR

Inside Sales

ESTATE OF E. W. HUNT*

Facts

At his date of death, March 17, 1944, E. W. Hunt owned 199 shares of the capital stock of the First National Bank of Olney, Texas. The authorized issued and outstanding capital stock consisted of 500 shares. This stock was not listed on any stock exchange. From January 7, 1941, to January 15, 1945, there had been five sales of this stock, as follows:

Date of sale	Shares sold	Price per share
January 7, 1941	10	$ 400
January 11, 1941	10	400
January 14, 1941	10	400
March 31, 1944	20	400
January 15, 1945	10	400

The sale of the 20 shares on March 31, 1944, was by the bank's vice-president to a director of the bank. The vice-president had obtained employment in a bank in Abilene, Texas, and informed the director that his stock in the Olney Bank was for sale. The price of $400 was agreed upon and paid. The shares had been purchased by the vice-president in 1935 for $300 per share, when its book value was $337.62 a share.

In 1945, Viola Hunt, wife of the deceased, sold 10 shares of the bank stock to the bank's cashier, for a consideration of $400 per share.

The invested capital of the bank at the beginning of the year, net profits after

---

*11 TC 984 (1948). Adopted from the court's statement of facts and opinion thereof.

income taxes paid, and dividends paid for the years 1939 through 1943, were as follows:

Year	Invested capital at beginning of year	Net profits after income taxes paid	Dividends per share
1939	$ 195,855	$ 29,449	$ 38
1940	$ 206,294	$ 30,268	$ 38
1941	$ 218,697	$ 29,981	$ 38
1942	$ 230,192	$ 23,646	$ 38
1943	$ 234,114	$ 24,393	$ 38
Average	$ 217,030	$ 27,547	$ 38

The book value per share of the stock was as follows:

Date		Book value
December 31, 1940	$	437.39
December 31, 1941	$	460.39
December 31, 1942	$	469.07
December 31, 1943	$	479.56

It is necessary to determine the value of the 199 shares held by E. W. Hunt on his date of death, March 17, 1944, for transfer tax purposes.

Value

Contended by taxpayer	$ 400
Contended by government	$ 600
Determined by the court	$ 400

The notice of deficiency contained a statement by the Internal Revenue Service that the entire value of the 199 shares was $119,400, or $600 per share. Although no information is given as to how the Service computed its value, it appears that with the consistent dividend payment of $38 per year, an industry yield of 6.3 percent would produce a $600 per share value. Working backwards, the value of $600 would be as follows:

Annual dividend	$ 38
Industry dividend yield	÷6.3 %
Internal Revenue Service value	$ 600

The Tax Court did not agree with the Internal Revenue Service and in pertinent part stated:

"All the sales with which the period deals from 1941 to 1945 give this stock a market value of $400 per share. Within a few days after the death of E. W. Hunt, . . . the stock, which had been consistently selling for $400 a share, again sold for $400 per share, although there is substantial testimony that its market value was probably less at that time than it had been prior to the death of E. W. Hunt.

"The Commissioner contends that this value is less than the book value and less than its dividend-paying record and the financial records of the bank would justify. In view of the fact that there was a sale of twenty shares of this stock within a few days after E. W. Hunt's death from the vice-president of the bank to a director of the bank, both of whom were informed as to the value of the stock and neither of whom was under any compulsion to sell, and that there is no evidence that the vendor in that transaction had any purpose to make a gift to the vendee, we feel that $400 per share represents the true market value of the stock on that date. Also, on January 15, 1945, Viola Hunt herself sold ten shares of this stock at $400, which is convincing evidence that such a value correctly reflects the market value of this stock."*

Analysis

In today's valuation determinations, the $400 figure would provide a good starting point for the ultimate value needed. The sale of stock a few days after the value date provides a good "willing buyer-willing seller" transaction and would tend to substantiate a value in the $400 range, depending, of course, on the impact of other relevant data.

---

*Estate of E. W. Hunt v. Commissioner, 11 T.C. 984, 992 (1948).

SUMMARY

As can be seen from the foregoing, some weight should be given to representative transactions occurring before or after the valuation date. The amount of weight afforded such representative sales will depend upon the following elements:

(1) the proximity of the sale to the valuation date;

(2) the amount of disparity between the number of shares sold and the number of shares to be valued;

(3) the motives surrounding the sale, other than to determine a fair price; and

(4) the amount of intervening change in the financial condition of the business and environment from the sale date to the value date.

These conditions determine the degree of reliance which should be placed on representative sales.

NOTES FOR CHAPTER 5

1. Estate of Fitts v. Commissioner, 237 F.2d 729 (8th Cir. 1956).

2. Rev. Rul. 59–60, 1959-1 C.B. 237, Sec. 3.01.

3. Generally, see Walter v. Duffy, 287 F. 41 (3rd. Cir. 1923).

4. 13 T.C. 259 (1949), acq. 1949-2 C.B. 3.

5. First Trust Company v. United States, 3 AFTR 2d 1726 (W.D. Mo. 1958).

6. Estate of Katz v. Commissioner, 1968 P-H TC Memo ¶68,171.

7. See, generally, Julius G. Day, 3 B.T.A. 942 (1926), Reynolds v. United States, 338 F.2d 1 (2nd Cir. 1964), cert. denied 380 U.S. 977 (1965).

8. Louis v. United States, 369 F.2d 263 (7th Cir. 1966).

9. 4 T.C. 125 (1944).

10. True v. United States, 51 F. Supp. 720 (D.C. Wash. 1943), but cf. Estate of Kaye v. Commissioner, 1973 P-H TC Memo ¶73,270.

11. Kinney's Estate v. Commissioner, 80 F.2d 568 (9th Cir. 1935).

12. 11 T.C. 984 (1948), acq. 1949-1 C.B. 2.

13. Penn v. Commissioner, 1952 P-H TC Memo ¶52,243, aff'd 219 F.2d 18 (9th Cir. 1955); Wood v. United States, 29 F.Supp. 853 (Ct. Cls. 1939); Hansen v. Commissioner, 1952 P-H TC Memo ¶52,236.

14. See Righter v. United States, 439 F.2d 1204 (Ct. Cl. 1971), wherein evidence was introduced that the Internal Revenue Service had accepted valuation figures in other estates involving the same stock within several years prior to the value date.

6

Comparable Companies:
Prime Tool in the Valuation Process

The use of comparable publicly held corporations as a guide to valuation has appeared with frequency over the past several years and, as a practical matter, may be the most important and appropriate technique for valuing a privately held operating business. Obviously, finding a business *exactly* the same as the enterprise to be valued is an impossibility. The standard sought is usually one of reasonable and justifiable similarity. This degree of likeness is attainable in most cases.

Revenue Ruling 59–60[1] endorses the use of corporations engaged in the same or similar lines of business, having their stock actively traded in a free and open market, either listed on an exchange or over the counter. When neither selling prices nor bid and asked prices are available for shares of stock, the Income Tax Regulations, dealing with transfer tax valuation at death, include as a relevant factor comparison with similar companies listed on an exchange.[2] If hypothetical shares are created for valuing a noncorporate closely held business interest, a value would be assigned to that particular interest. This approach to valuing a noncorporate interest would then involve essentially the same techniques as valuing a closely held corporation, except that a different approach is used and some adjustments may be required.

The research required in identifying comparable companies is time consuming. The process requires computation of ratios, review of various sources of financial information, and substantial judgment when weighing information collected to determine its relevance. It is not as vital that statistics be developed and reviewed as it is that every possible approach be explored and either be accepted or rejected. Developing raw numbers is one thing, but applying statistics to an entity in order to arrive at a fair market value requires a thorough knowledge of the particular company, its industry, and the overall economy.

It is recognized that the use of "listed" corporations as comparable companies when valuing a closely held business cannot yield exact fair market value measures, since the risk factor involved in investing in an actively traded corporation is less than that of purchasing the shares of a company for which there is no ready market. The purpose of comparative analysis, however, is to arrive at a "relevant range" for valuation. Appropriate risk factors are then utilized to give recognition to the lack of a ready market. (See Chapter 9 of this book.)

The courts have provided guidelines for determining comparability. Although the more obvious guidelines are financial in nature, there are several considerations which reach beyond the statistics a company generates. These considerations will be dealt with prior to a discussion of the financial analysis necessary to identify comparable companies.

NONFINANCIAL ASPECTS

The Tax Court, in *Cecilia A. Tallichet*,[3] enumerated several items which should be considered in the search for comparable companies. Those items listed in *Tallichet* to be considered when searching for comparable companies include:

(1) capital structure,

(2) independent audit opinion status,

(3) depth of management,

(4) personnel experience,

(5) nature of competition, and

(6) business maturity.

These traits should parallel each other for the entity to be valued and for the comparable company or companies. Since exact matching is impossible, it must be kept in mind that reasonable similarity is being sought.

Depending upon the nature of the business to be valued, other factors will also need to be considered. Some of these would include the number and size of retail outlets, sales volume, product mix, territory of operations, and competitive standing. Clearly, the list of items to consider could go on ad infinitum. However, the list must be tailored to fit each individual case. The items set forth above are not intended to be comprehensive, but are designed to provide a general range of attributes which should be considered.

SOURCES OF FINANCIAL INFORMATION

In order to obtain an accurate analysis of comparable companies, several financial sources must be consulted. The various financial services listed below can usually be found at public libraries or at college and university libraries. Many times, college and university finance classes for business majors will require students to perform financial analysis on a selected industry or business line as a term project. Likewise, graduate studies at these institutions may involve similar analytical projects. Contact with professors at these schools may provide a shortcut, or at least an aid, to the financial information gathering process. Also, local investment companies normally have financial information on hand for their use and are willing to provide this data if requested.

Standard and Poor's compile various financial statistics relating to publicly held corporations which provide a good synopsis of potential comparable companies. Their "Corporate Record" and "Stock Guide" should be utilized in the search for comparable companies.

Dun and Bradstreet provide financial material relating to industry averages, based upon financial statements of companies. Dun and Bradstreet provide statistics for 125 lines of businesses, consisting of 71 manufacturing and construction categories, 30 categories of wholesalers, and 24 categories of retailers. This data gives significant financial ratios that will aid in the search for comparable companies.

Robert Morris Associates publishes *Statement Studies* annually, consisting of averages obtained from financial statements received by bank loan officers. These studies consist of 11 ratios and are for approximately 156 different lines of businesses.

The Dow Jones Financial Service also publishes additional financial information and reports that should be consulted. Likewise, Standard Research Consultants compile periodic reports that should aid in the determination of financial ratios and other financial information.

Various publications, such as the *Journal of Finance, Journal of Finance and Quantitative Analysis, Financial Management, Financial Analyst Journal,* and *Journal of Business,* provide additional sources of financial studies. The Securities and Exchange Commission (SEC) and the Federal Trade Commission likewise publish quarterly data concerning manufacturing companies. These reports are broken down into different areas, such as industry groups, asset-size, and financial statements in ratio form. If the entity to be valued is large enough, the *Fortune 500* provides an additional excellent source of information.

Individual publicly held corporations' annual reports should also be consulted. These reports are made available upon request from each of the individual companies. Once the search for comparable companies has narrowed the choices to a select few, more specific financial and nonfinancial information should be obtained. Reports filed by publicly held corporations with the SEC should be requested and obtained from the corporations.[4] These reports not only provide additional information not otherwise available, but they also provide excellent documentation when arriving at a value range.

CAVEATS TO FINANCIAL RELIANCE—COMPARABLE CORPORATIONS

In the valuation process there are items which make a company noncomparable, although on the surface the company may appear to possess similar attributes to the one being valued. One of the primary differences lies in the methods of accounting for similar business activities. In many cases, alternatives exist for the reporting and disclosure of financial information which make otherwise seemingly comparative information deceptive. The possible divergent treatment of expenditures, depreciation, income recognition, and other accounting items makes a thorough analysis imperative, and, in many cases, difficult. Quite frequently, the accounting data has been developed using methods different from those employed by the business to be valued. The notes to individual financial statements issued by a publicly held corporation should be reviewed carefully in order to ascertain the differences in accounting policies and methods which may exist. Adjustments may be needed (where the necessary information is available) in order to obtain comparable data.

ADJUSTMENTS DEPENDING ON THE ENTITY TO BE VALUED

Chapter 1 addressed the various closely held business forms which may require valuation. These entities include sole proprietorships, partnerships, joint ventures, and corporations. When using comparative corporate analysis, adjustments to the financial information of the business to be valued, if noncorporate, may be necessary due to differences in the entities' accounting procedures. As an example, in valuing a partnership, adjustments to the partnership earnings may be necessary to reflect salary expenditures, taxes, and similar items which have been deducted in computing ratios and pertinent data for a comparable publicly traded corporation. Similar types of adjustments may be necessary for other closely held business forms in order to achieve a proper degree of relationship between the business to be valued and publicly traded corporations.

FINANCIAL CONSIDERATIONS

In order to compare the business being valued, relevant financial data and ratios must be developed. In order for a company to be considered comparable, it should possess reasonably similar sales, net worth, dividends, net income, assets, and other meaningful financial characteristics. The amounts obviously do not need to be the same but should be within a relevant range.

There are several ratios which are considered significant in determining the degree of comparability between companies. The computation of these ratios provides information which will not only be useful when comparing publicly held companies, but also will provide a good analysis of the financial condition of the company to be valued. The strength, or lack thereof, of the subject company's financial condition will have a bearing on its ultimate value. As these computations are being made, it should be remembered that this analysis has a twofold purpose: 1) to provide numeric measurements necessary to identify comparable companies, and 2) to determine the posture of the entity to be valued within its industry and to comparable companies. These ratios should be used in addition to the above specific financial attributes. The ratios to be used are generally classified into five fundamental types:

(1) liquidity ratios,

(2) leverage ratios,

(3) activity ratios,

(4) profitability ratios, and

(5) market-oriented ratios.

Liquidity ratios reflect the firm's ability to meet its maturing obligations. Liquidity ratios are broken down into three specific ratios: current ratio, quick or acid-test ratio, and the basic defensive interval. The formulas are as follows:

$$\text{Current ratio} = \frac{\text{current assets}}{\text{current liabilities}}$$

$$\text{Quick or acid-test ratio} = \frac{\text{current assets} - \text{inventory}}{\text{current liabilities}}$$

$$\text{Basic defensive interval} = \frac{\text{cash} + \text{marketable securities} + \text{accounts receivable}}{\left(\dfrac{\text{cost of goods sold} + \text{selling and administrative expenses}}{360}\right)}$$

CASE FIVE

Liquidity Ratios — Comparable Corporations

DEANO CORPORATION

Facts

Deano Corporation is the entity to be valued. Deano Corporation manufactures various plastic components for automobiles. Deano's financial statements for the year ending December 31, 1981, are as follows:

DEANO CORPORATION
Balance Sheets
December 31, 1980 and 1981

	1980		1981	
Assets		(thousands)		
Cash	$ 48		50	
Accounts receivables	178		150	
Marketable securities (short-term investments)	106		100	
Inventories	350		300	
Total current assets		682		600
Property	500		500	
Plant and equipment	950		1150	
Less depreciation	(300)		(350)	
Total property, plant and equipment		1150		1300
Total assets		$ 1832		$ 1900
Liabilities				
Accounts payable	$ 85		90	
Notes payable	115		110	
Other accrued liabilities	15		20	
Current portion of long-term debt	10		10	
Taxes payable	115		120	
Total current liabilities		340		350
Secured bonds	640		600	
Debentures — 10 percent	150	790	150	750
Total liabilities		1130		1100
Stockholders' Equity				
Common stock (5000 shares, $10 par)	50		50	
Preferred stock (4500 shares, $100 par, 8 percent)	450		450	
Capital in excess of par — common stock	100		100	
Retained earnings	102		200	
Total stockholders' equity		702		800
Total liabilities and stockholders' equity		$ 1832		$ 1900

DEANO CORPORATION
Statements of Income
For the year ended December 31, 1981

Gross sales	$ 2,030,000	
Less returns and allowances	(30,000)	
Net sales		2,000,000
Cost of goods sold		(1,500,000)
Gross profit		500,000
Less expenses:		
General and administrative	(35,000)	
Selling	(20,000)	
Lease expense	(30,000)	
Depreciation	(100,000)	(185,000)
Net operating income		315,000
Other income:		
Dividend income	5,000	
Interest income	5,000	10,000
Gross income		325,000
Less:		
Interest on notes payable	(10,000)	
Interest on secured bonds	(60,000)	
Interest on debentures	(15,000)	(85,000)
Net income before income taxes		240,000
Federal income taxes (at 40 percent effective rate)		(96,000)
Net income after taxes		$ 144,000

DEANO CORPORATION
Statement of Retained Earnings
For the year ended December 31, 1981

Balance of retained earnings, December 31, 1980		$ 102,000
Add net income 1981		144,000
		246,000
Less dividends:		
Preferred stockholders	$ 36,000	
Common stockholders	10,000	(46,000)
Balance of retained earnings, December 31, 1981		$ 200,000

Liquidity Ratios: Deano's liquidity ratios for 1981 are as follows:

1. Current ratio $= \dfrac{\text{current assets}}{\text{current liabilities}}$

$= \dfrac{\$600,000}{\$350,000}$

$= 1.7$ times

This figure shows that roughly 50 percent (1/1.7) of the current assets would need to be liquidated to satisfy current liabilities. A comparable company should have a reasonably similar ratio or the difference should be readily explainable.

2. Quick or acid-test ratio $= \dfrac{\text{current assets} - \text{inventory}}{\text{current liabilities}}$

$= \dfrac{\$600,000 - \$300,000}{\$350,000}$

$= 86$ percent

This ratio depicts the firm's ability to pay off short-term debt without having to rely on the sale of inventory. Again, a comparable company should have a reasonably similar ratio or the difference should be readily explainable.

3. Basic defensive interval $= \left(\dfrac{\text{cash} + \text{marketable securities} + \text{accounts receivable}}{\dfrac{\text{cost of goods sold} + \text{selling and administrative expense}}{360}} \right)$

$= \left(\dfrac{\$50,000 + \$100,000 + \$150,000}{\dfrac{\$1,500,000 + \$35,000 + \$20,000}{360}} \right)$

$= \dfrac{\$300,000}{\$4,319.44}$

$= 69.45$ days

This figure represents the approximate number of days that a firm can operate without resorting to revenue from sales.

Analysis

In the search for a comparable company to Deano, such company would ideally possess, with some variation, ratios similar to those determined above. If a company is found which has other characteristics (e.g., line of business, volume of sales, etc.) which appear to make it comparable, but its financial ratios are not in line, the valuation process requires that the expert explain the ratio differences and then assess the impact of such explanation to see if the company can still be considered comparable.

Leverage ratios depict that portion of the firm's activity which has been achieved by debt. Creditors consider these ratios in determining their margin of safety. Owners, on the other hand, look upon this ratio as a measure of their effectiveness in using debt to achieve growth. Likewise, if the firm is able to earn more from borrowed funds than the cost of such funds, the return on owner's equity is increased. There are three specific liquidity ratios, as follows:

$$\text{Debt ratio} = \frac{\text{total debt}}{\text{total assets}}$$

$$\begin{array}{c}\text{Times interest earned}\\ \text{(common stock only)}\end{array} = \frac{\text{earnings before interest and taxes}}{\text{interest expense}}$$

$$\begin{array}{c}\text{Times interest earned}\\ \text{(preferred stock)}\end{array} = \frac{\text{earnings before interest and taxes}}{\text{interest expense} + \left(\dfrac{\text{preferred dividends}}{\text{1-tax rate}}\right)}$$

CASE FIVE (cont.)

Leverage Ratios — Comparable Corporations

DEANO CORPORATION

Facts

See beginning of Case Five for Deano Corporation's financial information.

Leverage Ratios: Deano's leverage ratios for 1981 would be as follows:

1. Debt ratio $= \dfrac{\text{total debt}}{\text{total assets}}$

$= \dfrac{\$1,100,000}{\$1,900,000}$

$= 58$ percent

This figure shows that approximately 58 percent of the cost of the company's assets is represented by debt. Conversely, 42 percent of the assets are financed by owners' equity.

2. Times interest earned $= \dfrac{\text{earnings before interest and taxes}}{\text{interest expense}}$
(common stock only)

$= \dfrac{\$325,000}{\$85,000}$

$= 3.8$ times

This figure depicts the ability of the firm to meet its interest obligations. Failure to meet these payments will result in legal action by the debt holders and could eventually lead to bankruptcy. This example assumes that there is only common stock or that there is no obligation to pay preferred shareholders their dividends.

3. Times interest earned $= \dfrac{\text{earnings before interest and taxes}}{\text{interest expense} + \left(\dfrac{\text{preferred dividends}}{1\text{-tax rate}}\right)}$
(preferred stock)

$= \dfrac{\$325,000}{\$85,000 + \left(\dfrac{\$36,000}{1\text{-}.40}\right)}$

$= \dfrac{\$325,000}{\$145,000}$

$= 2.24$ times

This ratio recognizes the obligation of payment of dividends to the preferred shareholders.

Analysis

These ratios show generally how heavily leveraged the firm is. These ratios for a possibly comparable company would have to be reasonably in line with the ratios of the company to be valued. If not, significant differences in the character of the two companies may exist which should be closely examined and explored.

Activity ratios represent the effectiveness of a firm in utilizing its resources. Such ratios generally deal with the turnover activity on certain assets. Activity ratios include such ratios as inventory turnover, average collection period, fixed asset turnover, accounts receivable turnover, and total asset turnover. Such ratios are computed as follows:

Inventory turnover $= \dfrac{\text{net sales}}{\text{year-end inventory}}$

Average collection period $= \dfrac{\text{accounts receivable}}{\left(\dfrac{\text{net sales}}{360}\right)}$

Fixed asset turnover $= \dfrac{\text{net sales}}{\text{net fixed assets}}$

$$\text{Accounts receivable turnover} = \frac{\text{net sales}}{\text{accounts receivable}}$$

$$\text{Total asset turnover} = \frac{\text{net sales}}{\text{total assets}}$$

CASE FIVE (cont.)

Activity Ratios — Comparable Corporations

DEANO CORPORATION

Facts

See beginning of Case Five for Deano Corporation's financial statement information.

Activity Ratios: Deano's activity ratios for 1981 would be as follows:

1. $\text{Inventory turnover} = \dfrac{\text{net sales}}{\text{year-end inventory}}$

$$= \frac{\$2,000,000}{\$300,000}$$

$$= 6.67 \text{ times}$$

This ratio shows the number of times the inventory is replenished during the year. If the ratio was low, this would indicate the possibility of excess inventory. However, care should be taken to review industry averages to determine whether the ratio is appropriate or inappropriate.

2. $\text{Average collection period} = \dfrac{\text{accounts receivable}}{\left(\dfrac{\text{net sales}}{360}\right)}$

$$= \frac{\$150,000}{\left(\dfrac{\$2,000,000}{360}\right)}$$

$$= 27 \text{ days}$$

This ratio represents the average number of days Deano must wait after making a sale until the money is received. An assessment of the relative position of the firm's collection period should be made in view of industry averages and Deano's credit policy.

3. $\text{Fixed asset turnover} = \dfrac{\text{net sales}}{\text{net fixed assets}}$

$$= \frac{\$2,000,000}{\$1,300,000}$$

$$= 1.54 \text{ times}$$

This ratio reflects the effectiveness of a firm in utilizing its fixed assets. In essence, the result of this calculation is a determination of the return on the fixed assets. This return should be compared to Deano's industry average.

4. Accounts receivable turnover $= \dfrac{\text{net sales}}{\text{accounts receivable}}$

$$= \dfrac{\$2,000,000}{\$150,000}$$

$$= 13.33 \text{ times}$$

This ratio reflects the relationship of outstanding receivables to annual sales. This ratio should be compared to industry averages and evaluated in light of Deano's credit policy.

5. Total asset turnover $= \dfrac{\text{net sales}}{\text{total assets}}$

$$= \dfrac{\$2,000,000}{\$1,900,000}$$

$$= 1.05 \text{ times}$$

This proportion of sales to total assets demonstrates the relationship of sales to total assets. This ratio provides a benchmark for comparison to other companies to determine overall comparability.

Analysis

These activity ratios provide good indicators of management's effectiveness in utilizing the firm's assets. The ratios also indicate the relative sales which a company is generating on such assets. These ratios provide a valuable analytical tool in the evaluation of the quality of a firm's management and its performance within its industry.

Profitability ratios represent a measure of management's effectiveness as shown by returns on sales and investments. These consist primarily of four ratios as follows:

Income from sales $= \dfrac{\text{net sales} - \text{cost of goods sold}}{\text{net sales}}$

Profit margin on sales $= \dfrac{\text{net profit after taxes (net income)}}{\text{net sales}}$

Return on total assets (investment) $= \dfrac{\text{net profits after taxes (net income)}}{\text{total assets}}$

Return on common equity $= \dfrac{\text{earnings available for common stockholders}}{\text{common stockholders' equity} + \text{unrestricted retained earnings}}$

CASE FIVE (cont.)

Profitability Ratios — Comparable Corporations

DEANO CORPORATION

Facts

See beginning of Case Five for Deano Corporation's financial information.

Profitability Ratios: Deano's profitability ratios for 1981 would be as follows:

1. Income from sales $= \dfrac{\text{net sales} - \text{cost of goods sold}}{\text{net sales}}$

$= \dfrac{\$2,000,000 - \$1,500,000}{\$2,000,000}$

$= 25$ percent

This ratio reflects that portion of sales which represents gross profit. In other words, $0.75 out of every dollar is the cost of producing that dollar, and $0.25 of every dollar contributes toward the firm's other expenditures and net profit.

2. Profit margin on sales $= \dfrac{\text{net profit after taxes}}{\text{net sales}}$

$= \dfrac{\$144,000}{\$2,000,000}$

$= 7.2$ percent

This ratio reflects the ratio of net income to sales. In this case, 7.2 cents of every dollar represents net income that is available for dividends or retained earnings.

3. Return on total assets (investment) $= \dfrac{\text{net profits after taxes}}{\text{total assets}}$

$= \dfrac{\$144,000}{\$1,900,000}$

$= 7.6$ percent

This ratio represents the return a firm is realizing on its total investment and indicates the relationship of net profits after taxes to total assets. This return demonstrates the company's profit as a percentage of total investment.

Analysis

These profitability ratios determine the effectiveness of management and give an insight into the operating style and philosophy of the company.

Market-oriented ratios consist of those ratios listed and discussed when dealing with intrinsic valuation factors. These ratios are listed below, but will be discussed in more detail in Chapter 7:

$$\frac{\text{Book value}}{\text{per share (common)}} = \frac{\text{total assets at historical cost} - (\text{liabilities} + \text{preferred equity})}{\text{number of common shares outstanding}}$$

$$\frac{\text{Earnings per share}}{\text{(common)}} = \frac{\text{earnings available for common shareholders}}{\text{number of common shares outstanding}}$$

$$\frac{\text{Earnings per share}}{\text{(preferred)}} = \frac{\text{earnings available for preferred shareholders (net income)}}{\text{number of preferred shares outstanding}}$$

$$\text{Dividend payout} = \frac{\text{cash dividends paid per share}}{\text{earnings per share}}$$

CASE FIVE (cont.)

Market-Oriented Ratios—Comparable Corporations

DEANO CORPORATION

Facts

See beginning of Case Five for Deano Corporation's financial information.

Market-Oriented Ratios: Deano's market-oriented ratios are as follows:

$$\text{1. } \frac{\text{Book value per share (common)}} = \frac{\text{total assets at historical cost} - (\text{liabilities} + \text{preferred equity})}{\text{number of shares outstanding}}$$

$$= \frac{\$1,900,000 - (\$1,100,000 + \$450,000)}{5000}$$

$$= \$\underline{70}$$

This represents total liquidation value stated *at historical cost (which may be higher or lower than fair market value)*. Certainly, this value is not representative of the true fair market in almost all cases. Nevertheless, this ratio needs to be at least considered in analyzing the subject company and possible comparable companies.

$$\text{2. Earnings per share (common)} = \frac{\text{earnings available for common shareholders}}{\text{number of common shares outstanding}}$$

$$= \frac{\$144,000 - \$36,000}{5000}$$

$$= \frac{\$108,000}{5000}$$

$$= \$\underline{21.60}$$

This represents how much was earned for each share of common stock during the past year. Certainly, this ratio is relevant in identifying comparable companies and evaluating the company to be valued.

3. Earnings per share (preferred) $= \dfrac{\text{earnings available for preferred shareholders}}{\text{number of preferred shareholders equity}}$

$$= \frac{\$144,000}{4500}$$

$$= \underline{\$32}$$

This represents how much was earned for each share of preferred stock during the past year.

4. Dividend payout $= \dfrac{\text{cash dividends per share}}{\text{earnings per share}}$

(Common) $= \dfrac{\$2.00}{\$21.60}$

$$= \underline{9.3} \text{ percent}$$

(Preferred) $= \dfrac{\$8.00}{\$32.00}$

$$= \underline{\underline{25}} \text{ percent}$$

These ratios reflect the cash return, as compared to earnings, which each share of stock is receiving.

Analysis

These ratios, as will be discussed in Chapter 7, are representative of the market perception of the company. These ratios are generally quite important in determining the value of an entity. As has already been indicated, earnings are perhaps the most important element to consider in valuing operating entities. Accordingly, the data developed through these ratios assumes great importance in most valuation cases.

A synopsis of the ratios listed here is given in Appendix C, entitled *Table of Significant Ratios.* The table also briefly states the importance of each ratio in analyzing financial data.

TREND ANALYSIS

Trend analysis provides an additional trait that ratio analysis does not. Trend analysis entails graphically comparing the firm to be valued with industry averages and comparable companies. Ratios provide good indicators of the position of a firm at a particular point in time, whereas trend analysis displays the ratios over an expanded period of time. Trend analysis involves taking the numbers computed under the preceding ratio section, combining them with ratios in the years past (assumed in the following example), and plotting them on a graph. An example of trend analysis for selected ratios of Deano Corporation is given in Figure 6–1.

**DEANO CORPORATION
TREND ANALYSIS**

Liquidity Ratio

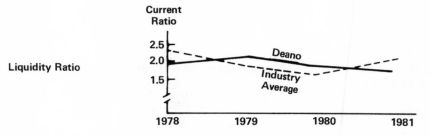

Leverage Ratio

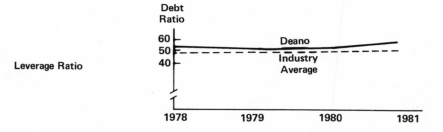

Activity Ratio

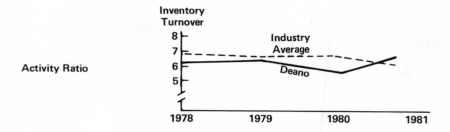

Profitability Ratio

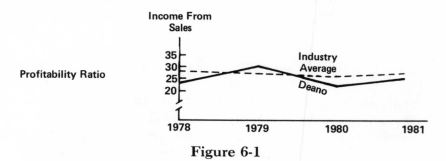

Figure 6-1

COURTS' ATTITUDE

There are a number of tax valuation cases involving the use of comparable publicly held corporations which should be considered in valuing the stock of a closely held business. These cases provide a relative benchmark to determine the degree of similarity considered to constitute comparability between a company to be valued and publicly traded corporations. An active market for the trading of shares of comparable corporations is indicative of public sentiment regarding the value of an ownership interest in that corporation (and, presumably, a comparable corporation). The degree of comparability when using comparative corporate analysis is expressed in other contested tax areas besides valuation litigation. Cases involving determination of what constitutes reasonable, or unreasonable, compensation in closely held corporations have employed the comparative company approach with success.[5] Hence, the comparable corporation approach permeates many areas of the tax law. Basically, each time comparable corporate analysis is utilized, the principles outlined herein are used to identify comparable companies.

In many valuation cases, the courts have concluded that a sufficient degree of similarity did not exist between a publicly listed corporation and the company to be valued. Such cases have generally involved a corporation, or corporations, in a line of business too divergent to be considered comparable. "Corporations engaged in the same or similar lines of business" and "comparable corporations" are considered by the Tax Court, and implied by other courts, to be terms that parallel each other.[6] Obviously, the specific nature of the business to be valued and a comparative corporation's characteristics also need to resemble each other in a justifiable and logical manner. The facts of each case dictate the latitude afforded in achieving comparability.

The cases discussed below will provide some examples of situations in which a court determined that comparative corporate analysis was not appropriate. These cases, and the discussion of the *Cochran*[7] case which follows, indicate the peripheral boundaries within which comparative corporate analysis can be considered as a major valuation technique.

In the valuation of a corporation which operated a grain elevator business, the district court, in *Bader* v. *United States*,[8] stated that since no grain elevator company's stock was traded on any exchange it would be impossible to use comparative analysis. One district court, when confronted with the proper value of a corporation whose business consisted of trading in coarse paper products at wholesale, held that a corporation whose sales were four times that of the corporation whose stock was to be valued and whose operations did not include extensive wholesaling was not sufficiently similar to be considered a comparable company.[9] Likewise, the Tax Court, when determining the value of a real estate holding and development company, held that several suggested comparable companies were not appropriate since they were not operating in the relevant geographical area and since their assets were considerably different.[10] In *Central Trust Company* v. *United States*,[11] the Court of Claims held that the performance and value of stock in such giant corporations as American Can Company and Continental Can Company were the result of operations on a significantly larger scale than the smaller can company to be valued. The lack of comparability was, in the judgment of the court, due to the disparity of the attributes (such as the level of automation and manufacturing business line) of proposed comparable companies and the company being valued.

The courts do look closely at contentions that one company is exactly comparable to another. Even if companies are in the same business, the courts recognize the fact that very rarely will one company be exactly identical to another. The rare case, where the Tax Court considered the company to be valued and two comparable companies as being "triplets of the industry," is found in *Drayton Cochran*.[12] The court in that case recognized that comparability of companies is a standard valuation test and proceeded to rely heavily on the value of shares of the comparable companies. Subsequent court decisions recognize that the degree of similarity found in *Cochran* will rarely exist.[13] Additional cases and factors considered by the courts in determining comparability are given in Appendix D, *Cases Using Comparative Corporate Analysis.*

For a company with significant diversification of operations, the search for comparable corporations is more difficult. The Tax Court, in one instance, has relied upon data that were derived from several publicly traded corporations in determining the ultimate value for one single diversified close corporation.[14] For a further discussion of how to value a diversified business entity, see Chapter 12.

SUMMARY

Comparing a closely held business to a corporation whose stock is actively traded on an open market provides a good scale upon which the value of the closely held business can be weighed and analyzed. In searching for a comparable company, a more thorough understanding of the entity to be valued and its business will be obtained. Further, use of this approach is essential in most cases since the general trend toward relying on comparable companies when valuing a closely held business is evident from the more recent valuation court decisions.

NOTES FOR CHAPTER 6

1. 1959-1 C.B. 237, Sec. 4.01(h).

2. Reg. Sec. 20.2031-2(f).

3. Tallichet v. Commissioner, 1974 P-H TC Memo ¶74,255.

4. SEC disclosure requirements are stringent. SEC reports which should be requested for potential comparable corporations include: 10-K (which is the annual report filed with the SEC) and 10-Q (which are quarterly reports filed with the SEC). These and other reports can be requested from the comparable corporation. For more information relating to the SEC and reports filed by publicly held companies, see K. Fred Skousen, *An Introduction to the SEC*, South-Western Publishing Company, Cincinnati, 1976.

5. See, for example, Schneider v. Commissioner, 500 F.2d 148 (8th Cir. 1974); cert. denied, 420 U.S. 908 (1975); R. J. Reynolds Tobacco Co. v. United States, 138 Ct. Cl. 1 (1957), cert. denied, 355 U.S. 893 (1957); Giles Industries, Inc. v. United States, 496 F.2d 556 (Ct. Cl. 1974); Patton v. Commissioner, 168 F.2d 28 (6th Cir. 1948).

6. Clarke v. Commissioner, 1976 P-H TC Memo ¶76,328.

7. Cochran v. Commissioner, 1948 P-H TC Memo ¶48,094.

8. Bader v. United States, 172 F. Supp. 833 (S.D. Ill. 1959).

9. Worthen v. United States, 192 F. Supp. 727 (D.M. Mass. 1961).

10. Estate of Tompkins v. Commissioner, 1961 P-H TC Memo ¶61,338.

11. Central Trust Company v. United States, 305 F.2d 393 (Ct. Cl. 1962).

12. See note 7 supra.

13. See note 11 supra, at 404.

14. Estate of Wilson v. Commissioner, 1951 P-H TC Memo ¶51,247.

7

Intrinsic Factors
in the Valuation Process

Intrinsic factors are those items which relate to the financial condition of the entity to be valued. Such factors include earnings capacity, dividend-paying capacity, book value or net asset value, and goodwill or other intangible assets. These factors are used in conjunction with comparison to similar companies and with expert testimony (see Chapters 6 and 10). The factors are to be viewed against the background of the history of the business, its economic outlook, and the outlook of the industry as a whole. The three factors most frequently used for intrinsic valuation are dividend-paying capacity, earnings, and book value or net asset value.

In order to obtain the maximum amount of information regarding the financial condition of a company, examination of the company books and records is necessary. If financial statements have been prepared on a yearly basis, it is wise to obtain these statements for each year since the inception of the business. Prior years tax returns, loan statements with financial institutions, financial agreements, and any additional information that would be beneficial to the collection of intrinsic information should be located and assembled.

DIVIDENDS PAID VS. DIVIDEND-PAYING CAPACITY

Revenue Ruling 59–60[1] sets forth the premise that dividend-paying capacity, rather than actual dividends paid, should be given substantial consideration in the valuation process when dealing with shares of closely held corporate stock. The reason for this position is that a prospective purchaser would be more concerned with present and future earnings and dividend-paying capability, than with past dividends paid.

The position of the Internal Revenue Service recognizes the fact that min-imization of dividends is attractive because it avoids double taxation. The dividend history of the firm may therefore be deceptive due to higher than normal salaries or bonuses being paid in lieu of dividends. Excessive travel and entertainment expenses or high rental paid for the use of property owned by an owner or family may also distort the dividend history. While the Service's position is sound and is often referred to in court decisions, the term "dividend-paying capacity" has not been adequately defined. Nowhere are guidelines proffered which enable a taxpayer to determine with any certainty the "dividend-paying capacity" of a particular company within the meaning of Revenue Ruling 59–60. The liquidity, current and retained earnings, and the capital structure of the subject company must all be considered in this type of analysis. Further, expansion plans, capital needs, or other needs for the accumulation of earnings by the entity may explain a relatively low dividend-paying history.[2]

Stock dividends may have some impact on this analysis. In a 1962 case, the Court of Claims indicated, in dictum, that some element of value should be attributed to the stock dividend.[3] In theory and in real terms, however, a stock dividend gives a shareholder nothing to which he is not already entitled.[4]

While the Service is quick to construct a hypothetical dividend rate when it considers a dividend too low, it shows no reluctance in considering actual dividends paid which are higher than the normal rate.[5] The Tax Court has, however, found the Service's heavy reliance on high dividends in error, holding that if the value of stock is determined using only dividends, then the Service has effectively ignored other relevant factors.[6]

Once "dividend-paying capacity" is estimated, such capacity must be capitalized in a manner similar to that of earnings. The primary difference is that a company does not pay out all of its earnings in dividends. While this approach, like the capitalization of earnings, is conventionally applied to operating companies, an interesting application of the principle was proposed by a taxpayer attempting to determine the value of a holding company owning substantial tracts of undeveloped land in Florida. In this case, *Estate of Heckscher,*[7] the company to be valued controlled a large amount of undeveloped land through a wholly-owned subsidiary. The taxpayer's expert justified his use of dividend-paying ability for valuation of real estate, saying that liquidation value was irrelevant since the owner of the minority interest being valued could not force liquidation. He projected the dividend-paying ability of the company after selling all of the real estate, basing his calculations on present dividends. He then chose a price from a range of prices producing an 8 percent dividend yield. The range ran from a price reflecting the current dividends to a price reflecting his estimate of the maximum dividend. The Tax Court took issue with his not considering book value and with his use of an 8 percent dividend yield, which was relatively high considering the assets of the company. However, the court did acknowledge the basic soundness and validity of the expert's method and assumptions.

Dividend capitalization rates of varying amounts have been approved by the courts. In *Bader* v. *United States*,[8] rates of 6 percent and 5.45 percent for the two years in question provided by the taxpayer's expert witness were accepted, even though the rates evidently came from yield tables rather than from comparative companies. In *Central Trust Company* v. *United States*,[9] however, the Court of Claims disallowed the taxpayer's expert witness's assertion that a hypothetical purchaser would require a 7 percent yield and looked to yields of comparable companies which produced a rate one-half the rate asserted by the witness. Obviously, actual market yields for comparable securities on the valuation date will have significant influence on the rate finally utilized.

Although dividend-paying capacity has not been given controlling weight by the courts, the absence of any testimony regarding such capacity may have an adverse effect on the credibility of the valuations offered. At least one court has criticized a witness for failure to consider dividends when computing comparative company statistics.[10]

An example of the computation of stock value using dividends as the only factor is given in *Case Six—Dale Toy Corporation*.

CASE SIX

Dividend-Paying Capacity

DALE TOY CORPORATION

Facts

Dale Toy Corporation (DTC) is a closely held toy manufacturing corporation with 5000 common shares outstanding and held by Dale S., its owner and founder. Because Dale S. owns all of the stock, it is his desire to initiate a gift program for the benefit of his children in 1982. DTC's dividends and earnings (per share and total) and the payout ratio (dividends to earnings) are as follows for the past seven years:

year	Dividends total	Dividends per share	Earnings total	Earnings per share	ratio (%)
1975	$ 12,500	$ 2.50	$ 50,000	$ 10	25.0
1976	20,000	4.00	75,000	15	27.0
1977	21,250	4.25	100,000	20	21.3
1978	21,250	4.25	125,000	25	17.0
1979	21,250	4.25	150,000	30	14.0
1980	21,250	4.25	175,000	35	12.0
1981	21,250	4.25	200,000	40	11.0
	$ 138,750		$ 875,000		18.2

In examining various financial services (e.g., *Moody's, Standard & Poor's,* the comparable companies' annual reports, etc.; see Chapter 6), it is determined that the following publicly traded companies are comparable in size to DTC:

	Comparable company	1981 Dividend	1981 Earnings	Payout ratio
1.	Beasley Playthings, Inc.	$ 130,500	$ 450,000	29.0%
2.	Puppydog Toys, Inc.	36,000	120,000	30.0%
3.	Rogers Toy Mfg., Inc.	285,000	760,000	37.5%
4.	Happy Tot Toys, Inc.	136,500	525,000	26.0%
		$ 588,000	$ 1,855,000	31.7%

Also, based on examination of the comparable companies' financial information and in conjunction with industry averages, it is determined that payment of dividends in relation to the market price of the stock is yielding approximately 8 percent (i.e., $8 dividend on $100 market price).

SITUATION A

DTC has no plans for expansion of its facilities and has limited its dividend payments since the year 1975, because of Dale S.'s desire to keep his personal tax liability at a lower level.

Value

Using the comparative companies' averages as an index, if DTC had paid an approximate comparable amount of its earnings (say 30 percent instead of its average of 18 percent) as dividends in 1981, and its earning trend approximated the comparables used, then its capacity to pay dividends in 1981 would have been, at the industry average yield of 8 percent, $150:

DTC earnings, 1981	$	200,000
Approximate comparable average payout ratio	×	.30
Comparable dividends		60,000
Shares held	÷	5,000
Dividend per share	$	12
Comparable dividend yield		.08
Value based on dividend yield ($12 ÷ .08)	$	150

This value represents "would have been" or a "dividends paid" figure. If, however, the earnings trend of DTC continues to increase at the rate of $25,000 per year, a value figure of $169 would be determined which would have some relationship to the "dividend-paying capacity" for 1982, the year Dale S. desires to initiate his gift program. This figure is computed as follows:

DTC earnings, 1981	$	200,000
Projected increased earnings over 1981		25,000
Projected DTC earnings, 1982		225,000
Approximate comparable average payout ratio	$\times$	.30
Comparable dividends		67,500
Shares held	$\div$	5,000
Dividends per share	$	13.50
Comparable dividend yield		.08
Value based on dividend yield (projected) ($13.50 $\div$ .08)	$	169

This value would be one basis for approximating the fair market value of the shares gifted in 1982. Other influential factors would obviously need to be considered.

SITUATION B

Value

If, however, DTC entered into expansion negotiations with regard to its present facilities in 1977, committed itself financially to expansion in 1978 (proved by minutes, contracts, etc., of DTC), and decided to limit its dividends paid to $4.25 per share in order to have the necessary capital for expansion, the computation of value of the shares could possibly be based on, at the 8 percent average industry yield, a value of $53 ($4.25 $\div$ 8 percent yield = $53). Obviously, other considerations would probably cause this figure to be adjusted.

EARNINGS AND EARNING CAPACITY

Section 5(a) of Revenue Ruling 59–60 states that earnings should be the most important valuation criterion when appraising an operating company.[11] Operating companies are differentiated from holding companies in that the former sells products or services to the public, whereas the latter relies primarily on the return on its underlying assets for its income. For further discussion of the problems of valuing these two different types of companies, see Chapter 4. In the majority of instances when an investor purchases shares of an operating company, the decision is based upon an estimate of the future earnings potential of the company. For this reason, the courts have accorded primary importance in valuation of operating companies to earnings and earning power.[12]

Earning averages and trends are considered when intrinsic analysis is employed. The best method in analyzing these trends is to develop and plot comparative income statements for the past several years. Trends of items on the income statement should be analyzed (e.g., income from operations, sales, operating expenses), as should net income. Adjustments to income should be made if there exist nonrecurring items that are not reflective of the true income. Likewise, any reason for probable deceptiveness of an income figure should be determined. For example, in *Estate of Nathan* v. *United States*,[13] the court determined that adjustments should have been made to the financial statements of the business to be valued due to low interest loans to the owners. Failure by the taxpayer to make these adjustments caused the court to totally disregard the value based on earnings. Also, items considered extraordinary, unusual in nature, and infrequently occurring should be discounted.[14] Revenue Ruling 59–60 states that while averaging earnings may be useful in smoothing fluctuations, if averaging is used without regard to current trends or future prospects, the procedure will not produce realistic results.[15] Further, no arbitrary five- or ten-year period should be used without reason.[16] The Court of Claims, in *Central Trust Company* v. *United States,* weighted the earnings trend from the most recent to the most remote period.[17] The Fourth Circuit considered a similar approach in *Estate of Snyder* v. *United States.*[18] The courts are quick to make adjustments in recorded earnings to account for obvious abnormalities. In fact, a loss in the first year of operations of the company was completely disregarded in *Estate of Clarke.*[19] In *Korslin* v. *United States,*[20] the district court lengthened the averaging period to mitigate the possible distortion of inventory adjustments made by the Internal Revenue Service. The Tax Court gave less weight to the abnormally high profits of war years than to profits of normal years in *Estate of Goar.*[21] The Tax Court also has ignored the testimony of an expert witness because he considered only the earnings of a single, admittedly abnormal, year.[22]

Once a representative earnings figure is determined, it may be capitalized at an appropriate rate to obtain an estimate of the entity's value. Revenue Ruling 59–60 states that the more important factors to be taken into consideration in deciding upon a capitalization rate are:

(1) the nature of the business,
(2) the risk involved, and
(3) the stability or irregularity of earnings.[23]

A useful estimate of the effect of these factors on the capitalization rate can be derived from the study of comparable companies. (See Chapter 6.) In fact, price-earnings ratios of truly similar publicly held companies are probably the best starting point for establishing a valuation based on capitalized earnings. This method of determining capitalization ratios was used in *Inga Bardahl*[24] and *Central Trust Company* v. *United States.*[25] While earnings and earning capacity are of primary importance in determining the value of closely held operating entities, they must not be considered to the exclusion of other relevant factors.[26]

An example of capitalization of earnings as explained in the preceding paragraphs is given in *Case Seven—Dewey Corporation.*

CASE SEVEN

Capitalization of Earnings

DEWEY CORPORATION

Facts

Dewey Corporation (DC) is a closely held corporation which Rab Company is considering acquiring. Accordingly, Rab Company wants to determine how much it should pay Mr. Dewey for his 2000 shares, being all of the outstanding stock of DC. The valuation date is February 15, 1981. DC's prior years earnings per share have been as follows:

1976	1977	1978	1979	1980	Total
$ 2.10	$ 2.10	$ 2.40	$ 2.90	$ 3.05	$ 12.55

The average five-year earnings for DC is $2.51 ($12.55 ÷ 5).

The only truly comparable corporation to DC is Bernie Corporation, whose shares are listed on the New York Stock Exchange and were traded on February 15, 1981, for an average price of $68 per share. The earnings per share for Bernie Corporation (computed under the same accounting method as Dewey), for the same years, are:

1976	1977	1978	1979	1980	Total
$ 4.60	$ 4.80	$ 5.00	$ 5.20	$ 5.40	$ 25.00

The average five-year earnings for Bernie Corporation is $5.00 ($25.00 ÷ 5).

Value

At a market price of $68 per share, Bernie's stock traded at 13.6 times its earnings. Applying this multiplier to DC's shares, an approximate value of $34.15 (13.6 × $2.51) per share results.

Analysis

Of course, a weighted average could be afforded the earnings to smooth out any fluctuation as recommended by *Central Trust Company* v. *United States.* But, in our example, both companies had increasing earnings over the years. Other factors would need to be utilized and alternative techniques should be used to compare the earnings value figure determined.

BOOK VALUE OR NET ASSET VALUE OF UNDERLYING ASSETS

"Book value" is the stated assets less the liabilities of an entity, commonly referred to in accounting circles as "owner's equity." On the other hand, "net asset value" is the fair market value of the net assets (fair market value of all assets less liabilities) underlying the stock of the corporation. Revenue Ruling 59–60 states that net asset value is an important criterion for valuation of closely held investment or real estate holding companies.[27]

Book value is a poor indicator of the worth of stock in an operating company. Only in isolated circumstances has it been used as the primary consideration for valuing the stock of an operating company. In *Estate of Banac*,[28] the Tax Court determined the value of the stock to be book value only because no other guidance was offered. While the courts pay lip service to book value, they frequently express their lack of reliance on that figure. The prevailing lack of reliance on book value is seen in *Mathilde B. Hooper, Admnx.*:

> *A prospective buyer would give some consideration to the book value of $145 a share. He would realize, however, that the company was a going concern, and that, even if it be assumed that the book value could be realized upon the liquidation of the corporation, there was no indication that it was to be liquidated.*[29]

A decision which similarly discounts the importance of book value can be seen in *Bader* v. *United States*.[30] The corporation being valued in that case was engaged in the grain, feed, and elevator business. The business had been founded and was managed by the decedent. After stating that the major valuation factors were book value, earning power, and dividend capacity, the district court elaborated on the lack of importance of book value in operating companies:

> *Book value is a factor to be considered, still it is not a reliable measure of fair market value. I am certain the investor is inclined to give earning power and dividend prospects much more weight in appraising the worth of any security. What the buyer is acquiring are the profits and dividends which the business will provide in the future.*[31]

In *Hansen*,[32] the Internal Revenue Service primarily considered the book value of a corporation engaged in developing film, finishing photographs, and wholesaling film and cameras. The Service gave little weight to factors such as labor costs of the company, intensive competition in the industry, obsolete equipment, and the lapse of several years without dividend payments by the company. The Tax Court noted this exclusion of important evidence from the Service's arguments and stated that considering book value alone, or even primarily, was an error if other significant factors existed.

An operating corporation's ownership of a large, liquid portfolio of marketable securities has not been treated consistently by the courts. In *Schlegel* v. *United States*,[33] the district court decided that a readily saleable portfolio owned by a manufacturing company constituted a relevant factor in valuation of that company's stock. However, in *Schroeder*,[34] surrounding circumstances compelled the Tax Court to rule that a large portfolio of marketable securities was not primarily determinative of the value of the closely held operating company holding that portfolio.

Revenue Ruling 59–60 does suggest that in "computing the book value per share of stock, assets of the investment type should be revalued on the basis of their market price and the book value adjusted accordingly."[35] It therefore becomes necessary for either an operating company or an investment holding company to consider the value of investment assets (i.e., assets not utilized in the trade or business of the corporation) in arriving at a value of the entity or an interest therein. This is not required for physical assets used in a trade or business. Such approach is logical for an operating company since the primary emphasis is on earnings and the actual value of operating assets could not be realized without ceasing operations and liquidating the business. On the other hand, value of underlying assets is one factor to consider in arriving at the overall value of the entity or an interest therein.[36]

If net asset value is determined for an operating company, some question exists as to whether a multiple should be applied against such net asset value once it is determined. Some authority exists that a price/net asset value per share ratio, obtained from comparable companies holding like assets, should be multiplied against the net asset value to obtain a new representative value.[37] Similarly, a price/book value ratio has been given judicial support when book value has been used.[38] However, there is authoritative support that the net asset value per share computation is sufficient to allow analysis of that factor's impact on overall value.[39]

An example of net asset value as applied to a pure investment company, without applying the comparable price/net asset value per share ratio, is given in *Case Eight—Oscar Corporation*.

CASE EIGHT

Net Asset Value — Investment Company

OSCAR CORPORATION

Facts

Oscar Corporation is a personal holding company having 2,000 outstanding shares. Oscar Corporation owns the following listed securities, as its only assets which are selling for the following prices on the date of valuation:

5,000	shares W Corporation at $100	$ 500,000
20,000	shares X Corporation at $25	500,000
10,000	shares Y Corporation at $35	350,000
8,000	shares Z Corporation at $50	400,000
	Total value	$1,750,000

Oscar's liabilities are $750,000.

Value

The net asset value per share of Oscar Corporation is $500 ($1,750,000 — $750,000 ÷ 2,000).

Analysis

There is no need to inquire into the dividends which W, X, Y, and Z pay to Oscar Corporation since earnings are not particularly relevant in this case. A certain discount should be allowed (at least on minority shares) due to the corporate blanket of Oscar. See Chapters 4 and 14.

Little mention is made specifically of net asset value in cases concerned with valuation of closely held companies. This appears to be caused in part by an apparent confusion in the courts between the terms "book value" and "net asset value." As indicated above, book value is the acquisition cost of resources used by the company and does not reflect specific price changes nor price-level fluctuations.[40] While book value appears on the financial statements of a corporation, it does not purport to represent current market value of the firm's assets. On the other hand, net asset value generally refers to the value of the entity's assets reduced by the entity's liabilities. Such current market value can be determined by appraisals of the company's assets.

The courts do, from time to time, mention liquidation value as a guide.[41] In most well-established operating companies, however, liquidation of the company's assets and their subsequent distribution to the shareholders are highly unlikely events. The preponderance of evidence points toward the continuance of the enterprise into the indefinite future when 1) a company's earnings steadily grow and its activities expand, 2) the industry of which it is a part is cast in a key role in economic development, and 3) the company makes far-reaching plans and substantial commitments for future operations. Hence, to give liquidation value or "net asset value" more than token weight in the valuation of a vigorous operating company is mere speculation.

The speculative nature of "net asset value" or liquidating value has been recognized by the Supreme Court. In *Olson* v. *United States*,[42] the issue involved was the valuation of land in determining a fair condemnation award. In establishing viable valuation criteria, the Court stated:

> *Elements affecting value that depend upon events or combinations of occurrences which, while within the realm of possibility, are not fairly shown to be reasonably probable should be excluded from consideration for that would be to allow mere speculation and conjecture to become a guide for the ascertainment of value—a thing to be*

condemned in business transactions as well as in judicial ascertainment of truth.[43]

This reasoning was echoed by the Tax Court in *Estate of Ethel C. Dooly,*[44] involving the valuation of a ranching corporation. The Internal Revenue Service based its value on the underlying assets of the corporation, establishing a hypothetical "higher use" value for the land of the ranching company. The court rebuked this conjecture in a reference to *Olson.* The court further found the Service to be erroneous in its reliance on Section 5(b) of Revenue Ruling 59–60 as support for its heavy dependence on net asset value since that section of Revenue Ruling 59–60 refers only to closely held investment companies or real estate holding companies, not operating companies.

In *Cochran,*[45] the Tax Court stated that net asset value should be considered, but when the problem is to value the stock of a going concern, other factors play a larger and more important role in the determination of value. The court emphasized the point by quoting Paul, *Federal Estate and Gift Taxation,* Vol. II, p. 1297:

> *The capital stock of a corporation, its net assets and its shares of stock are entirely different things. The value of one bears no fixed or necessary relation to the value of the other.*[46]

In *Estate of Heppenstall,*[47] the Tax Court stated that liquidating value is not a sound measure for valuing shares in a going concern. A similar view concerning the liquidating value is expressed in *Hooper.*[48] However, liquidation value does play a significant role in the valuation of preferred stock. (See Chapter 11 and the discussion related to planning considerations in Chapter 14.)

Perhaps the most important reason why liquidating value is not considered particularly relevant in valuing an operating company is that the valuation process *does not* require liquidation of the entity being valued. Further, unless the interest being valued has control and, hence, the power to liquidate, the "net asset value" has little meaning in the valuation of an interest in the entity. As a practical matter, in any case involving a going concern having employees, customers, and ongoing business obligations, consideration of values which might be realized in liquidation should receive minimal weight. For these reasons, the courts have found "net asset value" of secondary importance in valuing operating companies. However, since the courts have given this value some consideration at times, it cannot be totally ignored.[49]

GOODWILL OR OTHER INTANGIBLE ASSETS

When an earnings or dividends capitalization approach is used to determine the value of a closely held corporation, it is not appropriate for additional goodwill to be considered in valuing such stock. Goodwill results from excess earnings power. If an analysis of earnings is thoroughly performed, goodwill will be reflected automatically.

Goodwill is relevant, however, if an entity is, for some reasons, valued by aggregating the market value of its individual assets. If earnings exceed a normal rate of return on recorded assets, then those earnings are often attributed to goodwill. The specific facts must be considered in each case, according to Revenue Ruling 68–609.[50] (See Appendix B.) If the facts indicate that other identifiable factors, such as skills of salesmen under no binding contracts or the reputation of the decedent, caused the excess earnings, then no value should be given to goodwill.

Intangible assets such as customer lists, favorable location of business, and the like, may receive some positive or negative consideration, but these have not been dealt with specifically by the courts.

WEIGHTING VARIOUS INTRINSIC FACTORS

After the important factors have been considered in intrinsic analysis, it is quite improbable that the various methods of valuation will produce exactly the same results. They must be weighted in some manner depicting relative importance. Revenue Ruling 59–60 and numerous court decisions indicate that earnings, dividend-paying power, and book value (or net asset value) are of primary importance.

Section 7 of Revenue Ruling 59–60 states that while these factors should be weighted, the use of any formula should be discouraged since such averaging will serve only to exclude other significant factors. This approach is the one most courts take. The courts do not detail their mathematical computations in their opinions, but rather discuss the various factors, and then state in effect that, after having given due weight to each, a value of a certain amount has been determined.[51]

However, in some recent cases, the courts have quantified their formulas. In *Central Trust Company* v. *United States*,[52] the Court of Claims used a weighted average value of three figures derived from different approaches. Weight was applied in the following manner: earnings—50 percent; dividend-paying capacity—30 percent; book value—20 percent. The intrinsic value, as determined by the Court of Claims, is illustrated in *Case Nine—Central Trust Company*. In *Bader*,[53] the district court attacked the problem in the same manner, weighting earning power at 50 percent, dividends at 25 percent, and book value at 25 percent. *Case Ten—Bader Corporation* portrays that court's approach to determination of fair market value. *Bader Corporation* shows the actual disparity in value between the taxpayer and the Internal Revenue Service. The court's final value determination is also shown. While the approach illustrated in *Case Nine* and *Case Ten* is fairly new and as yet not widespread, it could indicate the beginning of a trend toward acceptance of more quantitatively derived fair market values.

CASE NINE

Weighting Intrinsic Factors

CENTRAL TRUST COMPANY*

Value date	August 3, 1954	October 25, 1954
I. Earnings		
(a) Earnings per share	$ 1.93	$ 1.79
(b) Comparable price-earnings ratios**	9.45	9.84
(c) Adjusted "earnings per share" value of single share	$18.24	$17.61
(d) Weight attributed to earnings	× .50	× .50
(e) Single share value attributed to earnings	$9.12	$8.81
II. Dividends		
(a) Annual dividend per share	$ .50	$ .50
(b) Comparative dividend yield**	3.50%	3.56%
(c) Adjusted "dividend" value of single share	$14.29	$14.05
(d) Weight attributed to dividends	× .30	× .30
(e) Single share value attributed to dividends	$4.29	$4.22
III. Book Value		
(a) Book value per share	$33.15	$33.54
(b) Comparative book value to market value**	83.96%	86.39%
(c) Adjusted "book value" value of single share	$27.83	$28.98
(d) Weight attributed to book value	× .20	× .20
(e) Single share value attributed to book value	$ 5.57	$ 5.80
Intrinsic value of single share of Central Trust Company	$ 18.98	$ 18.83

*305 F.2d 393 (Ct. Cl. 1962).

**Represents companies that are similar in financial position, posture in industry, etc. See Chapter 6 for methods and techniques to ascertain comparable companies.

CASE TEN

Weighting Intrinsic Factors

BADER CORPORATION*

Taxpayer	Weight	May 2, 1949	June 2, 1951
(1) Earning power basis	50%	$ 550	$ 550
(2) Dividend basis	25%	$ 450	$ 450
(3) Book value basis	25%	$ 660	$ 730
Weighted average		552	570
Discount for lack of marketability (See Chapter 9)—25%		(138)	(142)
Fair market value		$ 414	$ 428

Internal Revenue Service

(1) Earning power basis	50%	$ 550	$1,650
(2) Dividend basis	25%	$1,375	$1,525
(3) Book value basis	25%	$1,320	$1,785
Weighted average		945	1,652
Discount for lack of marketability (See Chapter 9)—15%		(145)	(247)
Fair market value		$ 800	$1,405

Court

(1) Earning power basis	50%	$ 550	$ 710
(2) Dividend basis	25%	$ 450	$ 450
(3) Book value basis	25%	$ 792	$ 983
Weighted average		585	713
Discount for lack of marketability (See Chapter 9)—10%		(58)	(71)
Fair market value		$ 527	$ 642

*172 F. Supp. 833 (D.C. Ill. 1959).

NOTES FOR CHAPTER 7

1. 1959-1 C.B. 237, Sec. 4.02(e).

2. Arguments under such contention would be similar to defenses raised when the Service asserts an accumulated earnings tax under Code Sections 531–537. The taxpayer may, however, assert that failure by the Service to attempt to levy an accumulated earnings tax estops them from asserting such position in relation to the dividend history.

3. Central Trust Company v. United States, 305 F.2d 393, 406 n. 6 (Ct. Cls. 1962).

4. See Graham & Dodd, *Security Analysis, Principles and Techniques*, 3d ed., 1951, pp. 444–5.

5. O'Bryan Bros., Inc. v. Commissioner, 127 F.2d 645 (6th Cir. 1942), aff'g 42 B.T.A. 18 (1940), cert. denied 317 U.S. 647 (1942); Estate of Heppenstall v. Commissioner, 1949 P-H TC Memo ¶49,034; Cochran v. Commissioner, 1948 P-H TC Memo ¶48,094; Kline v. Commissioner, 130 F.2d 742 (3rd Cir. 1942), aff'g 44 B.T.A. 1052 (1941), cert. denied, 317 U.S. 697 (1942).

6. Cochran, note 5 supra.

7. 63 T.C. 485 (1975).

8. 172 F. Supp. 833 (D.C. Ill. 1959).

9. See note 3 supra.

10. Louis v. United States, 369 F.2d 263, 265 (7th Cir. 1966).

11. See note 1 supra.

12. Hansen v. Commissioner, 1952 P-H TC Memo ¶52,236; Central Trust Company v. United States, note 3 supra; Estate of Dooly v. Commissioner, 1972 P-H TC Memo ¶72,164; Harrison v. Commissioner, 1958 P-H TC Memo ¶58,157; Wishon v. Anglim, 42 F. Supp. 359 (N.D. Cal. 1941); Laird v. Commissioner, 38 B.T.A. 926 (1938) acq. and nonacq. 1939-1 C.B. 20, 53.

13. 166 F.2d 422 (9th Cir. 1948).

14. Such criteria are similar to the standards set forth in "Accounting for Contingencies," *Statement of Financial Accounting Standards No. 5*, Stamford, Conn., FASB, March 1975. Adjustments should also be made to income if preferred shares exist, when a value is being determined for the common shares, in an amount equal to dividends of the preferred stock. Likewise, tax considerations for any future years must be considered. Prior years earnings may also have unrepresentative factors that affected the earnings at that time but have no significance in the present valuation (e.g., retirement of debt or preferred stock).

15. Rev. Rul. 59–60, note 1 supra, Sec. 4.02(b).

16. Revenue Ruling 59–60 does specify at least five years. Ten or more years have been used in the following cases: Bartol v. Commissioner, 1952 P-H TC Memo ¶52,162; Estate of McDermott v. Commissioner, 1953 P-H TC Memo ¶53,154; Estate of Montgomery v. Commissioner, 1953 P-H TC Memo ¶53,389.

17. See note 3 supra.

18. 285 F.2d 857 (4th Cir. 1961), rev'g. 182 F. Supp. 71 (D.C. N.C. 1960).

19. 1976 P-H TC Memo ¶76,328.

20. (No official citation) 31 AFTR 2d 73-1390 (E.D. Wis. 1973).

21. 1950 P-H TC Memo ¶50,242.

22. Aufiero v. Commissioner, 1954 P-H TC Memo ¶54,061.

23. Rev. Rul. 59–60, note 1 supra, Sec. 6.

24. 1965 P-H TC Memo ¶65,158.

25. See note 3 supra.

26. Julia Ann Schroth, Exec., 5 B.T.A. 326 (1926), acq. VI-I C.B. 5; Augustus E. Stanley, 41 B.T.A. 752 (1940), acq. 1940-1 C.B. 4.

27. Rev. Rul. 59–60, note 1 supra, Sec. 5(d); Maxcy v. Commissioner, 1969 P-H TC Memo ¶69,158, rev'd on other issues 441 F.2d 192 (5th Cir. 1971).

28. 17 T.C. 748 (1951), acq. 1952-1 C.B. 1.

29. 41 B.T.A. 114 at 119 (1940), acq. and nonacq. 1942-1 C.B. 9, 24.

30. See note 8 supra.

31. Ibid. at 838.

32. 1952 P-H TC Memo ¶52,236.

33. 71 F. Supp. 495 (D.C. N.Y. 1947) aff'd 164 F.2d 276 (1947).

34. 13 T.C. 259 (1949), acq. 1949-2 C.B. 3.

35. Rev. Rul. 59–60, note 1 supra, Sec. 4.02(c).

36. Ibid., Sec. 5(b).

37. Pabst v. Commissioner, 1947 P-H TC Memo ¶47,300; Colonial Trust Co. v. Kraemer, 63 F. Supp. 866 (D.C. Conn., 1945); Estate of Jenner v. Commissioner, 1977 P-H TC Memo ¶77,054.

38. Central Trust, note 3 supra; Bader, note 8 supra.

39. Richardson v. Commissioner, 1943 P-H TC Memo ¶43,496, aff'd 151 F.2d 102 (2nd Cir. 1945), cert. denied, 326 U.S. 796 (1946); Estate of Cruikshank v. Commissioner, 9 T.C. 165 (1947).

40. However, replacement cost data related in substance to price level adjusted financial statements are now required by the Securities and Exchange Commission. The acceptance of such data is becoming more

widespread. See *Financial Statements Restated for General Price-Level Changes,* APB Statement No. 3, New York: AICPA, 1969; Staff of Accounting Research Division, *Reporting the Financial Effects of Price-Level Changes,* Accounting Research Study No. 6, New York: AICPA, 1963; and *Financial Reporting and Changing Prices,* Statement of Financial Accounting Standards No. 33, Stamford, Conn., FASB, November 1979.

41. See Weber v. Rasquin, 101 F.2d 62 (2nd Cir. 1939), rev'g 23 F. Supp. 523 (D.C. N.Y. 1938).

42. 292 U.S. 246 (1934).

43. Ibid. at 257.

44. 1972 P-H TC Memo ¶72,164.

45. See note 5 supra.

46. Ibid. at 328.

47. 1949 P-H TC Memo ¶49,034.

48. See note 29 supra.

49. Schroth, note 26 supra, and Cochran, note 5 supra.

50. 1968-2 C.B. 327. See also, Forward Communications Corporation v. United States, 42 AFTR 2d 78-5334 (Ct. Cls. 1978); VGS Corporation v. Commissioner, 68 T.C. 563 (1977); Walter G. Andrews et. ux. v. Commissioner, 1976 P-H TC Memo ¶76,106.

51. See, for example, Estate of Ewing v. Commissioner, 1950 P-H TC Memo ¶50,296.

52. See note 3 supra.

53. See note 8 supra.

Valuation of
Minority and Majority Interests

A value can be estimated through contemporaneous sales or exchanges, comparison with similar companies, and/or through intrinsic factor evaluation. After determining value through one of these methods, it is generally appropriate to apply some form of discount or premium to such value. This chapter and Chapter 9 will deal with additional considerations necessary to determine ultimate value.

The level of ownership necessary to be considered a majority interest holder has generally been, for valuation purposes, ownership of greater than 50 percent of the voting rights. The level of control may, however, be greater if the Articles of Incorporation of the business, or the founding business agreement, require greater than 50 percent of the voting rights to be in agreement to liquidate the business. Likewise, if the entities' business documents are silent as to this degree of control, state law may require a greater percentage of ownership interest to agree to liquidate the entity.[1] In each fact situation it is necessary to examine the business ownership documents and, if necessary, applicable state statutes to determine what level of ownership interest will constitute control. Control of a business is generally considered to be the ability to dominate the decision-making process, including the decision to liquidate.[2]

Ownership rights in a closely held business can generally be classified into three elements of value:

(1) liquidation value—the right to a proportionate share of the assets upon termination of a business,

(2) income value—the right to a proportionate share of any distributions during the life of a business, and

(3) control value—the proportionate right of participation in the management of the business.[3]

The minority interest holder will generally be considered to enjoy the liquidation value (although not possessing the power to realize such value) and income value. However, if he is an outsider, the ability to enjoy the control value is normally nonexistent. A significant discount is generally allowed to reflect this negative factor. A majority shareholder would, on the other hand, generally be considered to possess the benefits of all three elements. Hence, the value otherwise determined may be increased.

MINORITY DISCOUNT

If the interest to be valued is a minority interest, the value determined using intrinsic factors or other valuation methods will usually be discounted. The justification for this value reduction is the lack of power to significantly influence management, compel dividends, or cause liquidation. Substantive support exists for the contention that a minority stock interest in a closely held business is usually worth less than the proportionate share of the assets to which it would attach.[4] The Internal Revenue Service concedes this point and lists as a factor to consider when valuing a closely held business the size of the block to be valued.[5] The "size of the block" factor pertains, specifically, to the number of shares in a closely held corporation and, generally, to the ownership percentage of other closely held business interests.

Revenue Ruling 59–60[6] states that a minority stock interest in an unlisted corporation is more difficult to sell than a similar block of listed stock. The ruling goes on to state that it is equally true that control of a corporation represents an additional element of value which would justify a higher value for a specific block of stock. The degree of discount afforded minority interests depends entirely on the facts of the case.

A minority interest discount may not apply if a majority of the shares are held by one family. This is based in part on the assumption that the family relationships will prevent a minority shareholder from being "frozen out."[7] Additionally, a recent Internal Revenue Service private letter ruling disallowed a minority discount to separate gifts of stock in a family relationship.[8] Likewise, a minority discount may not apply if the initial value was computed by the use of a representative sale that already considered the minority status of the shares traded.

If the minority interest holder is part of the group which has effective control over the entity's activities, he may be considered to possess the liquidation value, the income value, and the control value. If other minority interest holders are not considered to be part of the inside group, then the value of an inside minority shareholder may be enhanced by a premium through his ability to have a significant input into the operations of the business. The purpose of the valuation and the facts of the case will determine the presence or absence of this condition. The value attributed to an inside minority interest holder may therefore reflect liquidation value (if appropriate) or a value based on earnings and other factors. No direct authority or precedent exists with regard to the applicability of family attribution rules when valuing the shares of a closely held business although recent cases appear to reflect on such influential relationships.[9]

The discount afforded minority interest owners has increased over the past 50 years.[10] This discount is presently recognized as a justifiable reduction of a minority interest value. During the last decade discounts ranging from 15–55 percent[11] have been allowed, with an average discount in the 34–35 percent range.[12] The actual amount of discount given to a minority interest owner will depend upon the facts of the individual case.

Case Eleven—S. & C. Sporting Goods, Inc. provides an example of minority interest discounts that, although in the two situations are for the same number of shares, require different discount percentages depending upon each set of facts.

CASE ELEVEN

Minority Discount

S. & C. SPORTING GOODS, INC.

Facts

Billy Bob Buford owned 2,000 shares, out of 10,000 shares outstanding, in S. & C. Sporting Goods, Inc. (S & C) as of the date of his death. The initial value determination, using earnings and other intrinsic methods, is $75 per share of S & C stock.

SITUATION A

Billy Bob Buford's sisters, Beatrice and Betty, each own 4,000 shares of S & C. Billy Bob's interest receives a 20 percent minority interest discount valuing his interest at $120,000, computed as follows:

Initial value	$ 75
Less 20 percent minority discount	$ (15)
Value per share before other discounts	$ 60
Times number of shares held	× 2,000
Total interest value before other discounts	$ 120,000

SITUATION B

Billy Bob acquired the shares several years ago through his next-door neighbor who owns 5,100 shares. The remaining shares are owned by various relatives of his neighbor. Billy Bob's shares receive a 40 percent minority interest discount valuing his interest at $90,000, computed as follows:

Initial value	$ 75
Less 40 percent minority discount	$ (30)
Value per share before other discounts	$ 45
Times number of shares held	× 2,000
Total interest value before other discounts	$ 90,000

Analysis

Under Situation A, Billy Bob's interest was only discounted 20 percent due to Billy Bob's position as an inside minority interest holder. Although no family attribution rules directly apply to valuation cases, the tendency has been to allow a lesser discount for intrafamily interests that collectively control the business. It follows that a greater discount would be allowed in Situation B, in which Billy Bob had no association with control.

MAJORITY INTEREST DISCOUNTS AND PREMIUMS

The treatment of a majority interest is somewhat uncertain. An analysis of the case law indicates that a majority interest may be discounted, increased, or have no effect on the value otherwise determined.

A reduction in value of a majority interest holder (in addition to specific discounts that may apply; see Chapter 9) has generally been allowed in two different situations: (1) when the size of the interest has a limiting effect on the ability to dispose of such interest, and (2) when the nature of the entity's operations and assets reduces the potential market for disposition under what is called the "pyramid principle." The first of these reasons, the size limitation, exists if the market cannot smoothly absorb such a large interest.[13] This is, in essence, a discount for lack of marketability, as will be discussed in Chapter 9. It is also similar in nature to a "blockage" discount afforded publicly held corporate stock valuation.[14]

The second reason for a majority interest discount, the pyramid principle, is related closely to the first type of discount but has only recently received identification by the courts. The basic premise of the pyramid principle is that in a business with several different types of assets, or at least disparity between operations, there are fewer buyers interested in purchasing the entire business.[15] For a more detailed discussion of valuing a diverse closely held business, see Chapter 12.

There are several instances where a majority interest will receive a "premium." This control premium is the result of having the power to direct the actions of the enterprise. By owning such an interest, one possesses the ability to control the management and policies of a business entity, which has been held to enhance the value of such interest over the value of smaller interests.[16] Normally, this is in fact situations where the base value is determined using a comparable corporation or a representative sale or exchange of a smaller interest versus a computation utilizing the intrinsic approach. The determination of the amount of premium afforded control of a closely held business should, in part, be dictated by the premium being paid in public tender offers by willing purchasers for similar companies. There are, however, no clear-cut standards regarding percentage premiums for control.

The value of a majority interest otherwise determined may receive no additional adjustment if, as one court contended, a control premium negates any discount due to the lack of availability of a market.[17] The court indicated that while a majority interest might have a lower price due to the fact that a public offering would have to bear flotation costs (see Chapter 9), its value might be increased by an investor's desire to obtain control of a business through acquisition of a large ownership percentage.[18] This paradox can have a counterbalancing effect on the application of discounts and premiums.

Case Twelve—Rutherford Corporation provides an example of the pyramid principle which allows for a majority interest discount. *Case Thirteen— Hone's Furniture Corporation* depicts the application of a majority interest premium where the initial value determination was based on a representative sale prior to the value date.

CASE TWELVE

Majority Interest Discount

RUTHERFORD CORPORATION

Facts

J. R. is the principal shareholder of Rutherford Corporation (RC), owning 20,000 shares out of a total of 25,000 shares outstanding. J. R.'s only son, J. R., Jr., in anticipation of his vast inheritance, is curious as to the potential estate tax burden in the event that J. R. were to die in the near future. J. R., Jr., therefore, wants to compute the value of J. R.'s shares as of the year end 1981. The net worth of RC, using fair market asset values as of December 31, 1981, is $1,880,000, computed as follows:

Assets
Cash	$ 8,000
Accounts and notes receivable	400,000
Inventories	3,500

Stocks and bonds	2,000
Cattle	17,000
Horses	3,500
Citrus groves	400,000
Acreage and undeveloped lots	900,000
Flying "J. R." Ranch	350,000
Plant and equipment	80,000
Total assets	$ 2,164,000

Liabilities

Accounts payable	70,000
Notes and mortgages payable	200,000
Income taxes payable	14,000
Total liabilities	284,000
Net worth	$ 1,880,000

Value

J. R., Jr., computes the net asset value per share (net worth ÷ total outstanding shares) as follows:

Net worth	$ 1,880,000
Total outstanding shares	÷ 25,000
Net worth per share	$ 75.20

J. R.'s total shares would have a pre-discount value of $1,504,000 ($75.20 × 20,000 shares). J. R., Jr., being knowledgeable in the estate valuation area, recognizes that due to the diverse nature of RC, his father's majority interest might receive a discount. J. R., Jr., applies a 15 percent discount for such reasons, making J. R.'s ultimate value $63.92 per share for a total value of $1,278,400 in the RC.

Analysis

Because RC possessed such an array of differing assets, the "pyramid" majority interest discount would apply. In *Maxcy**, the court recognized such discount in a situation similar to RC on the premise that the determination of value is the price a willing seller of an interest to be valued could obtain from a willing buyer, not what the buyer may eventually realize. For a more detailed discussion on valuing a diverse closely held business, see Chapter 12. Obviously, the Internal Revenue Service would try to negate the discount by arguing that control should offset the impact of diversity of assets.

---

*1969 P-H TC Memo ¶69,158.

CASE THIRTEEN

Majority Interest Premium

HONE'S FURNITURE CORPORATION

Facts

Hone's Furniture Corporation (HFC) is an exquisite closely held furniture retailer catering primarily to the antique and upper-income class markets. HFC's shareholders are as follows:

Name	Shares
Ron Hone	501
Wilma Hone	124
Rhonda Hone	125
Lisa Hone	100
Laura Hone	100
Willie Smith	50
	1,000

Willie Smith, HFC's trusted night watchman and delivery man, recently sold 25 of his shares to Rhonda Hone for $400 per share, as Willie Smith wanted to make a down payment on a new house.

Ron Hone's banker, C. Robinson, has been discussing future personal financing for Ron Hone, and Ron has indicated his willingness to pledge all of his shares, if necessary, as collateral in order to secure a loan to satisfy Wilma's expensive habits. C. Robinson agrees that the recent sale of Willie Smith's stock is representative of an approximate value per share in HFC.

Value

Ron Hone and C. Robinson finally agree that due to Ron's majority interest his stock would receive a 15 percent premium over the sales price between Rhonda and Willie Smith. Ron's entire share value would be as follows:

Representative sale value per share	$ 400
Majority interest premium	× 1.15
Value per share	$ 460
Total shares held by Ron	× 501
Total value	$ 230,460

Analysis

The representative sale value indicates the sales price that a less than majority interest holder would receive for the sale of HFC's stock. Since Ron held a majority interest, his total interest should deserve a higher valuation due to the control represented by owning a majority interest. The facts of the case merited application of a premium. Obviously, however, other factors could have an impact on the final valuation.

SUMMARY

Although determination of a value, or value range, will be made using intrinsic methods, comparable corporate analysis, and/or representative sales or exchanges, discounts and premiums should be applied to such values depending upon the general level of ownership of the closely held business. The initial value computed under the various methods and the posture of the interest holder within the organization will both have a bearing on the application of a premium or discount.

NOTES FOR CHAPTER 8

1. See, for example, the Tax Court in Whittemore v. Fitzpatrick, 127 F. Supp. 710 (1954), and Estate of Damon v. Commissioner, 49 T.C. 108 (1967) discussing actual vs. effective control.

2. See Fellows and Painter, *Valuing Close Corporations for Federal Wealth Transfer Taxes: A Statutory Solution to the Disappearing Wealth Syndrome*, 30 Stan. L. Rev. 895 (May 1978).

3. See, generally, Field, *Current Techniques for Valuing Minority Stock Interests or Stock with Restrictions*, Taxation for Lawyers, January-February 1975, p. 244; and Whittemore v. Fitzpatrick, note 1 supra.

4. Pabst v. Commissioner, 1947 P-H TC Memo ¶47,300; Cravens v. Welch, 10 F. Supp. 94 (D.C. Col. 1935); Estate of de Guebriant v. Commissioner, 14 T.C. 611 (1950); aff'd and rev'd sub nom 186 F.2d 307 (2nd Cir. 1951).

5. Rev. Rul. 59–60, 1959-1 C.B. 237.

6. Ibid.

7. Blanchard v. United States, 291 F. Supp. 348 (S. D. Iowa 1968).

8. Ltr. Rul. 8010017. (See Appendix B.)

9. See Blanchard, note 7 supra, and discussion in Richardson v. Commissioner, 1943 P-H TC Memo ¶43,496.

10. Thomas W. Dant, Jr., *Courts Increasing Amount of Discount for a Minority Interest in a Business*, Journal of Taxation, August 1975, p. 104.

11. Discount of 15 percent allowed in Bollenbach v. Commissioner, 1974 P-H TC Memo ¶74,270; discount of 55 percent allowed in Gallun v. Commissioner, 1974 P-H TC Memo ¶74,284.

12. Dant, note 10 supra.

13. Schnorbach v. Kavanagh, 102 F. Supp. 828 (W.D. Mich. 1951).

14. Ibid. at 836.

15. See Estate of Salsbury v. Commissioner, 1975 P-H TC Memo ¶75,333, where 38.1 percent control premium was determined. See also Estate of O'Connell v. Commissioner, 1978 P-H TC Memo ¶78,191, where 12 percent premium was held to be insufficient. See also Estate of Maxcy v. Commissioner, 1969 P-H TC Memo ¶69,158, rev'd on other grounds 441 F.2d 192 (5th Cir. 1971); Whittemore v. Fitzpatrick, 127 F. Supp. 710 (D.C. Conn. 1954). Similar cases in concept, though not explicitly calling such discount a pyramid discount, are Williams v. Commissioner, 1973 P-H TC Memo ¶73,154, and Du Pont Dean v. Commissioner, 1960 P-H TC Memo ¶60,054.

16. Frank J. Kier, Executor, 28 B.T.A. 633 (1933); Estate of Brush v. Commissioner, 1963 P-H TC Memo ¶63,186 and Phillips v. United States, 12 F.2d 598 (W.D. Pa. 1926) rev'd 24 F.2d 195 (3rd Cir. 1928).

17. A. E. Staley, 41 B.T.A. 752 (1940); Driver v. United States, 38 AFTR 2d
    76-6315 (W.D. Wisc. 1976).

18. Ibid. Staley at 776.

9

Value Reduction
Through Discount Factors

The value determined using the valuation techniques set forth in the previous chapters will, in many cases, attract specific discounts in addition to those relating to the degree of ownership being valued. Such discounts may result from nonmarketability, existence of a restrictive agreement, intracompany human factors, or other unique characteristics of an entity.

DISCOUNT FOR LACK OF MARKETABILITY

An interest in a closely held business is not considered marketable (absent clear evidence to the contrary) due to the closely held nature of the ownership rights. Similar to the discount afforded a minority interest, a discount for lack of marketability is often utilized in valuing a closely held business interest. The general tendency, when valuing a minority interest, seems to be one of combining a nonmarketability discount with the minority discount, resulting in a single discount.[1] There are instances, however, where the facts warrant separate minority and nonmarketability discounts. In one such case, *Whittemore* v. *Fitzpatrick*,[2] a district court in Connecticut was indecisive as to the propriety of its valuation decision regarding a 600-share gift made to a trust for the benefit of the taxpayer's three sons. The court concluded that the gift was three separate 200-share transactions. However, in order to insulate itself from a redetermination of the value figure on appeal, the court also valued the entire 600 shares, applying a 50 percent discount for a lack of marketability. The 600 shares represented a controlling interest; however, when divided into three separate 200-share lots, each lot was considered to be a minority interest. Each share of stock, for the three 200-share blocks and the 600-share block, was determined to have a base value (before discounts) equal to each share's proportionate net asset value. The court allowed a 16 percent minority interest discount in addition to the 50 percent lack of marketability discount on each 200-share block. The court relied heavily on expert testimony in determining the amount of the discounts. Although the normal procedure is to combine minority and nonmarketability discounts, a nonmarketability discount, as witnessed in *Whittemore* v. *Fitzpatrick,* should generally apply to the valuation of a majority interest.

The use of the nonmarketability discount has increased over the years, in part due to the increasing number of smaller nonpublic firms. The early justification for such a discount was that it reflected the public offering expenses or "flotation costs" necessary to create a hypothetical market for a closely held interest. These costs are periodically published in percentage form by the SEC.[3] Such costs range from 5 percent for large offerings to 20 percent for smaller offerings based on the aggregate offer price. The rationale underlying discounts based on flotation cost percentages, however, has become suspect over the years as more and more smaller companies emerged where no public market could be created due to the increase in financial limits for public offerings. Therefore, in order to create a hypothetical public market for a closely held entity, it is necessary to use a discount greater than just flotation cost percentages. Such discount must recognize the virtual absence of a market for small private companies. The smaller the company, the larger the nonmarketability discount which is likely to be utilized. More recent nonmarketable discounts reflect the willing purchaser-willing seller attitude as to how saleable the interest really would be, taking into consideration earnings, dividends, posture of the entity, and the like, giving full effect to the nonpublic (lack of ease of disposition) status of the entity. Recent nonmarketability discounts have ranged from 20 to 30 percent,[4] and, when combined with minority discounts, have been in the 50 to 70 percent range.[5] There is now little question that the courts recognize the nonmarketable discount as a justifiable reduction of a previously determined value.[6]

Case Fourteen—Sasser Industries depicts the application of a nonmarketability discount as applied to a majority interest in a closely held corporation.

CASE FOURTEEN

Nonmarketability Discount

SASSER INDUSTRIES, INC.

Facts

Sasser Industries, Inc. (SII) manufactures certain surgical implements and medical equipment. Eric Sasser (Eric), sole shareholder of SII, is interested in determining the value of his 10,000 shares as he is contemplating selling his interest to a willing purchaser. Eric's preliminary valuation analysis utilizing comparable publicly traded corporations yields a value of $135 per share of SII stock.

Value

Eric's stock, since SII is a nonpublic company, is determined to have an ultimate per share value as follows:

Initial value	$ 135
20 percent reduction due to nonmarketability	(27)
Ultimate value	$ 108

Analysis

This figure should be compared with alternative computations of value under the intrinsic technique (Chapter 7). Likewise, the surgical implement and medical equipment industry outlook as well as other similar factors should be considered. The closely held status of the company and the lack of a ready market may justify a 25 to 30 percent reduction; however, the higher percentage discount is somewhat mitigated due to the purchase of the entire ownership interest. Therefore, a 20 percent discount is appropriate under these circumstances. Costs necessary to make SII stock marketable substantiate a portion of the discount applied.

RESTRICTIVE AGREEMENTS

Many times in the valuation of a closely held business interest, whether it be corporate or noncorporate, an agreement restricting the sale, transfer, or disposition of the ownership interest exists which must be considered. These agreements are primarily designed to maintain and protect ownership and control of the business. However, there are instances where the existence of a restrictive agreement will be the controlling factor in a valuation case. (For further discussion, see Chapter 14 and the planning necessary for a restrictive agreement to control value.) Such cases are usually where the restrictive agreement sets forth a designated purchase or sale price derived under a previously negotiated price or formula. If such price controls, it should negate the need for a formal valuation. On the other hand, a restrictive agreement may not control but rather only constitute an additional factor to be considered in determining ultimate value. In many cases, even if the restrictive agreement is not controlling, it will nevertheless suppress the potential trading of an ownership interest. Accordingly, even a noncontrolling restriction will generally serve as a basis for some discount in the valuation of the interest under consideration.

Revenue Ruling 59–60[7] discusses the impact of restrictive agreements in the valuation of closely held stock. The Ruling states that where the stock was acquired by a decedent and such stock is subject to an option reserved by the issuing corporation to repurchase the stock at a certain price, the option price is usually accepted as the controlling value for transfer tax purposes at death but is not controlling for lifetime transfer (gift) tax purposes.[8] Likewise, where the option is a result of voluntary action by the owner and is binding during life as well as at the death of the owner, such agreement does not necessarily determine the value. Where the owner is free to dispose of his interest at will, fair market value is not limited to the option price. The relationship of the parties, the percentage of ownership being valued, and other factors must also be considered.[9]

The Internal Revenue Service takes the position that it does not have to abide by the specifics of a restrictive agreement. The courts, however, are of the opinion that if qualifying characteristics are present, the agreement will control the value. In the majority of such instances, if the characteristics of the agreement are that 1) the price is either fixed or determined under a formula, and 2) the agreement represents a bona fide business arrangement with certain irrevocable rights (being absolute and nondiscretionary), the value under the agreement will be controlling.[10] If, however, the restrictions only apply at the death of the interest holder, the courts have determined that the fair market value, determined without regard to the restrictions (except to the extent that such restrictions are among the factors considered in determining such value), will control for transfer tax purposes at death.[11] Where the restrictions are binding both during the interest holder's life and at death, and are effective under all circumstances, the restricted price will control.[12] However, if the restriction is in effect during the life, as well as at the death of the interest holder, but is not binding under all circumstances, the restriction may not control.[13] Where the agreement is not controlling, it should nevertheless be considered a factor in arriving at a final value.[14] For a discussion of the specific types of restrictive agreements, see Chapter 14, which deals with planning opportunities.

The following brief discussion sets forth some areas where restrictive agreements were influential in a value determination. In *Helvering* v. *Salvage*,[15] the stock to be valued had been issued subject to an option to repurchase the shares at par value. In that case, the Supreme Court determined that the fair market value could not be in excess of the par value due to the controlling nature of the restrictive agreement. Likewise, the Tax Court, in *Phil Kalech*,[16] held that a book value restrictive agreement limited the value of the shares to the book value. It has also been held that a one-year restriction which did not prevent the sale but required the shareholder not to make a public offering had a depressing but not controlling effect on the value of the stock.[17]

With regard to partnerships, a partnership agreement which restricted the right of transfer or assignment of a decedent's partnership interest and allowed the surviving partners the option to purchase such interest after a partner's death at book value, limited the value of the decedent's partnership interest (for estate tax purposes) to the option-book value price even though it was less than the fair market value on the value date.[18] (See Chapter 14, relating to tax valuation planning for partnerships, for a more thorough discussion.)

An example of a restrictive agreement controlling the value of a business interest is given in Chapter 14, *Case Seventeen—Quast Contracting Company.*

HUMAN FACTORS

Certain discounts may be necessary when dealing with the human aspects of a business operation. Some influential factors in determining an ultimate value have been 1) business risk due to actions of officers or employees, and 2) loss of a key man within the organization.

The discountable risk associated with an employee's or officer's actions usually results in civil or criminal litigation involving the entity. The potential contingent loss of a business, assuming a willing purchaser is reasonably informed as to the loss, may warrant application of a percentage discount depending upon the degree of severity. Some circumstances may merely require an adjustment to the financial figures relied upon if the intrinsic valuation technique is utilized. (See Chapter 7, which deals with reliance on earning capacity, book value, dividends, and other factors used in the intrinsic valuation process.) However, if comparable corporate analysis or contemporaneous sales or exchanges are used, a percentage discount would be more appropriate. Litigation involving the company to be valued is discussed in more detail in Chapter 10. However, in one case discussed in that chapter, the Court of Claims recently allowed a 30 percent discount to the stock to be valued due to price fixing, illegal bid-rigging, and illegal corporate payments that occurred prior to the value date, although the full impact was not discovered until subsequent to such date.[19]

Dealing with the second human aspect discount, the future prospects of a business may be significantly diminished if the driving or motivating force behind the operations of the entity no longer exists. The loss of a key man in the organization may occur prior to a valuation date or may prompt a value determination for estate tax purposes. Under either of these instances, whether the gross value will be depressed as a result of such loss must be considered. A lower capitalization of earnings may result or a percentage discount may be required.

Revenue Ruling 59–60 indicates that key man insurance policies may have a mitigating effect on the depression of the value. Proceeds from insurance policies that are payable to the business entity are generally considered to be an asset of the entity for the purpose of determining the market value of an ownership in that business.[20] Such value can be reduced by the estimated loss sustained by the business because of the loss of a key man.[21] One valuation case has held that insurance proceeds are but one of many factors to be considered. This is contrary to the Internal Revenue Service position that the proceeds should be considered as an additional value to an otherwise determined figure.[22]

The general range of discount afforded to the loss of the key man appears to be 10 to 15 percent in instances where the continuation of the business is not in severe jeopardy.[23] If, however, the going concern nature of the business is doubtful, then a significantly greater discount may be allowed depending upon the technique used to determine the gross value. In cases where personnel loss is significant, it may be appropriate to consider net liquidation value as one of the key valuation measures.

Case Fifteen—Sanders Steel Corporation provides an example of a reduction of value due to the death of the dominant force in the business.

CASE FIFTEEN

Loss of Key Man Discount

SANDERS STEEL CORPORATION

Facts

Steve Sanders (Steve) was the founding father of Sanders Steel Corporation (SSC), a steel fabrication company which had been in existence for over 40 years. Steve died of a heart attack on March 16, 1981, while vacationing in the Bahamas. Steve was the president and treasurer of SSC, and was closely identified by the public with the corporation as the one person who came to mind when the SSC name was mentioned. Steve made all of the major decisions and negotiated all of the important contracts and sales. Steve was the majority shareholder, owning 9,000 out of 10,000 shares outstanding. Steve had, however, trained his son, Sam, as second line management to eventually take over the business.

Computation of value by using earnings and net asset value methods provides a figure of $75 per share.

Value

Because of the death of Steve and the effect on SSC, his shares are reduced as follows:

Initial value using earning and net asset value	$ 75
Loss of key man discount (12%)	(9)
Adjusted value per share	$ 66

Analysis

Steve was the dominant force in the business and his death reduces the value of the stock he held in SSC. The corporation has a competent person, Sam, to successfully assume Steve's duties. These two facts allow for a justifiable discount to the value otherwise determined. This key man discount should be made, however, in full view of other relevant facts, particularly in this case.

MISCELLANEOUS DISCOUNT FACTORS

There are several additional minor factors which may affect the ultimate value. One of these deals primarily with asset liquidation and is in essence a "taxes discount." This discount reduces an otherwise determined figure if such value has been developed relying upon the value of the underlying assets (the normal procedure for valuing an investment or holding type company; see Chapter 4). In this instance, the value given the underlying assets may be significantly above the acquisition cost of such assets. Liquidation of the entity would result in a substantial gain requiring the tax to be absorbed by the buyer. This tax could be considerable and inescapable due to the fact of retaining significant low cost basis assets. This "taxes discount," however, has recently been disregarded by the Tax Court for transfer tax purposes.[24] For other tax purposes, however, this tax should be considered and may be grouped with "other relevant factors" to consider.

Additionally, a "nonfinanceability" discount may be given if a company for some reason is deficient in its capital formation potential. These discounts may generally be with regard to the financial position of the company and are more specifically related to the analysis drawn under ratio and other financial considerations. (See Chapter 6.)

Another significant potentially discountable factor is that only unaudited financial statements are available for the firm to be valued. By not having the attest function performed by an independent certified public accountant, the credibility of the financial statements may be significantly diminished. Basic information to the valuation process may be misleading, misstated, or contain unintentional errors or omissions. A discount due to this lack of independent review of the fairness of the financial statements should be considered if the circumstances so warrant.

SUMMARY

Aside from the adjustments made with regard to the level of ownership interest within a firm, an interest to be valued may receive other discounts depending upon the facts of each case. If justified, discounts for nonmarketability, presence of a restrictive agreement, influential human factors, or other considerations may be necessary. The facts surrounding the valuation process and the purpose for the value will dictate the appropriateness of these discounts.

NOTES FOR CHAPTER 9

1. Central Trust Co. v. United States, 305 F.2d 393, 405 (Ct. Cl. 1962); Estate of Goodrich v. Commissioner, 1978 P-H TC Memo ¶78,248.

2. 127 F. Supp. 710 (D.C. Penn. 1954).

3. Securities and Exchange Commission, *Statistical Bulletin*, U.S. Government Printing Office, 1978. See also, "Cost of Flotation of Registered Securities" for respective years published by the U.S. Government Printing Office.

4. See Estate of Clarke v. Commissioner, 1976 P-H TC Memo ¶76,328; and Gallun v. Commissioner, 1974 P-H TC Memo ¶74,284.

5. Estate of Kirkpatrick v. Commissioner, 1975 P-H TC Memo ¶75,244; and Central Trust Company, note 1 supra.

6. Central Trust, note 1 supra, at 433.

7. 1959–1 C.B. 237.

8. Citing Rev. Rul. 54–76, 1954-1 C.B. 194 and Estate of Salt v. Commissioner, 17 T.C. 92 (1951).

9. Rev. Rul. 59–60, note 7 supra. See also Rev. Rul. 189, 1953-2 C.B. 294 relating to gifts and Estate of Caplan v. Commissioner, 1974 P-H TC Memo ¶74,039.

10. See Estate of Bischoff v. Commissioner, 69 T.C. 32 (1977) and Rev. Rul. 59–60, note 7 supra.

11. Land v. United States, 303 F.2d 170 (5th Cir. 1962), cert. denied, 371 U.S. 862; but cf. Estate of Anderson v. Commissioner, 1977 P-H TC Memo ¶77,237.

12. Estate of Salt, note 8 supra; Estate of Littick v. Commissioner, 31 T.C. 181 (1958).

13. Mathews v. United States, 226 F. Supp. 1003 (D.C. NY 1964).

14. See Heiner v. Gwinner, 114 F.2d 723 (3rd Cir. 1940); Estate of Cotchett v. Commissioner, 1974 P-H TC Memo ¶74,031.

15. 297 U.S. 106 (1936).

16. 23 T.C. 672 (1955), acq. 1955-2 C.B. 714.

17. Goldwasser v. Nunan, 47 B.T.A. 445 (1942), acq. 1942-2 C.B. 8, aff'd 142 F.2d 556 (2nd Cir. 1944), cert. denied, 323 U.S. 765 (1944).

18. See Fiorito v. Commissioner, 33 T.C. 440 (1959).

19. Estate of Tully, Sr. v. United States, 41 AFTR 2d 78–1477 (Ct. Cl. 1978).

20. Newell v. Commissioner, 66 F.2d 102 (7th Cir. 1933).

21. Ibid. at 103–4.

22. Estate of Huntsman v. Commissioner, 66 T.C. 861 (1976).

23. See Huntsman, ibid.; Estate of Clarke v. Commissioner, 1976 P-H TC Memo ¶76,328; United States v. Land, note 11 supra, but cf. Estate of Drott v. Commissioner, 15 AFTR 2d 1359 (D.C. Wisc. 1965) and In re Patton's Will, 278 N.W. 866 (S. Ct. Wisc. 1938).

24. Gifts—Gallun, note 4 supra and Estates—Thalheimer v. Commissioner, 1974 P-H TC Memo ¶74,203. See also Obermer v. Commissioner, 238 F. Supp. 29 (D.C. Haw. 1964); Whittemore v. Fitzpatrick, note 2 supra.

Using Experts to Full Advantage
in the Valuation Process

The use of experts to develop the value of a closely held business entity is a sound and recognized approach. The courts have accepted expert opinion evidence as one of the principal methods of proving value. Expert testimony is often used in developing intrinsic values and in determining comparable companies. In contested tax valuation cases, both parties usually present expert witnesses whose valuations may vary widely. While sometimes the courts will rely heavily on one litigant's expert or experts, a value ranging somewhere between the upper and lower limits of the values suggested by the opposing testimony will generally be adopted. This chapter deals with questions, assumptions, and definitions with which an expert should be familiar when formulating a value. This chapter will set forth criteria utilized by courts in determining the weight afforded a "testified value." Examples of questions an expert might be asked in order to develop a value are also included.

EXPERT CRITERIA

The expert should generally be familiar with the "fair market value" concept as it applies to valuation of a closely held business. Such value is not a liquidated value or the value at which an estate might be forced to sell to satisfy a tax obligation. It represents the proximity of value which would be used by a willing buyer and a willing seller negotiating at arm's length in an informed and open market. Obviously, certain variations will be necessary depending upon the facts of each case. Therefore, the expert should have complete knowledge of the facts of each case. Dates, total number of shares outstanding, financial statements, etc., need to be part of the expert's working tools. Charts, exhibits, flow charts, and other visual aids may be necessary in order to depict those factors utilized in determining a value.

In *Estate of Alvin Thalheimer,*[1] the Tax Court set down criteria to be utilized when judging the testimony of an expert witness in a valuation case. The court stated that the witness's demeanor, familiarity with the subject company, knowledge of the company's underlying assets, selection of comparable companies, valuation methods, and skills employed in assembling, analyzing, and weighing supporting data should be considered in expert valuations. An expert should generally be familiar with the promulgations issued by the Internal Revenue Service dealing with the valuation of closely held business interests. The shortcomings of not knowing the criteria set forth in Revenue Ruling 59–60[2] were recognized in *Diefenthal* v. *United States.*[3] The government's witness in that case was not familiar with several provisions of Revenue Ruling 59–60. Instead of considering the general financial background of the company to be valued, he selected certain years and omitted others in an apparent attempt to select those which better suited his conclusions. The witness read his testimony from his prepared reports on direct examination and answered unconvincingly on cross-examination when his reports were not made available to him. The expert's report contained mathematical errors which when corrected could not justify his conclusions. The witness sought to adjust the financial information he utilized on the basis of what he was "told," not upon valid information. A similar shortcoming appeared in *Allerton J. McEwan,*[4] where the Tax Court rejected the testimony of the taxpayer's expert on the grounds that the expert had an interest in the outcome of the litigation and because his testimony was based on unjustifiable assumptions.

Witnesses who are well-qualified to testify as to value have been relied upon heavily by the courts.[5] The courts reflect a favorable attitude toward experts who have a substantial number of years of valuation experience, have seniority within a reputable firm, and whose credentials include relevant publications.[6]

The methods used by expert witnesses vary widely. Regardless of their primary method of appraising a closely held business, an expert witness's testimony must be the result of careful consideration and more than a casual expression of an opinion. The courts are quick to disregard testimony which ignores relevant facts, such as established market value, or uses obviously faulty measurements.[7] The courts have also rejected testimony which they consider to be biased.[8]

COURT RELIANCE ON EXPERT TESTIMONY

There are certain characteristics of testimony which seem to increase the strength of expert testimony in the eyes of the courts. Such factors include the relevancy and general comparability of data used by the expert in his or her testimony. Nonrecurring, uncharacteristic and unusual data should be eliminated. In *Central Trust Company* v. *United States,*[9] the court criticized the expert's use of financial statements which were not available at the valuation date, remote sales of stock made during a period of uncharacteristic losses, and stale financial data. The courts also have a tendency to give greater weight to the testimony of an expert who is familiar with the facts and circumstances relevant to a particular stock, rather than possessing only general expertise in the valuation of closely held securities. In *Estate of Marion Christie,*[10] the Tax Court observed that while the government expert was qualified in the valuation of securities generally, the taxpayer's expert was more familiar with the subject stock, the limited market in which it was traded, and the stock of similar companies in the same geographical area. A view the courts seem to always solicit from an expert witness is the price the expert would pay for the stock to be valued, or the price he would advise his client to pay for it.[11] If the taxpayer fails to use as a valuation witness the investment banking firm which underwrote a public offering of the subject stock shortly after the valuation date, a court would clearly view such action with disfavor.[12] For valuations of a closely held corporation where the value date precedes a public issue, see Chapter 12.

The courts have given weight to values solicited from experts who use statistics or methods that are employed or sanctioned by government agencies such as the Federal Trade Commission or the SEC.[13] A district court in one instance applied a discount figure which was similar to a witness's discount percentage derived from securities transactions reported to the SEC.[14]

The ultimate value determined does not have to be the value solicited from either party's expert witnesses. The courts are not bound by the formulas or opinions proffered by expert witnesses, but are free to reach a determination of value based upon their own analysis of all the evidence in the record.[15] In a Second Circuit case, in fact, the court stated that "valuation is . . . necessarily an approximation. It is not necessary that the value arrived at by the trial court be a figure as to which there is specific testimony, if it is within the range of figures that may properly be deduced from the evidence."[16]

EXAMPLES OF QUESTIONS WHICH MAY BE ASKED OF EXPERTS

Testimony dealing with determination of value will normally come from a person who is familiar with financial matters and who has the ability to analyze and interpret data to arrive at a reasonable value. The most likely candidates to serve as expert witnesses are investment bankers and accountants. The following question sets are guidelines which might be used in substantiating the value used for tax purposes.

Obviously, it is necessary for anyone serving as an expert to demonstrate his or her qualifications. Such questions are beyond the scope of this book. Once the qualifications of an expert have been established, the next step is to determine the factors, traits, and techniques utilized in valuing a closely held business entity. These can be broken down into nine major categories, all being representative of criteria contained in Revenue Ruling 59–60:

(a) nature and history of the entity,

(b) economic outlook and condition of the industry,

(c) book value and financial condition of the business,

(d) earnings capacity of the company,

(e) dividend-paying capacity,

(f) representative sales of stock,

(g) restrictive agreements,

(h) lack of marketability, and

(i) comparative corporations.

Nature and History of the Entity

If the entity to be valued is a closely held corporation, information should be solicited with regard to the expert's association with that particular corporation. For an accountant, this may involve preparation of tax returns, tax advice relating to a corporate inception or reorganization, or any other closely held business functions in which an accountant is utilized. For an investment banker, an association with the closely held corporation could involve registration of securities subsequent to the value date for public distribution or other financial endeavors. Questions to determine the familiarity of the expert with the entity might include the following:

1. Describe your relationship with the entity to be valued.

2. How long has this relationship existed?

3. What is your association with the officers and/or shareholders of the corporation? Or, if a closely held noncorporate business: What is your acquaintance with the owners?

4. What is the total number of shares outstanding in this corporation and what portion of that represents the shares to be valued? Or, if applicable: What is the percentage interest to be valued?

5. What are the classes and characteristics of the ownership interests in this entity?

6. List the owners and their respective interests in this entity.

7. What is the interest you are presently valuing and who is its owner?

8. Have you on a previous occasion been requested to determine the value of an interest in this entity?

9. If yes: When was that appraisal made and what was the purpose of it?

10. What is your understanding of the term "fair market value"?

11. What is the general and specific nature of the business of the entity to be valued?
12. What are the various markets of which this entity would be considered to be a part?
13. On what date was the entity founded, and by whom?
14. List the locations of this business entity.
15. What is the breakdown of sales volume and percentage of net income with respect to each location?
16. What is the nature of the clientele which this entity serves?
17. Who are its major customers?
18. What is the financial condition of its major customers and what are their future prospects?

The Economic Outlook and Condition of the Industry

A knowledge of the economic outlook and condition of the industry is necessary in order to determine the success, or lack thereof, of the entity and its competition within the industry. Questions asked in this area might be along the following lines:

1. As of the value date, describe the general financial and overall economic condition of the industry.
2. Describe the entity's position within this industry.
3. As of the value date, who were this entity's major competitors?
4. What was the position of those competing entities within this industry as of the value date?
5. Who is considered to dominate this industry?
6. How does this business compete with the dominating firms in this industry?

Book Value and Financial Condition of the Business

The book value and other financial considerations are likely to give a view of the general condition of the entity to be valued. An expert might be asked such questions as:

1. What is the method you used to determine the book value of the interest being valued?
2. Which financial statements did you use?
3. Did you account for the period of time between the date of the financial statement and the valuation date on which the book value was derived?

4. Did you use consistent accounting methods to bring the financial statement up to date?

5. What is your opinion of the entity's financial position on the value date?

6. List those ratios and/or other financial data that were used by you to determine the financial position of this entity.

7. List any adjustments to the financial statements that you deemed necessary in order to properly reflect the value.

8. What is the justification for these adjustments?

Earning Capacity of the Entity

The earning power and history of the entity will be significant in determining the value which a willing buyer and willing seller would place on an operating company. Questions which could be asked in determining the earning power and history of the subject entity might include:

1. How did you compute the earnings per share and what is the amount for each of the last five years?

2. What, if any, adjustments were made in arriving at these figures?

3. What weight was afforded each year's earnings figures?

4. Do you consider earnings a significant factor in determining the fair market value for this entity (or an interest in this entity)?

Dividend-Paying Capacity

An investor is obviously concerned with that amount of money which will represent a return on his immediate investment. Therefore, dividends (or cash distributions) play a significant role in the determination of a fair market value. Questions regarding dividend-paying capacity might be:

1. Describe the dividend (or cash distribution) history of this entity.

2. If the earning trends reflected an upward movement, would that necessarily cause an increase in the payment of dividends (or cash distributions) in the future?

3. In your examination of the past record of distributions, how did you arrive at a dollar per share figure that would represent the dividend-paying (or cash distribution) capacity?

4. What are the factors that are deemed to affect distributions by a closely held entity versus distributions by a publicly traded entity?

5. What are the names and salary amounts received by the officers of this entity?

6. In your opinion, do such amounts represent reasonable compensation?

Representative Sales

Generally, a good indicator of fair market value is the existence of a representative sale of an interest in the entity before or after the value date. Questions to solicit this testimony from an expert could include the following:

1. What is your opinion about how sales of similar interests on or about the value date affect the determination of fair market value of the interest to be valued?
2. Were there any sales of interests in this entity within the last several years?
3. Describe the dates, prices, and amounts at which similar interests were sold.
4. Did you use the sales when determining the value of this interest?

   (*Note:* If yes, the answer should indicate why the sale was comparable.)

Restrictive Agreements

Restrictive agreements, as was shown in Chapter 9, oftentimes determine the fair market value of an interest in a closely held business. The existence of these agreements should be made known to the expert. Questions in this area might be as follows:

1. What are the restrictions and/or limitations with regard to this business interest?
2. Due to the nature of these restrictions and/or limitations, what is your determination as to the fair market value of the subject interest?
3. Does this restrictive agreement have a bona fide business purpose?

Lack of Marketability

Since a closely held business interest is not freely marketable, certain discounts are commonly afforded such interests. This lack of marketability discount was discussed in the previous chapter. Questions regarding the lack of marketability might be along the following lines:

1. On the basis of the cash distribution capacity, earnings, and book value, what amount of discount due to a lack of marketability did you allow?
2. What is the basis for such discount?

Comparable Entities

As was set forth in Chapter 6, comparable entities have an impact upon the determination of fair market value. The normal method used by a security analyst would be that of the comparative appraisal method. In this area, the questions along the following lines could be used:

1. What method did you use in determining comparable entities?
2. What are your guidelines for selections of comparable companies?
3. What companies did you consider in your comparative analysis?
4. Of the companies you considered, which ones did you choose for comparison with the company to be valued herein?
5. Why were the other companies eliminated?
6. What is the principal business line of the companies that were selected?
7. Why were some entities selected that manufactured a product different from the one manufactured by the entity to be valued?
8. In your collection of data from comparable entities, what were the significant items that you used?
9. In determining the fair market value, did you apply a discount for a lack of marketability to comparable figures?
10. Show the figures and computations that you used in determining the comparable entities.

Analysis

The above questions give nothing more than a quick synopsis of certain factors that should be considered by an expert witness. They are not intended to be comprehensive, but are designed to give merely an idea of the approach an expert might use to analyze the significant valuation factors in a particular case.[17]

SUMMARY

Expert witnesses play an important role in the valuation process due to 1) the technical difficulties encountered in the formulation of a value, and 2) the need for authoritative support for a value figure. Expert testimony is generally viewed with favor by the courts if the expert is qualified to testify about a value. The benefits of a well-versed expert in utilizing valuation techniques can many times provide the additional factor necessary to substantiate a value contention.

NOTES FOR CHAPTER 10

1. 1974 P-H TC Memo ¶74,203.

2. 1959-1 C.B. 237.

3. 343 F. Supp. 1208 (E.D. La. 1972).

4. 1956 P-H TC Memo ¶56,027, aff'd per curiam, 241 F.2d 887 (2d Cir. 1957).

5. Frank v. Commissioner, 54 T.C. 75 (1970), aff'd 447 F.2d 552 (7th Cir. 1971); Anderson v. Commissioner, 1970 P-H TC Memo ¶70,271; and Estate of Reynolds v. Commissioner, 55 T.C. 172 (1970).

6. Central Trust Company v. United States, 305 F.2d 393 (Ct. Cl. 1962); Nelson A. Elsasser, 12 B.T.A. 681 (1928) (acq. VII-2 C.B. 12); Estate of Thompson v. Commissioner, 1959 P-H TC Memo ¶59,183; and Kanawha Banking & Trust Company, 29 B.T.A. 376 (1933).

7. Frizzelle Farms, Inc. v. Commissioner, 61 T.C. 737 (1974); aff'd 511 F.2d 1009 (4th Cir. 1975); and Rodman v. Commissioner, 57 T.C. 113 (1971).

8. Frank, note 5 supra.

9. See note 6 supra.

10. 1974 P-H TC Memo ¶74,095.

11. Roberts v. Commissioner, 1945 P-H TC Memo ¶45,263; Estate of Stroh v. Commissioner, 1943 P-H TC Memo ¶43,031; Colonial Trust Company v. Kraemer, 63 F. Supp. 866 (D. Conn. 1945).

12. Silverman v. Commissioner, 1971 P-H TC Memo ¶71,143.

13. Estate of Thompson, note 6 supra.

14. Clark v. United States, 36 AFTR 2d 75-6417 (E.D. N.C. 1975).

15. Helvering v. National Grocery Co., 304 U.S. 282, 294 (1934); Palmer v. Commissioner, 523 F.2d 1308 (8th Cir. 1956) and Penn v. Commissioner, 219 F.2d 18, 21 (9th Cir. 1955).

16. Silverman v. Commissioner, 538 F.2d 927, 930 (2nd Cir. 1976).

17. For an example of jury instructions on factors to consider in the valuation of a close corporation see Medlock v. United States, 28 AFTR 2d 71-6239 (D.C. Neb. 1971).

11

Preferred Stock
Valuation Techniques

The general guidelines set forth in the previous chapters relating to the valuation of common shares in a closely held corporation also apply to the valuation of preferred shares within a closely held corporation. Certain adjustments and/or additional considerations regarding this separate level of ownership interest are necessary in order to arrive at a proper value.

The valuation of preferred stock has gained increased significance over the past several years, including its importance for contributions to Employee Stock Ownership Plans.[1] In many cases, preferred stock may be subject to restrictive agreements. If a restrictive agreement exists, then the agreement, if satisfying the elements set forth in Chapter 9, should be representative of the fair value of the preferred stock. For a further discussion pertaining to the utilization of restrictive agreements in the valuation process, see Chapter 14. The issuance of preferred stock in a corporate recapitalization is also an effective technique in freezing the value of a closely held corporation. See Chapter 14, which deals with planning opportunities and the use of preferred stock in corporate recapitalizations.

Little precedent has been established by the courts or Internal Revenue Service for valuation of preferred stock. Hence, no general rules exist for valuation of preferred stock other than the paralleling techniques used to value common stock. Typical of the conclusions drawn by the courts in cases involving the valuation of preferred stock is that of the Tax Court in *Alvin H. Behrend*.[2] In *Behrend*, the court was confronted with the task of ascertaining the value of nonvoting, noncumulative, redeemable class B preferred stock in a closely held corporation which had been given to a charitable foundation. No dividends had been paid on the stock up to the date of the contribution. The taxpayer contended that the value of the stock was $100 per share. The Internal Revenue Service contended that the stock was worthless. The Tax Court determined the value of the stock to be $57 per share, but failed to give the details as to how the value was determined, saying that "it would serve no useful purpose to discuss . . . the many arguments and theories advanced by both sides in this purely fact-finding question."[3] It is unfortunate that the courts have provided no guidelines for valuing preferred stock.

PREFERRED STOCK CHARACTERISTICS

Characteristics, restrictions, and rights of preferred stock in a closely held corporation should be determined at the outset of the valuation endeavor. A preferred stock generally will contain a combination of the following characteristics:

(1) subordinate or senior to other preferred stock issued,

(2) nonconvertible or convertible into other securities of the corporation,

(3) nonvoting, possessing a voting fraction, or voting pro rata with common shares,

(4) nonparticipating or participating in the profits of the corporation,

(5) noncumulative or cumulative with regard to nonpayment of dividends,

(6) possessing liquidation preference or redemption (call) feature, and

(7) possessing other contingent rights in the event that dividends are not paid.

The particular characteristics involved in each case need to be considered in their entirety to ascertain the power and level of rights afforded the preferred stock since such factors will bear on the ultimate value of such stock.

PREFERRED VALUE ATTRIBUTES

Preferred stock of a closely held corporation will generally have characteristics that are similar to publicly traded preferred shares for which current dividend yield and published market prices are available. Therefore, one method to be used to determine the value of preferred stock is the comparison of dividend rates and dividend yields of similar publicly traded stocks. This involves the consideration of financial and nonfinancial information to identify comparable companies as set forth in Chapter 6. In *Kirshaw Manufacturing Company, Inc.,*[4] an expert witness made a comparison of preferred stock of a closely held corporation with preferred stock of five publicly traded corporations based on earnings and assets of the respective corporations. The preferred stock of the closely held corporation was given as a bonus and was being valued for compensation purposes. The expert concluded that the closely held stock should yield 5.75 percent on the valuation date and determined a tentative value based upon such yield. He then reduced that value by 15 percent to reflect the lack of marketability of the closely held stock. The discount was based upon statistics compiled by the SEC covering the cost of flotation and distribution of the new stock. The Tax Court criticized the expert's method on two grounds: 1) the use of book values of the various corporations as a criterion of comparison, and 2) the comparison of the stock to stock with different voting and preference rights without making allowances for such variations. However, the court did not criticize the expert's reliance on dividend yield and, in fact, arrived at a value which was only 5 percent less than that of the expert.

The holding in the *Kirshaw* case paralleled somewhat the holding in a 1931 Court of Claims case, *Oxford Paper Company* v. *United States.*[5] The Court of Claims in that case held that the selling price of publicly traded preferred stock with an equivalent dividend rate was a relevant fact and should be considered together with all the other evidence in the case. In *Oxford Paper Company*, the court was confronted with a corporation engaged in cutting timber and selling pulpwood for the manufacture of paper. The court was critical of the government's valuation which relied entirely on the value of the underlying assets allocable to the preferred stock. The court determined a fair market value somewhat less than the value of the assets due to the necessity of considering the presence of common stock and relevant comparable market prices.

Par value limitations have also been considered by the courts in the determination of a preferred stock value. In *Elihu B. Washburne,*[6] the Tax Court considered the value of a minority owner holding $100 par value, 5 percent, noncumulative, nonvoting preferred stock (on which dividends had never been paid), and $1.00 par value common stock. The Internal Revenue Service issued a notice of deficiency for compensation received by the taxpayers upon receipt of preferred stock and common stock based upon the par values of such stock. The Internal Revenue Service subsequently changed its position in its brief, arguing that the value was proportionate to the amount which had been paid by another shareholder to obtain a controlling interest. The Tax Court dismissed the revised method as unrealistic. The court considered the net asset value of the preferred stock and common stock, along with other valuation factors. However, it discounted the importance of net asset value in determining the value of a minority interest, as compared to controlling interest. The value determined by the Tax Court, however, was not allocated between the preferred and common stocks.

In *William H. Mauldin,*[7] the taxpayer contended that a charitable contribution of preferred stock should be valued at the par value of such stock. The preferred stock was 5 percent, noncumulative, nonvoting, $100 par, with the redemption price of $105. The Tax Court applied a 33 1/3 percent discount to the par value based on " . . . the rate of return and the absence of any concrete evidence as to how (the corporation) was to operate and what its profits would be . . ."[8]

In *Estate of Joseph E. Salsbury,*[9] the Tax Court determined that class A common stock was essentially voting preferred stock. The stock to be valued constituted 51.8 percent of the voting control of a corporation engaged in manufacturing drugs and health products for poultry and other animals. All of the expert witnesses and the court valued the stock by dividing the stock into two elements: 1) preferred stock value, and 2) the control value. The values determined by the parties were widely divergent due to the differing amounts of control value to be applied. However, all parties assigned to the stock, for its "preferred stock value," an amount equal to par, plus the preference in liquidation. From the testimony at the trial, it appears that in determining the "preferred stock value" of the class A common shares, more than one expert witness noted the fact that the values of stock, if based on a dividend yield factor of comparable quality stock, would not vary markedly from par value. One witness stated that if the stock were straight preferred, it would sell for 85 to 90 percent of par. However, he, like others, used par value as the "preferred stock value." The court applied a control premium of 38.1 percent to the preferred stock value to arrive at the final value.

Liquidation value, when valuing preferred stock, has also been used as a valuation base. In *Rank* v. *United States*,[10] the taxpayer received cumulative preferred stock with liquidation preference to the extent of $50 per share and paying annual dividends of $3.50 per share in exchange for his interest in a partnership. During the same period of time as the valuation date, packages of one share of preferred and five shares of common stock were sold to the public at $50 per unit. The directors of the corporation had authorized the sale of the common stock at $3.00 a share, but no shares were sold. The Internal Revenue Service initially contended that the consideration received in the form of the preferred stock was equal to the guaranteed liquidation value ($50 per preferred share). In revising the amount of consideration received by the taxpayer, the Internal Revenue Service subtracted from the liquidation value of the preferred stock ($50) the offering price of five shares of common stock ($15), to arrive at a value of $35 per share. The court affirmed the value as determined by the Internal Revenue Service.

As can be seen from the case law, preferred stock valuation encompasses basically the same factors as valuation of common stock. However, the preferred share value takes into heavier consideration basic quantifiable value figures such as par, liquidation, and comparable preferred values. *Case Sixteen— Petty Corporation* presents a preferred stock valuation fact situation.

CASE SIXTEEN

Valuation of Preferred Stock

PETTY CORPORATION*

Facts

Petty Corporation (PC) is a closely held real estate holding company organized by Willis Petty (Willis). Willis has decided to make a charitable contribution of

---

*Based on *Estate of Lee,* 69 T.C. 860 (1978).

25,000 shates of preferred stock, representing one-half of the total preferred stock issued, and outstanding, all being held by Willis. In addition, Willis holds 4,000 shares of the common stock with 1,000 shares being owned by Willis's two daughters. The preferred shares are 7 percent noncumulative, nonparticipating, and nonvoting, with a par value of $100 per share. In addition, these shares have a liquidity preference of two times par or $200. Willis donated his shares on December 30, 1980, to a qualified charitable organization.

The amount of the contribution is being contested by the Internal Revenue Service. Both parties agree that PC should be valued on the basis of its net assets and have stipulated that the value of PC as of December 30, 1980, is $5,000,000.

Value

Contended by Willis	$ 100
Contended by IRS	$ 40
Determined by court	$ 72

The Internal Revenue Service contended that since the preferred stock has no power to force distribution through dividends, redemptions, or liquidation, it had a nominal value. However, the Internal Revenue Service is willing to concede a value of $40 per share.

Willis, on the other hand, argues in part that the common and preferred shares of PC should be valued on a per share basis. The common shares would be of nominal value since, although the common shareholders have control of the corporation, the common shareholders have no reasonable anticipation of a monetary return in the foreseeable future because all appreciation up to $10,000,000 in net assets would accrue to the benefit of the preferred shareholders. For this reason, the preferred shares should be assigned the net asset value of PC, or $100 per share ($5,000,000 ÷ 50,000).

The court determined the final value as follows:

Net asset value	$ 5,000,000
Times 80 percent interest in common shares held by Willis	× .80
Value to Willis	4,000,000
Less 10 percent lack of marketability	(400,000)
Adjusted value to Willis	3,600,000
Divided by total preferred shares held by Willis	÷ 50,000
Preferred share value	$ 72

Analysis

This case illustrates the arbitrary approach usually taken to arrive at final value in cases involving a complex capital structure. This approach to valuation of preferred stock by the courts, rather than a logical, well-reasoned approach, is illustrative of why no sound valuation rules exist for preferred stock.

SUMMARY

Valuation of preferred stock in a closely held corporation entails careful consideration of the particular characteristics and rights of such stock in each case. Preferred stock can play an important role in valuation planning, as will be seen in Chapter 14.

NOTES FOR CHAPTER 11

1. Section 409A(a) (3). The Valuation Committee of the ESOP Association of America recently adopted Rev. Rul. 59–60, with modifications, as the valuation guideline for ESOPs and TRASOPs.

2. 1961 P-H TC Memo ¶61,064.

3. Ibid.

4. 20 T.C.M. (CCH) 443 (1961), rev'd and rem'd on another issue, 313 F.2d 942 (5th Cir. 1963).

5. 32 F.2d 1008 (Ct. Cl. 1931).

6. 1968 P-H TC Memo ¶68,122.

7. 60 T.C. 749 (1973), acq. 1974-2 C.B. 3.

8. Ibid. at 759.

9. 1975 P-H TC Memo ¶75,333.

10. 73 F.2d 813 (5th Cir. 1934).

Handling Special Situations
in the Valuation Process

This chapter will deal with certain special problems which arise from time to time in the valuation process. First, the perplexing but common problem involving facts in existence on the valuation date which are unknown, or about which little is known, will be addressed. Second, the basic valuation considerations pertaining to a closely held business which holds assets unrelated to its principal business endeavors will be explored. Third, the provision of the Internal Revenue Code dealing with small business real property valuations for estate tax purposes will be examined. Next, the impact on the valuation process of community property laws, unique to several states, will be discussed. Likewise, the effect of governmental controls on the business to be valued will be analyzed. Finally, the problems of valuations preceding a public offering of stock identical to that to be valued will be considered.

LACK OF INFORMATION UNTIL AFTER VALUATION DATE

The courts and the Internal Revenue Service have consistently stated that failure to consider all relevant facts and circumstances is an error in the valuation process.[1] Accordingly, in order to value a closely held business for tax purposes in accordance with the criteria set forth by the Internal Revenue Service and the courts, no relevant fact can be excluded from consideration. Nevertheless, there are definite parameters to the universe of facts and circumstances which can be considered. A primary question is whether the valuation expert is to look past the valuation date to determine the ultimate impact of facts which may not have appeared significant on the valuation date. This situation is best explained by the following question: "Are we required to limit ourselves to the facts known on or prior to the critical date, or may we look to the future to see what happened to the property under valuation after the critical date?"[2]

If a fact is known prior to or on the valuation date, there is little question that such a fact must be considered in the valuation process.[3] It is also well-accepted that a fact occurring after the valuation date and independent of any previous act (even though known prior to the determination of the ultimate value) cannot be considered in the valuation process.[4] Certain facts in existence on the valuation date do not fall into either of these categories. Such facts are those about which little or nothing is known until an event occurring after the valuation date clarifies the importance of the previously obscure fact. On several occasions the courts have been required to evaluate the effect of such facts. In these cases, the courts have recognized that such facts must be given due consideration in reaching a final value.

In *United States* v. *Simmons*,[5] the Fifth Circuit was confronted with the effect of a fact existing on the valuation date about which little was known. Prior to the decedent's death, the Internal Revenue Service conducted an investigation of possible tax fraud. As a result of the investigation, the decedent had paid a deficiency in the amount of $43,000. The decedent passively conceded to the payment of the deficiency and did not file a claim for refund for any part of the payment. Shortly after the decedent's death, the executors retained special tax counsel to investigate the possibility of refund of the tax, penalties, and interest paid by the decedent. Approximately ten months after the decedent's death, the special tax counsel discovered a pencil memorandum among the effects of the decedent which tended to disprove the possibility of fraud. Shortly after the discovery of this memorandum, a claim for refund was filed for years which would have been closed except for the asserted fraud. The claim was filed prior to the filing of the estate tax return so that the executor included the claim in the estate tax return. The claim was given a zero value on the premise that since no one knew about the cause for the claim or the important pencil memorandum on the valuation date, the claim had no ascertainable value. The Internal Revenue Service contended that the claim did have a value which should have been included, even though no one knew on the valuation date that the basis for such claim existed. The jury found the claim valueless at the time of the decedent's death. The Fifth Circuit reversed the decision and held that there was no rational basis for the jury's finding that the claim was without value on the valuation date. The Fifth Circuit suggested that the district court charge to the jury that "'reasonable knowledge of all relevant facts'. . . includes knowledge of documents in existence at the time of death and later discovered by the estate's attorney."[6] The Fifth Circuit concluded that ignorance of an existing fact at the date of death did not make such fact irrelevant for purposes of valuing property on that date.

In *Estate of Isaac W. Baldwin*,[7] the executors of the estate and others filed an action in equity against the decedent's brother, G. Daniel Baldwin, and others. The suit was based primarily on an alleged fraud and breach of trust committed by G. Daniel Baldwin during the decedent's lifetime in operating a partnership between Isaac and G. Daniel Baldwin and in managing the property of Isaac and others. The fraud and breach of trust upon which the suit was based was discovered by the executors during the course of the administration of the estate. The court held that the claim subsequently filed by the executors should be included in the estate. By doing so, the court endorsed the premise that a fact existing on the date of valuation should be considered in establishing the value of a decedent's estate, even if little or nothing is known about such fact at the date of death. The Tax Court distinguished between 1) events occurring on or prior to the valuation date, thus being probative of value, and 2) events occurring after the valuation date which could not have been anticipated at the value date, thus having no effect on valuation.

In a recent Court of Claims case, *Estate of Tully* v. *United States*,[8] the court allowed a 30 percent reduction of an otherwise determined value due to the company's disreputable practices in the construction contracting business. The company to be valued was a construction firm involved in an illegal activity which started before the decedent's death. However, it was not discovered publicly until four years after the date of death. The firm had been involved in illegal bid-rigging and price fixing involving its primary customer, Consolidated Edison Company of New York. The court determined that a potential purchaser of the stock on the value date would have conducted a reasonable prepurchase investigation which would have uncovered the illegal business dealings between the company to be valued and representatives of Consolidated Edison. Although the estate subsequently contended that the stock to be valued was worthless, the court stated that the illegal activities were simply business risks that should be taken into consideration in determining the probable future profitability of the business. The illegal nature of the relationship, and its subsequent discovery, was determined to have an adverse impact on a willing purchaser's desire to purchase the business. The court placed on the estate the burden of proof that a reasonable investigation of the facts in existence as of the value date, although not being made public, should disclose an act about which little or nothing was known. Although the court stated that the use of hindsight is not permissible in making valuations, the court used hindsight to determine the magnitude of the illegal activity, the impact of which was not fully known until four years subsequent to the value date.

Several cases support the contention that relevant facts to be considered in the valuation process are those existing at the moment of valuation, whether or not actually known at that time. The courts appear to focus on a "relevant facts discoverable" standard. Facts qualifying under this test are those capable of being discovered by a hypothetical buyer in the course of obtaining reasonable knowledge of all relevant facts. In a valuation endeavor, therefore, investigatory questions, interviews, and other discovery methods must be utilized so that all relevant facts will be considered.

MISCELLANEOUS ASSETS OR OPERATIONS

It is not uncommon for a closely held business to hold miscellaneous assets or have numerous seemingly unrelated operations. As stated in Chapter 4, in the valuation of operating and holding companies, controversies may exist as to the true character of the entity to be valued. This is especially true when the entity is an operating company owning valuable assets or is a holding company in control of operating companies.

An operating company which holds substantial investment assets must be valued, according to the courts, by considering the operations separate from the investments.[9] The investment assets should be valued and such value should be taken into consideration along with the value determined for the operating portion of the entity. The valuation of the operating portion involves the application of intrinsic factors to determine a value. The underlying asset value is generally used for the investments or other passive holdings. Also, when an operating company has several diverse subsidiaries or division lines, segmental valuation may be necessary. Under segmental valuation, each portion (or segment) of the business is valued and the aggregate value of the segments represents the overall entity value. However, if there exists a fair degree of diversification between the segment lines, the pyramid discount (Chapter 8) may apply. The pyramid discount may also apply to an investment company holding diverse investments.

The justification of the pyramid discount is that the more diverse a business to be valued, the more difficult the disposition thereof due to such diversification. Underlying this premise is the fact that such diverse assets are held in corporate form. The valuation entails valuing the stock, or the ownership interest, and not each separate asset. The Internal Revenue Service has attempted to argue that any owner possessing a majority interest is able to cause the business entity to liquidate and sell the assets piecemeal at their fair market value.[10] The courts have rejected this argument and stated in one case that "whether or not a purchaser of a controlling interest . . . could liquidate the corporation and sell its assets is immaterial, as there must still be found a purchaser of the stock who would be willing to undertake such a procedure."[11] This statement recognizes the fact that the ownership interest of the entity is being valued and not the underlying assets themselves, although the underlying asset value may provide a good benchmark for the computation of a value for the stock.

SMALL BUSINESS REAL PROPERTY

There is a special exception to the general fair market value determination in the transfer tax area for a decedent's estate dealing with qualifying small business real property. Under the general definition of fair market value, one of the most important factors utilized is that of the presupposition that the value is the "highest and best" use to which the property can be put, rather than the actual use of the property at the time it is to be valued. Valuation on the basis of the highest and best use, rather than actual use, may result in the imposition of a substantial transfer tax at death. In recognizing that the potential transfer tax liability may be so severe as to jeopardize the continuation of the closely held business, legislation was passed allowing an alternate valuation using a special use valuation technique.[12]

The special use valuation election is available when the following conditions are satisfied:

(1) at least 50 percent of the adjusted value of the gross estate consists of real or personal property devoted to a closely held business at the time of the owner's death,

(2) the real property devoted to qualifying use comprises at least 25 percent of the adjusted value of the gross estate (for the purposes of satisfying both the 50 percent test and the 25 percent test, the qualifying property would be considered at its "most suitable use" value or its otherwise determined fair market value),

(3) the qualifying property passes to a qualifying heir or heirs of the decedent; the qualifying heir or heirs would be the individual's ancestors or lineal descendants, a lineal descendant of a grandparent of such individual, the spouse of such individual, or the spouse of any such descendant, including a legally adopted child,

(4) the real property had been owned by the decedent or his family for five out of the eight years ending on the date of the decedent's death and was devoted to qualifying use during such period of time, and

(5) the decedent or a member of the decedent's family had participated materially in the operations of the business during the period determined under the preceding requirement.[13]

Additionally, there is a requirement that the special use valuation cannot reduce the value of the property by more than $500,000 from the "highest and best use" valuation. For example, if the decedent's estate contains qualifying property valued at $750,000 at its "highest and best use," and the same property is valued at $150,000 at its current use, the gross estate will be reduced by only $500,000, not $600,000.[14]

In passing this legislation it was recognized that it would be a windfall to the beneficiaries of an estate to allow the real property used for the closely held business purpose to be valued under the "special use" criteria unless the beneficiaries continued to use the property for the business purpose for a reasonable period of time after the decedent's death. Therefore, there is a provision providing for recapture of the tax benefit where the real property is prematurely sold or is converted to nonqualifying uses.[15]

The methods listed in the Internal Revenue Code (and explained in the proposed regulations) for determining the value of the closely held business qualifying property are as follows:

(1) the capitalization of income which the property can be expected to yield over a reasonable period of time under prudent management,

(2) the capitalization of fair rental value of the property for closely held business purposes,

(3) assessed land values in a state which provides a differential or use value assessment law for closely held businesses,

(4) comparable sales of other closely held business land in the same geographical area far enough from a metropolitan or resort area so that nonagricultural use is not a significant factor in the sales price, and

(5) any other factor which fairly values the closely held business value of the property.[16]

A special election to have this provision apply is required and must be made not later than the time for filing the estate tax return.[17] A qualified attorney or accountant can assist the taxpayer in making this special election, and should be consulted prior to adopting the "special use" valuation technique.

COMMUNITY PROPERTY LAWS

Several states have community property laws which can sometimes complicate the valuation process.[18] Normally, in the valuation undertaking, the community property laws will affect the determination of majority or minority interest (Chapter 8). At one time, it was believed that each spouse's community half should be included as part of one aggregated interest.[19] The result of this aggregation was severe when a deceased spouse was deemed to have a majority interest regardless of the fact that such spouse individually possessed only a minority interest in the business. Accordingly, no minority discount could be used in valuing the deceased spouse's interest.

The Internal Revenue Code now provides a fair market value basis for "property which represents the surviving spouse's one-half share of community property held by the decedent and a surviving spouse under the community property laws of any state . . . if at least one-half of the whole community interest in such property was includible in determining the value of the decedent's gross estate."[20] The courts have held that such statutory language does not require valuation of the entire community interest as one aggregated interest. Such provision only requires that the decedent's community interest be included in determining the value of the decedent's gross estate. Hence, although in the aggregate the marital community may hold a majority interest, for transfer tax purposes at death the spouse should be deemed to own only a minority interest.[21] However, a Fifth Circuit decision has questioned this position and determined it to be insufficient as a matter of law.[22]

GOVERNMENTAL CONTROLS

There are very few valuation cases which address the question of the effect of governmental control on the business to be valued. One explanation may be that the effect of such control is adequately reflected in factors which would otherwise be considered for valuation purposes, such as the intrinsic factors set forth in Chapter 7. However, there are valuation cases, particularly those involving valuation dates during World War II, which indicate that the presence of substantial governmental regulations on the business to be valued may have a depressing effect on the value of an interest in that business.

In a 1950 Tax Court case, the court determined that a net asset valuation of a real estate holding company was justifiably reduced on account of governmental wartime controls. The corporation in that case was required to have a special license from the U.S. government to operate its normal business since some of its stock was held by French and Belgian nationals.[23] Along similar lines, wartime controls were cited as a factor in *Estate of Anna C. Ewing*.[24] The court observed that the company's problems attributable to the lack of labor and its dependence upon imported raw materials were accentuated by the war on the value date and production was limited because of governmental restrictions.

For the most part, present-day governmental controls should be properly reflected by the valuation techniques specified in the previous chapters. Evidently, in the eyes of the courts, governmental regulations are not as severe now as during wartime due to the lack of any current litigation using this theory. Nevertheless, unusual or inordinately severe governmental regulation and control should be given special consideration. Depending upon the form of governmental control, its impact may depress value or increase value. For example, governmental subsidies and aid may cause a premium since, no matter how bad the posture of the entity, the government will prevent it from going out of business. On the other hand, a discount may apply for price control or an adverse tax structure.

VALUATION PRECEDING PUBLIC ISSUE

On occasion, the valuation date will precede a public offering of an interest in the business to be valued. This may take the form of a closely held corporation subsequently offering its stock to the public, or may involve incorporating a previously noncorporate entity and selling the stock to the public. Often, contingencies will exist which create a great degree of uncertainty on the valuation date as to whether or not the public offering will be consummated. The existence of certain factors will determine, in part, how reliable the subsequent public price is as a measure of fair market value on the valuation date. The presence of indemnifying contracts with promoters and the presence of SEC approval of the offering on the valuation date may be positive indicators. Likewise, obtaining credit from financial institutions may also be indicative of the importance of the public price as a measure of value on the valuation date.[25]

In a 1967 case, the Tax Court held that gifts made four months prior to a public offering could be valued substantially below the public offering price.[26] Stock had been sold to underwriters at $10 per share some three months prior to the gift. In the same period as the gifts, the taxpayer sold a large block of shares to his son at $10 per share. The Internal Revenue Service contended that 1) the value of the gifted shares should equal the subsequent public offering price ($36.66), and 2) the difference between the public offering price and the sales price to his son constituted a gift and should be taxed. The Tax Court determined that the intervening developments between the gift and the public offering date were of marginal significance in the valuation of the shares. The court, however, recognized the fact that "many a contemplated public offering never sees the light of day and that, because of factors affecting the market at the particular moment of the public offering, the offering price can be radically different from the price originally contemplated."[27] The court subsequently valued the gifted shares at $13 per share, taking into consideration improvement in the company's financial posture subsequent to the sale of the stock to the underwriters. The court also ruled that the Internal Revenue Service failed to carry the burden of proof that the shares sold to the son should be treated as a gift in the amount of the difference between the public offer price and the sales price to the son. Therefore, such transactions had no gift tax implication.

In a 1974 case, *Tallichet*,[28] the Tax Court determined that the fair market value of a gift of stock two months after a registration statement was sent to the SEC, was significantly lower than the subsequent offering price to the public. One month following the last gift, the registered stock was offered for sale in a public offering for $17.50 per share. The court determined that the fair market value of the stock on the date of the gift was $12.00 per share.

Along a similar line of reasoning, a recent Revenue Ruling now requires a taxpayer to consider a proposed merger of a closely held corporation with a publicly held corporation in valuing stock of the closely held corporation.[29] The Revenue Ruling states that this consideration is necessary because:

> *(a) prospective seller would inform a prospective buyer of all favorable facts in an effort to obtain the best possible price, and a prospective buyer would elicit all the negative information in order to obtain the lowest possible price. In this arm's length negotiation, all relevant factors available to either buyer or seller, known to both, provide a basis on which the buyer and seller make a decision to buy or sell and come to an agreement on the price.*[30]

SUMMARY

As can be seen by the above discussion, several special situations exist which require particular attention by the valuation expert. These situations are unique to each individual set of facts but each can have a significant impact on the final value determination.

NOTES FOR CHAPTER 12

1. Schlegel v. United States, 71 F.Supp. 495 (D.C. NY 1947), aff'd 164 F.2d 276 (2nd Cir. 1947); and Cochran v. Commissioner, 1948 P-H TC Memo ¶48,094.

2. Angell, *Valuation Problems*, Practicing Law Institute, New York, 1957, p. 6.

3. Champlin Refining Co. v. Commissioner, 123 F.2d 202 (10th Cir. 1941).

4. James Couzens, 11 B.T.A. 1040 (1928); Ithaca Trust Co. v. United States, 279 U.S. 151 (1929); Estate of Tully v. United States, 41 AFTR 2d 78-1477 (Ct. Cl. 1978). See also Bader v. United States, 172 F.Supp. 833, 840 (D.C. Ill. 1959).

5. 346 F.2d 213 (5th Cir. 1965).

6. Ibid. at 219.

7. 1959 P-H TC Memo ¶59,203.

8. See note 4 supra.

9. Estate of Donald M. Hayes v. Commissioner, 1973 P-H TC Memo ¶73,236; Schlegel v. United States, note 1 supra; Gallun v. Commissioner, 1974 P-H TC Memo ¶74,284.

10. Estate of Gregg Maxcy v. Commissioner, 1969 P-H TC Memo ¶69,158, rev'd 441 F.2d 192 (5th Cir. 1971).

11. Ibid. at 793.

12. Section 2032A.

13. Section 2032A.

14. Section 2032A(o)(2).

15. Section 2032A(h)(2). See also Prop. Reg. Sec. 20.2032A-3 (7/19/78).

16. Section 2038A(e)(7)-(8).

17. Section 2032A(d).

18. The following states have a community property system in effect: Louisiana, Texas, New Mexico, Arizona, California, Washington, Idaho, and Nevada.

19. See S. Rept. 1013, 80th Cong., 2d Sess. (1948), 1948-1 C.B. 283,304.

20. Section 1014(b)(6).

21. See Estate of Lee v. Commissioner, 69 T.C. 860 (1978), for a discussion of the legislative history of the applicable estate tax provisions dealing with community property.

22. See Bright v. United States, 1980 P-H ¶151,091 (5th Cir. 6-18-80), where the court remanded the case to district court to consider evidence of whether the seller would have sacrificed the control premium and disposed of the deceaseds' and the living spouses' blocks of stock separately.

23. Estate of de Guebriant v. Commissioner, 14 T.C. 611 (1950), acq. 1950-2 C.B. 2. But see Claflin v. Commissioner, 186 F.2d 307 (2nd Cir. 1951).

24. 9 T.C.M. 1096 (1950).

25. See Berckmans v. Commissioner, 1961 P-H TC Memo ¶61,100.

26. Messing v. Commissioner, 48 T.C. 502 (1967) acq. 1968-1 C.B. 2.

27. Ibid. at 509.

28. 1974 P-H TC Memo ¶74,255. See also Silverman v. Commissioner, 1974 P-H TC Memo ¶74,285, aff'd 538 F.2d 927 (2nd Cir. 1976).

29. Rev. Rul. 78–367, 1978-2 C.B. 249. See Appendix B.

30. Ibid. at 250.

Planning Opportunities—Generally

The burden of valuation, when finally required, can be lessened in many cases by utilizing various valuation planning tools and techniques. The objectives of value planning generally are to preserve the select ownership of the entity (continuity), while maintaining the closely held status of the business (stability). Additionally, liquidity for persons affected by the plan, or for surviving family members not active in the business, is a common goal. Lastly, but certainly not unimportant, is minimization of the owner's overall tax burden by value planning.

The following chapters will discuss value planning techniques which 1) "freeze" the value of a business interest so that such interest will not require an in-depth value determination at a later date, or 2) transfer ownership rights in the closely held business to selected parties (whether family members or others). In order to implement these plans, the assistance of an attorney and an accountant well-versed in such techniques is essential. Potential tax ramifications necessitate the use of a specialist knowledgeable of the specific facts of each circumstance. The discussion of planning tools and techniques in the subsequent chapters is designed to provide an overall grasp of available alternatives. *These methods will not apply in all situations. The facts and circumstances of each case must be analyzed by an experienced attorney and accountant to determine which, if any, of the techniques can be used.*

GENERAL VALUATION PLANNING CONSIDERATIONS FOR VARIOUS FORMS OF CLOSELY HELD BUSINESSES

As stated in Chapter 1, a closely held business can take the legal form of a corporation, association, partnership, joint venture, or sole proprietorship.[1] Certain techniques may apply to one form, but not to another. Likewise, some techniques can and will apply equally to each of the different forms. The discussion of value planning opportunities which follows should not be construed as a recommendation to change ownership forms. Such discussion is merely an analysis of tools and techniques which can be utilized to simplify the valuation process for a closely held business and reduce potential tax liability. It must be kept in mind that in the value planning endeavor the underlying considerations are to 1) allow for an orderly transfer of property between parties, 2) provide stability and continuity of the closely held business, and 3) provide a source of liquidity to specified owners. Maximum flexibility is essential for each plan. Further, such plan must be revised periodically to reflect changes in personal and economic conditions.

Value planning can generally be broken down into two broad classifications: 1) entering into or executing agreements fixing or limiting a value, and 2) changing ownership to avoid valuation problems. The specifics of these planning activities will be discussed in the following chapters. Before discussing in detail the value planning tools available within a closely held business, a brief example depicting the advantage of utilizing one of the plans in reducing transfer taxes is given in *Case Seventeen—Biggs Corporation*.

CASE SEVENTEEN

Advantage of Value Planning

BIGGS CORPORATION

Facts

Biggs Corporation (BC) is a wholesale distributor of various athletic supplies and equipment. BC was founded by Walton Biggs in the early 1930s and has steadily increased its position within the wholesale athletic supply and equipment market. Walton Biggs's two sons, John and Mike, are active in the business and intend to continue the business indefinitely into the future. There are a total of 2,000 shares of stock in BC outstanding. By utilization of intrinsic methods and comparative corporate analysis, it is determined that each share of stock is worth approximately $1,000, as of May 26, 1982, the date of death of Walton Biggs.

Situation A: At the time of his death, Walton Biggs held the entire 2,000 shares of BC. The aggregate value of Walton Biggs's holdings in BC amounts to $2,000,000. This ownership interest alone results (assuming no deductions or credits, if any) in a transfer tax liability to Walton Biggs's estate of $780,800.

Situation B: If, however, Walton Biggs had:

(1) undertaken a recapitalization of BC when the value of the stock was at $500 per share, or

(2) shifted shares to his sons and subsequently entered into a restrictive

agreement which limited the disposition of his stock to anyone but his sons for a total price of $1,000,000, or

(3) formed a personal holding company with the shares he possessed when the value of the stock was $500 per share, or

(4) implemented a gift program with his two sons and decreased his holdings to 1,000 shares over an extended period of time, or

(5) sold a portion of his stock as an installment sale to his sons, or utilized a private annuity, so that his holdings only amounted to 1,000 shares, or

(6) utilized various trust arrangements, whereby he shifted all but 1,000 shares out of his estate for the benefit of his sons,

then the value attributable to BC in Walton Biggs's hands would be decreased to approximately $1,000,000, before discounts or other adjustments. The transfer tax liability would, therefore, be approximately $345,800 attributable to BC. Assuming that little or no transfer tax is paid under the method used to decrease the value of stock held by Walton Biggs, by utilizing these value planning techniques a savings of greater than 50 percent in potential transfer taxes can result.

Analysis

The last situation described above is an oversimplification of the role of value planning. Additional considerations are required in each situation depending on the facts and circumstances. Several tax advantages and disadvantages are present in each method mentioned. The purpose in the chapters that follow is to examine these advantages and disadvantages and to discuss some of the practical aspects involved in value planning.

NOTES FOR CHAPTER 13

1. For tax purposes, the term "association" refers to an organization whose characteristics require it to be classified as a corporation rather than another type of organization. For valuation planning purposes, an association will be presumed to enjoy those valuation planning opportunities applicable to the closely held corporate form. See Reg. Sec. 301.7701-2; Morrisey v. Commissioner, 296 U.S. 344 (1935); Larson v. Commissioner, 66 T.C. 159 (1976).

Value Limiting Techniques

Several techniques are available which can lock in or freeze the value of an ownership interest in a closely held business. These techniques, if properly utilized, can be very beneficial in establishing and limiting the value of an interest in a closely held business for transfer (estate and gift) or other tax purposes. Early use of these techniques not only results in a savings of time and taxes, but can also assist in preserving the closely held business as an ongoing entity. However, if these techniques are not properly utilized, the attempted value freeze may fail.

The purpose of using a value limiting technique is to freeze the value of an interest in a closely held business so that it will not vary with changes in the business environment over time. More specifically, the goal is to have a readily determinable value at any point in time regardless of business or economic trends. The most commonly used techniques for freezing the value of an interest in a closely held business are 1) agreements restricting the right of disposition, 2) recapitalizations of ownership by issuing limited value rights, and 3) creation of corporations which constitute personal holding companies for federal income tax purposes.

RESTRICTIVE AGREEMENTS—GENERALLY

Agreements restricting the right of disposition of a closely held business interest are generally for the purpose of maintaining the going concern status of the entity and preserving selected ownership. For transfer tax purposes, these agreements can be useful in providing liquidity to a decedent's estate for satisfying tax and other financial obligations. Of primary importance, however, is the fact that these agreements may establish a value which would otherwise have to be determined by use of intrinsic valuation techniques, comparable corporate analysis, and/or representative sales or exchanges. (See Chapters 5–7.) By fixing value through an agreement, conjecture is eliminated. Hence, such an agreement reduces the possibility of litigation as to value. For these reasons, restrictive agreements are considered effective tools in a taxpayer's arsenal to control and/or reduce taxes that are based upon "fair market value."

Authoritativeness of Restrictive Agreements

For transfer tax purposes at death, a binding restrictive agreement can freeze value if the guidelines outlined in Revenue Ruling 59–60 and the cases involving this issue are followed.[1] Revenue Ruling 59–60 briefly sets forth guidelines for creating a restrictive agreement which will control value.[2] However, the rules set forth in the ruling have not necessarily been followed by the courts.

Revenue Ruling 59–60 provides that, for transfer tax purposes at death, where a closely held business interest is acquired by a decedent subject to an option reserved by the business to repurchase such interest at a certain price, the option price controls the value of the interest.[3] The ruling also states that where a restrictive agreement is the result of a voluntary action by the interest holder, the agreement may or may not control depending upon the facts and circumstances of each case. The Internal Revenue Service, in Revenue Ruling 59–60, basically treats restrictive agreements in such cases as one "factor to consider," but not necessarily the controlling factor.

The courts agree with the "factor to consider" contention as stated in the ruling, but appear only to apply such standard to circumstances where there exist restrictions that apply at death, but which are not in effect during the life of an interest holder.[4] Similarly, if the restriction is binding both during life and at death, but not under all circumstances, the courts consider the restrictive agreement to be only a factor to consider.[5] Most importantly, however, for purposes of this discussion, the courts have held that an agreement which is binding during life as well as at death *and* under all circumstances (assuming adequate consideration exists) will control value for transfer tax purposes at death.[6] This judicially determined rule provides a more definitive standard for restrictive agreements than does Revenue Ruling 59–60, with its generalization that such an agreement is merely a "factor to consider."

Using the judicially developed standard, if the owner of an interest in a closely held business is willing, both during life and at death, to limit 1) the price he can receive, and 2) the person or persons to whom he can transfer his interest, significant tax benefits can be obtained. The agreement can be between the owner and his or her beneficiaries so as to preserve family ownership. However, if the purchaser under the agreement is the "natural object of the deceased's bounty," the agreement will be subject to close scrutiny by the Internal Revenue Service.[7]

Adequate Consideration

Even if an agreement is in effect under all circumstances, the value still may not be frozen for transfer tax purposes at death. The transfer tax regulations dealing with a decedent's estate point out that if there is no business purpose in the execution of the agreement, the agreement may be viewed as simply a device to avoid transfer taxes at death and such agreement may be disregarded.[8]

As an example, a New York district court in *Slocum* v. *United States*[9] held that one restrictive agreement, as applied to one of two corporations to be valued, was a bona fide business arrangement whereas another agreement pertaining to the second corporation was not. The former agreement was included in the Articles of Incorporation for the purpose of keeping control of the business in its present management. The court recognized such agreement as having a bona fide business purpose sufficient to control value. However, the later restrictive agreement was entered into under circumstances that inferred a testamentary disposition preceding the death of the owner and, as such, the agreement did not control, making the value a question of fact subject to trial determination.

In a recent Tax Court case, *Estate of Bischoff*,[10] two partners entered into an agreement which placed an absolute prohibition upon inter vivos transfers of their partnership interests. The agreement specified that a partnership interest could only be redeemed by the partnership and further provided a mandatory settlement or buy-out of a partner's interest upon the death of a partner at a price computed in accordance with a formula contained within the agreement. This formula was based upon the retiring partner's capital account as adjusted for partnership income and withdrawals. The restriction upon such transferability was intended to accomplish two objectives. First, it was intended to maintain ownership and control of corporations in which the partnership was the majority stockholder, and second, the restriction was intended to provide continuity of management to assure that the members of the partners' families would remain in control of the company after the death or retirement of the partners. The court held maintenance of family ownership to be a legitimate business for the restrictive agreement.

Based upon the foregoing discussion, it can be concluded that, at least for estate purposes, an agreement restricting the right of disposition and setting a fixed value for an interest in a closely held business in order to maintain family ownership will be deemed to have a valid business purpose and will achieve a value freeze.[11]

Normally, restrictive agreements provide a formula for adjusting price to reflect a reasonable value at the time when the agreement becomes operative. In some cases, however, the agreement specifies a fixed price and no adjustment formula is provided. In such cases, the adequacy of consideration is tested at the time when the agreement is executed and not at the time when it becomes operative (e.g., at death).[12] In any event, fixed price agreements should be reviewed periodically to be sure that the price provided therein is realistic. Also, state law should be reviewed to be sure that the agreement provides adequate consideration.[13]

Gift Purposes

Restrictive agreements do not achieve the same status for lifetime (gift) transfer tax purposes as they do for transfer tax purposes at death. It has consistently been held that binding restrictions in buy-sell agreements do not fix the value for lifetime transfer tax purposes.[14] This is due primarily to the difference between the valuation circumstances for estates and those for gifts. When valuation is necessary for a decedent's estate purposes, the event triggering the sale of the interest has already occurred. Comparatively, at the time of valuation for gift purposes, if the purchase is contingent upon death, the event that will trigger the agreement has not yet occurred. The donor enjoys selection of the time of transfer of his interest, while the donee possesses an indefinite right of retention.[15] For lifetime transfer tax purposes, therefore, the agreement is but one factor to consider.

Categories of Restrictive Agreements

Broadly classified, restrictive agreements fall into one of three categories. These categories generally apply whether the closely held business is a corporate or noncorporate entity.

First, buy-sell agreements can be created under which the owner (or his heirs) is required to sell his interest to a purchaser who is obligated to buy such interest at a given price, contingent upon the occurrence of a specified event.[16] As an example, the death of the owner or the termination of an employee could be the event which triggers the agreement and causes the purchase to occur. This type of agreement operates to restrict the sale of the interest to anyone except the party specified in the agreement.

Second, restrictive agreements can take the form of option agreements whereby an owner of a closely held business interest grants an option to purchase the business interest at a given price, exercisable at the will of a prospective purchaser, upon the occurrence of certain events, such as the retirement or death of the owner.[17] The existence of such an option would preclude the owner from selling the interest to another party at a different price so long as the option holder retained such option. This type of agreement is similar to the first except that the purchaser is not obligated to purchase the interest. However, the seller is obligated to sell if the purchaser desires to buy.

Third, there can exist contingent agreements or rights of first refusal which are agreements providing that if an owner (or his estate after death) desires to sell the business interest, it must first be offered at a certain price to a specific person or to a select group. Under this type of agreement, the owner is not forced to sell, but if he desires to sell, a first refusal right exists in a specified party.[18]

Generally, under a contingent or first refusal agreement, the restriction will not freeze a value but will merely be a factor to consider in the valuation process.[19] The first two types of agreements, however, may freeze value if a fixed price or a specified formula for determining the price is included in the agreement.[20]

RESTRICTIVE AGREEMENTS—TYPES, PRICE, AND PAYMENT

Types

Although restrictive agreements can be broadly classified into three different categories, in the two value controlling categories (the buy-sell and option agreements) three specific types of agreements are available. Such types are 1) a redemption agreement, 2) a cross-purchase agreement, and 3) a "combination" agreement.

Under a redemption agreement, the closely held business is obligated to purchase the subject interest upon the occurrence of the event or events specified in the agreement. The second type of agreement, the cross-purchase agreement, requires the remaining interest holders, rather than the closely held entity, to purchase the interest. The third type of agreement, the combination agreement, combines the other two agreements and allows for the remaining interest holders to have an option or obligation to purchase a portion of the subject interest, with the closely held business being obligated to purchase the remainder, or vice versa.[21] In a combination agreement, it may be preferable to grant the closely held business the option to acquire all the interest, with the remaining interest holders having the option to purchase any part not acquired by the entity. This arrangement takes into consideration the attractiveness of the redemption by the entity through the use of liquidity created by the business and avoids the risk of adverse federal income tax consequences (i.e., constructive dividend in the case of a closely held corporation) from having the entity satisfy an owner's obligation to purchase an additional interest in the entity.[22]

The facts and circumstances of each case will dictate the type of agreement to be used. Legal counsel will need to design each agreement to be sure that the desires of the parties and the relevant federal income and transfer tax consequences are properly reflected in the agreement.

Price

There are several methods by which the purchase price of the ownership interest can be determined. Normally, the circumstance of each valuation situation will determine the method to be used. The valuation method should be specifically set forth and described in detail in the restrictive agreement. In order for a restrictive agreement to be effective for fixing value, such value must be 1) readily ascertainable from the agreement, and 2) reasonable in light of the facts and circumstances existing at the time it was executed.[23]

One of the most common methods of setting purchase price in a restrictive agreement is by the use of net book value, or a multiple of net book value. This value can be determined as of the end of the last accounting period preceding the date upon which the need for valuation is triggered. The net book value of stock or the partnership capital account may be adjusted to reflect life insurance, appreciated property, or other similar factors to obtain a more representative value.[24] Such adjustments should be considered when the agreement is executed so that the precise meaning of "net book value" or "capital account value" is clearly ascertainable from the terms of the agreement. If the price is to be based upon "net book value" under historical cost accounting concepts, without adjustment for underlying asset values, the agreement should so state to avoid differences of opinion at a later date. Also, the purchase price can be fixed by setting forth a specific dollar value for each owner's interest in the agreement. If such an approach is used, the agreement should provide for a periodic review of the prices to be sure that the agreement always provides reasonably adequate values. It may be desirable to provide an alternative method of valuation if a review of the specified values has not occurred for a specified period of time before the date upon which the agreement becomes operative with respect to an owner's interest.[25]

Alternatively, the value of a closely held business can be fixed by providing a capitalization of earnings formula within the restrictive agreement. If this method is used, the agreement should specify 1) the number of years of earnings to be considered, 2) the method of averaging or weighing prior earnings, 3) whether pre-tax or after-tax earnings are to be used, 4) the source of earnings (in-house statements or audited statements), and 5) the earnings capitalization rate.[26] Use of a capitalizaton formula, however, may not be as preferable as the previously discussed methods, since 1) the drafting of provisions to allow for unusual and abnormal conditions is somewhat difficult, 2) the withdrawal of the interest holder from the closely held business may have an adverse material effect on the future earning power of the business, 3) the earnings history of the company may not be truly reflective of its value due to salaries and expenses of interest holders therein, and 4) valuation of an ownership interest under this method in the early years of a business may not be indicative of its true potential.[27]

Another price alternative involves utilizing independent appraisers. Although frequently used and effective for certain purposes, this method is not an effective technique for freezing value. The owner may have a good idea of the value of his interest. However, the appraiser's view after the agreement becomes operative may vary considerably from the preconceived value and result in a transaction which is not equitable to the buyer or to the seller.[28]

The purchase price could also be computed by a combination of the above methods. Again, the facts and circumstances of each case should determine the preferable method.

Payment

Payment for a closely held ownership interest under a restrictive agreement is usually made in one of two ways: 1) a lump-sum cash payment, or 2) installments.[29] The financial burden of the buyer may be eased by providing for installment payments. If such provision is used, the terms of the indebtedness should be described in the agreement, including such items as interest rate, security, and number and timing of payments. The general rules relating to installment sales will be discussed in more detail in Chapter 15.

If a lump-sum cash payment is required, such payment is usually funded by the purchase of life insurance on the owner.[30] As an example, under the cross-purchase agreement, it is not uncommon for the owners to acquire insurance on each other in order to have the necessary cash to meet their obligations under such agreement. If there is disparity in age among the different owners, an inequitable financial burden can arise. As an example, a younger owner would have to pay a higher premium on the life of an older owner than the older owner would pay on the life of the younger owner. Additionally, an administrative burden can result from the complexity of insuring each owner. A large number of policies may be needed in order for all owners to be covered. As an example, two owners would require two policies. However, six owners would require a total of 30 policies as each owner would have to insure each of the five other owners. If a cross-purchase agreement is utilized, a method of alleviating the administrative problem would be to establish a trust to acquire, hold, and pay for one policy on each owner's life. In structuring this type of trust, it is imperative that no owner have incidents of ownership in the policy on his life so as to avoid the inclusion of the proceeds in his taxable estate. If this type of trust can be utilized, it would simplify the procedures for paying premiums and reduce the total number of policies which would otherwise be required. A positive aspect of utilizing the insurance funding for cross-purchase agreements is that the creditors of the entity do not have a claim against such policies, whereas they probably would if the policies were owned by the entity.[31]

Case Eighteen—Quast Contracting Company sets forth an example, dealing with a partnership, in which a restrictive agreement controlled the value of a decedent's interest.

CASE EIGHTEEN

Restrictive Agreements

QUAST CONTRACTING COMPANY

Facts

Gerald Quast and his two adult sons, Quick and Quin, were partners in a general contracting business under the name of Quast Contracting Company. Due to the success of their business and the amount of capital investment in the partnership, on November 1, 1977, the partners entered into an agreement whereby upon the death of one of the partners the surviving partners could purchase the deceased partner's interest by paying, in cash, 10 percent of the amount on the partnership books representing the deceased partner's interest (capital account) and executing a promissory note to the estate for the balance. The option would be exercisable for a period of 180 days after the death of one of the partners. Additionally, the partners were restricted in the disposition or assignment of their interest during their life.

On January 21, 1981, Quin Quast was accidentally killed on a contracting job. On his date of death, Quin's capital account was $175,000. The surviving partners, Gerald and Quick, subsequently made payment and executed the note pursuant to the terms of the agreement. An appraisal of the business as of Quin's date of death indicates that Quin's aliquot part of the total value of the partnership was $300,000.

Value

The value of Quin's interest in the partnership for transfer tax purposes was the amount determined under the partners' agreement, or $175,000.

Analysis

The agreement was executed by the parties to ensure continuity of business both during the life and after the death of a partner, providing the surviving partners so elected. The option was irrevocable and without rights of assignment. Accordingly, the agreement should control since the concern is valuing the decedent's partnership interest at the time of his death, not determining the fair market value of the net partnership assets at the time of his death.*

---

*See Angela Fiorito, 33 T.C. 440 (1959), citing Helen S. Delane, 6 T.C. 1188 (1946).

RECAPITALIZATIONS—GENERALLY

One of the most effective value freezing techniques available to a closely held business is that of the recapitalization. Although primarily associated with closely held corporations, there has been recent discussion utilizing "recapitalizations" in the area of partnership estate planning. A discussion of the technique as it applies to partnerships will follow the discussion of the technique as it applies to closely held corporations.

Objectives in Recapitalizing

Basically, recapitalizing is the restructuring or reshuffling of the capital structure within the framework of an existing closely held business.[32] As an example, for a closely held corporation, a recapitalization may entail the division of common stock into two or more classes of common stock and/or preferred stock and the exchange of the newly created classes of stock for the presently outstanding stock. Under specific Internal Revenue Code sections and related regulations, recapitalizing a corporation can be tax free if properly structured.[33] Because of such treatment, recapitalizations have been used to accomplish several objectives with a great deal of success.

Recapitalizations are used to freeze the value of stock held by a principal shareholder by issuing to him or her securities in the recapitalization that have a fixed and permanent value. Such fixed value securities, however, provide the shareholder with a suitable amount of dividend income and can provide for retention of control of the business, if desired. At the same time, the future appreciation in value of the corporation is shifted to selected present or potential owners (usually family members) who receive a different class of stock in the recapitalization. Further, the recapitalization ensures the preservation of ownership to such designated parties upon the death of the principal shareholder. If properly planned, these goals can be achieved with minimal transfer and income tax consequences. In the proper case, the recapitalization "fits like a glove, and can turn a tax burden into a tax boon."[34]

Despite all of the apparent advantages, corporate recapitalizations do have some drawbacks. First, and very importantly, the owners of the business must consider the serious financial implications of the potentially heavy dividend requirement created by the preferred stock. The holder of the senior securities will also be receiving large amounts of ordinary income in the form of dividends. If dividends are received, it must be kept in mind that the income utilized to pay the dividends has been previously taxed at the corporate level. Second, the stock received in a recapitalization may be classified under the Internal Revenue Code as Section 306 stock. If such stock is subsequently disposed of, whether by sale or redemption, certain serious income tax ramifications may result. Avoiding this tax treatment is discussed in more detail in the stock design section on page 153. These risks of potential unfavorable income taxation may be so significant to a taxpayer as to preclude further consideration of value planning.

To prevent abuses in the reorganization area generally and the recapitalization area specifically, Congress and the Internal Revenue Service have created several exceptions to the general rule of nontaxability of corporate recapitalizations.[35] One particular Code provision, however, deals specifically with a possible exception in an otherwise tax free recapitalization. Section 305(b) was added to the Code to prevent the substitution of potential capital gain income for current ordinary income through the use of stock dividends and similar transactions.[36] Section 305(c) includes in the ambit of Section 305(b) transactions such as a corporate recapitalization in which a shareholder's proportionate interest in the earnings and profits or assets of a corporation is increased.[37] However, it is clear from the Congressional deliberations that such provision does not apply to a "one time" recapitalization of a closely held corporation. The Regulations, Revenue Rulings, and private rulings have given extensive support to treating a recapitalization as a "single and isolated transaction" entitled to tax free treatment.[38] Nevertheless, before undertaking a recapitalization plan for a closely held corporation, Section 305 and the Regulations thereunder should be carefully reviewed to ensure that no unintended problems arise.[39]

CONSUMMATING THE RECAPITALIZATION

Successfully completing a recapitalization takes very few steps. Basically, the corporation must 1) adopt a plan of recapitalization, 2) amend its Articles of Incorporation, as necessary, to provide for the issuance of the new securities, and 3) exchange its presently outstanding stock for the new securities. However, potential tax and legal hazards exist in each of the steps required to consummate the recapitalization. The execution of these steps requires the utmost care to avoid potential tax liability. For these reasons, the advice and services of an experienced attorney and accountant must be utilized. Additionally, when dealing with recapitalizations it is prudent to file a private ruling request with the National Office of the Internal Revenue Service to be sure that favorable tax treatment will result from the recapitalization. An experienced attorney or accountant can facilitate the processing of such a request. The following discussion sets forth the principles involved in corporate recapitalizations, but because of the intricate problems involved in each case, professional guidance is needed to accomplish each specific plan.

Plan of Recapitalization

A recapitalization is not defined per se in the Internal Revenue Code or the Regulations. However, a recapitalization is deemed to be subject to Section 368(a)(l)(E), by virtue of examples given in the Regulations thereunder and published interpretations thereof over the years.[40] Since a recapitalization is considered to be a reorganization, if the requirements of the Code regarding reorganizations are followed, the transaction should be tax free under Section 354. Additionally, the basis of new shares received should be the same as the basis of the old and the holding period should be deemed to include the holding period of the surrendered shares.[41]

The plan of recapitalization must be adopted by the Board of Directors of the corporation and approved by its shareholders. A copy of the plan, together with a statement executed under penalties of perjury stating the purpose and details of the transaction, must be attached to the corporation's tax return for the year in which the recapitalization takes place.[42]

As with all reorganizations,[43] a recapitalization must have a business purpose other than to avoid taxes.[44] Fortunately, the Internal Revenue Service has held that the desire to increase the proportionate holdings of a younger shareholder by decreasing the holdings of an older shareholder constitutes a valid business purpose.[45] As previously mentioned, in substantiating a recapitalization as being tax free and possessing an adequate business purpose, it is not uncommon for private rulings to be filed with the Internal Revenue Service. Recent valid business purposes, according to such rulings, have been to provide incentives to key employees,[46] motivate management,[47] encourage participation of children,[48] minimize business interruption on retirement,[49] and prevent dilution of an equity interest.[50]

Issuance

Once the plan of recapitalization has been approved, the Articles of Incorporation and other relevant legal documents must be modified to allow the issuance of the new securities.

At this point, perhaps the most critical step in the recapitalization must occur. The parties must value 1) the securities to be issued, and 2) the securities to be surrendered, to be sure that the values are approximately equal. If the values are not equal, potential adverse tax consequences may result from the recapitalization exchange.[51]

If the value of the securities issued exceeds the value of the stock surrendered, such excess may be a constructive dividend or compensation if the stockholder is also an employee.[52] On the other hand, if the value of the securities issued is less than those surrendered, the party relinquishing value may be deemed to be making a gift of the excess. For instance, in a family corporation the excess of the fair market value of surrendered common stock over the fair market value of newly issued preferred stock may constitute a gift to a remaining old common shareholder.[53] However, to intentionally overvalue the preferred stock to avoid the potential transfer tax is not advisable, as this will defeat the objective of freezing the estate of the recipient shareholder at its lowest possible value and might possibly constitute a constructive dividend or compensation to the transferor shareholder.[54]

An Internal Revenue Service private letter ruling will not overcome the problem faced in valuing the shares as each ruling presently contains the caveats that 1) the ruling is effective only to the extent that the fair market value of the stock surrendered is approximately equal to the stock received, 2) no opinion is expressed concerning the tax treatment of the amount by which the values of the stocks are unequal, and 3) a determination of the fair market value of the stock in question is reserved for a field agent's determination.

In order to guard against adverse transfer or income tax consequences if it is later determined that the value of the securities surrendered did not approximately equal the value of securities issued, it is advisable to include a "revaluation" or "adjustment" clause within the formal plan of recapitalization. Generally, such a clause provides that if a future determination by a court or administrative agency finds that the value of stock issued was not equal to the value of stock surrendered, 1) additional shares of stock will be issued if the originally issued stock had too little value, or 2) shares of stock will be returned to the issuing corporation if the stock issued had too much value. Such stock issuance or return should, by agreement, be treated as if it had occurred on the date of the original exchange.

The effectiveness of a revaluation or adjustment clause in avoiding potential unintended tax consequences is not clear from the decided cases. The concept of the revaluation clause was challenged by the Internal Revenue Service in a 1976 Colorado district court case, *King* v. *United States*,[55] that was subsequently affirmed by the Tenth Circuit. In *King*, the taxpayer sold his closely held stock to trusts for the benefit of his children in exchange for a private annuity. The sale agreement contained a revaluation clause which provided that in the event that the Internal Revenue Service later determined that the value of the stock exceeded the consideration received, the purchase price was to be adjusted to the value of the stock determined by the Internal Revenue Service. The Internal Revenue Service subsequently contended that the value of the stock was in excess of the value of the annuity received, thereby creating a gift in the amount of such excess. The district court determined that the revaluation clause was valid for use in overcoming the difficulty in equating values. The Internal Revenue Service, on appeal, contended that the revaluation clause was contrary to public policy.[56] The Tenth Circuit held that the clause was not contrary to public policy as it did not operate to negate a previously valid transaction but merely adjusted the transaction in the event that tax consequences arose. The court further found the intended purpose of the revaluation clause proper in view of the inherent uncertainty in valuing shares of a closely held family corporation. The holding in *King* should be correct since the revaluation clause does nothing more than reaffirm the absence of intent by the transferor to make a gift as part of the exchange. If intent is absent, the taxpayer should be allowed to protect himself both from 1) an unwarranted tax liability, and 2) an unintended loss of value in the exchange. The use of a revaluation or readjustment clause to avoid unwanted and unintended tax consequences appears justified in view of the reasoning in the *King* decision and that of analogous authority.[57]

In summary, in undertaking a recapitalization it is necessary to utilize the valuation techniques set forth in the previous chapters in order to arrive at the fair market value of the securities involved. The importance of the valuation process to these techniques cannot be overemphasized.

RECAPITALIZATION STOCK DESIGN

Assuming that only common stock is issued and outstanding prior to a recapitalization undertaking, as is the usual case, all or part of existing common stock is generally exchanged for a new class of preferred stock. New common stock is generally issued to owners designated to receive the future appreciation of the corporation or such owners may simply retain the common stock already owned.[58] A recapitalization does not have to constitute an exchange of stock for the same class of stock, and generally does not.[59] The alternatives available in formulating the features of the newly issued preferred stock are virtually unlimited. The main objective in designing the recapitalization is to achieve a value freeze of a select class of the newly issued stock. This "frozen value" stock will be placed in the hands of the retiring or senior owner or owners. Ancillary considerations must not be overlooked. For example, providing a source of income (e.g., through dividends to the senior shareholder) may be necessary for the success (or acceptability) of a recapitalization.

The classes of stock to be issued and the voting rights thereof depend somewhat on state law. State law may require that only common stock be voting and not allow for voting preferred stock.[60] Again, the need for an experienced attorney is evident so that applicable state law requirements can be met. Also, a major factor in deciding the classes and voting rights of the new stock is the owner's desire and future intention of divesting or retaining control of the closely held business. This is illustrated in the following examples dealing with multiple classes of stock.

Multiple classes of stock may be useful in gift programs intended to transfer appreciation to designated shareholders at virtually no tax cost. In many instances multiple classes of stock also present the best value planning technique. As an example, assume that a senior family member as a principal shareholder desires to retain control, but wants to recapitalize to freeze the value of his interest in the corporation. New common and new preferred stock would be issued with only the preferred stock having the controlling voting rights. The preferred stock would contain certain features to freeze its value (e.g., fixed redemption value, etc., discussed infra and in Chapter 11). If the preferred stock value is approximately equal to the value of the old common stock surrendered therefor, the new common stock would be of nominal value. The senior family member would receive the preferred stock in exchange for his old common stock and cause all the new common stock to be issued to junior family members for cash or in exchange for old common stock which they already own. In the alternative, the junior members may just keep the old common they already own. The issuance of the new common stock, because of its nominal value, should have minimal lifetime transfer (gift) tax ramifications to the senior family member. The preferred stock would receive dividends, but should have a frozen fair market value despite its voting control.[61] The common stock should receive the future appreciation of the value of the business as the preferred stock would have a frozen value. While authority indicates that the preferred stock might receive some premium above its purportedly fixed value due to voting control, the plan should nevertheless substantially limit the value of the older family member's interest while allowing him to maintain control during life.[62]

Another possible alternative would be to have the new preferred stock possess full voting rights with such rights lapsing upon the death of the senior family member, causing a shift of the voting power from the preferred to the common stock at the moment of death.[63] This should cause a lower value for the preferred stock at the date of death since a prospective purchaser who acquires the stock could not obtain voting control.[64] Nonvoting preferred stock should not be deemed to have a value in excess of its redemption value since it does not possess voting control.[65]

The last example represents liberal utilization of voting control to effect an estate plan. Although such plan has not been considered by the courts, its conceptual soundness has been supported by authorities in the recapitalization area.[66]

At one time, disposition of preferred stock was an effective tool for converting ordinary income into capital gain. To cure such abuse, Congress enacted Section 306 of the Internal Revenue Code. Section 306 stock is stock (other than common stock) issued with respect to common stock and is received by a shareholder as a nontaxable stock dividend at a time when the corporation has undistributed earnings and profits.[67] If Section 306 stock is redeemed by the corporation, the amount received by the shareholder is to be included in the shareholders' income as ordinary (dividend) income.[68] If Section 306 stock is sold or otherwise disposed of, the amount received is treated as ordinary income to the extent that the stock's fair market value on the distribution date was covered by corporate earnings and profits.[69] Ordinary income will not result, however, if certain exceptions and exemptions apply.

Disposition of Section 306 stock will not result in the above recognition or ordinary income if:

(1) the transaction terminates the shareholder's entire interest in the corporation (considering attribution rules),[70]

(2) the stock is redeemed in a distribution which qualifies as a partial or complete liquidation,[71]

(3) the transaction is not considered to be an avoidance of income taxes,[72] or

(4) the disposition is nontaxable.[73]

Generally, Section 306 will not apply to a recapitalization when only preferred stock is received in exchange for all of a shareholder's common stock. The problem arises in the tax treatment of a recapitalization when both common stock and preferred stock are exchanged for common stock.

The Code is rather explicit that Section 306 can apply to stock (other than common stock) received in certain wholly or partially tax free corporate reorganizations if the effect of the transaction is substantially the same as receipt of a dividend.[74] The Regulations do, however, provide some guidance, by virtue of an example, in avoiding Section 306 applicability when only preferred stock is received in a recapitalization. Under such example, where two shareholders own common stock and preferred stock and, pursuant to a recapitalization, exchange the existing preferred stock for new preferred stock (which is not substantially different from the preferred stock previously held), such new preferred stock is not Section 306 stock unless the preferred stock surrendered was itself Section 306 stock.[75] This position was confirmed by Revenue Ruling 77–108.[76]

Section 306 does become a problem when the recapitalization results in receipt of preferred and common by all shareholders or if some of the shareholders receive preferred stock and retain the common stock already owned. This creates the appearance of the preferred stock distribution being essentially equivalent to a dividend and could jeopardize the nonapplicability of Section 306. Even though favorable private rulings appear to be easily obtainable, stating that Section 306 will not apply to recapitalizations in most situations,[77] it is advisable to consult an accountant and an attorney to determine the potential tax impact involved in each set of facts. If possible application of Section 306 is bothersome when contemplating a recapitalization, an alternative may be formation of a new corporation under Section 351. Section 306 may also be avoided by the use of a personal holding company, as discussed infra.

Avoiding Section 306 by Use of Section 351

The basic definition of Section 306 stock does not include stock received in the formation of a corporation under Section 351. The transfer of property in forming a corporation must comply with the requirements of Section 351 so that gain or loss does not result. A transfer will avoid recognition if 1) the transferor controls the corporation after the transfer (control being 80 percent voting power and 80 percent of each class of nonvoting stock), and 2) the conveyance is not a transfer of property to an "investment company." If a gift of stock is made to family members immediately after the formation of the new corporation, the control requirement should not be endangered as long as such gift is not pursuant to a binding prearrangement and is made without consideration.[78] With regard to the "investment company" problem, if the transfer results directly or indirectly in diversification of the transferor's interest and is made to a regulated investment company, a real estate investment trust or a corporation whose assets consist of 80 percent or more of investment property or marketable securities, recognition of gain or loss will result.[79] In most instances, the transferee does not meet the above definitional requirements and no diversification of the transferor's interest is deemed to occur. It should also be noted that "diversification" is deemed to occur only if two or more persons transfer nonidentical property to a corporation (unless the property is insignificant in relation to the total value of the property transferred).[80] In a typical family recapitalization, identical property (stock of the existing corporation) is transferred to the new holding company. Many times, if a question exists, it is advisable to obtain a private ruling in order to be assured of nonrecognition treatment.

In forming a new corporation to avoid Section 306 treatment, stock of an existing closely held corporation would be transferred to a newly created corporation in exchange for preferred stock and common stock in the new corporation. The common stock is then gifted to the closely held members who can, from a tax and practical standpoint, benefit from the future appreciation of the business.

A possible problem exists with this alternative since creation of the new corporation may be viewed as a reorganization.[81] A Section 306 problem could then arise as receipt of the preferred stock could be viewed as essentially equivalent to a dividend. However, an exception to Section 306 is available to cure this problem which, in simplified terms, poses the question: "If cash was received in the exchange instead of stock, would the cash constitute a taxable dividend?"[82] If the answer is no, the stock is not Section 306 stock. The focal point of answering this question is whether or not the issuing (new) corporation has earnings and profits from which to pay a dividend. Existence of earnings and profits makes a dividend fully taxable and, in this discussion, would result in the preferred stock being classified as Section 306 stock. The Internal Revenue Service recently addressed this situation in Revenue Ruling 79–274.[83]

Under the facts of Revenue Ruling 79–274, Corporation X had outstanding 3,000 shares of common stock which were owned 1,500 shares each by individuals A and B, and was engaged as an ongoing business. For valid business purposes, A and B organized Corporation Z and transferred all the stock of X to it. In exchange therefor, A and B each received 500 shares of Z voting preferred stock and 1,000 shares of Z voting common stock. The Internal Revenue Service determined that such transaction was subject to both the reorganization section and Section 351 of the Code. Since there were no prior legislative or administrative directives as to the tax treatment when the 1) reorganization, *and* 2) transfer of property in formation of a company provisions apply, the Internal Revenue Service required the voting preferred stock to be classified as Section 306 stock. However, the preferred stock was Section 306 stock only to the extent that Corporation Z had earnings and profits at the end of the tax year in which the transaction was consummated, due to the above exception involving the "cash received in lieu of" question.

It can be concluded, based on the holding in the Ruling, that if the new corporation has no earnings and profits in its first year, the dividend equivalency test will apply and Section 306 treatment can be avoided even though a reorganization has occurred. By electing an appropriate fiscal year end, earnings and profits can be avoided. As an example, using the facts in the above Revenue Ruling, if Corporation Z were formed on the next to last day of the year (i.e., December 30), Corporation Z could close its tax year the next day and have no earnings and profits and, hence, no Section 306 stock. However, if preferred stock which has a Section 306 taint is transferred to a corporation, the newly issued preferred stock will be deemed to be Section 306 stock and the old preferred Section 306 stock will retain its taint within the new corporation, regardless of the level of earnings and profits.[84]

In summary, proper timing of the formation of a corporation can result in the complete avoidance of Section 306 if desired. Additionally, formation of a new corporation under these circumstances presents an excellent vehicle for introducing preferred stock into a corporate framework. Multi-classes of stock, both voting and nonvoting, could be issued as well. The combinations of stock design are virtually unlimited, thus making the formation of a corporation under Section 351 very attractive.

As a side note, even if newly issued preferred stock is deemed to be tainted by Section 306, once such stock passes through a decedent's estate, the taint is removed. This is due to the step-up in basis to fair market value as of the date of death.[85] Therefore, as a practical matter, the receipt of Section 306 stock in a recapitalization would not pose a problem if the recipient shareholder intended to retain the preferred stock until death. It should be noted, however, that Section 306 stock will not lose its taint by gifting the stock to another family member. The taint remains with the stock even though the stock is gifted away.[86]

Characteristics of the New Issue

The following discussion will focus on stock features normally associated with newly issued preferred stock received in a recapitalization. The characteristics of preferred stock and their relationship to value determination are discussed in Chapter 11. The principles discussed in Chapter 11 apply to the recapitalization area by virtue of the value to attach to the newly issued preferred shares and the necessity of future valuation for transfer or other tax purposes. It must be remembered that labeling stock by a certain name does not necessarily control its classification. For example, one Revenue Ruling classified newly issued class A common stock as, in actuality, preferred stock due to its features.[87]

An effective and normal means of freezing the value of preferred stock is to provide a liquidation or redemption value for each share. The fixation of value by use of liquidation value recognizes the superiority of the preferred shareholder to that of common or other shareholders in the event of liquidation. However, their participation above that amount yields to other shareholders.[88] A redemption or callable feature allows the corporation to "call in" the stock at its option at a certain price, usually par. Many times the ultimate value will be below that specified as a redemption or liquidation value.[89] The redemption or liquidation amount, however, will provide a base or range within which the ultimate value would fall if liquidated.[90]

In view of the fiduciary duty the courts consider the corporate directors to owe to minority shareholders, the redemption amount and events necessitating redemption should not be solely for the purpose of maintaining or shifting control of the corporation or obtaining other personal benefits for the directors or majority shareholders.[91] A valid business purpose should exist for attaching a redemption feature to stock. Such purpose must have a substantial value limiting effect on the stock in order for the redemption price to control the tax value of the shares.[92] The value of preferred stock can be further substantiated as a "frozen" figure by executing a stock purchase agreement in harmony with a recapitalization. The purchase agreement would immediately trigger the redemption of the stock by the corporation at a stated value upon the occurrence of a specified event. The value of the shares under the stock purchase agreement, if equal to the liquidation or inter vivos redemption value attached to the shares, would result in a double value limiting technique. (See the discussion of restrictive agreements at the beginning of this chapter.)

The dividend rate of the new preferred will depend on two primary factors: 1) current yields on comparable publicly traded preferred stock (market temperance), and 2) the desire of the senior shareholder for receipt of dividend income. The dividend yield given to preferred stock obviously affects the value of such stock. A significant factor in determining the fairness and/or appropriateness of a dividend yield is the market yield of similar publicly traded preferred shares. (See comparable corporate analysis in Chapter 6.) Another consideration in setting the rate is to see that the senior shareholder, who is foregoing future appreciation, receives a comfortable level of income through payment of dividends on the preferred stock he receives in a recapitalization. This steady source of income can be eroded by inflation in future years. One alternative in solving this problem is to allow the dividend rate to fluctuate with an appropriate government inflation index. This would keep the level of income at a constant purchasing power level by allowing for inflation.[93] The cost of such adjustment, of course, must be considered by the corporation in determining if it can afford to have the preferred stock outstanding.

As long as the senior shareholder possesses control of the corporation, attachment of a cumulative feature to the shares of stock should be unimportant as the shareholder can obtain dividends by exercising his voting rights. A cumulative dividend feature is generally deemed to increase the value of stock and may frustrate a low estate valuation.[94] A noncumulative feature coupled with no voting rights, however, would greatly depress the value of preferred stock. Care must be taken in valuing noncumulative, nonvoting preferred stock which is exchanged in a recapitalization since it may have a very low value in comparison with other classes of stock. Depending upon the business and its volatility or elasticity to general economic trends, the presence or absence of a cumulative feature rests on the desires of the parties.

Convertibility of the shares may make the valuation endeavor more difficult. Additionally, convertibility may cause the "frozen value" to vary as the common stock appreciates in value. The desires of the owner and the facts of each case will dictate whether a conversion feature should be utilized. Generally, however, the conversion feature should be avoided in value planning since it has a negative impact on efforts to fix value.

It must be remembered that a caveat to any recapitalization technique utilized in value planning is that the various classes of stock are required to be created for a valid business purpose. Avoidance of taxes is not deemed to be a valid business purpose.[95] Likewise, the economic and legal characteristics of the stock will determine the true nature of the stock. In other words, the label attached to such stock does not necessarily control its potential tax treatment.[96]

The main point of the above alternatives is to demonstrate that the use of various classes of stock in a recapitalization allows the placement of value and control in accordance with the wishes of the parties with minimal tax cost, provided careful planning is utilized.

Case Nineteen—Kelman Company, Inc., provides a hypothetical example of a closely held corporate recapitalization.

CASE NINETEEN

Recapitalization

KELMAN COMPANY, INC.

Facts

Kelman Company, Inc. (KC) is a closely held corporation engaged in the farming business. KC presently has outstanding 410 shares of $100 par value common stock held as follows:

Name	Shares
John Kelman	400
Jack Kelman (John's son)	10

John Kelman (Kelman) gifted the 10 shares of stock to his son, Jack, when Jack was a minor. The present net worth of KC is $717,500. This amount is based on current value versus historical cost. This also represents the entire value of the common stock ($1,750 per share).

Kelman is anxious for Jack, now an adult, to participate actively in the management of KC, and believes strongly in the work incentive derived through equity ownership in a business. For this reason, Kelman would like to create circumstances that would permit him to retain voting control in KC but have the flexibility to make available to Jack further investments in the equity of KC.

Analysis

To create a circumstance whereby the foregoing business objectives may be accomplished, KC's Certificate of Incorporation is amended to provide for the authorization of 7,500 shares of preferred stock (new preferred). The rights of the new preferred stock will be as follows:

Dividends: Noncumulative dividends at the rate of $9 per year (9%).

Voting rights: One vote per share.

Redemption: Redeemable at par value $100. Additionally, a purchase agreement is executed which is binding both during life as well as at death of any preferred shareholder. The agreement provides for the purchase of the preferred shares from a decedent estate.

Preference in liquidation: Par value ($100).

Convertibility: None.

Kelman will exchange each of his common shares for 18.75 shares of preferred stock. Jack will retain his common stock. Kelman will receive 7,000 shares of the new preferred stock which will have a total redemption value of $700,000. The 400 common shares exchanged have a fair market value of approximately $700,000 prior to the exchange, which is roughly equal to the value of new preferred received. If the values are approximately equal no tax consequences should result. It is believed that although the 9 percent dividend yield is less than the current yield on comparable publicly traded preferred stock, the presence of voting control on the preferred stock offsets any decrease in value due to the low, noncumulative dividend rate. Accordingly, the value of preferred stock should closely approximate its redemption or liquidation value.* This conclusion has not been fully tested in the courts and the Internal Revenue Service may not accept such rationale in all cases. Nevertheless, such position should be correct since voting control should clearly mitigate any deficiency in the dividend structure.

Periodic sales, or gifts, of the preferred stock can be made to Jack to increase his equity position. The 9 percent dividend right assures Kelman of a fixed dividend income of $63,000 per year. Most importantly, the future appreciation of KC should accrue to Jack.

---

*See Abrams and Morgan, "Recapitalizing a Closely-held Corporation," 25 Prac. Law. 11 (No. 6, Sept. 1979).

PARTNERSHIP RECAPITALIZATION

As mentioned at the outset of the recapitalization discussion, recent attention has been given to the use of family partnerships to achieve a value freeze.[97] Generally, under a partnership capital freeze a new partnership is created (or an existing partnership restructured) so that two classes of partnership interests result. The first interest, the "regular partnership interest," is the normal type of partnership interest providing participation in profits and losses. The other partnership interest, the "frozen partnership interest," has a preferred 1) liquidation value, and 2) income distribution position. The latter interest is owned by the senior partners while the former interest is owned by the younger partner. Receipt of such interest by a junior partner could either be by gift or be dependent upon contributions of property and services.[98] The preferred income position could either be a fixed amount or a percentage of the liquidation value. If the amount is fixed, it should be considered a guaranteed payment.[99] However, it may be advantageous to avoid guaranteed payments if it is beneficial for the frozen interest holder to enjoy the tax character of specially treated items (e.g., capital gains and losses) realized by the partnership. Alternatively, the frozen interest holder could receive a preferred position as to partnership profits up to a stated percentage of its liquidation value. The technique of recapitalizing a partnership to achieve a value freeze can be applied to either limited or general partnerships.

The use of a partnership arrangement, rather than various corporate techniques, has several advantages. First, a more constant cash flow can result if a preferred cumulative position (guaranteed payment) is held by the frozen interest partner. This guaranteed amount would be required to be paid by the partnership regardless of the sufficiency of earnings. If there are insufficient earnings, the guaranteed payments are, in essence, borne by the normal partnership interest holder. However, in the agreement, an allocable amount of any deficiency may be chargeable to the frozen interest holder.[100]

Second, a number of tax problems can be avoided by use of a partnership rather than a corporation. Such problems include the avoidance of double taxation on income received, unreasonable accumulation of earnings, and thin capitalization.[101] Additionally, the Section 306 "preferred stock bail out" problem and possible Section 305 taxable stock dividend treatment can be avoided by use of the partnership freeze. Also, in the event that a corporation is liquidated, additional taxes are imposed which would not exist in a partnership liquidation. This is because, as a general rule, a partner will recognize a gain upon liquidation only to the extent that the cash received exceeds his basis.[102]

Third, state law requirements for recapitalizing a closely held corporation may be complex. Additionally, more flexibility is allowed when structuring the buy-out of ownership interest between a partnership and a retiring partner or a deceased partner's estate than is allowed for corporations.

Despite its many advantages, there exist a number of traps in the partnership recapitalization area which can catch the unwary. These problems include:

(1) the possibility of reclassifying the partnership as an association taxable as a corporation,[103]

(2) the unlimited liability of the general partners,[104]

(3) the rather complex partnership rules governing taxation of family partnerships,[105]

(4) the "substantial economic effect" which must undergird the allocation of profits and losses,[106]

(5) potential taxable transfers, as gifts, resulting from valuation errors,[107]

(6) the exchange of a general partnership interest for a limited partnership interest which may not be a tax free like-kind exchange,[108]

(7) a sale or exchange of 50 percent or more of the total interest in partnership capital and profits which terminates the partnership for income tax purposes,[109] and

(8) the fact that the frozen partnership interest has the potential to be treated as debt.[110]

Even with these drawbacks, a partnership recapitalization can be an advantageous method of restructuring a business relationship. However, even though such an undertaking appears to be meritorious for successfully freezing a partnership value, it has yet to be considered by the courts.[111]

PERSONAL HOLDING COMPANY

An alternative technique to freezing the value of the business portion of one's estate is the use of a personal holding company (PHC). Under such technique, the personal wealth of an individual, usually property with the potential for moderate to significant levels of appreciation, is transferred to a newly created PHC in exchange for preferred and common stock of the newly formed corporation. Attractive appreciating property to transfer to the PHC would be the stock of a closely held business, publicly traded stock, and/or real estate held by an individual. The fundamental benefit from the formation of a PHC is that appreciating property can be exchanged for nonappreciating classes of stock (i.e., stock that is limited in value). These classes of stock, in turn, represent ownership of the company that owns the appreciating property. The PHC, therefore, is an effective means of reducing the value of an individual's estate. Additionally, the PHC stock, if a minority interest in a decedent's estate, is subject to two value discounts.

Although achieving minority status appears unattractive from the standpoint of not possessing control, it can easily be achieved through the manipulation of ownership interest while still retaining, in essence, a controlling interest. See Disappearing Wealth, in Chapter 15. The two discounts the PHC interest receives would be 1) lack of marketability discount of the interest (common to all minority interest holders, discussed in Chapter 9), and 2) the holding company discount. The holding company discount recognizes that an extra layer of insulation exists around appreciated property in the form of a holding company. Therefore, the value of the underlying assets is reduced because the free transferability of the assets is impaired.[112] By accumulating an individual's assets under a corporate blanket, the value otherwise achieved on the sale of the assets is reduced to a lower level.

In utilizing the PHC as a value freeze, it is not uncommon for the transferor of appreciated property to retain the newly issued preferred shares and gift the common shares to family members. Assuming that the preferred stock is nonparticipating, the common shares would absorb the appreciation in value of the PHC's underlying assets. This concept is based on achieving a value freeze by utilization of features to attach to the preferred shares as was discussed previously with respect to recapitalization.

Valuation is of the utmost importance in the formation of a PHC. Similar in nature to the necessity of valuation in a recapitalization, equating valuation is necessary in order to avoid transfer (gift) tax consequences in the exchange of the property for the newly issued stock. Valuation would be required at two different levels in the establishment of a PHC.[113] First, the value of the assets transferred to a PHC must be determined. If stock in a closely held corporation is transferred to the PHC, then the valuation endeavor would encompass utilization of representative sales or exchanges, comparative corporate analysis, and/or intrinsic valuation factors (discussed in Chapters 5–7). The second valuation would entail determining the relative values of the various classes of stock in the new corporation. (See valuation of preferred stock, Chapter 11; the previous discussion of valuation in recapitalizations; and representative sales or exchanges, comparative corporations in the valuation process, and/or intrinsic factor, Chapters 5–7.) The class of stock that would receive future appreciation would be gifted, purchased, or subscribed to by other family members. As in the recapitalization area, if the family members receive more in value than is contributed or paid, unnecessary tax consequences may arise that will frustrate an effective estate valuation plan. The Section 306 problem discussed in the recapitalization area can be avoided in the formation of a PHC if proper planning is done.

Tax Benefits

Formation of a PHC can achieve several tax benefits. First, corporate dividends received by the PHC enjoy an 85 percent deduction.[114] In other words, 85 percent of the dividends paid to a PHC are not included in the taxable income of the corporation. (However, this deduction is disallowed for purposes of the PHC undistributed income tax, discussed infra.) Therefore, the PHC may have no income tax liability, and may in fact generate a net operating loss if the shareholder-owner's salary and operating expenses exceed the income of the corporation. Such loss for the PHC can be carried back for three years and forward for seven years. Similarly, capital losses can be carried back three years while no such provision exists for individuals.[115] Second, to the extent that the shareholder-owner is reasonably compensated through a salary, dividend income with a maximum tax rate of 70 percent is being converted into earned income with a maximum tax rate of 50 percent—a potential 20 percent tax reduction. Third, by making gifts of PHC stock to family members, versus marketable securities otherwise gifted, the senior shareholder of the PHC has discretion as to distributions, cash or otherwise, to be made on the gifted shares. This, coupled with the significant limited marketability of such shares, can effectively prevent the disposal by a junior family member of his PHC shares. This may be contrary to the junior family member's desires if he held gifted readily marketable securities.

Although a PHC appears extremely advantageous in achieving a lower potential transfer tax liability at death and value freeze, it does have some major drawbacks. One significant negative feature is the confiscatory penalty tax levied on undistributed passive income. The tax is a harsh 70 percent straight rate. The tax may be levied if 1) greater than 50 percent of the PHC stock is owned by five or fewer individuals, and 2) 60 percent of its ordinary income, with certain adjustments, consists of passive income such as dividends, interest, royalties, and rents. The dividends received deduction is disallowed in computing the income amount.[116]

Tax Planning in PHC

The PHC tax can be avoided by failing to satisfy either the ownership test or the income test. Avoiding the stock ownership test can be done by disposing of stock. However, one must guard against the stock attribution rules, unique to the PHC tax.[117] Staying below the income test can be satisfied by decreasing the PHC (passive) income or increasing the adjusted ordinary gross income for the year, as the 60 percent level is calculated by dividing the PHC income by the adjusted ordinary gross income. The adjusted ordinary gross income is the gross income less 1) gains from the sale or disposition of capital assets, 2) gains from the sale or disposition of property used in the trade or business, or 3) expenditures attributable to production of income from rents and royalties (i.e., interest expense, property tax, depreciation, and the like).[118] Because of the items that constitute adjusted ordinary gross income, it is preferable to hold low yield securities or high growth stock (versus heavy dividend or interest securities) within a PHC. Property with the potential for appreciation is especially attractive since the capital gain from the sale of such property is not included in the computation. Additionally, interest income from tax exempt securities is excluded.

Since the purpose of the PHC tax is to require a corporation to pay dividends, dividend payments are allowed to reduce the amount subject to tax. Specific rules apply to the allowance of the deduction of dividends and should be adhered to carefully.

An ancillary consideration in the establishment of a PHC is the possibility that it might cause the loss of the privilege to make installment payments of transfer taxes upon the death of a shareholder. Under Section 6166A, tax payments can be deferred if the decedent's estate consisted of a certain portion of closely held business interests. (See more detailed discussion in relation to possible limitation of shifting of ownership interests in Chapter 15.) The definition of a "closely held business interest" under this section requires that the entity be carrying on a trade or business. Whether a PHC is an active trade or business by retention of appreciating passive assets and receipt of passive income has yet to be determined. The Internal Revenue Service has indicated, however, that mere management of investment assets does not qualify under the extension to pay provisions.[119]

SUMMARY

The advantages of having a readily determined value are numerous. Not only will speculation regarding a value be significantly decreased, but personal financial planning can take a more concrete form. Coinciding with the benefits of having a fixed value is the reduction of potential transfer taxes upon the death of a senior owner and allowance of any increase in value of a business to accrue to younger owners. Additionally, preservation of the closely held status of the business and continuation of the business as a going concern can be maintained by utilization of value limiting techniques. The tools available consist of restrictive agreements, recapitalizations (both corporate and partnership), and formation of a personal holding company for federal income tax purposes. These methods operate to stabilize a value regardless of business environmental changes.

NOTES FOR CHAPTER 14

1. Rev. Rul. 59–60, 1959-1 C.B. 237. The applicable case law is specified in the footnotes below.

2. Ibid., Section 8.

3. Citing Rev. Rul. 54–76, 1954-1 C.B. 194.

4. Land v. United States, 303 F.2d 170 (5th Cir. 1962), cert. denied, 371 U.S. 862 (1963); Estate of Anderson v. Commissioner, 1977 P-H TC Memo ¶77,237; Giannini v. Commissioner, 2 T.C. 1160 (1943), aff'd on other issue, 148 F.2d 285 (9th Cir. 1945), cert. denied, 326 U.S. 730 (1946).

5. Mathews v. United States, 226 F. Supp. 1003 (E.D. N.Y. 1964).

6. Estate of Salt v. Commissioner, 17 T.C. 92 (1951); Estate of Littick v. Commissioner, 31 T.C. 181 (1958); Estate of Weil v. Commissioner, 22 T.C. 1267 (1954); Lomb v. Sugden, 82 F.2d 166 (2nd Cir. 1936); Wilson v. Bowers, 57 F.2d 682 (2nd Cir. 1932); Broderick v. Gore, 224 F.2d 892 (10th Cir. 1955); Estate of Davis v. Commissioner, 1978 P-H TC Memo ¶78,069; Estate of Minnie Caplan v. Commissioner, 1974 P-H TC Memo ¶74,039.

7. Rev. Rul. 59–60, 1959-1 C.B. 237, Section 8, citing Rev. Rul. 157, 1953-2 C.B. 255 and Rev. Rul. 189, 1953-2 C.B. 294.

8. Reg. Sec. 20.2031-2(h).

9. 256 F. Supp 753 (D.C. N.Y. 1966).

10. 69 T.C. 32 (1977).

11. Estate of Bischoff v. Commissioner, ibid. See also Estate of Reynolds v. Commissioner, 55 T.C. 172 (1970); Estate of Littick v. Commissioner, note 6 supra; Baltimore National Bank v. United States, 136 F. Supp. 642 (D.C. Md. 1955); Broderick v. Gore, note 6 supra.

12. O'Neal, *Close Corporation: Law and Practice,* 2nd edition, Vol. 2, Chapter Sec. 7.29, citing Ness, *Federal Estate Tax Consequences of Agreements and Options to Purchase Stock on Death,* 49 Colum. L. Rev. 796, 806, 814 (1949).

13. For a discussion relating to the adequacy of consideration and effect of state law, see Stechel, *Restrictive Buy-Sell Agreements Can Limit Estate Tax Value of a Business Interest,* Journal of Taxation, June 1976, p. 360.

14. Rev. Rul. 59–60, note 1 supra, Section 8; Krauss v. United States, 140 F.2d 510 (5th Cir. 1944); James v. Commissioner, 3 T.C. 1260 (1944), aff'd 148 F.2d 236; Moore v. Commissioner, 3 T.C. 1205 (1944); McDonald v. Commissioner, 1944 P-H TC Memo ¶44,096; Commissioner v. McCann, 146 F.2d 385 (2nd Cir. 1944).

15. Rev. Rul. 59–60, note 1 supra; Rev. Rul. 189, 1953-2 C.B. 294; Baltimore National Bank v. United States, note 11 supra. See also O'Neal, note 12 supra, Chapter Sec. 7.29.

16. Kornel, *Valuation For Estate Tax Purposes,* 30th Annual N.Y.U. Institute, (1972), p. 197. See also Stechel, note 13 supra.

17. Ibid.

18. Ibid.

19. See Kornel, note 16 supra, p. 198 citing James v. Commissioner, 3 T.C. 1260 (1944), aff'd 148 F.2d 236; City Bank Farmer's Trust Co., 23 B.T.A. 663 (1931); Estate of Fry v. Commissioner, 9 T.C. 503 (1947). See also Estate of Reynolds v. Commissioner, 55 T.C. 172 (1970); Worcester County Trust Co. v. Commissioner, 134 F.2d 578 (1st Cir. 1943); Michigan Trust Co. v. Commissioner, 27 B.T.A. 556 (1933); for gifts see Rev. Rul. 189, 1953-2 C.B. 296; Berzon v. Commissioner, 63 T.C. 601 (1975), aff'd 534 F.2d 528 (2nd Cir. 1976).

20. See Kornel, note 16 supra, pages 197–198 citing Commissioner v. Bensel, 100 F.2d 639 (3rd Cir. 1938); Armstrong's Estate v. Commissioner, 146 F.2d 457 (7th Cir. 1944); Lomb v. Sugden, 82 F.2d 166 (2nd Cir. 1936); Estate of Littick v. Commissioner, 31 T.C. 181 (1958); Knipp Estate v. Commissioner, 25 T.C. 153 (1955), aff'd 244 F.2d 436 (4th Cir. 1957), cert. denied, 355 U.S. 827.

21. Apolinsky, *Devices for Pegging Values of Business Interest for Estate Tax Purposes,* Tax Planning for the Closely Held Corporation, 1979, Practicing Law Institute, Course Handbook Services Number 139. See also Willis, *Partnership Taxation,* Vol. 2, Chapters 48–49; and O'Neal, note 12 supra, Chapter 7.

22. Rev. Rul. 69–608, 1969-2 C.B. 42; Smith v. Commissioner, 70 T.C. 651 (1978).

23. Baltimore National Bank v. United States, note 11 supra.

24. Willis, note 21 supra, Chapter Sections 48.02–48.10; O'Neal, note 12 supra, Chapter Section 7.42(a); Fiorito v. Commissioner, 33 T.C. 440 (1959).

25. Willis, note 21 supra, Chapter Sec. 48.08; O'Neal, note 12 supra, Chapter Sec. 7.24(b).

26. Willis, note 21 supra, Chapters 47–48; O'Neal, note 12 supra, Chapter 7.24.

27. O'Neal, note 12 supra, Chapter Sec. 7.24(d).

28. Willis, note 21 supra, Chapter Secs. 48.04–48.06; O'Neal, note 12 supra, Chapter Sec. 7.24(e).

29. Apolinsky, note 21 supra, p. 585 and O'Neal, note 12 supra, Chapter Sec. 7.25.

30. See Thomas, *How to Use a Buy-Sell Agreement to Protect a Client's Business and to Save Estate Taxes,* Estate Planning, September 1979; and O'Neal, note 12 supra, Chapter Sec. 7.25.

31. Tobisman, *Corporate Buy-Sell Agreements,* Estate and Financial Planning for the Closely Held Corporation, Practicing Law Institute, No. 97, p. 69.

32. Adapted from the Supreme Court's definition of a recapitalization as it applies to a closely held corporation in Helvering v. Southwest Consolidated Corporation, 315 U.S. 194, 202 (1942).

33. See Sections 368, 358 and 354 generally. Also Section 1036.

34. Cooper, *A Voluntary Tax?: New Perspectives on Sophisticated Estate Tax Avoidance,* Brookings Institute, Washington, D.C., 1979, p. 19. Originally published as an article by the same name, 77 Colum. L. Rev. 161 (1977).

35. See Sections 302, 305, 306, and related Regulations.

36. S. Rep. No. 91-552, 91st Cong., 1st Sess. 151 (1969); H. Rep. No. 91-413 91st Cong., 1st Sess. 113 (1969), 1969-3 C.B. 200.

37. Reg. Sec. 1.305-7.

38. 115 Cong. Rec. Sec. 16,221; Reg. Sec. 1.305-3(3), example 12; Rev. Rul. 77–19, 1977-1 C.B. 84; Rev. Rul. 75–93, 1975-1 C.B. 101; Ltr. Ruls. 8005059, 8005047, 7948103, 7942033 and 7937082. But see Ltr. Rul. 7941009.

39. See, for example, Reg. Sec. 1.305-7(c).

40. See Reg. Sec. 1.368-2(e)(3) and the case law that follows. See also Golomb, *Recapitalization: The Definition Problem,* 7 Tax L. Rev. 343 (1952).

41. See Sections 358 and 1223.

42. Reg. Sec. 1.368-3(a).

43. Reg. Sec. 1.368-1(c).

44. Gregory v. Helvering, 293 U.S. 465 (1935).

45. Rev. Rul. 74–269, 1974-1 C.B. 87.

46. Ltr. Rul. 7923069.

47. Ltr. Rul. 7928084.

48. Ltr. Ruls. 7927051 and 7928068.

49. Ltr. Rul. 7927053.

50. Ltr. Rul. 7925043.

51. Rev. Rul. 74–269, note 45 supra.

52. See Reg. Sec. 1.162-7 and Prop. Reg. Sec. 1.86-6(d).

53. Rev. Rul. 74–269, note 45 supra, and Section 2511(a)4(6).

54. Ibid. See also Abrams and Morgan, *Recapitalizing a Closely Held Corporation,* The Practical Lawyer, Vol. 25, No. 6, September 1979, for an excellent recapitalization discussion.

55. In Re John M. King, District Court of District of Colorado, D.C. No. 71-B-1630, decision unreported, affirmed King v. United States, 545 F.2d 700 (10th Cir. 1976).

56. The Internal Revenue Service based such position on Commissioner v. Procter, 142 F.2d 824 (4th Cir. 1944), cert. denied, 323 U.S. 756, which held that a limitation provision on a transfer of interests in trust to satisfy debt obligations was a condition subsequent and invalid as being contrary to public policy.

57. Estate of Dickinson v. Commissioner, 63 T.C. 771 (1975); Soter v. Commissioner, 1968 P-H TC Memo ¶68,043; Rev. Rul. 72–570, 72-2 C.B. 241; Arrowsmith v. Commissioner, 344 U.S. 6 (1952); Rees Blow Pipe Mfg. Co. v. Commissioner, 41 T.C. 598 (1964), aff'd per curiam, 342 F.2d 990 (9th Cir. 1965); Turco v. Commissioner, 52 T.C. 631 (1969).

58. See, generally, Abbin, *Gift, Estate and Income Tax Exposure From Recapitalizing Closely Held Companies*, U. Miami, 10th Inst. on Est. Plan. para. 1208.1 (1976), wherein various combinations of such classes are examined and explained. Additionally, Section 1036 provides for no gain or loss when exchanging common stock for common stock or preferred stock for preferred stock.

59. Rev. Rul. 72–206, 1972-1 C.B. 104.

60. Abbin, note 58 supra, pages 12-25.

61. Salsbury v. Commissioner, 1975 P-H TC Memo ¶75,333.

62. Ibid.

63. See Abrams and Morgan, note 54 supra for comprehensive example involving a lapsing vote and Abbin, note 58 supra, pages 12–27 for a general discussion.

64. Abrams and Morgan, note 54 supra, and Kenter, *Marketable Securities: Some Estate Planning Techniques and Approaches*, 35 N.Y.U. Inst. on Fed. Tax 1105, 1170 (1977). See also Ltr. Ruls. 7905096 and 7918124.

65. Whittemore v. Fitzpatrick, 127 F.Supp. 710 (D.C. Conn., 1954).

66. See Abbin, note 58 supra, and Abrams and Morgan, note 54 supra.

67. Section 306(c).

68. Section 306(a)(2).

69. Section 306(a)(1).

70. Section 306(b)(1)(A) and (B). Attribution rules (Section 318) are generally as follows: a person is deemed to own the stock actually owned by spouse, parents, children, and grandchildren (no attribution between brothers and sisters).

71. Section 306(b)(2).

72. Section 306(b)(4).

73. Section 306(b)(3).

74. Section 306(c)(1)(B).

75. Reg. Sec. 1.306-3(d), example 2.

76. 1977-1 C.B. 86.

77. Lt. Ruls. 7928084, 7928068, 7928010, 7927053, 7927051, 7927050, 7927033, 7927023, 8001022, 8001029 and 8001050. But see Lt. Ruls. 7926166, 7926042, 7925078, 7925026 and 7924017.

78. Apolinsky, note 21 supra citing D'Angelo Associates, Inc. v. Commissioner, 70 T.C. 121 (1978); Wilgard Realty Co. Inc. v. Commissioner, 127 F.2d 514 (2d Cir. 1942), cert. denied, 317 U.S. 655 (1943); but see Fahs v. Florida Machine and Foundry Co., 168 F.2d 957 (5th Cir. 1948).

79. Reg. Sec. 1.351-1(c)(1).

80. Reg. Sec. 1.351-1(c)(6) and Lt. Rul. 7936076.

81. Reorganization under Section 368(a)(1)(B).

82. See Section 306(c)(2) and Reg. Sec. 1.306-3(d).

83. 1979-2 C.B. 131. See also Ltr. Rul. 7923069 and Corry, *Preferred Stock Issued in Tax Free Exchanges: Does Section 306 Apply?*, Tax Law Review, Fall 1979, p. 113.

84. Rev. Rul. 77–108, note 76 supra.

85. Reg. Sec. 1.306-3(e).

86. Ibid.

87. Rev. Rul. 75–236, 1975-1 C.B.106.

88. Estate of Lee v. Commissioner, 69 T.C. 860 (1978) and Rank v. United States, 345 F.2d 337 (5th Cir. 1965).

89. Estate of Mundy v. Commissioner, 1976 P-H TC Memo ¶76,395; Van Hagke v. Commissioner, 43 AFTR 2d 79-1310 (E.D. Wisc. 1979).

90. Van Hagke, ibid.

91. See Mundy, note 89 supra; Zahn v. Transamerica, 162 F.2d 36 (3rd Cir. 1947); Van Hagke, note 89 supra.

92. Mundy, note 89 supra.

93. See, for example, Ltr. Rul. 7932048.

94. Abrams and Morgan, note 54 supra.

95. See note 44 supra. See also Driver v. United States, 38 AFTR 2d 76-6315 (W.D. Wisc. 1976); Tully v. United States, 41 AFTR 2d 78-1477 (Ct. Cl. 1978); Riss v. Commissioner, 56 T.C. 388 (1971).

96. Carnahan v. United States, 188 F.Supp. 461 (D.C. Mont. 1960); Rev. Rul. 57–132, 1957-1 C.B. 115; Rev. Rul. 75–236, 1975-1 C.B. 106.

97. Abbin, *The Partnership Capital Freeze—An Alternative to Corporate Recapitalization*, U. Miami 13th Inst. Est. Plan. (1979); Nash, *Family Partnership—A Viable Planning Alternative*, U. Miami 13th Inst. Est. Plan. (1979); Apolinsky, note 21 supra.

98. See, generally, Sections 721–723, Section 83, and Section 2512.

99. Section 707(c).

100. Abbin, note 97 supra.

101. Sections 531–537.

102. Section 731(a)(1). But see Sections 736 and 751.

103. Morrissey v. Commissioner, 296 U.S. 344 (1935); Reg. Sec. 301.7701-2; Larson v. Commissioner, 66 T.C. 159 (1976).

104. Ibid.

105. Section 704(e) and related Regulations.

106. Section 704(a) and (b). Reg. Sec. 1.704-1(b)(2); Orrisch v. Commissioner, 55 T.C. 395 (1973); Cooper, note 34 supra.

107. Abbin, note 97 supra.

108. Estate of Meyer v. Commissioner, 503 F.2d 556 (9th Cir. 1974); Rev. Rul. 78–135, 1978-1 C.B. 256.

109. Section 708(b)(2).

110. Abbin, note 97 supra.

111. Nash, note 97 supra; Abbin, note 97 supra.

112. Whittemore v. Fitzpatrick, 127 F. Supp. 710 (W.D. Conn. 1954); Oshins and Lawther, note 62 supra; Gallun v. Commissioner, 1974 P-H TC Memo ¶74,284; Estate of Piper v. Commissioner, 72 T.C. 1062, (1979).

113. Apolinsky, note 21 supra.

114. Section 243.

115. Sec. 1212(a)(1)(A). However, this provision does not apply to Subchapter S corporations. See Milefsky, *How to Use a Personal Holding Company as an Effective Estate Financial Planning Tool*, Journal of Taxation, April 1975, p. 202.

116. Sections 541–547.

117. Section 544.

118. Section 543(b)(1) and (2).

119. Rev. Ruls. 75–365, 1975-2 C.B. 471; 75–366, 1975-2 C.B. 472; 75–367, 1975-2 C.B. 472.

15

Tax Planning Opportunities by Shifting Ownership

Shifting ownership within a closely held business is a well-recognized estate planning technique. The obvious desire to pass ownership rights to a family member so that the closely held business will remain in family control makes ownership shifts a practical and effective means of reducing potential taxes. The unification of estate and gift taxes into a single transfer tax has made inter vivos shifts of ownership somewhat less attractive for tax purposes than under prior law. Nevertheless, there still are techniques available which effectively shift ownership and avoid, or at least minimize, the transfer tax.

As shown in *Case Seventeen—Biggs Corporation* in Chapter 13, the transfer of ownership rights to the natural and intended future owners of the business can result in meaningful transfer tax savings. But how are ownership rights transferred to a family member without adverse tax consequences? The answer to this query is the focal point of this chapter. The tools available to successfully achieve an ownership shift with a minimum of tax liability include utilization of 1) gift programs, 2) installment sales, 3) various trust arrangements, and/or 4) private annuities. Each of these methods can be utilized to achieve value planning through ownership shifts. The use of gifts, as will be shown later, has decreased in attractiveness due to the unification of the estate and gift tax rates. However, there are still advantages in utilizing a gift program. All of the techniques listed are considered to be effective in reducing income and transfer taxes by 1) shifting income to a lower tax bracket family member, and 2) allowing future appreciation of the closely held business to accrue to the recipient of the ownership rights. Before discussing these techniques in detail, the concept of changing ownership to reduce transfer taxes will be considered.

DISAPPEARING WEALTH

In evaluating the ownership given to various family members, the principal owner's desire to retain control must be considered. The indefinite time of death precludes exact estate planning. Nevertheless, it is possible to achieve a significantly lower transfer tax liability at death through the use of lifetime ownership shifting techniques.

It is recognized that a premium may be attached to the interest of a controlling or majority owner in a closely held business. Conversely, a discount may be applied to the interest of a minority owner. (See Chapter 8.) The maneuvering of the ownership interest can result in each interest holder receiving a discount, with no concomitant application of a control premium to the value of any shares. This is a highly favorable result for estate planning purposes. Prevention of the use of a premium in valuing any interest results in what has been termed "disappearing wealth."[1]

As an example, a senior shareholder owns 60 out of 100 outstanding shares of stock in a closely held corporation. An independent third party holds the remaining 40 shares. In such an arrangement, the senior shareholder's holdings would be given a premium due to the control it enjoys. If, however, the senior shareholder transferred 15 shares to a relative, then the senior's holdings no longer represent a majority. (This assumes that more than 50 percent ownership is needed for control and that the new owner is actually independent of the senior shareholder to avoid the problems discussed on pages 88 and 89.) The transfer would be made to a party the senior shareholder could confide in so that his desires and wishes would be given serious attention during his lifetime. The value attributed to control should disappear and, in fact, allow all owners to enjoy a decrease in taxable value due to the application of a minority discount. The implementation of the decrease in ownership, however, rests strictly on the senior owner's willingness to fragment his ownership interest and (at least potentially) see the direction and philosophy of the business change.

CAVEATS IN SHIFTING OWNERSHIP

The fragmentation of an ownership interest, if too severe, can cause the loss of favorable tax advantages which might otherwise be available. For example, if a Section 303 redemption of stock in a closely held corporation is being considered in order to pay estate taxes, the decedent's (former senior owner's) level of ownership retention may fail to meet the required level to be afforded this favorable treatment. Section 303 requires that in order for favorable redemption treatment to be available, stock representing 50 percent or more of the adjusted gross value of the decedent's estate must be included in the estate. Fragmentation of ownership may cause loss of the availability of Section 303.

Additionally, under Section 6166 and 6166A, certain levels of ownership by a decedent are necessary in order to qualify to elect to pay the decedent's estate taxes on the installment method. Under the provisions of Section 6166, the decedent's interest in a closely held business must exceed 65 percent of such decedent's adjusted gross estate (gross estate less certain allowable deductions). A partnership interest will qualify under this requirement if 1) the partnership has 15 or fewer partners, or 2) 20 percent or more of the total capital of the partnership is included in the gross estate of the decedent. Stock held by the decedent in a corporation will qualify if 1) there are 15 or fewer shareholders, or 2) 20 percent or more of the voting stock was held by the decedent.[2] Interests in two or more closely held businesses may be combined if more than 20 percent of the value of each is includible in the decedent's gross estate. If the above criteria are met, the representative of the estate may elect, under Section 6166, to pay the estate tax attributable to the closely held business in up to ten equal annual installments with the first installment deferred up to five years after the original tax due date. Interest will be charged at the rate of 4 percent on the transfer tax attributable to the first $1,000,000 of closely held business value ($345,800 of tax liability). Interest on the excess tax payable, the payment of which is extended, is 12 percent for periods after February 1, 1980 (see discussion under Section 6166A below).

Under the alternate provision, Section 6166A, the value of the closely held business must exceed 1) 35 percent of the gross estate, or 2) 50 percent of the taxable estate, in order to receive installment treatment. Under this provision, the maximum number of partners or shareholders allowable in the closely held business is ten. Interests in two or more closely held businesses may be combined if more than 50 percent of the value in each is included in the gross estate. If a closely held business interest qualifies under Section 6166A, the transfer tax attributable to such interest can be made in ten equal annual installments, with the first payment due on the normal due date. The interest rate on the unpaid tax varies depending upon fluctuations of the prime rate charged by banks. The rate for periods after February 1, 1980, is 12 percent. This rate, applicable under Section 6166 and 6166A, will remain in effect until January 1982, at which time it will be adjusted to a more current rate.[3]

It is clear from the foregoing that fragmenting ownership requires consideration of the possible loss of positive tax features as well as the practical aspects of disposing of ownership rights. The tools and techniques in this chapter are structured to fragment a senior owner's holdings in a closely held business. However, care should be taken to fully analyze the positive and negative tax aspects of such plans, as well as the business considerations attendant to the proposed ownership changes.

CLASSES OF OWNERSHIP SHIFTING RIGHTS

As indicated above, shifting ownership rights can be a highly advantageous estate planning method. In most closely held business tax planning situations, the desire is to shift ownership rights from a senior family member to a junior family member (hereinafter referred to as "senior member" or "junior member"). As mentioned in Chapter 1, a closely held business generally will be either a corporation, partnership, or sole proprietorship. The disposition of rights in these various forms of organizations requires an understanding of the "interests" available for ownership shifting within each kind of organization. The following brief discussion analyzes such "interests" in each type of entity.

Corporations

The application of ownership shifting is most easily seen and understood in the area of closely held corporations. Closely held stock is a prime candidate for disposition to junior members because of the ease of transferring stock certificates to such members. Additionally, the ownership of stock provides at least an intangible "numeric" interest in a closely held corporation. Because a value, even though possibly difficult to determine, can be ascribed to each share owned, stock is an excellent medium for shifting ownership rights in a closely held business.

Partnerships

With regard to partnerships and ownership shifting, a disposition of partnership interests creates a more complex valuation endeavor. Partnership interests can generally be categorized as either 1) a capital interest, or 2) a profits interest.[4] Tax minimization when dealing with the fragmentation of partnership rights requires compliance with applicable Code provisions relating to the classification and characteristics of a partnership. Similar to a shareholder's interest in a corporation, a partner's interest in a partnership can be sold or exchanged in whole or in part. Unlike a shareholder, however, a partner, for tax purposes, is considered to 1) own a proportionate interest in each of the individual assets, and 2) owe a proportionate amount of each of the partnership's liabilities. Disposition of a partnership interest results in a capital gain or loss and may result in recognition of ordinary income or loss. With regard to relationship of partners, partnerships can take the form of 1) a partnership with unrelated partners, or 2) a family partnership. For federal income tax purposes, a family partnership is made up of husband and wife, ancestors, lineal descendants and/or any trust for the benefit of such persons (but not brothers and sisters).[5] The following discussion of fragmentation of a partnership interest is limited to family partnerships since many closely held business partnerships are categorized as family partnerships and subject to the federal income tax rules attributable thereto.

Three elements must be satisfied in order for a partnership to be recognized as a legitimate family partnership for federal income tax purposes. First, each partner must, in fact, actually own the interest attributable to him or her. Second, the interest must be a capital interest. Third, capital must be a material income-producing factor (i.e., substantial amounts of partnership gross income must result from the use of capital). The steps necessary for a parent or other senior family member to satisfy these elements when disposing of a family partnership interest include:

(1) the transferor must relinquish, and the transferee must acquire, the entire ownership interest (full and absolute control of the interest transferred),

(2) the transferee must be entitled to share in the assets in the event of withdrawal or liquidation of the partnership, and

(3) the transferee must be held out to the public, customers, creditors, and others as a partner.[6]

Sole Proprietorships

As applied to sole proprietorships, ownership shifting primarily encompasses disposition of assets owned by the senior owner and used in the closely held business. This transfer to junior members usually involves assets intended to remain a major part of the closely held business as the business passes to successor generations (e.g., buildings, land, equipment, and the like).

GIFTS

Prior to 1977, an owner could gift all or a portion of his closely held business interest to a junior member and, assuming that the gift was not made in contemplation of death, have the gift taxed at substantially lower rates than the estate tax rates which would apply at the owner's death. Thus, gifts were very attractive estate planning tools since the property gifted would be taxed at a lower rate than if it passed through a decedent's estate. Presently, however, the unified transfer tax taxes gifted property and property in a decedent's estate at the same rate. Although the unified transfer tax has diminished the advantages of gift programs, the benefits of such programs have not been totally eliminated. There still exists the $3,000 annual exclusion (hopefully to be increased in the near future by Congress to a more reasonable level based upon today's economy). This $3,000 annual exclusion has several benefits that are not readily apparent. For example, gifts made in excess of $3,000 to a donee 1) require the filing of a gift tax return, and 2) if made within three years of death will be includible in the gross estate of the decedent (whereas, a gift of $3,000, even one day prior to a decedent's death, will not be includible in the gross estate or require the filing of a return). The most important aspect of gifting closely held business ownership rights, as mentioned at the beginning of this chapter, is that they operate to 1) shift income to a lower tax bracket family member, and 2) allow future appreciation of the gifted property to accrue to junior members. While this latter objective requires some degree of speculation, such speculation is not particularly risky in today's economy.

As stated above, the value of property as of the gift date is taxed at a rate set forth in the Transfer Tax Table[7] (see Appendix E). Where property is gifted for less than adequate and full consideration, the amount by which the value of the property exceeds the value of the consideration is deemed to be a gift.[8] Gift tax returns are to be filed on or before April 15 of the year following the year in which the gifts are made. If, however, total taxable gifts during the first three-quarters of the year exceed $25,000, then the gift tax return is due on or before the 15th day of the second month following the calendar quarter in which the gift exceeds the $25,000 amount.[9]

As previously mentioned, there is an annual exclusion from the transfer tax of $3,000 per year per donee ($6,000 if spouse joins) for gifts of present interests in property.[10] If more than $3,000 is gifted to a donee in one year, there still may be no transfer tax liability if the donor has not exhausted his or her lifetime transfer tax credit. This lifetime transfer tax credit is $42,500 per donor for gifts made in 1980, and $47,000 for gifts thereafter. This credit amounts to equivalent gift value of $161,563 for 1980, and $175,625 for subsequent years. This credit, as is the tax rate, is unified for lifetime and death transfers. In other words, any portion of the credit used to offset the lifetime transfer tax reduces the credit available for use against the transfer tax at death.[11] The use of the credit is mandatory and not elective in the order in which lifetime transfers (gifts) are made.[12] Under maximum application, for years after 1980, a married couple could conceivably gift a one time total of $357,250 to one donee in one year and not be subject to tax. (The tax credit equivalent of $175,625 for each donor, plus the $3,000 annual exclusion—both taken twice because of spouse joining—equals $357,250.) Once the transfer tax credit and $3,000 per donee annual exclusion are depleted, further noncharitable gift giving is subject to tax. However, if the donee is the donor's spouse, there is also allowed a $100,000 transfer tax marital deduction for lifetime transfers.[13]

It may appear at first glance that gifting property (valued in excess of the annual exclusion) during the life of a donor is unnecessary even though protected by the credit, since the property will be taxed at exactly the same rate for gift purposes as it will for estate purposes (due to the unified transfer tax and related credit). However, as stated earlier, this is true only if the value of the property when the gift is made is equal to its value when it is included in the taxable estate of the donor. Gifts remain advantageous when 1) the value at the time of the gift is anticipated to be less than the value of the gifted asset at any time in the future, and 2) income can be shifted to a lower tax bracket family member. An example would be the gifting of shares of a closely held corporation which are not frozen as to value when gifted (see the discussion of corporate recapitalizations in Chapter 14), since such shares are the sole recipients of future increases in corporate value.

NET GIFTS

Donors often wish to make a significant lifetime gift of appreciated property (e.g., stock in a closely held corporation) but the resultant transfer tax liability is so burdensome as to preclude such a gift. This is usually the case where payment of the transfer tax liability would cause the donor to sell property not otherwise considered for sale in order to satisfy such liability. A solution to this dilemma is to make the gift, either expressly or by implication, conditional upon the donee's payment of the tax resulting from the transfer. This method, whereby the person receiving the gift (the donee) pays the transfer tax, is known as the "net gift" technique.

In the net gift arrangement, the transfer tax paid by the donee is deducted from the value of the gifted property, resulting in a gift of the net value. A circular problem arises as the net value of the gift is dependent upon the amount of tax, which in turn is dependent upon the value of the gift. In order to compute the actual tax on the amount of the net gift, the following formula is used:[14]

$$\frac{\text{Tentative tax}}{1 \text{ plus (rate of tax*)}} = \text{Actual tax}$$

*Usually shown as percentage of excess over the lowest range amount on the Transfer Tax Table (see Appendix E).

The actual tax is then applied against the donor's transfer tax credit.[15] According to a recent Revenue Ruling, the donor does not have the option to use his or her transfer tax credit as desired in the net gift area, but rather is required to use the credit available when a net gift is made.[16] An example of the computation is given in *Case Twenty—Capini Corporation.*

In the net gift area, the Internal Revenue Service has been quick to contest instances where a gift is made of property the value of which is so significantly in excess of the donor's basis that the gift tax paid by the donee exceeds such basis. The Service contends that in such circumstances the gift should be viewed as part sale and part gift under the rationale that since the gift tax is the obligation of the donor, the donee's payment of this obligation constitutes income to the donor.[17] The donor would therefore recognize gain in the amount of the excess of the taxes paid over the basis in the property. This contention, however, has not been approved by the courts except in cases where there was a preexisting obligation on property transferred to a trust and the trust subsequently satisfied such obligation for the donor.[18] The Tax Court, and the higher courts by affirmation, adhere to the opinion that no taxable income is realized as a result of a conditional transfer where the tax liability exceeds the donor's basis.[19]

Under a net gift arrangement, it is essential that the donee's payment of the transfer tax be an implied or expressed condition of the transfer.[20] If there is no obligation of the donee to pay the transfer tax (i.e., the donee pays the transfer tax voluntarily), then the net gift computation (actual tax) will not be used and the gift will be taxed at its gross amount.[21]

CASE TWENTY

Net Gift Technique

CAPINI CORPORATION

Facts

Pat Capini, as donor, desires to make a gift of 20,000 shares of stock in Capini Corporation (value $200,000) to his son, Fred Capini. However, Pat Capini is hesitant to make the gift as his cash flow is negligible due to the recent purchase of a summer cottage. Fred offers to pay the transfer tax. Pat agrees and makes the gift conditional on Fred paying the transfer tax. Pat subsequently makes the gift on March 28, 1981.

Actual Tax:

Tentative transfer tax base:		
Gross transfer		$ 200,000
Less: Annual exclusion		(3,000)
Tentative transfer tax base		$ 197,000
Computation of tentative tax:		
Transfer tax on $150,000		$ 38,800
Transfer tax on $47,000 at 32%		15,040
Total tentative transfer tax		53,840
Less: 1981 Unified transfer tax credit		(47,000)
Tentative tax		$ 6,840

Computation of actual tax:

$$\frac{\text{Tentative tax}}{\text{1 plus rate of tax}} = \text{actual tax}$$

$$\frac{6,840}{1.32} = \$ 5,182$$

Reporting the transfer tax:		
Gross transfer		$ 200,000
Less transfer tax for quarter	$ 5,182	
Annual exclusion	3,000	(8,182)
Taxable gift for quarter		$ 191,818

Tax on gift for quarter:

Transfer tax on $150,000	$ 38,000
Transfer tax on $41,818 at 32%	13,382
Transfer tax liability	52,182
Less: 1981 transfer tax credit	(47,000)
Transfer tax due	$ 5,182

Analysis

Fred would pay the actual tax due. All of Pat's unified transfer tax credit is depleted because of the amount of the transfer tax liability. Pat does not have the option to defer his credit until his death, or for some later gift. He must use the credit available at the time of the net gift.

INSTALLMENT SALES AND GIFTS

The use of an installment sale, alone or in conjunction with a gift program, may also operate to freeze the value of gifted property. Stock owned by a senior shareholder which has significantly appreciated in value in relation to its basis is enticing for installment sale treatment, especially when the future prospects of the business are good. Along similar lines, if a sole proprietor owns land which his family business is built on, such property is a good candidate for sale to a junior member if the business is to be continued. As the shares of stock or parcel of land continue to appreciate in value, the installment sale becomes even more attractive.

The installment transaction can effectively:

(1) avoid immediate recognition of capital gain by the transferor (senior member),

(2) allow the transferor to convert appreciating property into income-producing property,

(3) shift ownership to selected parties,

(4) freeze the value of transferred property in the hands of the transferor, and

(5) allow ease in structuring payments for the transferee (junior member).

The basic fact pattern in an installment sale is to have the present holder of appreciated, and hopefully appreciating, property transfer his ownership rights to a junior member. The junior member, in turn, executes an instrument of indebtedness for the fair value of the property payable over a set number of years in specific amounts each year. Further, the annual payment could be set with an eye to the gift tax provision allowing a $3,000 annual per donee exclusion so as to allow for the senior owner the option of forgiving up to $3,000 annually of the installment obligation. Care must be taken that the forgiveness is not a foregone conclusion, as the Internal Revenue Service might treat the transaction as a gift in the full amount of the property transferred on the transfer date.[22] As a side note, if an installment obligation is disposed of other than by sale, satisfaction, or exchange, such as by gift, gain or loss is recognized in an amount equal to the difference between the basis of the obligation and its fair market value at the time of disposition. The character of this gain or loss (capital or ordinary) is dependent upon the nature of the property the sale of which resulted in the obligation.[23]

Installment sales are governed by Section 453 as modified by the new installment sales provisions signed into law on October 19, 1980.[24] Specific attention must be given to the rules in such legislation regarding installment sales to related parties.[25]

In actuality, there is no substantial transfer tax savings to the transferor from an installment sale until several years after the transaction has taken place. This results from the fact that the property sold is initially replaced by an obligation of equal amount. However, the sales price freezes the value to the senior shareholder, allowing future appreciation in the property transferred to accrue to the junior member. Additionally, the present value of the obligation in the hands of the senior member is incrementally reduced each year until such time as its value is significantly below that of the property previously transferred. This assumes that the payments received by the senior member are not invested in assets which would result in a value in excess of the value of property previously sold.

THE USE OF TRUSTS

A common and effective means of reducing the size of an estate is to transfer the property out of the estate prior to death. Many times such a transfer is made to a trust. However, even if a transfer of property is deemed to be complete in form, such property may nevertheless be included in the gross estate if the transaction lacks substance.

In most instances, if the settlor (creator of the trust) has the power to control the beneficial enjoyment of the property transferred, at death, such property will be includible in his or her estate under Section 2036 and/or Section 2038 of the Code.

Section 2036 is commonly referred to as the "grantor section." This provision becomes operative when the decedent previously owned and transferred property during his or her lifetime for less than adequate consideration if there was retained:

(1) the right, either alone or in conjunction with any other person, to designate the persons who shall possess or enjoy the previously transferred property or the income from such property, or

(2) the possession or enjoyment of, or the right to the income from, the property previously transferred.

Section 2038 requires that if property is transferred during an owner's life and if at the time of the owner's death the enjoyment of the property remains subject to a change through the exercise of a power held by the owner to alter, amend, revoke, or terminate the transfer, then such property will be included in the owner's (decedent's) gross estate. Section 2038 transfers are commonly known as "revocable transfers."

Sections 2036 and 2038 apply only to the power held by the decedent at his or her time of death. The decedent will be considered to fall under the ambit of Sections 2036 and 2038 if he has the unrestricted right to remove or discharge a trustee at any time and appoint himself as trustee of a trust containing property he previously owned and transferred to the trust.[26] Generally, according to case law defining the application of these Sections and their related Regulations, it can be assumed that 1) if the transferor is a trustee, the value of the trust may be included in his estate, depending upon the trustee's powers (i.e., sole trustee or multiple trustees who can override the transferor trustee), 2) similarly, if the transferor has the right to remove or discharge the trustee and appoint himself as trustee, the value of the trust may be included in his estate, depending on the trustee's power, and 3) the power of the transferor to remove one trustee and replace such trustee with another will not cause the value of the trust to enter into his estate. Presently, there exists a question as to the third assumption relating to the transferor's power to remove and replace trustees. The Internal Revenue Service recently stated, in Revenue Ruling 79–353,[27] that the transferor's power to appoint trustees will cause the trust to be includible in the decedent's (transferor's) estate. This position appears erroneous in view of the case law and legislative activity that exists in this area, as discussed below.

The landmark decision in which the transferor retained the power to replace a trustee is the 1972 U.S. Supreme Court decision of *Byrum* v. *United States*.[28] The Supreme Court determined that where the decedent had irrevocably transferred closely held corporate stock to a trust reserving the power to 1) vote the stock in the trust corpus, 2) veto the transfer by the trustee of any of the shares, and 3) remove and appoint a successor trustee at will, such power did not merit the inclusion of the value of such trust in the decedent's gross estate. The Court held that the decedent did not possess beneficial enjoyment of the property transferred.

The Supreme Court's decision in *Byrum* was legislatively overruled, in part, by the Tax Reform Act of 1976, and the Revenue Act of 1978. The change, however, pertained only to retention of voting rights in transferred stock, which makes such stock includible in the decedent's gross estate. Until recently, the right to remove and appoint a successor trustee at will was not a sufficient power to justify inclusion in the settlor's estate as set forth in *Byrum.* However, as previously stated, the Internal Revenue Service, by virtue of Revenue Ruling 79–353, now contends that reservation by the transferor of the power to remove the trustee at will and appoint another trustee is equivalent to retention of powers vested in a trustee and, therefore, requires the inclusion of the trust assets in the estate of the transferor.

The Service bases the above contention, in part, on a 1958 First Circuit case, *Van Beuren* v. *McLoughlin*,[29] which stated, in dictum, that the "unrestricted . . . power to remove a trustee and replace him . . . is an extremely potent power."[30] However, in *Van Beuren* the grantor had the power to appoint herself as trustee. Revenue Ruling 79–353 is completely contrary to *Byrum* and prior assumptions made by parties forming a trust when there is reserved the right to replace or remove a trustee but there is no right to appoint one's self as trustee.

It is understood that the Internal Revenue Service is considering modifying or withdrawing Revenue Ruling 79–353. It appears that, as it presently stands, the only way to avoid an argument with the Internal Revenue Service over the inclusion of the value of the trust in an estate is to have the grantor (settlor) renounce his or her power to remove and replace trustees.

GENERATION-SKIPPING TRUSTS

Prior to the Tax Reform Act of 1976, substantial tax benefits were obtainable by transferring property to a trust for the benefit of future generations. The tax advantages were generally twofold. First, income from the transferred property was shifted from a higher tax bracket senior member to a lower tax bracket trust, or junior member as beneficiary under the trust. Second, if properly structured, the property transferred to the trust was excluded from the senior and junior members' estates upon their deaths. The 1976 Act preserved the first of these advantages; however, the second has been materially changed.

A generation-skipping transfer of an interest in a closely held business would require that 1) a senior member create a trust with the closely held interest, and 2) the income from the trust be payable to the junior member or members for their lives with the corpus passing to their children (i.e., the senior member's grandchildren) upon the death of the junior member or members. In essence, the income interest and remainder interest are split for the benefit of two (or more) generations (beneficiaries) which are younger than the generation of the creator of the trust. Thus, except for the gift tax incurred upon creation of the trust, the senior member, prior to 1977, was able to pass property from himself to his grandchildren, and allow his children to enjoy income benefits during their lives without incurring any estate tax at the children's death. This type of transaction raised an inequity in the eyes of Congress since a transfer from parent to child, and then from child to grand-child, created two taxable transfers, whereas utilization of the generation-skipping trust arrangement created only one transfer tax (when the trust was established) and accomplished an identical result. Due to the possibility that substantial wealth could escape transfer taxes, a generation-skipping transfer tax now exists.[31]

Basically, the generation-skipping tax taxes the transfer from the junior member or members to the succeeding generation. However, the tax is not imposed until the death of the last surviving junior member if the trust is for the benefit of several junior members.[32] Even though the tax would be determined as if it passed through the last survivor's estate, the tax is paid from the assets of the trust.[33] The tax reformers did, however, allow a $250,000 value per child exclusion on property transferred from the junior member to the senior member's second succeeding generation (i.e., grandchildren).[34] This exclusion creates the ownership shift planning avenue available for closely held business interests.

In present-day estate planning involving generation-skipping transfers, the fact pattern will be the same; however, the $250,000 exclusion must be kept in mind. The valuation is made at the time of the transfer to the senior member's third generation (i.e., grandchildren) versus when the trust is created.[35] Additionally, it must be kept in mind that the transfer tax covers only situations involving trusts, or trust equivalent arrangements, where beneficial interests pass from a second to a third generation. Thus, a direct transfer from a grandparent to a grandchild does not create a beneficial interest to the grandparent's child and no generation-skipping tax is imposed.

As can be seen, the generation-skipping trust now has limited utility. Nevertheless, it remains an item which should be considered in appropriate cases.

PRIVATE FAMILY ANNUITIES

An often discussed but seldom used ownership shifting technique is the private family annuity. Many practitioners feel that there is still an element of risk in this area due to a lack of legal unanimity. A discussion of the legal inconsistencies involving private family annuities is beyond the scope of this text. The general principles and practical considerations in the private family annuity area are discussed below.

Under a private family annuity transaction, a senior member of a family (usually elderly) transfers appreciated property to a junior member. The junior member in turn contracts to make periodic payments to the senior member for life. Although similar in nature to installment transactions, the private family annuity results in payments to a senior member for life versus a specific number of years (as in an installment sale). The private annuity arrangement, also like installment sale transactions, readily lends itself to use when 1) stock within the closely held corporation should be shifted to a junior member, 2) portions of partnership interests, profits, or capital can be disposed of under state law advantageously to a junior member, and 3) a sole proprietorship possesses high value property expected to remain as a portion of the family business that is to be passed along to future generations.

Private annuities differ from commercial annuities in that the transferee in a private annuity is a family member not normally in the business of selling annuities. Likewise, appreciated property is usually the subject of transfer in a private annuity, whereas cash is the usual medium in a commercial annuity transaction. Also, under commercial annuities, actuarial tables are used by commercial firms to develop the terms of payment, whereas private annuities are subject to specific tables under the income tax Regulations.[36] Private annuities, unlike general commercial annuities, possess potential gift tax consequences based upon the values determined.

The most important item to consider in a private family annuity is how the proceeds received by the senior member are invested. If the money received is used to purchase property that is equal to or in excess of the value of property disposed, then the primary advantage of reducing the value of the senior member's estate is quickly defeated.

In general, a private family annuity achieves, from a tax advantage standpoint, the following objectives:

(1) avoids tax liability to the senior member on the transfer if the present value of the annuity agreement (based on the tables in the Regulations) is equal to the fair market value of the property transferred,

(2) avoids transfer taxes on the property transferred at the death of the senior member as the property will not be included in the estate by reason of the prior transfer,

(3) transfers income from the senior member's probable high income tax bracket to a junior member's lower tax bracket if the property transferred is income-producing,

(4) avoids recognition of all but a pro rata portion of gain in the year of the transfer, and

(5) a portion of each payment received is tax free as a return of the basis with ordinary and capital gain rates applying to the remainder.

Each annuity payment received by the senior member is divided into two segments.[37] The first portion represents a return of capital and is excluded from income. The second portion represents the gain which is in turn subdivided into two subportions, one being capital gain and the other being ordinary income. The exclusion ratio determines the percentage of each annual payment that is a tax free return of capital. This ratio is computed by dividing the senior member's (transferor's) adjusted basis in the property by the total of the amount of annual payment multiplied by the senior member's life expectancy. The capital gain subportion is computed by dividing the capital gain realized (present value of annuity payment minus adjusted basis of property) by the senior member's life expectancy. The present value of the annuity payments is determined under the regulations as is the life expectancy rate.[38] The other subportion of the gain, the amount taxed as ordinary income, is simply determined by subtracting the excluded return of capital amount and capital gain amount from the annual amount received. These rather complicated calculations are illustrated in Figure 15-1.

Once the senior member reaches his or her life expectancy under the federal tax annuity tables, the capital gain realized will have been fully taxed. As the senior member outlives his or her life expectancy, the amount previously taxed as capital gain will be considered ordinary income and taxed as such.

The document creating the payments between the parties should possess all of the basic elements necessary to constitute a legal obligation. However, this obligation should not provide a security interest in any form. In order for a private family annuity to be successful, the annuity should be unsecured.[39] A recent Tax Court case, *212 Corporation*,[40] confirmed that a secured annuity results in immediate and full taxation at the time of the transfer. The theory behind this contention is that, if an obligation is secured, then there is no uncertainty as to collection and therefore the transaction is closed and completed.[41] The present tax treatment of an annuity is based on an "open transaction" theory which applies if the annuity is unsecured.[42] If the annuity is secured, then the transferor is required to recognize gain in the year of the transfer in the amount of the difference between the original basis and the present value of the annuity.

The basis to the junior member (transferee) is relevant for determining gain or loss on future disposition of the property and present depreciation expense. A 1955 Revenue Ruling sets forth the basic rules, assuming no gift is present.[43] The amount of depreciation to be taken on the property, if it is depreciable property, by the transferee depends upon whether the depreciation period is before or after the date of death of the transferor. If depreciation is being computed before the date of death of the transferor, the depreciation basis will be the present value of the annuity obligation on the date of the transfer. Once the payments have exceeded the present value of the annuity on the day of the transfer, the basis in the property is increased. If depreciation is being computed after the date of death of the transferor, then the basis in the property is merely the total payments which were in fact made. For

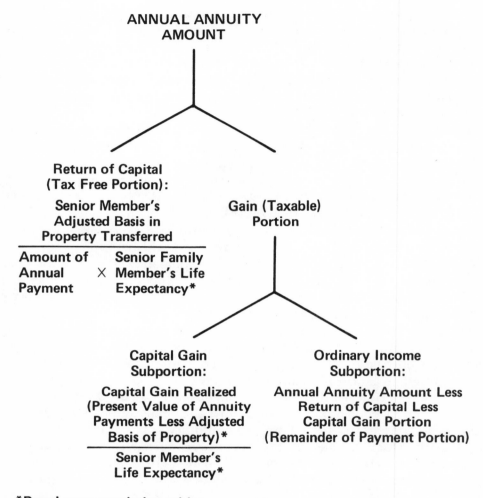

*Based upon regulation tables.

Figure 15–1

gain purposes, if the property is sold before the date of death of the transferor, the basis will be the sum of the actual payments made plus the then present value of the future annuity payments. If at a later date the sum of the payments actually made exceeds this amount, such amount or amounts are recognized as losses in the years paid. If, however, the sum of actual payments never equals the amount of payments plus the present value, then the excess will result in recognition of income in the year of the transferor's death. If the property is sold after the date of death of the transferor, the basis is merely the amount of the annuity payments actually made by the transferee. For losses, the determination of the amount of loss at the time of sale will encompass only the amount actually paid. Thereafter, additional loss will be recognized as future annuity payments are made. As a result of the different basis computations for gains and losses, it is possible that neither a gain nor a loss will be recognized at the time of the sale of the transferee. In such case, it is necessary to wait until future periods to determine whether gain or loss is ultimately recognized.

Private family annuities are complex and possess certain amounts of risk. There is a risk as to the uncertain economic return and the lack of definitive legal requirements to be followed in this area. Private family annuities, however, can produce desired results under proper circumstances. However, these circumstances will need to be examined in full by a practitioner knowledgeable of 1) the facts at hand, and 2) the present status of the law relating to private family annuities.

SUMMARY

By shifting ownership within a closely held business, transfer taxes can be minimized and sometimes completely avoided. Favorable tax methods available to achieve ownership shifting include 1) gift programs, 2) installment sales, 3) normal trust arrangements, 4) installment trusts, 5) generation-skipping trusts, and 6) private family annuities. Also, larger estates may use certain charitable devices, including charitable lead trusts, to shift ownership. However, due to the complexity of such vehicles and their very limited utility for transfers involving closely held businesses, a detailed discussion of such techniques has not been included herein. Although some of the techniques discussed herein have not been explicitly defined from a tax standpoint, these methods do operate to preserve the closely held status of the business. This factor, coupled with the minimization of income and transfer taxes, makes these ownership shifting devices attractive planning opportunities during the life of a closely held business.

NOTES FOR CHAPTER 15

1. Fellows and Painter, *Valuing Close Corporations for Federal Wealth Transfer Taxes: A Statutory Solution to the Disappearing Wealth Syndrome,* 30 Stan. L. Rev. 895 (May 1978); Cooper, *A Voluntary Tax? New Perspectives on Sophisticated Estate Tax Avoidances,* The Brookings Institute, Washington, D.C., 1979, based on an article by the same name appearing in 77 Col. L. Rev., 161 (1977).

2. However, attribution rules have been adopted for Section 6166 under Sec. 512 of the Revenue Act of 1978.

3. Rev. Rul. 77–411, 1977-2 C.B. 480. See also Blum and Bienemann, *Deducting Interest on Deferred Estate Tax Payments,* The Tax Adviser, March 1980, p. 132.

4. See United States v. Frazell, 335 F.2d 487 (5th Cir. 1964), reh. denied 339 F.2d 885 (5th Cir. 1964); cert. denied 380 U.S. 961 (1965), on remand see 269 F. Supp 885 (W.D. La 1967); and Diamond v. Commissioner, 56 T.C. 530 (1971), aff'd 492 F.2d 286 (7th Cir. 1974).

5. Family partnerships fall under the rules of Sec. 704. The parties necessary to constitute a family partnership are set forth in Sec. 704(e)(3).

6. See, generally, Reg. Sec. 1.704-1(e).

7. Section 2001.

8. Section 2512.

9. Section 6075.

10. Section 2053(b). Additionally, generally, transfers made by a decedent within three years of death are included in the decedent's estate. However, the Revenue Act of 1978, Sec. 702(f), provides an exception to the inclusion rule where no gift tax return was required to be filed with respect to the gifts (e.g., gifts less than $3,000 in value). See General Explanation of the Revenue Act, prepared by the Joint Committee on Taxation, March 12, 1979. Therefore, proper documentation for satisfying the $3,000 limit is imperative.

11. HR 94-1390.

12. Ltr. Rul. 7842068.

13. Section 2523(a). The Tax Reform Act of 1976 allows an unlimited gift tax marital deduction of the first $100,000 of lifetime gifts to the spouse. After the first $100,000, there is no deduction for the next $100,000. There is a 50 percent deduction for spousal gifts in excess of $200,000.

14. Rev. Rul. 75–72, 1975-1 C.B. 310, Rev. Rul. 76–49, 1976-1 C.B. 294; Rev. Rul. 76–57, 1976-1 C.B. 297.

15. Ltr. Rul. 7842068.

16. Rev. Rul. 79–398, 1979 I.R.B. No. 49-12.

17. See note 16 supra.

18. Johnson v. Commissioner, 59 T.C. 791 (1973), aff'd 495 F.2d 1079 (6th Cir. 1974), cert. denied 419 U.S. 1040 (1974) and Evangelista v. Commissioner, 71 T.C. 1057 (1979).

19. Henry v. Commissioner, 69 T.C. 665 (1978); Krause v. Commissioner, 56 T.C. 1242 (1971), appeal dismissed (nolle pros) (6th Cir. 1972); Estate of Scheaffer v. Commissioner, 1966 P-H TC Memo ¶66,126; Estate of Morgan v. Commissioner, 37 T.C. 981 (1962), aff'd 316 F.2d 238 (6th Cir. 1963), cert. denied 375 U.S. 825 (1963); Estate of Scheaffer v. Commissioner, 37 T.C. 99 (1961), aff'd 313 F.2d 738 (8th Cir. 1963), cert. denied 375 U.S. 818 (1963); Estate of Staley, 47 B.T.A. 260 (1942), aff'd 136 F.2d 368 (5th Cir. 1943), cert. denied, 320 U.S. 786 (1943); Hirst v. Commissioner, 63 T.C. 307 (1974), aff'd 572 F.2d 427 (4th Cir. 1978) and Turner v. Commissioner, 49 T.C. 356 (1968), aff'd per curiam 410 F.2d 752 (6th Cir. 1969).

20. See Rev. Rul. 75–72, note 14 supra, and Harrison v. Commissioner, 17 T.C. 1350 (1952).

21. Affelder v. Commissioner, 7 T.C. 1190 (1946).

22. Rev. Rul. 77–299, 1977-2 C.B. 343; Deal v. Commissioner, 29 T.C. 730 (1958); de Goldschmidt-Rothchild v. Commissioner, 9 T.C. 325 (1947), aff'd 168 F.2d 975 (2nd Cir. 1948); Davies v. Commissioner, 40 T.C. 525 (1963), acq. 1966-1 C.B. 2; Haygood v. Commissioner, 42 T.C. 936 (1964), acq. 1965-1 C.B. 4, nonacq. 1977-2 C.B. 2 and Kelley v. Commissioner 63 T.C. 321 (1974), nonacq. 1977-2 C.B. 2.

23. Section 453(d)(1)(B).

24. Installment Sales Revision Act of 1980 (H.R. 6883) October 19, 1980.

25. Ibid., Sec. 2(a).

26. Reg. Sec. 20.2036-1(b)(3) and Reg. Sec. 20.2038-1(a).

27. 1979-2 C.B. 325.

28. 408 U.S. 125 (1972).

29. 262 F.2d 315 (1st Cir. 1958), cert. denied 359 U.S. 991 (1959).

30. Ibid. at 323.

31. Section 2601 et seq.

32. Sec. 2602.

33. Sec. 2603.

34. Sec. 2613(a)(4), (b)(5), and (6).

35. Ibid.

36. Reg. Sec. 1.72-9.

37. Rev. Rul. 69–74, 1969-1 C.B. 43.

38. Reg. Sec. 1.72-9.

39. Estate of Bell v. Commissioner, 60 T.C. 469 (1973).

40. 70 T.C. 788 (1978).

41. Burnet v. Logan, 283 U.S. 404 (1921); Rev. Rul. 239, 1953-2 C.B. 53 but compare Rev. Rul. 69–74, 69-1 C.B. 43.

42. Ibid.

43. Rev. Rul. 55–119, 1955-1 C.B. 352.

Appendix

A

Internal Revenue Service Appeals Officer Valuation Training Program Coursebook

AUTHOR'S NOTE

This appendix contains relevant excerpts from the *Appeals Officer Valuation Training Program* Coursebook. The Internal Revenue Service developed this manual to assist its Appeals Division members in valuing property that has no readily determinable fair market value.

This manual was revised in 1980, and serves as a useful guide to grasp those tools and techniques the Internal Revenue Service relies upon in valuing closely held business interests. The reader is cautioned, however, that the individual facts and circumstances of each situation will control the value determination. No one method will apply in all instances. Certainly, this manual is slanted toward the view of the Internal Revenue Service and *care should be taken not to follow it as the law.*

Appeals Officer Valuation Training Program

Coursebook

This material was designed specifically for training purposes only. Under no circumstances should the contents be used or cited as authority for setting or sustaining a technical position.

Department of the Treasury
Internal Revenue Service

Training 6126-02 (10-80)
TPDS 87221

Preface

This training course has been developed for Appeals Officers stationed at Appeals offices and suboffices in the seven regions. Primary beneficiaries of the valuation training will be Appeals Officers who negotiate settlements of income, estate or gift tax cases in which valuation of real or personal property is necessary.

Historically, this course was conceived and presented by the Special Services Branch of the National Office Appellate Division, predecessor to the Appeals Division. This Branch also provided valuation assistance to Appeals Officers on complex valuation issues. Effective January 1, 1980 the Special Services Branch was abolished. The valuation assistance responsibility is now administered by Valuation Analysis Section of the Engineering and Valuation Branch and other branches under the Assistant Commissioner (Technical) in the National Office. Since these branches service all components of the Service, Appeals will need to hold valuation advice requests to the necessary minimum.

This updated course has one primary purpose, to provide a source of on-the-spot knowledge on a wide range of valuation issues for Appeals Officers handling such issues. It is designed to enable Appeals Officers to successfully dispose of the great majority of all such issues coming before them for consideration.

Table of Contents

197

Case Studies

      Industrial stock valuation – Case Study # 1

      Investment Company Valuation – Case Study #2

LESSON 8 –– Minority Interests - Multi-Product Businesses - Partnerships

    Objectives

    Family owned Minority Interests

    Multi-Product Businesses

    Partnerships

      Modification of Stock Valuation Techniques

      Sales Agreements Among Partners

LESSON 10 - Common Errors in Valuation - Non-recognized Methods; Formulas

    Objectives

    Introduction

    Using methods not recognized

    Use of formulas –– Denial of the Judgment Factor

      Typical Approaches

      A.R.M. 34

      Example

      Comparing Stock Market Evaluation to Formula Approach

Lesson 1

INTRODUCTION

CONTENTS

COURSE OBJECTIVES

At the end of this course you will, when faced with valuation questions during case settlements, be able to:

1. Make preliminary valuations of closely-held securities and other business interests as a check on methods used and analyses furnished by Internal Revenue personnel or by taxpayers or their experts.

2. Identify methods or approaches used by taxpayers, their experts, or Internal Revenue personnel which are incorrect, used improperly or not recognized by the investment community.

3. Identify valuation problems in the fields of closely-held securities, business interests, intangibles, real estate, blockage, and art objects or similar unique items where additional expert advice, either written or oral, is needed at the Appeals level.

4. Evaluate the relative strengths and weaknesses of taxpayer's or their expert's valuations or of the Government's appraisals skilfully enough to settle more than 90% of all such issues coming before you on bases fair to taxpayers and the Government alike.

APPEALS PHILOSOPHY

The appeals philosophy of the Internal Revenue Service is to resolve tax controversies, without litigation, on bases which are fair and impartial to both the Government and the taxpayers (P-8-1 of IRM 1218). In accomplishing this mission Appeals Officers have the objectives of granting prompt conferences and making prompt decisions, reaching high quality decisions in each case, and achieving a satisfactory number of agreed settlements. The goals in considering valua-

201

tion issues are the same but because of their diversity and complexity, achievement of these goals is often more time consuming, difficult and fraught with frustration.

Recognizing the particular need for special effort and training to maximize successful settlements of valuation questions, the Appeals Division instituted a training program beginning in 1960 to focus on these issues. Earlier seminars had identified the problem of lack of adequate guidance on settling valuation issues.

The reaction of the participants to this limited program was that there was a real need for such information in the day-to-day operations of the Appeals offices, and a singular lack of such material where it was needed. In many cases, it was stated that the information presented would have greatly facilitated and simplified work on valuation cases had it been available. It is for the purpose of clarifying valuation concepts and techniques and enabling the Appeals Division to more easily and yet more effectively handle such cases, that this course has been published.

MAJOR PROBLEM AREAS

The issues we will be concerned with arise most often in estate tax and gift tax cases. The essence of these taxes is valuation, and it is the valuation of securities, business interests and other properties of no readily ascertainable fair market value which will be emphasized in this course. The concept of "fair market value" as stated in the applicable provisions of the Estate Tax and Gift Tax Regulations (Treas. Reg. §§ 20.2031-1(b) and 25.2512-1) issued under the Internal Revenue Code of 1954 (IRC §§ 2031 and 2512), is familiar to most Internal Revenue Service personnel. To be specific, the fair market value is that price at which a willing buyer will buy and a willing seller will sell a certain item of property, neither being under any compulsion to buy or to sell and both having a reasonable knowledge of all relevant facts. This concept is applicable to all Federal taxes and has been restated many times over by the Tax Court and other Federal and State tribunals.

The question of value is one of fact and therefore subject to solution only in the light of all circumstances having a bearing on the issue as of the valuation date. It is, furthermore, a matter which is to be resolved in all cases on the basis of sound judgment and common sense. There is no mathematically "right" answer, only a range of possible right answers which can be supported by convincing and logical reasoning. We cannot expect another appraiser to come up with the same conclusion that we do on a valuation issue. However, we must be sure that there is ample justification for the value placed on the property in each case.

CLOSELY-HELD CORPORATE SECURITIES, PARTNERSHIPS AND OTHER BUSINESS INTERESTS

Experience has shown that problems involving the valuation of closely-held securities make up the majority of valuation issues arising in the estate and gift tax fields. This type of question concerns corporations which are owned by a small number of individuals, usually within one or more family groups, and which have none of their capital stock held or traded publicly. The normal means for ascertaining fair market value such as sale prices or bid and ask quotations are missing. Thus, as was pointed out in the Estate Tax and Gift Tax Regulations, we have to use alternative bases on which to form an opinion of value. Such alternatives are discussed in detail in Lessons 4 through 7, but we may mention for illustration purposes the key factors of earnings, dividend paying capacity, tangible asset value and comparable security selling prices.

Because of the frequency with which these problems arise, a large part of this text will be given over to a consideration of them. Related to closely-held security valuations are appraisals of other kinds of business interests. These include partnership or sole proprietorship interests, associations, joint ventures, etc. Most of the same factors used in valuing closely-held stocks apply equally well to the valuation of such other business interests.

The essence of value in such assets is their income-producing ability; past, present and potential. In their appraisal therefore, we give a great deal of attention to earnings and expectations. The experience of the investing public in dealings involving comparable assets gives us a significant clue as to how the hypothetical willing buyers and willing sellers might react if the property were being marketed. Neither earnings nor comparable sales however, are the sole controlling factor in these issues. Both the Internal Revenue Code and the related regulations contain the injunction that all relevant facts must be considered.

Later lessons in this course suggest methods and approaches to use in analyzing these types of problems. Typical case situations are included in the text for analysis and study. We cannot stress too strongly the importance of viewing all of these comments as guideposts or possible lines of attack rather than inflexible rules to be applied universally. Each valuation problem is unique; the facts are infinite in variety. For example, an approach which is reasonable in valuing the capital stock of a retail department store may be useless in appraising the stock of an automobile dealership. A partnership interest cannot be valued in exactly the same manner as the capital stock of an incorporated business even in the same industry. We must, of necessity, bring individual judgment to bear on every valuation problem and exclude religiously any stereotyped approach.

SUMMARY

In summary, the objectives of this training material and the training sessions are:

1. To identify those valuation problems which because of their frequency of occurence or their complexity, make up the bulk of the more troublesome issues in this field coming before the Appeals offices;

2. To discuss and illustrate the accepted methods and approaches to be applied by Appeals Officers in their consideration of such valuation questions, as well as to provide some suggested procedures for testing appraisals offered in evidence during Appeals conferences; and

3. To describe and furnish examples of the more common errors which are encountered in valuation work, indicating how and why such methods are incorrect.

Lesson 4

METHODS AND APPROACH - VALUATION OF CLOSELY-HELD SECURITIES

REFERENCES

Rev. Rul. 59-60, 1959-1 C.B. 237
Rev. Ruls. 65-192 and 65-193, 1965-2 C.B. 259, 370

CONTENTS

Introduction
Objectives
Extent of Such Corporations
Rev. Rul. 59-60, Background and Scope
Factors to Consider
    Type of Business
    Industry Survey

INTRODUCTION

The first lesson identified and described briefly the major areas to be explored in this course. The valuation of closely-held securities will be given considerable attention in this and subsequent lessons. Experience has shown that a majority of the controversial valuation questions will fall into this category or one of the other areas discussed during the course. We now take up the closely-held stock valuation problem.

OBJECTIVES

At the end of this lesson you will be able to:

1. List the eight key factors to be considered when valuing closely-held securities.

2. Describe the purposes of Rev. Rul. 59-60, 1959-1 C.B. 237, Rev. Ruls. 65-192 and 65-193, 1965-2 C.B. 249, 370.

3. Explain the relevance of factors 1 and 2, company history and industry survey, in valuing corporate stock.

EXTENT OF SUCH CORPORATIONS

A recent estimate states that there are roughly two and one-half million corporations in the United States of which about two percent or approximately 11,000 have any part of their capital stock held by the public. This leaves around 2.49 million corporate entities with closely-held ownership. The relatively small percentage of publicly-owned securities which are actively traded can be pointed out by the following facts. The New York Stock Exchange listed 642 preferred stocks and 1,552 common stocks in December 1978. The Exchange estimates that about 1,600 corporations have securities of one type or another traded on its floor. The National Quotation Bureau quotes prices on almost 25,000 securities which are traded over-the-counter. The over-the-counter market handles all the securities business in the country except that which is done on the New York and other stock exchanges. The daily trading over-the-counter involves on the average about 5,000 of these securities. It is evident, therefore, that probably no more than 10,000 corporate stocks held publicly are subject to any degree of active trading.

As might be expected with the majority of American corporations owned privately, the question of the valuation of the securities of such firms is frequently involved in Federal tax cases. The Federal estate and gift tax are based upon the value of the property transferred. Thus, closely-held stock valuation issues often arise in the examination of estate or gift tax returns.

REV. RUL. 59-60 -- BACKGROUND AND SCOPE

Before October 1953, all examinations of estate and gift tax returns were conducted in the National Office. In the case of gift taxes this constituted the original, and in the majority of instances, the final examination. Valuation problems including the valuations of the stocks of closely-held corporations were referred to a special section for consideration. A staff of valuation specialists were employed in that office to pass upon such matters.

With the decentralization of the estate and gift tax audit activities in 1953 it became necessary to provide a general guide for examination personnel as to the approach and methods to use in the valuation of closely-held securities. This was done by the issuance of IR-Mim. No. 338, dated December 28, 1953, entitled "Valuation of Stock of Closely-Held Corporations in Estate and Gift Tax Returns." Rev. Rul. 54-77, 1954-1, C.B. 187, incorporating all of the Mimeograph except certain procedual paragraphs, in March 1954. A later revision, Rev. Rul. 59-60, 1959-1 C.B. 237 made a few substantive changes in the original ruling. Because of its pertinence to the subject of this lesson, Rev. Rul. 59-60 is included in its entirety as Appendix A at the end of this text.

The principal changes to the earlier ruling reflected in the revision were an updating of references to the 1954 Code sections and corresponding sections of the new Estate Tax and Gift Tax Regulations and a restating of the factor "Goodwill" to read "Whether or not the enterprise has goodwill or other intangible value" (Sec. 4.01(f) of the Rev. Rul.). Additionally, the discussion of the goodwill or intangible value factor was revised with the objective of eliminating any possible implication that a formula approach such as A.R.M. 34 was valid in evaluating securities (Sec. 4.02(f) of the Rev. Rul.). The term "family or personal holding company" was clarified and broadened to read "closely-held investment or real estate holding company whether or not family owned" (Sec. 5(b) of the Rev. Rul.). Finally, a critical improvement was made by including language emphasizing the requirement of IRC § 2031(b) that similar companies be considered in evaluating closely-held stocks. The ruling now pointed out that securities traded over-the-counter were to be used for comparison purposes as well as those traded on stock exchanges, and the important critieria of <u>active trading</u> in a <u>free and open market</u> were injected into the picture (Sec. 4.02(h) of the Rev. Rul.).

A very important amplification of Rev. Rul. 59-60 occurred in 1965 with the issuance of two rulings, Rev. Ruls. 65-192 and 65-193. The first of these rulings indicated that the general approach, methods and factors outlined in Rev. Rul. 59-60 for use in valuing closely-held corporate stocks for estate and gift tax purposes were equally applicable to valuations of such stocks for <u>income tax and other tax purposes</u>. An added broadening of the applicability of Rev. Rul. 59-60 was also included by making its provisions relevant in determinations of the fair market values of <u>business interests of any types</u> and of <u>intangible assets for all tax purposes</u>.

One more notable change in Service position was the statement in Rev. Rul. 65-192 that henceforth the formula approach set forth in A.R.M. 34, 2 C.B. 31 and A.R.M. 68, 3 C.B. 43 had no <u>valid</u> application in determining the fair market value of corporate stocks or of other business interests. These two rulings will be referred to in more detail in Lesson 10 when we discuss the erroneous use of formulas in valuation.

As a framework, Rev. Rul. 59-60 is good. It is concise, yet reasonably comprehensive. It serves the purpose for which it was issued and in addition places the Internal Revenue Service on record, both before the public and internally, as an advocate of sound valuation standards which have been recognized by the appraisal profession, exercised by the investing public, and formalized by the courts. It is, however, only a framework and therefore leaves an infinite amount of material on the subject to individual judgment. The paragraphs to follow will, it is hoped, add a little flesh to the skeleton of the ruling.

FACTORS TO CONSIDER

In the valuation of closely-held securities it is essential to consider all factors. This requirement is stated in the applicable provisions of the Internal Revenue Code, and the Estate and Gift Tax Regulations. Also, there are a number of court cases in which the judge's opinion includes a restatement of this policy. Two of the earliest of these are <u>Bradley Estate</u>, 2 T.C.M. 609 (1943); and <u>Laird, et al. v. Commissioner</u> 85 F. 2d 598 (3rd Cir. 1936), 29 B.T.A. 196 (1933) on rehearing. The Tax Court stated in the <u>Bradley</u> memorandum decision that, "Net worth, earnings and income capacity, and all other factors having a bearing are to be considered in valuations of closely-held stock." The decision in <u>Laird</u> included a comment to the effect that ". . . valuation of a stock must consider all factors..., including assets, earnings, dividend-paying capacity, etc."

A complete listing of factors is not feasible since each issue will involve circumstances or items unlike any other. There are, however, broad areas which are present in closely-held security valuations which must be examined in practically every case. We will merely list these factors at this point. The pages to follow will contain a more detailed discussion of each factor. The fundamental factors are:

1) the nature of the business including its history since organization,
2) the economic status of the industry and the nation at the critical date of valuation,
3) asset value,
4) earnings,
5) dividends and dividend-paying capacity,
6) the existence or lack of intangible value,
7) sales of the stock and the size of the block to be valued, and
8) the selling price of comparable securities relative to their earnings, dividends and asset values.

We will try to indicate, as we take up each factor, under what circumstances it becomes of prime importance in developing an opinion as to fair market value. Throughout the consideration of the factors of value, the essential ingredient of common sense and judgment on the part of the appraiser cannot be overemphasized. These are fact questions which must be decided by reasoning power after all pertinent data have been assembled. The ensuing paragraphs, therefore, are purely informational and are not to be construed as establishing strict guidelines to be followed in each case.

Type of Business

The nature of the business of a corporation is one of the first facts (if not the very first) to ascertain in valuation. The appraisal of the corporate stock will be made within the framework of the particular industry, and its characteristics will influence the weight accorded the various factors of value. There are peculiarities inherent in certain business enterprises which require attention in evaluating the stock. For example, the valuation of a newspaper publishing company will require the appraiser to find out the number of units of circulation for a period of years, the lineage of advertising, the amount of (and the accounting method used to show) prepaid subscriptions, and the type of competition in the area. On the other hand a security holding company will require such data as underlying investment market values and an anlysis of the security portfolio. The appraiser must be familiar with the industry, learn its economic status and its financial practices, and fit the specific company into this picture.

A study of the corporation's history, or that of any of its predecessor businesses, is part of this factor. We are interested in the growth and development of the business over the years preceding the valuation date. The products or processes in which it deals, the volume of business, the trend of operations, and the acquisitions or mergers it may have made, are all proper subjects of our investigation. At the conclusion of this part of the consideration of the issue we should be as well informed about the specific company and its past, present, and future outlook as the most prudent of investors would be prior to buying or selling such stock.

A list of stockholders and their relative interests in the stock of the corporation should be studied. The family connections of the individual stockholders should be set out so that the closely-held nature of the corporation is clear. The necessary data may not be available, in which case the appraiser must take steps to acquire it. An Appeals Officer should request the District Director's office to complete or further develop the case file in this respect. Any recent change in the product line or geographic scope of the corporation should be noted. Any major business change could cause past operating results to be invalid for predicting future earnings.

Industry Survey

In addition to ascertaining all essential data on the particular corporation involved, the appraiser should make a detailed analysis of the industry. There are many sources of information on the broad industry classifications which are in easy reach of the average appraiser. These include such commercial publications as Standard and Poor's Industry Surveys, Moody's Manual of Investments Standard and Poor's Analyst's Handbook, the Wall St. Journal and Barron's Weekly. The U.S. Department of Commerce issues industry studies and certain nonprofit organizations such as Harvard Business School prepare comprehensive studies under private grants covering important aspects of various industrial groups. Trade papers and trade associations are often excellent sources of an industry's own evaluation of its status and direction.

Such source materials provide a wealth of information which must be carefully screened to make sure that the data are pertinent to the specific stock valuation issue as of the critical valuation date. Just how much of this data should be developed is a matter of judgment. However, the more appraisers know about an industry the better prepared they will be to appraise the stock of a corporation operating in that industry.

It may be possible to isolate one segment of an industry for consideration. For instance we may wish to concentrate upon <u>participating</u> life insurance companies or consider only <u>high leverage</u> investment holding companies. To the extent that we can pinpoint our anlaysis our results will be correspondingly more reliable.

While surveying the industry trends we should also relate our valuation problem to overall economic conditions in the country. A corporation, or an industry, does not function in a vacuum. We will have to take into account the direction of the national economy prior to the valuation date in order to impart to our conclusion the essential elements of realism and practicality. Also, the relative prosperity or depression of the industry in question and competitive industries, e.g., plastics and textiles, or aviation and railroads, can be traced to economic cycles on a national scale. Often we will locate the underlying causes of hitherto unexplained fluctuations in earnings or costs of a company by referring to the "big" economic picture.

It is also important to analyze the status of the security investment market as of the valuation date. The stock exchanges or the over-the-counter market are the media through which a closely-held corporate stock will generate a public offering. Thus, the hypothetical willing buyer or willing seller would be viewing such stock not only in relation to its industry and financial position but also within the marketplace. We should not overlook the stock market's climate in evaluating these securities. For example, it would be mandatory that the state of the market be considered carefully if the valuation date fell between September 11, and November 14, 1978, when the New York Stock Exchange Index fell nine points or 15%. Any appraisal as of that period or thereafter would be patently defective if the effects and significance of the 1978 market break were ignored. Similarly any period of general market movement will have to be related to the valuation issue under study so that a realistic result can be possible.

Lesson 5

CLOSELY-HELD CORPORATIONS - FACTORS (CONT'D.)

CONTENTS

OBJECTIVES

At the end of this lesson you will be able to:

1. Compute and verify corporate common stock book value and net current asset value, and compute important balance sheet ratios.

2. Compute earnings per share of common stock and make significant income statement analyses.

3. Describe major kinds of specific industry data and analyses that should be examined by the security analyst.

ASSET VALUE

Moving now to the data pertaining to the specific corporation to be valued, we will study the balance sheet for the year ending nearest to, but not subsequent to, the valuation date. Constructing comparative balance sheets for a period of past years is most helpful and should be done if possible. This type of analysis enables the appraiser to ascertain the company's growth in several respects; expansion of plant and equipment, improvement in current position, increasing or decreasing long-term debt, etc. The importance of these facts is readily apparent.

Book Value

At the valuation date the stock of the corporation had a certain asset value or book value. Ordinarily we cannot find balance sheets as of the specific date, thus the alternative is to use the latest available statement. Computing book value per share is relatively simple. The important fact to remember is that <u>all</u> of the corporation's equity devolves upon the common equity holders. To illustrate:

<u>XYZ Corporation Equity Section</u> –

Common stock, no par, stated value $5, 200,000 shares issued and outstanding	$1,000,000
Paid-in-capital in excess of stated value	2,000,000
Retained earnings	7,500,000
Total Equity	$10,500,000

XYZ Corporation's book value is $10,500,000 and its common stock has a book value per share of $52.50 ($10,500,000/200,000 shares). If, however, the corporation had one or more outstanding preferred stock issues the computation would be as follows:

<u>XYZ Corporation Equity Section</u> –

8% Preferred stock, (Par $100), 20,000 shares issued and outstanding	$2,000,000
Common stock, no par, stated value $5, 200,000 shares issued and outstanding	1,000,000
Paid-in-capital in excess of stated value	2,000,000
Retained earnings	5,500,000
Total Equity	$10,500,000

Now, although total corporate equity remains the same, the common stock book value per share will be $42.50 ($8,500,000/200,000 shares).

If certain items are present on the balance sheet, adjustments to the book value per share computation must be made. For example, if there are any shares of the corporation's own stock held in the treasury (so-called treasury stock), then the cost of such reacquired stock should be deducted from the total net worth to get the book value of the common stock shares outstanding. The familiar "book value per share" figure is derived by dividing the total book value by the number of shares of common stock issued and <u>outstanding</u>. Of course, as indicated above, any preferred stock value has to be provided for before computing the common stock equity value.

Also, whatever amounts appear on the balance sheet as "Goodwill" or "Franchises" or other intangibles should be eliminated in order that the book value of <u>tangibles</u>, net of all liabilities, is obtained. This is necessary because essentially, in evaluating these stocks, the very

212

thing we are seeking to determine is to what extent, if any, intangible value exists or is indicated in this enterprise.

Although we need to determine a stock's book value per share we should recognize that this is not the stock's fair market value. Actually, book value in the ordinary industrial or mercantile company bears little direct relationship to fair market value. The relationship between the commercial value of a business and the so-called physical values of its assets is highly indirect and uncertain. Almost never does it justify an assumption that the "values" (that is, the depreciated costs) of the latter even roughly measure the value of the former. Book value, therefore, is merely the historical or accounting value of the corportation's assets in excess of all corporate liabilities.

Net Current Asset Value

Another key factor obtained from a balance sheet analysis is the amount of working capital or net current asset value. This is computed by deducting all current liabilities from current assets. Its significance is the clue it provides as to the ability of the corporation to meet day-to-day cash needs. Working capital in a business has been compared to the lifeblood of an organism. The greater the amounts of cash and equivalents available to a company in excess of its current obligations, the stronger it will be financially.

We may question the necessity for ascertaining a corporation's net current asset value when seeking to arrive at the fair market value of its capital stock. In fact current asset position is not that far removed from the investor's thinking and the professional investment services reflect this. Periodically Standard and Poor's Corporation will prepare an analsis of the publicly-traded common stocks which are selling currently at or below their respective net current asset value per share. The implication of this analysis is not necessarily that a stock should be bought if it is on this list. The point is made, however, that there may be some good investment bargains to be found among such securities that are so conservatively priced. Typically 100 or more such actively traded stocks exist at any point in time.

Balance Sheet Analysis

While it will be impractical to attempt to outline all of the elements on the balance sheet of a corporation which need analysis, certain of the more important items are:

a) Depreciation schedules of all principal classes of fixed assets--Study of these discloses the age of the assets, their cost, and remaining life; facts which aid in judging the need of the corporation for future capital asset expenditures.

b) Retained earnings analyses--These show the source of retained earnings, adjustments for extraordinary transactions and dividend disbursements.

c) Investments in subsidiaries--These should be analyzed and complete sets of financial statements obtained, so that the fair market value of these enterprises can be ascertained. Consolidated statements may be needed and will have to be prepared by the appraiser if they are not readily available.

d) Other investments in marketable securities and real property of an investment nature must be studied and their fair market value determined.

e) The amount of working capital and the working capital ratio, as well as the quick asset ratio--Quick assets are cash, receivables, and short term investments. Quick asset ratio relates these assets to current liabilities.

f) The capital structure of the business including the number of shares of the various classes of capital stock outstanding; the amount of long-term debt; the dividend and liquidation rights of preferred stocks; the maturity dates, call prices, and assets which are security for bonds or debentures of the company.

The above items are only a few of the balance sheet factors considered in a typical stock valuation. An important aspect of the asset value study is to compare such significant items as working capital ratio or ratio of long-term debt to total invested capital, to other firms in the same industry. Such a comparision gives greater meaning to the various balance sheet disclosures for valuation purposes. Circumstances in the individual companies and industries, however, will determine which analyses are the most useful and productive to make.

EARNINGS

The earnings of a business have been held by many valuation authorities to be the essence of its fair market value. Certainly investors have a primary concern with the earning power inherent in the securities they are buying or selling. People invest for the most part for two purposes; appreciation and potential return. The measure of these elements comes from the past and present income experience of the company. While it is future return or appreciation which the investor is buying or selling, the only tangible evidence of such future events is the past earnings history. And to the extent that the earnings data are current they are more reliable as an index of the future.

This concept has court acceptance as noted in Johnson (John E.) v. United States, 44 F.2d 224, 246 (Ct. Cl 1930)--"It is a matter of common knowledge that the market value of shares of stock, in the absence of something that tends strongly to show that the future will bring a change in the profits of the company, is largely determined by the earnings of the company in the present year."

Also see Robertson v. Routzahn, 1 F. Supp. 355, aff'd. 75 F.2d 537 (6th Cir. 1935), Cert. denied 295 U.S. 763 (1935), where the comment is made that "Latest earnings are the most significant in their effect on value."

Thus an appraiser should look first at the latest year's results and then at a suitable period of past year's earnings. The number of past years to consider will vary with each set of circumstances. Naturally, if a violent change in the corporation's income pattern has occurred, it may be that the years since this happened should be given the most attention. Earnings trend is important and is often the primary clue to future expectancy. As stated in Rev. Rul 59-60, arbitrary five- or ten-year averages are not to be used. Whatever period seems logical in view of the company's history, earnings trend or type of business, should be adopted. The opinion in appeal of Edward P. Mertz 5 B.T.A. 694 (1926), notes "Earnings which show a steady downward or upward trend should not be averaged over a past period to reflect anticipated earnings." In a later decision, Central Trust Co. v. United States, 305 F.2d 393, 424 (Ct. Cl. 1962), the court took into account the favorable earnings trend of the corporation to be valued by assigning mathematically greater weights to the most recent years' earnings.

Income Statement Analysis

Although we have entitled this factor "Earnings", included are all of the analyses necessary to a full understanding of the operating results of the company. Thus, comparative income statements for a suitable period of years should be developed in as much detail as the available data permit. Trends in net sales, operating costs, various classes of expense or income, and net profit, should be noted. These data tell much about the company's progress in the period preceding the valuation date. Percentages of profit and loss items to sales may be computed to indicate the relative importance of certain income or cost items. The rate of return on invested capital is a significant item in appraising a corporation's earning power. This statistic can be further revealing if it is compared to other businesses in the same industry, thus allowing us to evaluate the closely-held company in relation to its competitors. Not only these, but various other checks can be made in considering stock valuation issues; the nature of the industry involved determining the particular analysis which is needed. For instance we will study the amounts of contracts obtained each year in appraising a construction company, the amounts of timber cut annually in evaluating lumber companies, and the ratio of deposits to capital and surplus in bank valuations. As in the balance sheet analysis, the peculiarities of the type of business concerned will dictate the direction of the appraiser's research and analysis.

Often a closely-held corporation will own substantial nonoperating assets which are unnecessary in the conduct of its ordinary business. The income from such assets should be segregated from the operating net income since undoubtedly different rates of return are applicable to the two income sources. For example there is no logic in capitalizing the income from a large, long-standing investment in U.S. Treasury Notes at 15 percent when their established yield is 8 percent. One method of compensating for this situation is to capitalize operating earnings at a proper rate derived from consideration of all valuation factors, and then add to such value the fair market value of the nonoperating assets. The resultant value will then be a more realistic index of the fair market value of the whole business entity including its two distinct elements.

We cannot stress too strongly the care that should be exercised in analyzing the earnings data. This factor is of prime importance in all valuations and the financial statements used must be accurate representations of the company's earning history. In many instances an error in the final opinion of value can be traced almost entirely to a corresponding error in the earnings information or in the analysis of such information.

Earnings Per Share

The bulk of closely-held stock valuations concern common stocks. In computing the earnings available for the common stockholders we must deduct any preferred dividend requirements. These should be computed and deducted regardless of the possibility of nonpayment. It is the legal and probable annual net profit available to the common stockholders which is being sought. Of course, Federal tax liability should be deducted also in arriving at the net income.

Changes in the capital structure of the company may have resulted in certain annual income statements showing net profits which are not representative of the future earning potential. For example, if a sizable long-term debt or preferred stock issue had been retired two years before the valuation date, the earnings available for the common stock as reported for earlier years would be understated in terms of the current and future situation. Appropriate adjustments should be made in computing earnings per share.

Also, unusual outlays of receipts from nonrecurring causes should be investigated and removed if it appears that they distort the earnings picture. To illustrate, the gain from the sale of a plant building or the loss from a law suit are not normal events and may not be reasonably expected to recur in the future. Such gains or losses, and their offsetting tax effects, do not belong in operating income and should be eliminated for purposes of valuation.

VARIATIONS IN INDUSTRIES

As has previously been stated, both asset value and earnings analyses must be modified and directed in accordance with the company's industry category. There follows a brief discussion of five separate industries in which their unique characteritics require specific analysis. Also, where available, certain data sources are mentioned in which an appraiser can obtain comparative information on an industry basis.

216

Retail Stores

These enterprises require that we pay specific attention to certain key operating and financial factors. Our analysis should encompass at least the following:

a) Gross profit margin – computing the relationship between gross profit and net sales.

b) Inventory turnover – comparing average inventory to cost of goods sold to determine the degree of rapidity and the number of times that the company liquidates its inventory per year.

c) Bad debt experience – telling us how efficient the company's credit policies have been.

d) Common size income statement analysis – comparing key items of operating expenses and costs to net sales.

Supplementary information important in evaluating retail merchandising companies are the number of employees, the size of and number of retail outlets, and the categories of merchandise sold.

Manufacturing

Analysis of the financial data of manufacturing concerns will center on:

a) Costs of goods manufactured – ascertaining the respective importance of raw materials costs, direct labor costs and factory overhead in the production of goods.

b) Plant and equipment – determining how adequate fixed asset investments are to meet the company's needs and also to learn of any future expansion or modernization plans.

A primary subject to explore in ·valuing these corporations is the company's relationship with labor unions which represent segments of the work force.

Insurance

In these cases a number of factors peculiar only to the insurance industry require consideration. These include:

a) Amounts of insurance in force.

b) Types and amounts of insurance written in recent years.

c) Average premium received and average face value of policy written.

d) The policy lapse ratio – which informs us of the stability of the insurance business.

217

A critical element of insurance companies' balance sheets is the statutory reserves which are required by law to be maintained. These are established depending upon the amount of insurance in force and various formulas are permitted. It is necessary to find out what approach is being used by the corporation under appraisal since we learn something about the management philosophy of the company from this information.

An essential source to consult for comparative industry data is Best's Insurance Manuals. These can be found in most major city libraries.

Publishing

Newspapers and other periodical publishers are usually family owned and frequently need to be valued for tax purposes. Factors to analyze in this industry are:

a) Units of circulation.

b) Advertising lineage - in newspaper publishing we should note the ratio of lines of advertising to lines of news.

c) Relative amounts of revenue attributed to advertising and circulation.

Many situations exist where newspapers own broadcasting subsidiaries. If a radio station or television station are owned by the publishing company separate analysis of the broadcasting operations are needed.

Two sources can be mentioned here. N.W. Ayer & Son, Inc., Directory, which lists and includes much data about all but the smallest of newspapers and periodicals, and the public files of the Federal Communications Commission for data on broadcasters.

Banks

Because of the specialized nature of this type of business our analysis will again take some highly individualized approaches. We should study, along with the usual elements of corporate financial statements:

a) Amounts of total deposits in various types of accounts such as demand, time, certificates and money market.

b) Income from investments compared to other sources.

c) Number of branch banks.

Of particular interest in this industry are the state laws governing banking which may inhibit branch banking. Also, we should analyze the ratios of retained earnings, or undivided profits as banks traditionally refer to them, to capital. These analyses tell an appraiser much

218

about the financial strength of the company and also pave the way for comparisons with other banking companies.

SUMMARY

The efforts made by security analysts in examining the asset value and earnings of a corporation are essential if they are to reach defensible value conclusions. If this lesson has impressed the student with the imperative nature of such analyses it has achieved its purpose. In the investment world this is referred to as the fundamentalist approach. And this is exactly what we are talking about. The balance sheet and asset value - the income statement and earnings - these are the fundamentals upon which the valuation will be based.

Lesson 6

CLOSELY-HELD CORPORATIONS - FACTORS (CONT'D.)

CONTENTS

Objectives
Dividends
    Dividend Paying Capacity
    Court Decisions
Intangible Value
    Does It Exist?
    Approaches
Actual Sales of the Stock
    Case Citations
    Conclusion
Comparatives

OBJECTIVES

At the end of this lesson you will be able to:

1. Explain why dividend paying capacity is as important as the dividend record in appraising corporate securities.

2. Describe the relevance of intangible value to closely-held stock appraisals.

3. Analyze a cross section of court decisions cited in the text regarding the weight to accord sales of closely-held stock and explain the implications of those decisions.

4. List the principal steps to take in making a comparative analysis.

DIVIDENDS

Dividend Paying Capacity

The actual return on a stockholder's investment in a corporation is measured by the dividends received. Dividend payments out of current earnings make up the true yield realized by the stockholder. However, in the case of closely-held or family-owned corporations, the actual dividend record may constitute a gross understatement of the ability of the company to pay dividends. Recognition of this fact has resulted in emphasis being placed on dividend-paying capacity (as opposed to the actual dividend record) in Rev. Rul. 59-60. This does not mean that actual dividend history should be ignored, but it does inject into the dividend analysis the requirement that reason be used in relating these facts to the final valuation of the stock.

Court Decisions

Fortunately the Service has received some support from various courts for the "dividend paying capacity" theory.

The attitude expressed by the Tax Court and other Federal courts on this concept may be summarized in brief from the following excerpts:

> Colonial Trust Co. v. Kraemer, 63 F.Supp. 234 (1945); "Dividend paying capacity should be considered in appraising stock value." Brunswig (Marguerite Wogan), 9 B.T.A. Memo. Op., 40,401; "It is a matter of common knowledge that many stocks paying small dividends have considerable market value by reason of net worth of the underlying assets." Crowell (Benedict) 21 B.T.A. 849, aff'd. 62 F. 2d 51 (6th Cir. 1932); "Dividends must be considered in valuations, but a conservative dividend policy lessens their weight as a criterion of value." Rheinstrom v. Willcuts, 26 F.Supp. 306 (1938); "The future is speculative as to any company. The stock of one buttressed with . . . a conservative dividend policy, is obviously less speculative than a stock . . . where all earnings are paid out in dividends. . . ."

There is ambiguity in the phrase "dividend-paying capacity" which we should admit readily. Just how is this "capacity" to be determined? At the outset we might state that the corporation's earnings are the initial decisive factor in setting its dividend-paying capacity. There are, however, other important elements in the picture. The need for surplus funds for plant expansion or improvement, or the development of new product research, for example, are valid reasons for curbing dividends, and also for reducing our estimate of the company's capacity to pay dividends. A helpful device in analyzing this factor is to look at the experience in the industry as to dividends paid. Stated simply we will study the dividend payout ratios of a comparable cross section of the industry. This should provide us, in many instances, with a fair indication of the percentage of available earnings which the particular industry pays out in annual dividends. The advantage of this approach is that we then have tangible support for our contentions as to the closely-held corporation's real dividend-paying potential.

INTANGIBLE VALUE

Does It Exist?

The existence of intangible value in a going concern can result from one or more distinct sources. These include the ownership or rights in such things as patents, copyrights, trademarks, franchises, leasehold improvements, deferred advertising costs, deferred research and development costs and goodwill. The latter is generally the most important and the most frequently encountered of these intangible items. Demonstrated earning power is a prime evidence of such value. On the other

221

hand, intangible value, or goodwill, may be present in an enterprise although a series of loss years preceded the valuation date. We have knowledge of one newspaper publisher who sold out for a price reflecting several hundred thousand dollars for goodwill, where annual losses had been realized for over twenty-five years prior thereto and only modest tangible asset value existed. The reason for such price was, of course, the subscription lists and other attendant intangibles inherent in such a business. The point is that earnings are not the sole indicator of goodwill. As a matter of fact, even a favorable earnings record may not support the assigning of intangible value to an enterprise. In this latter respect the following two Tax Court opinions are cited:

> Savidge (S. Leigh) 4 T.C.M. 545 (1945)--It was held that the taxpayer received no goodwill from liquidation of an automobile distributing corporation holding franchises from an automobile manufacturer which were nonassignable and cancellable in event of dissolution of the agency company. The Commissioner's determination of a goodwill value based on capitalization of earnings was rejected.

> Vamvaks (Peter) 4 T.C.M. 733 (1945)--The Tax Court Judge concluded that convincing evidence showed that no goodwill existed with respect to the taxpayer's business in Miami, Florida, so testimony as to the value of goodwill based on capitalization of earnings was rejected.

Approaches

The general acceptance by the courts, however, of the premise that goodwill is attributable primarily to earnings is attested to by the citations below:

> McKee 116 F.2d 499 (6th Cir. 1940)--"Goodwill may have a value not shown by books of account, which value is best measured by capitalizing its earnings."

> Mitchell Camera Corp., 6 T.C.M. 719 (1947)--"Successful operation of a business is evidence that it has goodwill."

> Mossman, Yarnelle and Co., 9 B.T.A. 45 (1927)--"There are no well-known and universally accepted rules either for the determination of the existence of goodwill or for its valuation * * *. Reputation as a reliable concern increases value of goodwill. Successful operation of a business is substantial evidence of goodwill."

The meaning of the term goodwill has become blurred by common usage. For accounting purposes, a firm has goodwill when its expected future earnings exceed the earnings normally realized in its industry. It is not recorded on the books, however, unless it is bought or sold. The accounting definition does not cover the other nuances of meaning

222

which are often given to it. The existence of a regular clientele has been termed "Goodwill," as has an investment in long-range advertising campaigns. The Rev. Rul. mentions the brand name or locality aspects of goodwill. All of these possibilities should be explored by the appraiser of a closely-held corporation in order that the presence of substantial intangible value in the enterprise may not be overlooked.

ACTUAL SALES OF THE STOCK

The sale of closely-held corporate stock, if at arm's length and for reasonable consideration, will be a strong indication of the fair market value of such stock for Federal tax purposes. The admonition of the Rev. Rul. to look with suspicion on forced or distress sales as representing true fair market value should be heeded. We have to recognize, however, that the courts are more than ready, particularly in recent years, to rely on sales as the best evidence of value if the price is anywhere within reason. The Appeals Officer should have in mind, therefore, the weakness in the Government's position in the event of trial, if the opinion of value is contradicted by sales at substantially lower values between alleged unrelated parties apparently dealing at arm's length.

Case Citations

Sales Are the Best Evidence

There follow several comments taken from court decisions and other authorities in which the position is taken that <u>sales prices are the best evidence of fair market value</u>:

(a) Bonbright's <u>Valuation of Property, Vol. 1</u>—Comments are made to the effect that where market value is the objective, the courts quite generally admit recent sales of the property in question, or of similar property as evidence of value. In the valuation of ·securities or of commodities such sales are often taken as settling the whole question without more evidence. The inference here of present value from recent sales may be inaccurate, and a litigant usually has the opportunity to disprove its validity and to establish a different value. But despite these defects, actual sales are generally a far more reliable index of market value than are any available alternative forms of evidence, such as opinions of experts or estimates based on a capitalization of prospective earnings.

(b) <u>Blood (Philip W.) et al. Exrs.</u> 22 B.T.A. 1000 (1931)—The sale of a small number of shares of a closely-held corporation on a date near date of death was accepted as best evidence of value.

(c) <u>Burns (Wilbur F.)</u> 30 B.T.A. 163 (1933)—Value was determined as the price at which a large number of shares were sold in block to persons who knew the restrictions on resale and were familiar with the company's affairs.

(d) Chambers (In re) Estate, 155 N.Y. Supp. 153 (1912)--A very small number of sales within the prior year were held sufficient to establish the market value of the unlisted stock of a great corporation, of which this estate held a large block of stock.

(e) Chisholm (Est. of Arch. M.) 37 B.T.A. 167 (1938)--Exceptional circumstances must be proven rather than assumed, to demonstrate that sale price of stock is not its market value.

(f) Dowling (Robt. E.) 8 B.T.A. 676 (1927)--The price per share paid to buy out a minority stockholder was held to be better evidence as to value than bid and ask prices or offers not resulting in sales.

(g) Flynn (John J.) 35 B.T.A. 1064, 1068 (1937)--"Where sales of the property to be valued have been made they are preferred as evidence of value rather than opinion.

"The sales of the stock at par to buyers under no compulsion to buy support respondent's determination which is sustained."

(h) McFawn et al. v. Commissioner, B.T.A. Memo. Op.; 10/28/1941 (CCH 12, 158-D) Docket Nos. 103285 to 103287, and 104520 to 104523--"It is well established that the best evidence of fair market value of shares of stock is the price received on sales which are arm's length sales made at or about the time at which the valuation is to be determined.*** Where sales of a stock to be valued have been made they are preferred as evidence of value over that of opinion evidence."

(i) Newman (Matter of), 154 N.Y. Supp. 1107 (1915)--For the stock of a small and closely-held corporation the price at which decedent sold shares to employees was accepted as evidence of market value.

(j) Wright (Estate of Millie Langley) v. Commissioner, 43 B.T.A. 551 (1941)--Market price of McKesson & Robbins stock on stock exchange held to be fair market value, notwithstanding that such price "may have been due to concealments and misrepresentations subsequently discovered," i.e., discovered two years later.

(k) F.G. Inc. v. Commissioner, 47 F.2d 541 (7th Cir. 1931)--If a sale was at arm's length between parties conversant with factors underlying the stock value, the sale is best evidence of value even though buyer and seller were closely related.

If evidence of stock sales exists it will be necessary to examine all of the pertinent facts in order to assess the validity of the reported sales prices. Schedules of the transactions for a period of years preceding the valuation date should be prepared. These will show, among other facts, the names and family relationships of buyers and sellers, the number of shares transferred, the prices realized, the terms of each sale, and the date of each sale. Analysis of these data should aid the appraiser materially in ascertaining whether or not such sales established a representative market value for the stock. If we decide that they do not point to the fair market value, resort must be made to the alternative indices of value such as have been cited earlier. Regardless of the weight merited by the stock sales, the appraiser must be able to testify that he or she considered such sales in arriving at an opinion of value.

Sales Are Not Determinative

On the reverse of the coin we find many decisions setting aside sale prices as determinants of fair market value:

(a) Brooks, Exr., v. Willcutts, 78 F.2d 270 (8th Cir. 1935)--In a closely-held family corporation the Court disregarded sales and found a value for the shares of stock based upon other criteria such as earning power, net worth, and dividend-paying capacity.

(b) Bryan (C.A.), 19 B.T.A. 111 (1930)--Sales to buyers. uninformed of company's affairs, made by a high pressure sales organization, were not indicia of market value of stock. (The necessity for paying large commissions for selling the stock also made sale price poor evidence of value.)

(c) Coca-Cola Bottling Co. (Ill.) v. Commissioner, 22 B.T.A. 686,765 (1931)--"The stock sales made prior to March 1, 1913, are entitled to but little weight. The volume of stocks sold is not large enough to indicate clearly any market value. However, such sales should not be wholly ignored."

(d) Crosby v. Heiner, 12 F.2d 604 (W.D. Pa. 1926) aff'd, 24 F.2d 191 (3rd Cir. 1928)--"Sales are always evidence of † market price, . . . but the statute required . . . a 'fair market price.' Sales made at a particular time and place may be significant, but the price paid is not necessarily decisive of fair market price or value."

(e) Day (Julius G.), 3 B.T.A. 942 (1926)--There were small sales consistently over a considerable period, which was regarded as showing that stockholders were well-satisfied with their investment. The Board Tax Appeals considered also the assets behind the stock and sustained the $175 per share value determined by the Commissioner, notwithstanding the evidence that 106 shares were offered at $135 within a year and could not be sold and that there were sales of 2 and 25 shares at $100 per share.

(f) <u>Gillette Rubber Co.</u> 31 B.T.A. 483 (1934)--Sales of stock under restricted conditions to a limited class of purchasers without public offering, do not necessarily establish market value.

(g) <u>Lucas v. Alexander</u> 279 U.S. 573; 49 S. Ct. 426 (1929)--A forced sale or liquidating value is no criterion of fair market vlaue.

(h) <u>N. Amer. Teleg. Co. v. Nor. Pac. R.R. Co.</u>, 254 F. 417 (8th Cir. 1918)--"The term market value as the words fairly import, indicates price established in a market where the article is dealt in by such a multitude of persons and such a large number of transactions, as to standardize the price.

"Individual sales are not competent proof of such value although evidence of such sales and even of offers made in good faith may be received in evidence along with evidence of any other character which influences value.

"Private dealings in property can never be used to show market value in the primary sense, and, when used to show market value in the sense of fair and reasonable value, individual transactions can never be made the sole basis for ascertaining such value. No text writer or court has been discovered which supports any such doctrine."

(i) <u>Zouri Drawn Metals Co.</u> 8 B.T.A. 853 (1927)--A sale of stock to an insider was regarded as inadequate evidence of its value.

(j) <u>Acme Mills, Inc.</u> 6 B.T.A. 1065 (1927)--A sale at a long interval away from the basic date of valuation loses probative value since conditions may have changed greatly during the interval.

Conclusion

The foregoing citations disclose the complete lack of consistency in the treatment accorded this subject by the courts over the years. The Appeals Officer will, as always, have to depend in the final analysis, upon his or her own judgment and assessment of the merits of the case. The reaction of a given court to the valuation issue when questionable sales are present is impossible to foretell and the best we can do in this course is to indicate the extreme uncertainty which exists in this area.

COMPARATIVES

Under IRC § 2031(b) consideration must be given to the market value of corporations engaged in the same or similar business in evaluating a closely-held company. The question invariably arises as to the degree of comparability of the particular listed or traded corporations chosen. Exact comparability is an impossibility. Reasonable similarity is, however, both attainable (in most instances) and essential.

The Rev. Rul. cites some of the criteria to examine in judging comparability. We can suggest many other factors such as the number and size of retail outlets and the number of employees in the department store industry; the amount of insurance in force in the insurance company field; and the number and type of food packing plants in the food processing industry. In addition, volume of sales, working capital ratios, capital structure, and earnings trend are important factors in rating one corporation's similarity to another. Although the research required is time consuming, it will usually be worthwhile to investigate the major part of the industry involved so that all of the more valid comparatives can be found. Often several analyses of progressively narrower segments of an industry will be possible, with the last study covering just those few most nearly comparable corporations. (An illustration of this approach is contained in the Industrial Stock Valuation Case Study No. 1, Lesson 7). Such an intensive survey of the industry will, in addition to producing an authoritative comparative analysis, bring about in the appraiser an increased knowledge of the field. This should further enhance the value and quality of the opinion.

The primary product of the comparative analysis is the derivation of various ratios between the market price on or about the valuation date of the similar corporations' stocks, to:

1. The net earnings per share, (both in the latest year and for one or more periods of prior years),

2. The net tangible asset value per share of common stock as of the balance sheet date just prior to the valuation date, and

3. The current and average dividends per share paid to common stockholders for similar prior periods.

There may be other percentages which are called for in certain industries but the foregoing are basic to all. There will be certain instances, however, when one of the relationships will outweigh the rest in significance. For example, the investment holding company field necessitates emphasis on the market price to asset value ratio. But all elements must be studied in order to escape the charge that all pertinent factors had not been considered. From the analysis of these ratios the appraiser can begin to evolve an understanable range of possible market prices or range of values for the closely-held stock at issue. It should be remembered, however, that this analysis is only one of the many relevant factors entering into the final opinion of fair market value.

Lesson 7

TYPICAL CLOSELY-HELD STOCK VALUATION

CONTENTS

OBJECTIVES

At the end of this lesson you will be able to:

1. Apply the more important comparative analytical techniques used by security analysts to evaluate and verify the values of industrial and investment businesses.

2. Describe and compute the more important ratios and per share amounts which are used in security analysis.

3. Identify the major factors used in the two Case Studies in this lesson to arrive at fair market value.

COMPARATIVE ANALYSIS

Sources of Data

There are a number of excellent sources and reference services which provide the security analyst with all needed background market and financial data. Two kinds of data are used to make a comparative analysis--market information and financial information. Market data disclosing stock or bond prices and volume of trading on a daily basis are readily attainable in the Wall St. Journal or comparable sources. Financial data can be found in Moody's Manuals and Standard & Poor's Services.

Key Ratios

Once the information is assembled what is done with it? Certain key ratios and relationships are essential in appraising corporate securities. The majority of these relate a financial fact about a corporation or its security to a market factor. For example we will compute the ratio of earnings or book value per share to the market price per share. A variation on the so-called price/earnings ratio is called the capitalization rate, which is merely the reciprocal of the price/earnings ratio.

Relationship between dividends and market value will also be calculated. Also how much of the available corporate earnings were actually paid out should be noted.

Worksheet

In the final analysis the information concerning comparative corporations will be organized, condensed and combined into a specific worksheet. There is no single prescribed format that is used. Examples of the kind of presentations found satisfactory by Appeals Officers in the past are included in the two Case Studies which follow in this lesson.

The primary cautionary point to keep in mind is that the comparative analysis, although it is essential in most valuations of securities is still only one factor. The conclusion as to value must comprehend all factors to pass the test of judicial scrutiny.

MENTAL PROCESS IN VALUATION

The obvious question you will ask at this point is "What do I do with all this information?" We may be fully informed about the corporation to be valued and its industry. We may have completed a comprehensive comparative analysis. In other words, after following Rev. Rul. 59-60 explicitly we still do not have the fair market value of the stock. The reason for this is, of course, that the all important element of judgment is in the possession of the analyst or Appeals Officer or whoever is faced with the responsibility for making the determination of value.

Some attempt has been made in this course to come to grips with the mental process of valuation dilemma. Your instructor will take you through three increasingly more structured attempts to visually portray the process. Hopefully, the discussion will go at least part way towards answering the question posed in the prior paragraph.

CASE STUDIES

There are definite limitations upon the effectiveness of long dissertations upon such a theoretical subject as valuation. In the hope of overcoming some of these limitations we have devised several case studies on the more important phases of the work, which we think may facilitate an understanding of certain basic valuation techniques. The cases used are, in essence, actual situations, although some of the facts have been changed in order that a simpler and more direct example could be obtained.

The examples to be considered at this point, Case Studies No. 1 and 2, concern typical closely-held stock valuations of the "garden variety". Most of the elements in these studies will be familiar to the reader. We ask, however, that despite the apparent simplicity of the problems, you indulge the writers by giving careful consideration to them.

230

Suggestions and comments will be welcomed. The first illustration concerns the valuation of the common stock of a closely-held industrial corporation.

Industrial Stock Valuation – Case Study No. 1

Statement of the Issue

What was the fair market value on November 20, 1979, of 6,500 shares of the common stock of the Orchid Packing Company, included in the estate of John Aster?

The valuation date is the date of death.

The shares were reported on Schedule B of the Federal estate tax return at $100.00 per share.

The examining Estate Tax Attorney recommended a value of $919.44 per share for the stock, and the statutory notice has been issued on that basis.

The valuation question is the major issue in the case. The tax deficiency is $1,804,652.00.

Statement of Essential Facts

Basis of Valuation:

The taxpayer's representative contends that the returned value is the proper fair market value for the common stock of Orchid Packing Co. since it is based on actual sale prices. The agent's determined value is premised upon the book value of the stock as shown by the balance sheet dated October 31, 1979.

Corporate History:

The company was incorporated in Iowa in 1921, and is engaged in the meat packing and processing business. It operates two large meat packing houses in Iowa and a subsidiary conducts a meat packing business in California. It produces primarily beef, lamb, and pork meat products, as well as byproducts such as animal and plant foods and hides. The company leases several hundred railroad refrigerator cars and conducts its own purchasing, slaughtering, and marketing of fresh and processed meats.

The capital stock of the company consists of the following classes:

Class	Shares	Par Value
6% Cumulative Preferred.................	1,000	$100.00
Common Stock.........................	32,000	No Par

231

As of the valuation date all of the above shares were outstanding except for 100 shares of the common stock held in the corporation's treasury.

The preferred stock is nonvoting until dividends are five years in arrears. There are no accumulated dividends payable to preferred stockholders as of the basic date.

The two classes of stock are closely-held by members of the Aster and Lily families. The bulk of the voting common stock is owned by the Aster group.

The decedent, John Aster, was the corporation president at the time of his death. His father had founded the original business from which the present corporation had evolved. Two sons and one nephew of John Aster have been active in the firm since the end of World War II. His oldest son, Thomas, was assistant vice president in charge of production at the time of John's death, and the nephew, Matthew Aster, was sales manager.

The company has had a peaceful labor relations history and is currently setting up a profit-sharing plan for the benefit of its employees. It markets its products under the brand name "Orchid."

Sales of the Common Stock:

There is no record of any sales of the preferred stock. The following schedule lists the most recent sales of the common stock as shown by the corporate records:

Date	Shares	Price	Seller
Jan. 18, 1964.............	20	$100.00	A. B. Yew
Sept. 15, 1966............	30	100.00	George Lilac
Aug. 19, 1968.............	10	100.00	George Lilac
May 4, 1970..............	15	100.00	A. B. Yew
Dec. 2, 1974.............	25	100.00	Martin Ivy

The purchaser in all of the above transactions was the corporation. All sellers are employees or officers of the company. The shares acquired were not cancelled but were held in the corporate treasury. There was no record available of sales of the common stock prior to January 18, 1964.

Balance Sheet:

The company operates on a fiscal year ended October 31 basis. A condensed balance sheet as of October 31, 1979, follows:

Orchid Packing Company

Balance Sheet as of October 31, 1979

Cash on Hand and in Bank.................................... $3,930,000
Receivables (Net of a Reserve of $35,000).................. 6,800,000
Inventories.. 9,580,000
Municipal and U.S. Bonds................................... 3,200,000
Prepayments.. 150,000

    Total Current Assets............................... $23,660,000

Investment in Subsidiary................................... $100,000
Plant, Equipment and Machinery.............. $14,140,000
   Less: Reserve for Depreciation.......... 3,690,000   10,450,000
Other Assets... 20,000

    Total Assets....................................... $34,230,000

Accounts Payable... $2,750,000
Taxes Payable.. 1,950,000
Accrued Expenses... 100,000

    Total Liabilities.................................. $4,800,000

6% Preferred Stock (1,000 shares).......................... $100,000
Common Stock (32,000 shares).................. $3,200,000
   Less: Treasury Stock (100 shares)........ 10,000   3,190,000
Retained Earnings.. 24,540,000
Paid in Capital.. 1,100,000
Reserve for Contingencies.................................. 500,000

    Total Equity....................................... $29,430,000

    Total Liabilities and Equity....................... $34,230,000

Experience with receivables indicated the present nominal reserve was adequate. Inventories were valued for the most part on the LIFO method. Government bonds were shown at their fair market value on the balance sheet date. Investment in subsidiary is carried at cost based on the acquisition by Orchid in 1959. Plant and equipment consist mainly of buildings constructed and equipment acquired since 1956. Common stock is shown at the stated value of $100.00 per share.

Sales, Income and Dividends:

A schedule of sales, earnings and dividends paid follows covering the ten years preceding the valuation date:

Fiscal Year Ended 10/31	Net Sales	Net Income After Taxes	Cash Dividends on Common Stock
1970.........	$180,100,000	$1,840,000	$319,250
1971.........	191,200,000	1,980,000	319,250
1972.........	215,300,000	2,040,000	319,250
1973.........	212,300,000	1,910,000	478,875
1974.........	230,900,000	2,200,000	478,500
1975.........	281,000,000	2,350,000	638,000
1976.........	275,100,000	3,050,000	638,000
1977.........	290,000,000	3,810,000	638,000
1978.........	297,700,000	3,950,000	957,000
1979.........	312,500,000	4,100,000	638,000

Note: The above amounts include the sales and net income of the subsidiary.

Development and Interpretation of Facts

Taking our guides from Rev. Rul. 59-60, we will consider the important elements of value as they apply to the fair market value of the Orchid Packing Co. common stock.

The nature of the business is clearly stated and amplified enough so that an appraiser can get a general idea of the scope and character of its operations. Its operating history shows progress and substantial growth both as to sales and income. We can readily assume that management has been efficient and effective. Furthermore the existence of potential management personnel to succeed to the top executive positions in the company is suggested by the presence of two younger members of the family in high level jobs. The loss of the "key man" will probably not leave the corporation without capable management material.

The economic outlook for the meat packing industry at the time of death can be ascertained in a general fashion by reference to Standard and Poor's industry survey or similar publications.

Typical comments set forth in Standard and Poor's "current" industry analysis dated September 10, 1979 can be paraphrased as follows:

With larger cattle marketings in the final half likely to offset a prospective year-to-year dip in hog slaughter, overall sales of the meat packers are expected to improve in the fiscal year ending October 31, 1979.

The first half improvement suggests better full year profit margins for meat packers.

...the highly favorable first half assures meat packers of substantially higher earnings in 1978-79.

Referring to the "basic" industry analysis issued by Standard and Poor's the following statements are illustrative of the significant facts to be gleaned from such source materials:

Consumption of meat fluctuates directly with the volume of livestock slaughter, as packers must move their perishable inventories into consumption, regardless of price to avoid spoilage. The volume of livestock slaugher depends on such factors as the size of herds, the number of animals which have reached maturity, and prices which can be realized for meat animals. However, meat production varies only moderately from year to year, except when influenced by unusual factors, such as droughts.

The relationship of livestock prices to the cost of feeds and prices for other farm products competing for the use of land are the basic determinants of supply, but these factors take time to exert their influence.

Except for animals bought for stocking and feeding purposes, all livestock shipped to markets are purchased by packers and immediately slaughtered. Furthermore, most fresh meat is sold promptly, to avoid excessive shrinkage.

Between 1968 and 1978 civilian per capita consumption of meat rose 25.3 pounds to an annual total of 207.3 pounds.

Meat prices, as well as the volume of operations, are beyond the control of the packing industry. The packers can, however, regulate the prices paid for livestock, and these are adjusted on the basis of the returns which can reasonably be expected from meats and byproducts. Competition in the buying of livestock prevents purchases at prices low enough to provide wide profit margins.

"Despite the rapid inventory turnover, large supplies of meat and produce are constantly in the process of distribution. Although the curing and smoking of meats has been speeded up, supplies must still be accumulated during periods of seasonally heavy marketings and held for even distribution throughout the year. This condition has increased in importance with the growth in the market for canned and frozen meat products. Fresh meat, still providing the bulk of output and carrying the narrowest profit margins, usually is on hand less than two weeks.

The characteristically narrow profit margins of meat packers reflect competitive bidding for livestock supplies. Also, the percentage of sales carried through by domestic meat packing companies to net income has rarely exceeded 2%.

The inherent uncertainties of the industry, together with substantial capital leverage and narrow margins make shares of the meat packing companies' common stocks highly speculative. Price/earnings ratios normally are low.

Moving now from the industry picture to the company to be valued we can make some observations about the balance sheet and book value of the subject stock.

We can note readily that the company is in excellent financial condition by virtue of substantial cash or its equivalent on hand; its exceptional liquid ratio (that is the ratio of cash, receivables and marketable securities to current liabilities)) of 2.90 to 1; and its net current asset, or working capital, ratio (current assets to current liabilities) of 4.93 to 1. The dollar value of the working capital was in excess of $19.8 million.

Other corporations in the meat packing industry indicated working capital ratios at the end of the 1979 fiscal year as follows:

Corporation	1979 F.Y. Working Capital (in 000's)	Ratio
Armour & Co.	$191,241	3.2-1
Burns & Co., Ltd.	10,393	2.0-1
Canada Packers, Ltd.	41,447	2.2-1
Cudahy Packing Co.	14,153	1.7-1
Geo. A. Hormel & Co.	25,768	2.0-1
Hygrade Food Products Corp. ...	18,767	2.1-1
E. Kahn's Sons Co.	3,968	2.9-1
Oscar Mayer & Co., Inc.	35,705	3.4-1
Morrell (John) & Co.	35,968	2.6-1
Rath Packing Co.	14,509	3.3-1
Swift & Co.	260,680	3.5-1
Tobin Packing Co., Inc.	7,795	3.5-1
Wilson & Co., Inc.	73,149	4.9-1

Average Ratio.. 2.9-1

The book value per share of Orchid Packing Company's outstanding common stock is $919.44. The net current asset value of the common stock is $591.22 per share.

The inventories should be studied in detail to ascertain the amounts of each general type of meat products involved. Inventory turnover in the 1979 fiscal year averaged 16.7 times. A detailed schedule of the corporation's capital asset accounts, that is the building, machinery and equipment accounts and their respective depreciation reserves, should also be prepared and analyzed. The asset "Investment in Subsidiary" will have to be carefully investigated. Financial statements pertaining to its operations for a period of years as well as a balance sheet as of October 31, 1979, are required. For purposes of this example, we will assume that a value of $1,500,000 represents the fair market value of this investment as of the balance sheet date. Of course, much the same analysis as we are now making of the parent company, would be necessary before we could arrive at a conclusion as to the subsidiary's fair market value.

The consolidated book value of the common stock of Orchid Packing Company and its west coast subsidiary, reflecting the fair market value of such affiliate rather than its book value is computed to be $30,730,000, ($29,330,000, the parent company's book value plus $1,400,00, the excess of the fair market value of the subsidiary over its cost) or the equivalent of $963.32 per share. The consolidated net current asset value reflecting actual working capital of the California plant was $650.00 per share.

Next we will consider the earnings history of the business. We note that the corporation's sales of products have increased from a level of around $180 million in 1970 to an amount in excess of $312 million in the fiscal year 1979. Net income has recorded a similar rise, increasing from $1.8 million in the year ended October 31, 1970 to $4.1 million in the latest fiscal year. The following schedule shows the resultant earnings per share of common stock realized in the ten years preceding the valuation date:

Fiscal Year Ended 10/31	Net Income Per Share*	Fiscal Year Ended 10/31	Net Income Per Share*
1970	$57.49	1975	$73.48
1971	61.88	1976	95.42
1972	63.76	1977	119.35
1973	59.69	1978	123.64
1974	68.78	1979	128.34

*Computed after preferred dividends were deducted and on the basis of 31,900 common stock shares outstanding.

Average earnings for various periods before the date of death appear as follows:

Period	Total	Average
FY 1970 - 1979	$851.73	$85.17
FY 1975 - 1979	540.13	100.03
FY 1977 - 1979	371.23	123.74

Referring to the dividend record we find the following amounts paid per share of common stock outstanding at the time of declaration:

F.Y. 10/31	Dividend	F.Y. 10/31	Dividend
1970	$10.00	1975	$20.00
1971	10.00	1976	20.00
1972	10.00	1977	20.00
1973	15.00	1978	30.00
1974	15.00	1978	20.00

Average dividends for the ten-year and last five-year periods respectively amounted to $17.00 and $22.00 per share.

Appraisal Techniques

The comparative approach is used as a substitute when the best evidence of fair market value—namely representative sales of the closely-held corporation's stock—are lacking. By analyzing relative selling prices of similar stocks we are able to gauge with some degree of realism the probable range of values which a willing buyer would pay and a willing seller would take for the common stock of Orchid Packing Co.

The following Exhibits A and B contain a suggested method of presentation and analysis of the more significant financial information pertaining to the comparable corporations. It may be noted on Exhibit A that the ratio of the market prices of the various companies in the meat packing industry to earnings, current and average, and to tangible asset value have been computed. Exhibit B is a schedule of earnings of the comparative corporations recorded in the five years prior to the valuation date. The thirteen companies included in the analysis constitute firms in the industry on which reliable market quotations can be found and which realized a profit in the latest full year before the valuation date. Recognizing certain dissimilarities from the standpoint of size and magnitude of sales, earnings and working capital, a more representative group of five of the corporations were selected for further analysis. The result of this study appears later.

Attention is called to the fact that the comparative analysis is based not only upon the common stocks but also upon the total capital employed in each of the comparable corporations, including the capital secured by incurring long-term debt. We have also added interest on long-term debt to net income after taxes to arrive at the amount of earnings available to the total capital investment. Some such procedure is needed when we compare businesses with widely differing capital structures. This point will be discussed in greater detail in Lesson 12.

EXHIBIT A

In Re: [illegible] Packing Company Dubuque Iowa

Comparative Corporations of the Meat Packing Industry-Valuation Date-November 20, 19xx

Common Stock Traded	Corporation	Amount Outstanding	Market Value Per Unit 11/20/xx	Total Market Value	Net Tangible Asset Value	Latest Year's Earnings Applicable	Net Working Capital (in 000's)	Latest Year's Net Sales (in 000's)	Five Year Average Earnings	Ratios – Price to: Asset Value (%)	Latest Year's Earnings	Five-Year Average Earnings
NYSE	Armour and Company											
	Notes Payable (4½%)	40000000-	Face	40000000	40000000	1170000						
	First Mortgage Bonds	32266000-	Face	32266000	32266000	967830						
	Debentures	10000000-	Face	10000000	10000000	399000						
	Conv. Subord. Deb. 4½s, 1983	32648200-	117¼-118	38402445	32648200	1469169						
	Subord. Cum. Inc. Deb. 5s, 1984	54090000-	99⅜-99⅝	53751938	54090000	2724025						
	Income Deb. 3½s 19_8	1522000-	Face	1522000	1522000	116515						
	Common Stock	5536324sh	55-55⅝	306573942	232155546	22775000			16650427	13206	1346	1841
				482516325	402681746	29621539	191241	1887026	22706294	11983	1629	2125
TOR S.E.	Burns & Co., Ltd.											
	Bonds	2100500-	Face	2100500	2100500	112337						
	Common Stock	767083sh	15⅞-16	12177443	23241213	492017			630708	5240	2475	1931
				14277943	25341713	604354	10417	134922	819657	5634	2363	1742
TOR S.E.	Canada Packers, Ltd.											
	Common Stock Class A	400000sh	74½	29800000								
	Common Stock Class B	800000sh	75¼	60200000								
				90000000	68028260	4098720	41447	599970	5319954	13230	1476	1692
NYSE	The Cudahy Packing Co.											
	Long Term Debt	5773100-	Face	5773000	5773000	238600						
	4½% Cum. Preferred Stock	100000sh	67	6700000	10000000	450000						
	Common Stock	1540938sh	9-9½	14253677	20189650	1303659			✓	7060	1093	✓
				26726677	35962650	1992259	14153	329604		7432	1342	
ASE	Geo. A. Hormel and Co.											
	Common Stock	1195621sh	34⅞	41697282	52868258	5724527	25768	411827	3886321	7887	728	1073
ASE	Hygrade Food Products Corp.											
	Loans Payable	6000000-	Face	6000000	6000000	330000						
	4% A Preferred Stock	5822sh	60	349320	582200	23288						
	5% B Preferred Stock	16582sh	Par $100	1658200	1658200	82910						
	Common Stock	735711sh	23⅝-23⅞	17275109	28704485	2437011			818637	6018	709	2110
				25282629	36944885	2873209	18767	454333	1226235	6843	880	2062
OC	E. Kahn's Sons Co.											
	Common Stock	188294sh	B 31½	5931261	7651570	643886	3968	42647	586700	7752	921	1011
OC	Oscar Mayer & Co., Inc.											
	Notes Payable	3500000-	Face	3500000	3500000	173343						
	Common Stock	2236980sh	B 38-A 40½	87801465	66936451	7897362			5736519	13117	1112	1531
				91301465	70436451	8070705	35705	295966	5919330	12962	1131	1542

In Re: Oscar ... Packing Company, Dubuque, Iowa

Comparative Comparison of the Meat Packing Industry—Valuation date: November 20, 1974

Where Common Traded	Corporation	Amount Outstanding	Market Value Per Unit 11/20/74	Total Market Value	Net Tangible Asset Value	Latest Year Earnings Applicable	TPI Working Capital (in 000's)	Total Year Net Sales (in 000's)	Five Year Average Earnings	Asset Value (Tot)	Ratio-Price to Total Year Earnings	Ratio-Price to Five Year Average Earnings
NYSE	Morrell (John) & Co. Notes Payable Common Stock	11,804,000 - 1,221,251 sh	Face 27-27⅞	11,804,000 33,568,135 47,372,135	11,804,000 53,562,678 65,366,678	644,120 4,694,426 5,338,536	35,968	653,679	303,367 370/014	6,443 72,49	7,58 8,87	11,72 12,80
ASE	Rath Packing Company Notes Payable Common Stock	7,010,000 - 4,900,000 sh	Face 11⅝	7,010,000 11,508,750 18,518,750	7,010,000 28,982,782 35,992,782	300,956 6,028,87 7,038,43	14,509	267,080	3,557,110	4,483 52,61	28,57 26,31	✓ 51,86
NYSE	Swift & Company Debentures 2⅝%, 1962 Debentures 2⅞%, 1983 Other Long Term Debt Common Stock	22,655,000 - 1,144,000 - 74,314,250 - 5,999,444 sh	87⅞ 94 Face 54⅝-55⅝	20,191,269 1,075,360 74,314,250 331,467,281 427,050,160	22,655,000 1,144,000 743/4,250 402,534,130 507,647,380	4,572,697 251,035,385 296,476,082	260,680	261,0056	17,798,239 219,957,57	8,094 84,12	13,20 14,39	18,62 19,42
OC	Tobin Packing Co. Inc. Notes Payable Common Stock	1,421,000 - 884,268 sh	Face B23-A24%	1,421,000 21,111,899 22,532,899	1,421,000 19,113,665 20,534,665	78,960 18,74,765 1,953,725	7,795	79,265	20,42,415 21,43,530	11,045 10,973	11,26 11,53	10,34 10,51
NYSE	Wilson & Co. Inc. Long Term Debt Debentures 6½%, 1976 4.25 Cum. Preferred Stock Common Stock	484/868 - 11,550,000 - 17,200,00 sh 2,302,817 sh	Face 98-99 B93⅜-A95 52½-53½	484/868 11,374,750 16,211,000 122,047,301 159,478,919	484/868 11,550,000 14,275,685 94,504/174 125,171,727	259,732 500/56 736,967 11,828,942 13,325,797	731/47	766,373	4,675,143 8,362,542	129/5 123,61	10,32 11,57	18,28 18,47
	Total Common (13 Co.) All Securities			107,41,18365 449,687,245	104,657,842 458/37,765	91,274,377 106,626,992			63,178,036 77,024,444	11,6290 11,7959	16,953 17,739	17,085 22,553
	Total Common (... Co.) All 3 securities (... Co.)			107,655,118 420,960,568		Average Common only Arithmetic Weighted Median Average: All securities Arithmetic Weighted U. rights Median				8,965 9,934 7,887 7,372 9,958 7,887	13,04 12,02 11,2 13,65 13,59 11,59	15,55 16,92 14,92 18,74 18,25 17,17

1) In review of large price ranges losses to average in computed 2) Excluding the Dubuque Packing Co. and Rath Packing Company 3) Excluding the Cudahy Packing Co.

In re: Cur Pac Packing Company, Debtor, etc.

Computation of Average Earnings of Comparative Corporations in the Meat Packing Industry

Company		Net Income Available to All Securities and to Common Stock Only					Totals		Averages		Moody's Manual Page
		Fiscal Year 1975	Fiscal Year 1976	Fiscal Year 1977	Fiscal Year 1978	Fiscal Year 1979	All Securities	Common Stock	All Securities	Common Stock	
1. Armour and Company [1][3]	Total	2173681	1842313	21155306	2260/627	29621539	11353468	83252137	22770694	16650427	1150
	Common	16221237	13121000	14815000	16320000	22775008					
2. Bueno and Company, Ltd [3]	Total	1598471	812715	211760	794984	602354	4098284	3115641	819657	630708	2805
	Common	1362701	679182	17227	607644	492017					
3. Canada Packers Ltd. [3]	Total	5250231	4613871	4995590	5661339	4098720	26599771	26599771	5319954	5319954	2805
	Common										
4. The Cudahy Packing Company [2]	Total	1272151	33398	⟨4928057⟩	⟨1680957⟩	1992259	y	y	y	y	482
	Common	360976	⟨8245057⟩	⟨12887157⟩	⟨2434856⟩	1303659					
5. Geo. A. Hormel & Co.	Total	4532416	3147435	3062390	2744657	3724527	19431607	19311607	3886321	3886321	913
	Common										
6. Hygrade Food Products Corporation [2][3]	Total	2305483	⟨83147⟩	469706	567929	2873209	6131176	4093186	1224235	818637	161
	Common	1970410	⟨4695647⟩	23881	131731	2437011					
7. E. Kahn's Sons Co.	Total	6119627	625175	523432	523580	643896	2933500	2933500	586700	586700	631
	Common										
8. Mayer (Oscar) & Co. Inc.	Total	5868800	4740075	4502552	4608440	8070705	29596652	28682577	5919330	5736519	408
	Common	5476985	4565575	4315268	6227407	7077362					
9. Morrell (John) & Co.	Total	4244246	2915957	2948813	3117689	5338336	18565071	15168353	3701014	3033671	1005
	Common	3560852	2151466	2308041	2653778	4694216					
10. Rath Packing Co.	Total	1870029	⟨14738557⟩	⟨4608777⟩	1124411	703843	1785551	y	357110	y	2156
	Common	16114404	⟨1891726⟩	⟨2836887⟩	8044742	402887					
11. Swift and Company	Total	21814871	15764572	20899116	21736143	29476082	109778784	88991177	21955757	17778235	1578
	Common	18412767	12045688	16313927	17111430	25103385					
12. Tobin Packing Company, Inc.	Total	2318642	2054609	2294997	2092679	1963725	10717652	10212077	2143530	2042415	767
	Common	2191692	1944629	2195982	2005004	1874765					
13. Wilson & Company, Inc.	Total	3075210	8781798	8526376	8103527	13325797	41812708	33378916	8362542	6675643	87
	Common	1206631	7005708	6213653	6510781	11829942					

[1] In Canadian dollars.

[2] Calendar years 1974–1978 are used.

[3] Corporation has only common stock outstanding. In view of large participation in the average is simplified.

A summary of the analysis appearing on Exhibit A follows:

	Range	Arithmetic Mean	Median
1. Percent of asset value represented by market value-			
Common Stock..........	40.8% – 132.3%	98.5%	78.9%
Total Capital.........	52.6% – 132.3%	90.7%	78.9%
2. Number of times latest year's earnings represented by market value-			
Common Stock..........	7.1 – 28.6	13.0	11.1
Total Capital.........	7.3 – 26.3	13.7	11.6
3. Number of times five-year average earnings represented by market value-			
Common Stock[a]......	10.1 – 21.1	15.5	16.9
Total Capital[a]......	10.1 – 21.3	18.8	17.2

[a] Excluding Cudahy Packing Co. and Rath Packing Co. because large losses in prior years distorted the average earnings figures.

It is readily apparent from the above summary that a wide range of ratios results from all three phases of this analysis. After study of the companies used and the various items of financial information pertaining to them as shown on Exhibit A, a refinement of the basic comparative approch in this case seems warranted. A selection of the five most comparable meat packing companies has been made and the results summarized on the following tabulations:

Schedule 1 – (Common Stock Analysis)

Corporation	Price/Assets Ratio (%)	Price/Latest Yr.'s Earnings Ratio	Price/Five-Year Av. Earnings Ratio
Cudahy............	70.6	10.9	----
Hormel............	78.9	7.3	10.7
Hygrade..........	60.2	7.1	21.1
Mayer............	131.2	11.1	15.3
Morrell..........	66.4	7.6	11.7
	407.3	44.0	58.8
Arithmetic Average........	81.5%	8.8	14.7
Median...........	70.6%	7.6	13.5

Schedule 2 - (Total Capital Analysis)

Corporation	Price/Assets Ratio (%)	Price/Latest Yr."s Earnings Ratio	Price/Five-Year Av. Earnings Ratio
Cudahy............	74.3	13.4	----
Hormel............	78.9	7.3	10.7
Hygrade..........	68.4	8.8	20.6
Mayer............	129.6	11.3	15.4
Morrell..........	72.5	8.9	12.8
	423.7	49.7	59.5
Arithmetic Average........	84.7%	9.9	14.9
Median..........	74.3%	8.9	14.1

The results of the above analysis present a somewhat more consistent picture than was displayed by the survey involving all thirteen corporations. Before concluding the study, a tabulation of the market price/dividends ratios (or dividend yield) should be referred to. Exhibit C following sets forth the previous five-year dividend record and the ratios of market values of the comparative companies to the latest year's dividends and to the five-year average dividends.

A summary of the results of this analysis follows:

	Range	Arithmetic Mean	Median
1. Original complete analysis:* (a) Yields computed by relating latest year's dividends to market value of common stock (10 companies)	2.3% - 4.8%	3.5%	3.4%
(b) Yields computed by relating five-year average dividends to market value of common stock: (12 companies)	2.3% - 5.9%	3.5%	3.6%
2. Selected company analysis: (a) Latest year yields (4 companies)	2.7% - 4.2%	3.6%	3.7%
(b) Average latest five-year yield: (5 companies)	2.4% - 5.9%	3.8%	4.0%

*Cudahy paid no dividends in any year and Rath and Burns paid no current dividends.

Giving attention to all of the foregoing data, what is the fair market value on November 20, 1979 of 6,500 shares of the common stock of Orchid Packing Company?

Possible Solution

At the outset we must give attention to the reported sales of the subject stock, since if they are representative of market value a theoretical valuation will not be necessary. A cursory perusal of these data, however, should be sufficient to convince an appraiser and the Tax Court that the sales fail on several counts as determiners of fair market value. First, they involve nominal amounts of shares. Second, they are isolated transactions extending over a long period and in most cases quite remote in time from the valuation date. Third, the parties to the sales were in each case the corporation, its officers, or employees. Whether or not completely arm's length and bona fide sales took place may be subject to doubt in view of the relationship between the parties. Fourth, the selling price was identical from January 1964 to December 1974. This inflexibility of price during a period of exceptional progress and successful operations by the company indicates either an apparent lack of awareness on the part of the sellers involved, or the setting up of a purchase price by the corporation without regard for the actual fair market value of the stock. Because of the foregoing, the sales of themselves do not establish a market value for the shares of common stock to be valued herein.

We are forced, therefore, to rely on the financial and economic factors as they apply to Orchid Packing Co. in determining the fair market value of its common stock.

A summary of the most significant facts in the case might be as follows:

1. The stock is closely-held and therefore lacking in ready marketability.

2. The company operates a successful meat packing business with plants in Iowa and California.

3. The book value is $919.44 per share as reported and $963.32 per share on a consolidated basis.

EXHIBIT C

In Re: ____ Packing Company, Dubuque, Iowa

Schedule of Dividends Paid by Comparative Corporations in the Meat-Packing Industry

	Annual Amounts of Dividends Paid on Common Stock					Total	Average	Market Value of Common Stock	Yield (%) 19__	Average	Payout (%) 19__	Average
	FY1975	FY1976	FY1977	FY1978	FY1979							
1. Armour and Co.	$6,133,953	7,249,260	7,430,244	7,547,322	7,641,605	36,004,384	7,200,877	306,573,942	25%	23%	34%	43%
2. Burns & Co., Ltd. [1/]	615,666	383,541				997,207	498,604	121,777,443		4.1		79
3. Canada Packers, Ltd. [2/]	2,100,000	2,100,000	2,100,000	2,100,000	2,100,000	10,500,000	2,100,000	49,000,000	23	23	34	39
4. The Cudahy Packing Co.												
5. Hormel (Geo. A) & Co.	1,575,420	1,673,869	1,673,869	1,673,869	1,673,869	8,270,896	1,654,179	41,697,282	4.0	4.0	29	4.3
6. Hygrade Food Products Corp [2/]	546,469	684,090	697,269	712,523	725,642	3,415,993	683,199	17,275,109	4.2	4.0	30	83
7. E. Kahn's Sons Co	194,830	192,956	288,254	286,813	283,806	1,246,659	249,332	5,931,261	4.8	4.2	44	42
8. Mayer (Oscar) & Co., Inc.	1,746,008	1,762,077	1,937,886	2,206,361	3,030,262	10,682,594	2,136,519	87,801,465	3.5	2.4	38	37
9. Morrell (John) & Co.	835,128	905,394	926,066	941,187	961,469	4,569,244	913,849	35,568,935	2.7	2.6	20	30
10. Rath Packing Co.	990,000	371,273				1,361,273	680,637	11,508,750	3.0	5.9		
11. Swift & Co	11,048,396	11,069,790	9,596,048	9,590,046	10,499,027	51,812,307	10,362,461	331,449,281	3.2	3.1	4.2	58
12. Tobin Packing Co., Inc.	774,673	789,325	972,695	972,695	972,695	4,482,083	896,413	21,111,899	4.6	4.2	52	44
13. Wilson & Co., Inc. [4/]	3,623,149	3,638,259	3,645,586	3,665,574	3,678,579	18,260,197	3,652,039	122,049,301	3.0	3.0	3.1	55
Total 10 companies [4/]					31,564,904 [2/]		30,347,472 [5/]	1,059,978,475 [5/]	348	4.2.1	354	553
Total 11 companies							31,028,109	1,076,559,918				
Total 12 companies								1,081,461,668				
						Average:						
						Arithmetic			3.5	3.5	3.5	50
						Weighted			3.0	2.9	3.5	48
						Median			3.4	3.6	3.4	4.3

1/ In Canadian Dollars
2/ Amounts are for calendar years 1975–1979 inclusive.
3/ Two-year average
4/ Excluding Burns & Co. Ltd, Rath Packing Co and Rath Packing Co
5/ Including the Cudahy Packing Co and Rath Packing Co

245

4. The net current asset value per share is $591.22 using the parent company only and $650 per share in terms of a pro forma consolidation.

5. Sales and net earnings trends have been for the most part consistently upward.

6. An industry study indicates that Orchid ranks near the top in financial stability and growth.

7. Latest year's earnings were $128.34 per share and 10-, 5- and 3-year average earnings amounted to $85.17; $108.03; and $123.74 per share respectively.

8. Dividends paid average $17.00 per share over the ten fiscal years ended in 1974 and $22.00 per share during the latest five years.

9. Stocks of a selected group of comparable companies were selling on the average for 81% to 85% of tangible asset value; 9 to 10 times latest year's earnings; and 14 1/2 to 15 times last five years' average earnings.

10. Average dividend yields displayed by the comparatives centered around the 3 1/2% level.

Two points are worth mentioning regarding Orchid's earnings and dividend record. First, the upward trend in profits is clearly shown in the previous earnings schedules, and in view of the continued improvement in operating results the latest year's results prior to the basic date are believed to be most indicative of what to expect in the future. Second, in a closely-held corporation such as Orchid Packing Company, where a family group controls the company's policies, the dividend payments are secondary in importance to the dividend-paying capacity of the business. This latter consideration in turn reverts to the earning capacity of the business. We note from the earnings and dividend records that Orchid's management has evidenced a reluctance to increase dividends in proportion to the rise in net income. The reasons for doing this may be sound. However, the fact remains that the management of publicly-held corporations will be more receptive to the wishes of the stockholders than will the owners of a small, family held enterprise. Thus dividends actually paid by this closely-held firm bear little relationship to its normal capacity to make dividend payments.

In support of this statement, we will compare the rates of dividend payout of other meat packers to Orchid's record. The schedule below shows the payout ratios recorded by the selected group of comparable firms which paid dividends in the 1979 fiscal year.

Payout Ratios

Company	FY 1979 Earnings to Common	1979 Dividends	Ratio(%)
1. Hormel	$5,724,527	$1,673,869	29
2. Hygrade	2,437.011	725,642	30
3. Mayer	7,897,362	3,030,262	38
4. Morrell	4,694,216	961,469	20
Totals	$20,753.116	$6,391,242	117

Arithmetic Average...29.5%
Weighted Average...30.8%

Using the foregoing as an index we note that if Orchid had disbursed a comparable amount (say 30%) of its earnings in 1979, its dividend would have amounted to around $38.50 per share instead of the actual $20.00 paid. At the industry average yield of 3.5% a value of $1,100.00 per share is indicated for Orchid.

Based on Orchid's actual dividends paid in the current year the average yield of the four dividend-paying comparatives shown, produces an indicated value of $570.00 per share.

The more important price/earnings analyses indicate values for Orchid ranging from $1,027.00 to $1,155.00 per share using latest year's income, and from $1,458.00 to $1,512.00 per share in terms of average earnings.

The price/asset value ratio averaging out to approximately 90% for the entire industry, suggests a value of $867.00 per share for Orchid's common stock (on a consolidated basis).

Conclusion

The range of possible values is wide and all of the relevant factors do not point to any single figure as the market value of the stock. This is typical in these issues. If presented to us in the form as shown on the preceding pages, we would place a value of $950.00 per share on this stock. For settlement our recommendation would depend among other things upon the relative effectiveness of the taxayer's prospective valuation expert and his or her opinion. The reader may well ask how we reach such a conclusion as to value? The answer is the usual "It is a matter of judgment." There are two significant and definitive observations we can make, however, which weighed heavily in the final opinion of value.

A principle of our valuation approach is that latest year's earnings are most important. At a value of $950.00 we are capitalizing latest year's earnings of $128.00 per share at approximately 13 1/2%. Certain of the comparable securities were selling at lower capitalization rates (and therefore higher values per dollar of income), but these securities are marketed on the major stock exchanges or over-the-counter. Their apparent greater mobility should demand some premium, or to be more exact, Orchid's common stock lower mobility warrants some discount.

Secondly, the only factor suggesting values substantially higher than the $950.00 valuation is the price/average earnings analysis developed from the comparatives. The high ratios exhibited by these companies in this respect we find are a direct result of relatively large increases in their net profits during the five-year period. For example, Morrell advanced from a $2 million net profit in 1976 to over twice that amount, or $4.7 million net income in 1979. Hormel jumped from $2.9 million in 1978 to $5.7 million in fiscal year 1979. Hygrade rose from $470,000 loss in 1976 to $2.4 million profit in 1979, and so on. These changes naturally produce high ratios in terms of current market value when earnings are at the much higher level. Orchid recorded no such phenomenal increase in its earnings over the latest five years ($3.0 million in 1976, $3.8 million in 1977 and $4.1 million in 1979). Thus we must conclude that a substantially lower value than the average earnings analysis suggests will be reasonable for the stock in question.

Investment Company Valuation - Case Study No. 2

Before setting forth the second case study we would like to point out that the use of the comparative analysis may be of questionable validity in certain instances. Although the courts have accepted the concept in deciding many valuation cases, in one area, the valuation of family security holding companies, we have some doubts. Ordinarily, the comparison is made in these cases to closed-end investment companies which have their stocks traded publicly. The distinction between the purpose for which the two organizations were formed causes our concern. Contrary to the situation in the listed or traded company, the closely-held enterprise is formed to provide a convenient, and possibly a tax saving, receptacle for the family's investments. It is not formed ordinarily with the intent of marketing its stock to the public and it does not publicize the know-how of its management. These differences from the listed firm raise serious doubts about correlating the two. Until we can set forth these views in the successful trial of one of these valuation issues, however, we will have to take cognizance of the comparative approach in such valuations in an effort to obtain an equitable settlement. The following case study concerns a typical holding company appraisal.

Statement of the Issue

What was the fair market value on March 31, 1980, of 17,750 shares of the common stock of Cactus Investments, Inc., made the subject of gifts by donor Donald Pine on that date?

The shares were included in the Federal gift tax return filed by Mr. Pine for the calendar year 1980 at a value of $125.00 per share.

248

The taxpayer has offered to settle the issue on the basis of a value of $150.00 per share.

Statement of Essential Facts

Basis of Values:

The taxpayer and attorney base their contention that the returned value represents the fair market value of the common stock of Cactus Investments, Inc. as of the date of the gifts, on a formal appraisal furnished to them by a firm of security analysts. Such an appraisal compared the stock to certain investment company securities traded on the public market and applied certain discounts to the indicated results. The value determined by the agent had as its primary support the adjusted book value per share of the stock as disclosed by the balance sheet dated December 31, 1979.

Corporate History:

The Corporation was organized in January, 1934, under the laws of the District of Columbia and is a security investment holding company. It had 50,000 shares of no par common stock outstanding on March 31, 1980, of which the shares to be valued constitute 35.5%. Over 85% of the stock is owned by members of and relatives of the Pine family, the donor herein being the recognized head of this group. There have never been any bona fide sales of the stock.

Portfolio of Investments:

From information furnished by the taxpayer we find that Cactus Investments, Inc. owned the following marketable securities as of December 31, 1979:

Industrial Bonds

Units ($1,000 bonds)	Corporation	Cost	12/31/79 Market Value
50	National Steel 3 7/8% '86	$46,313	$46,500
100	Xerox Convertible 4% '84	135,000	134,000

Preferred Stock

Shares			
9,000	Chesapeake and Ohio R.R.	269,000	569,250
24,500	Southern Railway Co.	294,000	490,000

Common Stock

Shares			
5,000	American Cyanamid	97,100	344,375
18,500	Atlantic Refining	200,000	1,130,813
14,000	Continental Can	280,000	700,000
2,000	Dow Chemical	25,000	152,750
10,000	Florida Power and Light	156,000	755,000
12,200	International Business Machines	50,000	493,800
3,400	Libby-Owens-Ford	125,000	204,000
60,000	Potomac Electric Power	583,000	1,372,500
42,000	Pure Oil Co.	420,000	2,373,000
24,200	Sinclair Oil	240,000	1,379,400
32,000	Standard Oil of California	290,000	2,344,000
8,200	Texas Co.	115,000	718,525
40,000	Washington Gas Light Co.	520,000	1,405,000
6,000	Westinghouse Electric	185,000	259,500
Total		$4,030,413	$14,872,413

A search of various financial publications disclosed the following market values for Cactus' investments as of the date of gift, March 31, 1980:

Security	Price Range or Range of Bid and Ask Prices on or about 3/31/80		Mean Price
	High	Low	
National Steel 3 7/8% '86		93	93
Xerox Convertible 4% '84		145 1/2	145 1/2
Ches. and Ohio R.R. pfd.	60	59	59 1/2
Southern Railway Co. pfd.	20 3/8	20 3/8	20 3/8
American Cyanamid com.	76	75 1/2	75 3/4
Atlantic Refining com.	61 1/2	61 1/4	61 3/8
Continental Can com.	51 1/4	50 7/8	51
Dow Chemical com.	78 5/8	77 3/4	78 1/4
Florida Power and Light com.	77	76 3/8	76 5/8
International Business Machines com.	45 5/8	45	45 1/2
Libby-Owens-Ford com.	57	56 1/2	56 3/4
Potomac Electric Power com.	24	23 3/4	23 7/8
Pure Oil Co. com.	58 1/2	58 1/8	58 3/8
Sinclair Oil com.	53 1/4	52 1/2	52 7/8
Standard Oil of California com.	70 1/4	69 1/2	69 7/8
Texas Co. com.	77 1/8	75 7/8	76 1/2
Washington Gas Light Co. com.	34 5/8	34 1/2	34 1/2
Westinghouse Electric com.	48 1/8	47 3/4	48

Balance Sheet:

The company's balance sheet rendered as of December 31, 1979 appeared as follows:

250

Cactus Investments, Inc.

Balance Sheet as of December 31, 1979

Cash... $93,000
Receivables... 5,000
Marketable Securities (at cost)....................... 4,030,413

      Total Assets.................................... $4,128,413

Current Liabilities................................... $4,413
Capital Stock (50,000 shares).................. $500,000
Retained Earnings............................. 3,624,000

      Total Equity.................................... $4,124,000

      Total Equity and Liabilities.................... $4,128,413

The net worth of $4,124,000 indicates a value per share of $82.48.
The examining officer substituted the fair market value of the underlying securities on December 31, 1979, amounting to $14,872,413, for
the cost figure and thereby derived the adjusted book value of $299.32
per share upon which the tax deficiency was based. Since the valuation date is March 31, 1980, the fair market value of the securities
as of that date should be used in arriving at the revised book value
for the common stock. We find that there were no changes in the
investment portfolio in the period December 31, 1979, to March 31,
1980. A schedule of the market values of the investments as of the
valuation date follows:

Security	Units Held	3/31/80 Unit Value	Total Value	Percent to Total
National Steel 3 7/8% '86	50	93	$46,500	.31%
Xerox Convertible 4% '84	100	145 1/2	145,500	.98
Chesa. and Ohio R.R. pfd.	9,000	59 1/2	535,500	3.61
Sourthern Railway Co. pfd.	24,500	20 3/8	499,188	3.36
American Cyanamid	5,000	75 3/4	378,750	2.55
Atlantic Refining	18,500	61 3/8	1,134,438	7.64
Continental Can	14,000	51	714,000	4.81
Dow Chemical	2,000	78 1/4	156,500	1.05
Florida Power and Light	10,000	76 5/8	766,250	5.16
International Business Machines	12,000	45 1/2	546,000	3.68
Libby-Owens-Ford	3,400	56 3/4	192,950	1.30
Potomac Electric Power	60,000	23 7/8	1,432,500	9.64
Pure Oil Co.	42,000	58 3/8	2,451,750	16.51
Sinclair Oil	24,200	52 7/8	1,279,575	8.62
Standard Oil of California	32,000	69 7/8	2,235,000	15.06
Texas Co.	8,200	76 1/2	627,300	4.22
Washington Gas Light Co.	40,000	35 1/2	1,420,000	9.56
Westinghouse Electric	6,000	48	288,000	1.94
Total Market Value			$14,851.701	100.00%

A breakdown of the investments by industry groups shows the following:

Petroleum........................	52.05%
Public Utilities................	24.37
General Manufactueres...........	7.40
Railroads.......................	6.97
Electronic......................	5.61
Chemicals.......................	3.60
	100.00%

Substituting the fair market value of the marketable securities on March 31, 1980, for the amount appearing on the latest balance sheet, produces an adjusted book value of $14,945,288 or $298.90 per share.

Earnings and Dividends

The table below shows the net income of Cactus after taxes and the dividends paid for the ten years 1971-1980:

Year	Earnings After Taxes[1]	Dividends Paid[2]
1971	$391,000	$375,000
1972	410,000	400,000
1973	418,000	410,000
1974	403,000	400,000
1975	450,000	450,000
1976	460,000	450,000
1977	484,000	470,000
1978	450,000	470,000
1979	512,000	500,000
1980	560,000	550,000
	$4,538,000	$4,475,000
Average	$453,800	$447,500

[1]Before net income from sale of securities.
[2]Excluding amounts paid from profits on securities sold.

Appraisal Technique

As required by IRC § 2031(b), the appraiser should analyze comparable investment company stocks prior to arriving at an opinion as to the value of Cactus Investments common stock. Investment companies fall into several classes. The open-end investment company, sometimes called the Mutual or Boston type, is characterized by the continual issuance and/or redemption feature of its capital stock. Stockholders may at any time, and at their option, redeem their shares at the asset value of the stock, less a slight discount. The bid price for the stock is, in effect, maintained at a level close to its asset value. Closed-end investment companies, on the other hand, have no such stock redemption provision and operate in the conventional corporate manner

252

of having set amounts of capital stock issued at a given time. These companies are further classified as leverage or nonleverage. In leverage companies, (i.e., companies with one or more issues of securities senior to the common stock) the asset value and market value of the common stock may depend more on the amounts of senior capital outstanding than on the investment activities. Since Cactus Investments, Inc., has only common stock outstanding, the comparative analysis should be confined to the nonleverage closed-end investment companies.

The following list includes most of the companies similar to Cactus which were listed in Moody's Manual for 1979:

1. A.M. Capital Corp.
2. A. V. C. Corp.
3. Abacus Fund
4. Adams Express co.
5. American European Securities Co.
6. American International Corp.
7. American Research & Develop. Corp.
8. American-So. African Investment Co., Ltd.
9. Boston Personal Property Trust
10. Canadian General Investments, Ltd.
11. Carriers & General Corp.
12. Central West Co.
13. Consolidated Financial Corp.
14. Consolidated Investment Trust
15. Dominick Fund Inc.
16. Electric Bond & Share Corp.
17. Eurofund, Inc.
18. General Public Service Corp.
19. Hanna (M.A.) Co.
20. Holyoke Shares, Inc.
21. Imperial Equity Corp.
22. Investment Foundation Ltd.
23. Japan Fund, Inc.
24. Lang & Co.
25. Lehman Corp.
26. Louisville Investment Co.
27. Madison Fund, Inc.
28. Magnum Fund Ltd.
29. Midwest Securities Investment
30. Midwest Technical Development Corp.
31. National Aviation Corp.
32. Niagara Share Corp.
33. Pallas Corp.
34. Petroleum Corp. of America
35. Providence Investors, Inc.
36. Real Silk Hosiery Mills, Inc.
37. Southport Commercial Corp.
38. Southwestern Research & General Investment Co.
39. Spring Street Capital Corp.
40. Standard Holding Corp.
41. Standard Shares Inc.
42. Stanley Securities Co.
43. Sun Investment Co.
44. Toronto & London Investment Co., Ltd.
45. Tri-Continental Financial Corp.
46. United Corp.
47. U.S. & Foreign Securities Corp.

Of the 47 companies named above the ten which are underlined comprise those most comparable to Cactus from the standpoint of type of investment portfolio, level of earnings and total asset value. Market prices for the common stocks of these corporations as of March 31, 1980, are listed below:

253

	Company	Source of Quotation	High	Low	Mean
1.	Adams Express Co.	WSJ NYSE	27 5/8	27 1/2	27 9/16
2.	American European Securities Co.	Chr. Sup.OC	A26 1/4	B25 1/4	25 3/4
3.	American International Corp.	WSJ NYSE*	A16 1/2	B16 1/4	16 3/8
4.	Carrier & General Corp.	WSJ NYSE	36	36	36
5.	Consolidated Investment Trust	Chr. Sup.OC	A11 1/2	B11	11 1/4
6.	Dominick Fund, Inc.	WSJ NYSE	20 1/2	20 1/2	20 1/2
7.	General Public Service Corp.	WSJ NYSE	6 1/8	6	6 1/16
8.	Lehman Corp.	WSJ NYSE	30 7/8	30 3/8	30 5/8
9.	Niagara Share Corp.	WSJ NYSE*	A21 1/2	B21 1/8	21 5/16
10.	U.S. & Foreign Securities Corp.	WSJ NYSE	30 1/2	30 1/4	30 3/8

A – Ask price   *Not traded March 31, 1980, Bid and Ask prices used.
B – Bid price

Exhibit D following contains a ten-year record of the investment income of the ten corporations selected for analysis. Exhibit E sets forth the dividend record of each company for the same period. The most significant tabulations of price to asset value ratios are included on Exhibit F. Summaries of the various relationships between the market values of the comparable equities and the financial records of the respective companies follow:

Schedule A – Ratio of Market Price to Tangible Asset Value

Range	–	71.7% to 100.5%
Arithmetic Average	–	85.4%
Weighted Average	–	84.6%
Median	–	85.1%

Schedule B – Price/Earnings Ratios and Dividend Yields

Price to latest year's earnings: Range – 33 to 52 times
                                             Average – 40 times

Latest year's yields: Range – 1.8% to 3.0%
                                             Average – 2.5%

Price to last 5-years' average earnings – 46.5 times (average)
Last 5-years' average yield – 2.2% (average)

Based on the foregoing data, what was the fair market value on March 31, 1980, of the 17,750 shares of Cactus Investments, Inc. common stock?

Possible Solution

An initial factor to clarify in evaluating the stock of a family-owned investment holding company, is the status of the interest to be valued, i.e., whether it is a majority or a minority interest. If an

arithmetical majority of the outstanding shares are at issue there is
no question that control is a real factor to consider. This will be
so regardless of whether local statutory requirements for corporate
liquidation are met or not. Inasmuch as the company has demonstrated
a history of profitable operations, and barring tangible evidence of
an intent on the part of management to liquidate, we must appraise the
business as a going concern. The benefits accruing to uncontested
management of such a company carrying with it the essential responsibility for salaries, investment policies, dividend payments, etc., are
the ingredients entering into the increment in value attaching to
control stock.

In Re: [ ] Investments, Inc.

Earnings of Comparative Closed-End Investment Companies - Non-Leverage Only

Years 19[ ]-7[ ] inclusive

Corporation	1970	1971	1972	1973	1974	1975	1976	1977	1978	1979	10-Year Total	5-Year Total
1. Adams Express Co. Average	2244053	2758355	2877657	2514325	2561333	2529863	2395033	2463079	2572826	2867555	25784057 / 2578406	12823336 / 2563667
2. American Eur. Sec. Co. Average	424844	457091	423500	454590	448698	420444	357017	352260	362377	432967	4118728 / 411873	1905005 / 381001
3. American Intl. Corp Average	968485	1172778	1202368	1052124	1066174	1073021	1042571	1106678	1170661	1317933	11172793 / 1117279	5710864 / 1142173
4. Carriers & General Corp Average	454388	471364	482314	440464	471650	460307	468775	483151	483315	503783	4719511 / 471951	2399331 / 477866
5. Consolidated Investment Tr. Average	1787922	1859200	1849462	1744806	1894002	1981407	1924198	2013726	2100261	2261964	19417828 / 1941783	10281736 / 2056347
6. Dominick Fund Inc. Average	604498	668930	641294	653888	825206	865143	766069	790808	894818	973123	7683757 / 768376	4309961 / 861988
7. General Public Sv. Corp. Average	532495	703760	753807	760294	1173427	1284174	1473825	2014166	2107859	2193319	12997126 / 1299713	9075343 / 1815069
8. Lehman Corp. Average	4608633	5380764	5170940	5205770	5720372	5944566	5802238	6181635	6463194	7639657	58121789 / 5812179	32031290 / 6404258
9. Niagara Share Corp. Average	1103017	1082344	1081721	991015	1042616	1117731	1353076	1956777	1547325	1731528	12537350 / 1253735	7736637 / 1447327
10. U.S.&Foreign Sec. Corp. Average	3155553	3184765	2772176	2534097	2610939	2593336	2430678	2544756	2752850	3027120	27451150 / 2745115	13367640 / 2673528

Data covers fiscal years ending June 30.

Dreyfus & Associates Investments, Inc.

Dividends Paid by Comparative Closed-End Investment Companies - Non-Average Only

Years: 19__ inclusive

Corporation	1970	1971	1972	1973	1974	1976	1976	1977	1978	1979	10-Year Total	5-Year Total
1. Adams Express Co Average	2247366	2760296	2919932	2589727	2601657	2547538	2344013	2445816	2474844	2778490	25742497 2574850	12650319 2530064
2. American Brake Co Average	426086	466062	416618	462295	455319	423303	355473	331034	365886	439729	4141805 414181	1915425 353085
3. American Int'l Corp. Average	956760	1165316	1215324	1057453	1079702	1082505	1028310	1087275	1126697	1242960	11052302 1105430	5361747 1112349
4. Carrier & General Corp Average	443209	471250	476850	448800	448800	448800	448800	476850	476850	516120	4651329 465433	2367420 473684
5. Consolidated Invest Tr. Average	1784760	1876548	1835753	1743966	1876945	1856109	1948594	1989478	2092250	2224625	19391008 1739101	10243034 2042607
6. Dominick Fund, Inc. Average	648220	680371	639913	624400	599470	820352	718355	737437	828982	909169	7204669 720667	4014295 802857
7. General Public Ser. Corp. Average	524535	6939114	7434999	7434999	1115219	1224652	1500162	1942143	1970383	2179806	12659772 1265977	8839146 1767829
8. Lehmann Corp Average	4454401	5089541	5089542	5147621	5676141	5801071	5655616	5882743	6069225	7320014	56185135 5618514	30709889 6141578
9. Niagara Share Corp Average	1011441	1045154	1028022	1027561	822785	1067356	1402738	1323638	1470222	1596384	12055281 1205528	7060138 1412028
10. U.S.& Foreign Sec. Corp Average	3031122	3218622	2825218	2328947	2612516	2578258	2406942	2552638	2747976	3014976	27374975 2737498	13303530 2660506

1/ Includes 28882 preferred dividends.
2/ Data covers fiscal years ending June 30.
3/ Dividend policy change from 1945 provides for a single payment in January of each year.
4/ Computed.

In Re: Castow Investments, Inc.
Comparative Used-End Investment Companies - Npn-Leverage Only

Stock Traded	Corporation	Shares Outstanding	Market Value per Share Mar 31/1980	Net Tangible Asset Value per Share	Ratio Market Value to Asset Value	Earnings per Share Total Year	Earnings per Share Five-Year Average	Dividends per Share Total Year	Dividends per Share Five-Year Average	Investment Securities Owned	Investment Securities Owned Set of Latest Year	S. Major Classification Holding Trade
NYSE	1. Adams Express Co. Common Stock	37197000.sh	27.5625	32.09	85.89	0.74	0.69	0.77	0.68	5072986	5160653	
OC	2. American Employer Ins Co. Common Stock	7725571.sh	26.75	33.53	79.80	0.57	0.67	0.60	0.60	876402	877196	
NYSE	3. American International Corp. Common Stock	28930318.sh	16.375	1.860	88.04	0.48	0.57	0.45	0.58	2308110	2347814	
NYSE	4. Carriot General Corp. Common Stock	56100000.sh	36	39.43	91.30	0.70	0.96	0.92	0.86	656731	670030	
OC	5. Consolidated Investment Trust Common Stock	6744442.sh	11.25	1.336	84.21	0.34	0.30	0.33	0.30	1510947	1743562	
NYSE	6. Dominick Fund, Inc. Common Stock	17560597.sh	20.5	25.44	80.58	0.52	0.44	0.48	0.41	2034160	1894103	
NYSE	7. General Public Service Corp. Common Stock	13147603.sh	40.25	7.22	83.45	0.16	0.13	0.17	0.13	3841781	4359613	

In Re: [...] Investment, Inc.

Comparative Closed-End Investment Companies - Non-Leverage Only

Stock Traded	Corporation	Shares Outstanding	Market Value per Share Mar. 31/19..	Net Tangible Asset Value Per Share (b)	Ratio Market Value to Asset Value (b)	Earnings per Share Latest Year	Earnings per Share Five-Year Average	Dividends per Share Latest Year	Dividends per Share Five-Year Average	Income from Securities Earned last year	Income from Sale of Securities Distributed last year	5- Major Classification of Investments
NYSE	B. Lehman Corp. Common Stock	12200023.dl	30.625	33.86	91.25	0.63	0.53	0.60	0.50	14,728,890	15,738,029	Oil&Gas 15.0, Pub.Util. 14.4, Chem. 10.2, Drugs 9.3, Off. Equip. 9.0
NYSE	A. Niagara Share Corp. Common Stock	4,996,320.8	2/3/.25	21.20	100.53	0.41	0.34	0.38	0.34	6589184	2289750	Petroleum 18.9, Chem 16.8, Off. Equip. 13.4, Election 11.2, Equip Tools 9.7
NYSE & U.S.A	Foreign Securities Corp. Common Stock	3,3108158.8	30.375	42.35	71.72	0.91	0.81	0.91	0.80	3336579	3340068	Oil&Gas 32.9, Pharm&Drug 21.1, Mfg etc 13.6, Mkt+Mrg 8.2, Pub.Util. 7.3

(a) As of December 31/19.. (b) Data for March 31/19.. not available

259

The mere fact of family ownership does not, however, attribute to all shares owned by the members of that family the essence of control. The courts have traditionally viewed real minority interests as just that, despite continuity of control between the shares to be valued and the remaining family stockholders (See Lesson 8). The block involved in this case is therefore considered to be a minority interest.

The principal factors affecting the fair market value of the shares transferred by the taxpayer are: (1) the underlying asset value of $298.90 per share; (2) latest year's and 10-year average earnings per share of $11.20 and $9.08 respectively; (3) latest year's and 10-year average dividends of $11.00 and $8.95 per share respectively; (4) the market price/asset value ratios disclosed by comparable investment company stocks averaging approximately 85%; and (5) the indicated price/earnings ratios and dividend yields of the comparatives ranging between 30 and 50 times and averaging about 2.5% respectively.

We can compute corresponding market values for the stock of Cactus Investments using the ratios obtained from the comparative analysis. These range from $253.00 per share based on price/asset value percentages, to $480.00 per share (price/latest year's earnings) and $440.00 per share (price/latest year dividends). Taking all of the valuation factors into account, and considering such tenuous elements as marketability and the caliber of the investment management, an opinion of $240.00 per share for the subject stock may be derived. The weighing of all the facts is a process distinctive to each appraiser. Honest differences of opinion are the rule in valuation issues. Therefore, any suggested value here is only the best answer in the judgment of the writer and should be viewed as a possible result rather than the one, correct result. The fact that reasonable persons may differ in their approaches is not to suggest that there are no fundamental principles or body of acceptable practices of valuation. As will be developed further in subsequent lessons the discipline is both an art and a science, but is nevertheless learnable.

Lesson 8

MINORITY INTERESTS - MULTI-PRODUCT BUSINESSES - PARTNERSHIPS

CONTENTS

Objectives
Family-Owned Minority Interests
Multi-Product Businesses
Partnerships
    Modification of Stock Valuation Techniques
    Sales Agreements Among Partners

OBJECTIVES

At the end of this lesson you will be able to:

1. Explain probable reaction of the U. S. Tax Court and other courts
    to the minority interest factor in family corporate stock valua-
    tion cases.

2. State the primary concern of appraisers when evaluating multi-pro-
    duct or multi-service companies, and suggest possible solutions to
    the problem.

3. Describe the major changes in comparative analysis techniques used
    in making stock valuations to adapt them to partnership valua-
    tions.

FAMILY-OWNED MINORITY INTERESTS

What is the traditional position taken by the courts on minority
interests in family controlled enterprises? The citations and excerpts from the decisions set forth below present a rather consistent
picture of the Tax Court's opinion on this issue. As will be noted
later, however, there is at least one exception to this apparent
uniformity on the part of the courts to be found in a District Court
decision.

Fred Pabst, Sr., 6 TCM 1186 (1947).

"Minority stock interests in a closed corporation are usually
worth much less than the proportionate share of the assets to
which they attach."

This case involved the valuation of the stock of a family
holding company owning family controlled common and preferred
stock of Pabst Brewing Co. The court held that the full
underlying asset value should be computed; denying discounts
for blockage and a relatively inactive market; but found a
value for the holding company stock of $212.00 per share.
Underlying asset value per share was $286.20. The court

261

viewed the block to be valued as a minority interest although it was owned by a member of the Pabst family which controlled both the holding and operating companies. Judge Harlan deciding.

Estate of Lloyd R. Smith, 9 TCM 907 (1950).

"The respondent points out that Investment Company (a family holding company) was organized and existed for the purpose of holding a controlling stock interest in Smith Corporation for the convenience and benefit of the Smith family who, either directly or by way of trusts, owned all of the stock in Investment Company ... he urges that the basic and proper criterion for the valuation of Investment Company stock is the net asset value of Investment Company stock predicated on the market value of Smith Corporation stock . . . the estate's 408 shares of Investment Company stock represented a minority interest of only 21.94 percent thereof and alone could not compel . . . liquidation. A purchaser of the stock would be without assurance that he could liquidate it for a proportional part of Investment Company's assets."

In this case the underlying asset value was $7,317.28 per share. The petitioner contended for a value in the range of $3,200 to $3,350 per share. Decision per Judge Turner was $5,700 per share.

Estate of Jessie Ring Garrett, 12 TCM 1142 (1953).

"The Ring Company was a family holding company organized in November, 1946 to hold certain assets . . . The fair market values of the assets of these two concerns are stipulated. The respondent has valued the Ring Company stock at the proportionate share of the stipulated fair market value of the underlying assets. We do not think these values are necessarily determinative of the value of the Ring Company stock . . . We are here concerned with a minority interest in a family holding company . . . Under certain circumstances it has been held that such interests in family corporations or ventures have a fair market value less than the proportionate share of the underlying assets. We think the circumstances here require a similar conclusion."

The Commissioner valued the Ring Company stock at $82.00 per share based on adjusted asset value. The estate returned the stock at $48.80 per share and had witnesses testify to $41.40 and $29.97 per share. Judge Tietjens found a per share value of $55.94.

Estate of Hazel K. Bakewell, 14 TCM 144 (1955).

Valuation of a family holding company was involved. Stock to be valued was 333 shares out of 1,000 outstanding. Net adjusted asset value per share $1,508.63. Commissioner used $1,500.00 value. Petitioner returned stock at $864.00 per share. Expert testimony was taken but not disclosed in decision. A summary of all factors in two paragraphs is the extent of Judge Tietjens' opinion. Value of $1,100.00 found.

Estate of Irene de Guebriant, 14 TC 611 (1950).

"Where stock of a family corporation has never been listed on an exchange or sold, valuation is extremely difficult. We recognize that stock in such a closed corporation is hard to sell, there being no other market except that afforded by the few other stockholders. Wood v. U.S., 29 F. Supp. 853, . . . we note that the 511 1/2 shares constituted a minority interest, approximating one-seventh of the total outstanding stock at the time of Irene de Guebriant's death. Respondent argues that the existence of a minority interest is not, by itself, sufficient grounds for holding that the fair market value of the stock was not equal to its asset value. But minority stock interests in a "closed" corporation might be worth less than the proportionate share of assets to which they attach."

Judge Hill held a value of $32.02 per share was the fair market value of estate's stock. The returned value was $28.46 per share and the Commissioner's value was $42.69 per share, which was adjusted underlying asset value.

From the foregoing it would appear that the Tax Court will certainly give great weight to arguments that a minority block of stock in a family corporation will be viewed as just that. The weight of precedent suggests that if we attempt to increase the value of such interests as being part of control, we will experience great difficulty in the courts. One prior decision, however, injects an intriguing factor into the family corporation picture. The case of Baltimore National Bank and Zenvyl Krieger v. U.S., 56-1, USTC 11576, involved the valuation for Federal estate tax purposes of the closely-held stock in a family-owned brewing company. In his decision Judge Thomsen of the U. S. District Court, Maryland District, had this comment to make:

"These cases" (prior citations not repeated here for sake of brevity) "stressed the sale value of the stock, giving little if any weight to the retention value, i.e. the right of the legatee, derived from the decedent at his death, to hold the stock subject to the restrictive agreement and to collect dividends thereon. But the retention value is important in both of the cases at bar . . .

"In <u>Worcester County Trust Co. v. Commissioner</u>, 134 F.2d 578, 582 (1st Cir. 1943) the restriction was against sale during life, but did not apply to transfers to legatees or next of kin in distribution of a stockholder's estate. In that respect it was similar in effect though not in form to the agreement in the case at bar, which permitted the creation of trusts to last during the term of the agreement. The First Circuit held that the retention value as well as the sale value should be considered; that the restriction did not impose a ceiling on value for estate tax purposes; but that since the restriction did affect the market value of the stock it should be considered as one of the 'relevant factors having a bearing' on that question.

"In gift tax cases, where the owner may continue to hold his shares if he wishes to do so, the courts have emphasized the value of the right of retention, and have held that such a restriction on the right to transfer does not limit the valuation, but is a factor which should be considered along with other elements affecting value.

"<u>Kline v. Commissioner</u>, 3 Cir., 130 F.2d 742, 743; <u>Krauss v. U.S.</u>, 5 Cir., 140 F.2d 510; <u>Commissioner of Internal Revenue v. McCann</u>, 2 Cir., 146 F.2d 385; <u>Spitzer v. Commissioner</u>, 8 Cir., 153 F.2d 957, 5 A.L.R.2d 1114; <u>Raymond J. Moore</u>, 3 T.C. 1205; <u>O'Neal, Stock Transfer Restrictions</u>, 65 Harv. L.R. 773, 813.

"Both the sale value and the retention value of the stock must be considered. In determining the latter, particular weight must be given . . . earning record over the years . . . Earnings are the principal element to be considered in determining retention value."

The District Court advances a persuasive line of reasoning in the foregoing decision and it is our opinion that some recognition of the judge's logic is warranted. Both on the basis of deductive reasoning and from the actual evidence we may see that the taxpayer holding the stock, be it an estate or beneficiary, would not be willing to sell the family interest at any price. On the other hand we must face the fact that the statutes and the courts impose and accede to the hypothetical willing buyer--willing seller concept in valuation. Thus we have to assume such parties' existence. Our task is to ascertain the dollar value at which these fictional individuals will agree to transfer the shares of a closely-held corporation as of the valuation date.

To sum up our conclusions on this factor:

1) We can be certain that the Tax Court will be inclined in all but the most exceptional cases to view a minority block of stock in a family-owned corporation as a strict minority interest.

2) The attributes of control stock may attach to such shares because of the retention value to the willing sellers, but only a strong evidentiary factual case can be expected to have a chance to prevail on this point.

MULTI-PRODUCT BUSINESSES

To an increasing extent corporations, both publicly-held and closely-held, tend to branch out into other unrelated business activities. Diversification in products or services has become very attractive to corporate managements looking for investment opportunities. Valuation of a diversified company presents unique problems to the security analyst. In your consideration of Case File 5, Handout 8-1, you should take particular note of the methods suggested for coping with the valuation of a diversified corporation.

PARTNERSHIPS

In many respects the valuation of a partnership interest, or for that matter any noncorporate business interest, will necessitate a knowledge and analysis of the same basic financial information as outlined in Lesson 4 on closely-held stock valuations. We will discuss in this lesson therefore, those aspects of partnership interest appraisals which require some modification of the corporate valuation approach. We should like to call attention at this time to the provisions of IRC †§ 1372 whereby small business corporations may elect to be taxed as an alternative type of organization. The wording of this section makes the election usable by closely-held organizations only, hence the tax effects of these provisions of the law may need consideration in appraising closely-held enterprises regardless of organization. Certainly in those instances where an election has been made it will be essential to reflect the provisions of Subchapter S of the Internal Revenue Code in an appraisal of the business.

Modification of Comparative Analysis

At the outset the study of the various financial statements of a partnership business will have to be made in the light of recognized partnership accounting methods. Thus the various partners' capital accounts should reflect the annual amounts of salaries withdrawn, profit shares, and bonus or interest credits for each of the selected period of years preceding the valuation date. The exact amount of the partnership interest to be valued, i.e., in terms of percentage of profits to which the partner was or is entitled, is an essential fact. The index of earning capacity of a partnership enterprise is the net income determined before salaries to partners and, of course, without regard for the partners' personal tax liability on their shares of the profits. Contrary to the case in corporation valuations, taxes are not properly a deduction of the business. Similarly, the salaries paid to the partners may not represent reasonable amounts for the services they perform and should be eliminated if they were reflected in the net income reported.

The Appeals Officer may well ask how do we transform the basic data about a partnership into a value determination for a given interest? Partnerships are not bought or sold on stock exchanges. In fact, even private sales of such enterprises on which accurate information is available are practically nonexistent. One method which has proved helpful is the industry comparative approach with appropriate adjustments made for differences in accounting procedures.

In brief, the earnings of comparable, listed or quoted corporations, before taxes, are related to the market prices of their securities. These ratios are compared to the partnership earnings, after estimating reasonable executive salaries, to provide some idea of the rates of capitalization suitable to a business in this particular industry. Also the ratio of market value to book value of the comparable corporations may be of interest. Although this type of analysis furnishes only rough indications of fair market value, it does permit the partnership interest to be brought into some degree of relationship with similar business equities on which market valuation is available.

It is helpful also to convert the partnership earning history to a hypothetical corporation picture by estimating taxes and executive salaries for the years analyzed. The resultant corporate basis earnings can then be compared to the actual price/earnings ratios computed for the corporations in the industry. Actually, the two approaches should not produce materially different results.

The task of intelligently estimating the amount of executive salaries which would be fair and reasonable for a particular business entity is not easy. One method used with some success is to compare the salary expenditures of similar corporations using the Internal Revenue Service Statistical Source Book as a source. These data are tabulated by corporate size as well as by industry thus permitting a meaningful analysis. Once estimates of executive salaries and corporate taxes have been deducted from the actual earnings of the partnership we obtain income figures suitable for comparison with the publicly traded stocks' price/earnings ratios. One word of caution is needed. The above adjustments to be made to the partnership's reported profits are used only for the purpose of developing a comparison with publicly-held corporations. The earnings factor which is used in valuing a partnership interest will, of course, reflect the amounts earned by the business as shown by its financial statements.

As you can see from the foregoing, the appraisal of partnership interests (and other business interests as well) does not depart very far from the accepted approach used in evaluating closely-held corporate stocks, except for the attention given to the fundamental accounting distinctions. The following paragraphs, however, do cover an element quite often present in partnerships which can prove troublesome to the appraiser.

Sales Agreements Among Partners

On occasion the members of a partnership will enter into agreements which set forth the basis on which their respective interests will be sold to the remaining partner or partners in the event of death or retirement. Where such an agreement exists and where, possibly, an actual sale of a partnership interest has taken place under the terms of such agreement the question invariably occurs, is the value for the business established conclusively by this fact? We cannot argue about the sale price if the transaction has been closed on the agreed upon basis, but we can determine a value other than that sale price if the facts so warrant. The courts have affirmed the position that although a partnership agreement may establish a selling price at, for instance, "not more than book value," such agreement is not binding on the Commissioner in fixing value for estate tax purposes. This point is stressed in the Tax Court decision in the Estate of George Marshall Trammell, 18 T.C. 662 (1952) wherein the Court sustained the Commissioner in the above contention and referred to a prior case in which a similar ruling was made (City Bank Farmers Trust Co., Executor, 23 B.T.A. 663 (1931).

Of interest also is the decision in the Estate of Robert Gannon, 21 T.C. 1073 (1954), wherein the partnership agreement provided that upon the death of a partner the surviving partners had the right to exercise an option to purchase the decedent's interest at an amount fixed annually by supplementary agreement of the partners. The partnership agreement contained no provisions for fixing the value of the partner's interest for the purpose of a lifetime transfer and there were no optional provisions for lifetime transfers. Upon the authority of the Trammell case the court found that the agreed valuation of decedent's partnership interest was not binding for Federal estate tax purposes.

The contention is frequently made that there is no goodwill in a partnership when the partners have committed themselves by contract to sell out at book value. In the memomorandum decision in the case of Estate of Samuel H. Straus v. Comm., 8 T.C.M. 442, (1949) the Tax Court held that a written agreement between partners to sell their interests in the event of death at book value without any allowance for goodwill was not binding on the Commissioner. The Court approved goodwill in this instance over and above the net asset value of the interest involved. It should be noted that in both this decision and the Trammell case, cited above, the partnerships involved were retail sales outlets owning no specific patents or franchises to which intangible value could be attributed. Thus the court was asserting that goodwill in the true sense of the word was conceivable in partnership enterprises regardless of existing agreements as to value between the partners.

By contrast the following citations should be noted:

Estate of Lionel Weil, 22 T.C. 1267 (1954). Under the terms of agreements among the members of a partnership, the decedent was prohibited from disposing of his partnership interest during his lifetime, and the surviving partners were authorized and obligated to purchase decedent's interest at a determinable price based on book value at his death, the amount payable under those agreements is the proper valuation of decedent's partnership interest for estate tax purposes. The previous recommendation for appeal was rejected by the Solicitor General, who decided that the surviving partners' promise imposed a legal liability, and decedent's agreement not to sell was the consideration in this respect.

Brodrick v. Gore, 224 F.2d 892, (10th Cir. 1955). Executors under deceased partner's will were bound to sell to surviving partners and they to purchase decedent's interest in partnership per book value thereof. Under the partnership agreement, such interest had no value to decedent's estate in excess of its book value, so that Federal estate tax should be based on such value, rather than the possibly higher fair market value of the interest. In the Action on Decision, it is pointed out that a local court had held agreement valid; this, coupled with absence of collusion, bad faith, or a non-adversary proceeding, was a judicial determination of book value. No certiorari.

It must be pointed out in summary that a bona fide sale of a partnership interest, whether based on an agreement or not, may afford an adequate basis for the valuation of the asset, since under the Regulations the fair market value of the estate's property is defined as the price at which the asset will change hands between a willing buyer and a willing seller neither being under any compulsion to buy or to sell. The applicable facts affecting value must be considered in either case, and the final determination must be supported by such facts.

In conclusion, if a sales agreement between partners provides for mutual commitment, adequate consideration and reflects a normal business intent, it will probably be held enforceable, in which case the probabilities of the agreement limiting value for tax purposes will be improved.

Lesson 10

COMMON ERRORS IN VALUATION – NON-RECOGNIZED METHODS; FORMULAS

CONTENTS

OBJECTIVES

At the end of this lesson you will be able to:

1. Describe the A.R.M. 34 approach to valuing business intangibles.

2. Explain why A.R.M. 34 and all such formula approaches to the valuation of business interests are invalid.

INTRODUCTION

As occurs so often in a technical specialty area a body of typical errors have achieved popularity and acceptance by the uninformed in valuation of business interests for tax purposes. The more bothersome and recurring types of erroneous valuation methods or approaches include 1) using inapplicable methods, 2) using formulas, 3) relying on subsequent events, 4) making careless comparative analyses, 5) applying arbitrary discounts, 6) failing to consider nonrecurrent items, and 7) failing to adjust for nonoperating assets or income.

In this lesson we begin consideration of the more troublesome conceptual errors and of mistaken applications which are often found in practice. Some of these erroneous concepts are more persistent than others. For example, despite repeated efforts by such divergent institutions as the security analyst profession and the IRS, there is frequent adherence to the formula approach in making closely-held corporate stock valuation by taxpayers and tax practitioners. In fact it was only with the issuance of Rev. Rul. 68-609 that the Service was able to clearly direct examining officers to cease using the so-called A.R.M. 34 approach in valuing business interests.

A prime reason for Appeals Officers to object to valuation by formula is because such approach is not accepted by knowledgable people in the investment industry. We should be constantly on the lookout for methods that are inappropriate to the specific industry or not recognized by investors generally. This leads to the first so-called common error we will address in this course.

One of the primary premises of sound appraisal practice is that the methods and approach used by the appraiser should correspond to those used by the investing public and accepted in the particular industry involved. Appraisers who disregard this rule place themselves on dangerous ground. We have seen one instance where an appraiser relied upon nonstandard methods to arrive at his conclusions, then failed completely upon cross-examination to justify his appraisal or overcome the lack of a firm foundation for his opinion. And, as a result, his testimony was virtually ignored by the court. If the appraiser uses a method of appraisal which has a specific application, but applies it outside of its own particular field, the results are not reliable.

One of the first valuation cases which was heard by the Board of Tax Appeals shortly after it was formed involved the determination of the portion of the allowable depletion the lessor of certain iron mines could deduct each year. The law prescribed merely a reasonable allowance for depletion. In presenting the case the Internal Revenue Service advanced the following theory: (1) Depletion should be allowed in equal amounts per unit each year rather than in variable amounts which increased steadily or decreased steadily from year to year; (2) A sinking fund formula was the only basis upon which such an allowance could be accomplished; and (3) The Hoskold sinking fund formula which the Internal Revenue Service was using for mine valuation but not for any other type of valuation, was the proper valuation formula to use in this instance. It may be noted that the Hoskold sinking fund formula was used and accepted by the mining industry.

The Board decided the case in favor of the Commissioner. Since this decision, however, there has been widespread use of the Hoskold formula in appraisals for tax purposes of diverse properties where investors and members of the particular industry involved have never used it. This is a misapplication. The formula is effective if used by a person who knows what it does and how it should be applied, but it gives distorted results if it is used in strange fields by inexperienced appraisers.

Another illustration would be in the valuation of physical properties on the basis of cost of reproduction new reduced by observed physical deterioation. This approach is not apprpriate in most cases for determining fair market value. It is a method developed for insurance purposes primarily to inventory property and to estimate the cost of replacing it in its present condition in the event of its loss by fire or other casualty. For this purpose, it is a good and generally accepted method of appraisal. Many appraisal companies and appraisers specialize in this type of appraisal. However, any competent appraiser who uses this method would never hold that it produces fair market value as defined by the tax statutes. In this connection, see Soaper (R. H.), 3 B.T.A. 701 (1926), where the Board said "The statute does not ask what it would cost to replace the assets in their worn condition, but what price could be obtained for them in a fair market." Also note Supreme Court decisions <u>Western Union Telegraph Co. v. Taggart</u>, 163 U. S. 1 (1896), "The cost of the property, or of its replacement, is by no means a true measure of its value;" and <u>Standard Oil Co. of N. J. v. Southern Pacific Co. et al.</u>, 268 U. S. 146 (1925) "* * * Cost of reproduction as of the date of valuation constitutes evidence properly to be considered in the ascertainment of value. (however) It is to be borne in mind that value is the thing to be found, and that neither cost of reproduction new, nor that less depreciation is the measure or sole guide. The ascertainment of value is not controlled by artificial rules. It is not a matter of formulas, but there must be a reasonable judgment having its basis in a proper consideration of all relevant facts."

The principal defect of reproduction cost as a determiner of fair market value is that it ignores obsolescence. Most structures and equipment, machines, etc., are retired from use not because of wear and tear, but because of obsolescence. In other words, technological advances have resulted in the present machinery or equipment producing a less economical result for the manufacturer than would be possible if new machinery were employed. This, of course, will place owners of old equipment and machinery in less favorable positions with respect to their competitors, and if they are to remain in business they will eventually have to avail themselves of improved methods in order to earn profits.

There are other methods which can be easily misapplied by the imprudent appraiser. However, the two cited above should suffice to bring the point home. As in every other field, appraisals can best be made by informed and experienced persons who know the limitations of the methods they are applying and who know the standard and accepted procedure to use in a given valuation. To ignore these precepts is to invite a disastrous failure if the issue goes to trial.

USE OF FORMULAS--DENIAL OF THE JUDGMENT FACTOR

One of the most frequently encountered errors in appraisal is the use of a formula to determine a question of fact which on a reasonable basis must be resolved in view of all pertinent circumstances. A.R.M. 34,2 CB 31 and A.R.M. 68,3 CB 43, are the formulas we encounter most frequently although there are many others. A.R.M. (Appeals and Review Memorandum) 34 originally was a rule of thumb method or formula adopted for the purpose of computing the loss of goodwill value by breweries because of prohibition. It was provided as a means of determining the value as of March 1, 1913, or any other date, of such enterprises. While the ruling cautions that this formula is not to be regarded as controlling if better evidence is presented in any special case, nevertheless, A.R.M. 34 has been applied indiscriminately by tax practitioners and by members of the Internal Revenue Service since it was published. On occasion the Tax Court has recognized A.R.M. 34 as a means of arriving at a fair market value. The latest and most controlling decisions on valuation, however, relegate the use of a formula to a position of being a last resort. A.R.M. 34 was published

271

in 1920 but since that time it has continually appeared in the annals of tax valuation and resulted in many improper appraisals.

Typical Formula Approaches

The form of the computation prescribed by A.R.M. 34 is as follows:

Net tangible assets at date of appraisal		$100,000
Yearly earnings, first preceding year	$ 20,000	
Yearly earnings, second preceding year	30,000	
Yearly earnings, third preceding year	15,000	
Yearly earnings, fourth preceding year	40,000	
Yearly earnings, fifth preceding year	25,000	
Total	$130,000	
Average annual earnings for 5 preceding years		$ 26,000
Less: 8% of net tangible asset value ($100,000 x .08)- earnings attributable to tangible assets		8,000
Balance of earnings attributable to intangible assets		$ 18,000
Recapitulation:		
Value of intangible assets ($18,000 capitalized at 15%)		120,000
Add the value of the tangible assets		100,000
Value of the Business		$220,000

By such a formula the same value would be found in 1970 as in 1933 although values per dollar of earnings actually were very different in those two years. The basic defect is apparent; the rates of return which are applied to tangibles and to intangibles are completely arbitrary and have no foundation in fact. For this reason the application of this, or for that matter any other formula, leaves the appraiser wide open to embarrassing cross-examination.

The 8% rate, or any other arbitrary rate of earnings as a normal return on tangible assets in any and all industries, cannot be demonstrated to have a reasonable basis. Similarly, the 15% rate or any specific rate on intangible assets is not in itself a supportable figure. If there were a somewhat comparable business which had earned $50,000 per year as an average for five years and which had been sold for $400,000 cash it could be said that there was a 12 1/2% indicated rate of return on total investment but no one could ascertain what had been the rates of return on the tangible and intangible assets. All that can be said for A.R.M. 34 or a similar formula method of capitalization using two rates of interest, is that you hope to get a good answer based upon two bad guesses. It is difficult enough to get one reasonably accurate rate of capitalization using normal appraisal methods such as the comparison with market prices for publicly-held stocks. To get two fairly accurate rates, one for tangibles and the other for intangibles, other than by the use of pure guesswork, is impossible.

In the illustration above, the computed value for the business of $220,000 represents a rate of capitalization of 11.5% and 12% in terms of latest years or average earnings. Such rates may not even be adequate returns on the <u>tangible</u> assets of the business. By rate of capitalization we mean the number of times the earnings figure used, average or current, that the business is worth. Of course, any capitalization of earnings must take into consideration the economic conditions prevailing at the specific date of appraisal, including those conditions controlling in the industry, in this particular company's geographical area, and even in the national economy. By a rate of capitalization of 12% we are saying that the value of the company represents approximately 8 1/2 times the average earnings. In this case the average earnings were $26,000 and 8 1/2 times this figure results in $221,000.

It has been observed for example in patent valuations that the use of A.R.M. 34 results in the following erroneous assumptions: (a) the business has intangible value based on an application of A.R.M. 34, and (b) this intangible value must be attributed to the patents because the business owns patents.

There is no direct logic which attributes all intangible value in a certain enterprise to any particular asset which it owns whether that asset be tangible or intangible. Consequently, the practice of automatically applying whatever intangible value is found for a business to such assets as the patent or the copyright or the trademark or similar intangible item has no basis in fact.

Should we assume that a business does have intangible asset value, say of $120,000, and that it owns patents having unexpired remaining lives, there still is no evidence that this intangible value pertains to the patents in whole or in part. It may be attributable to some extent to better than average management, extraordinary location of the business which enables it to earn greater than customary profits, the effects of prior or current advertising, the going concern value which results from efficient selection and organization of personnel, or any one of a number of factors other than the patents. The patents themselves might be given away or sold for a nominal sum without affecting future earnings one iota.

An illustration of just how the A.R.M. 34 formula will result in a nondefensible appraisal will be given later.

The courts have said that formulas may be used to appraise fair market values only in the absence of better evidence or possibly as a check on the other evidence. There follows citations and extracted comments from decisions which clearly indicate the position of the Courts on the use of formulas: In <u>Georgia Railway Co. v. The Railroad Commission,</u> 262 U. S. 625 (1922) the Supreme Court said, "The value cannot be determined solely by application of a formula." The most explicit statement on this subject was made by the Board of Tax Appeals in <u>(Jas.) Couzens,</u> 11 B.T.A. 1040, 1165 (1928) where it stated "There may

273

be no slavish adherence to a formula (in determining value) . . . ."
Also, see the opinions in <u>Crawford v. Helvering,</u> 70 F.2d 744 (D.C.
Cir. 1934) where it was observed that there is no definite formula for
determining fair market value and the question is one of fact to be
determined by the evidence; <u>Mills (W.P.),</u> 5 TCM 730 (1946), which
found capitalizations by formula of earnings and dividends were not
accepted as evidence of market value; <u>Hotel de France Co.,</u> 1 B.T.A.
28 (1924) where the Board stated (formulas) "can only serve to tie
together the evidentiary facts. Alone they are helpless;" and in
<u>Minnesota Rate Cases,</u> 230 U.S. 352, 434 (1912) where it was held that
the ascertainment of value is not a matter of formula "but there must
be a reasonable judgment having its basis in a proper consideration of
all relevant facts."

I.R.S. Clarification of Use of A.R.M. 34

The Service has made several important efforts to try and control the
usage of the A.R.M. 34 approach for tax valuation purposes. Revenue
Rulings 65-192 and 65-193, CB 1965-2, 259 and 370, which were referred
to in Lesson 4 set forth the areas of applicability of the formula.
The rulings, incidentally, also put the Service on record to the
effect that Rev. Rul. 59-60 is fully applicable in the valuation of
closely-held stocks for Federal <u>income</u> tax purposes. Rev. Rul. 65-192
states that:

> "The formula approach set forth in A.R.M. 34, C.B. 2,31
> (1920), and A.R.M. 68, C.B. 3, 43 (1920), has no valid appli-
> cation in determinations of the fair market values of corpo-
> rate stocks or of business interests, unless it is necessary
> to value the intangible assets of the corporation or the
> intangible assets included in the business interest. The
> formula approach may be used in determining the fair market
> values of intangible assets only if there is no better basis
> therefor available. In applying the formula, the average
> earnings period and the capitalization rates are dependent
> upon the facts and circumstances pertinent thereto in such
> case."

By far the most significant development within the Service was the
issuance of the Rev. Rul. 68-609, 1968-2 C.B. 327 at last superseding
both A.R.M. 34 and A.R.M. 68. Although the "formula" is restated in
this ruling its usefulness was accurately described by the following
excerpt:

> "Accordingly, the "formula" approach may be used for determin-
> ing the fair market value of intangible assets of a business
> <u>only</u> if there is no better basis therefor available" (under-
> lining supplied).

An Example of Formula Application

As a case in point to illustrate the danger of unreasoning reliance upon formulas in the solution of valuation problems we will describe the valuation problem involved in the Estate of Richard Marigold, date of death February 6, 1979. Names and dates will be fictitious but the facts are taken from an actual case. This estate owned 172 shares out of a total 1,000 shares outstanding of the common stock of the Marigold Bookstore, Inc. A summary of the history of the company and the financial data available follows:

(1) The company was founded in 1891 by the father of the deceased. The company operated two book stores in Bakerville, Virginia, serving the student body of State University. The primary business was the retailing of text books and school supplies with an incidental trade in office equipment and athletic equipment. The stock was closely held by members of the Marigold family and a few employees.

(2) A balance sheet as of December 31, 1978, disclosed a book value per share of $119.86. This amount included $1.16 per share of intangible value entitled Goodwill and Copyrights which was carried on the books. Current assets totaled $142,938.89 consisting principally of cash ($43,022), Accounts Receivable ($30,637) and Inventory ($65,167). Current liabilities were $28,662.51 and working capital amounted to $114.276.38, or $114.28 per share. Net tangible asset value was $118.70 per share.

(3) Operating information covering the period 1974-1978, inclusive, was available only in condensed form. The schedule following discloses the pertinent facts obtained from such information:

Year	Sales	Taxable Income	Net Income	Earned Per Share	Dividends Per Share
1974	$390,440	$47,340	$27,280	$27.28	$13.95
1975	349,960	31,450	21,300	21.30	15.00
1976	323,230	26,360	18,220	18.22	15.00
1977	321,440	24,280	16,200	16.20	15.00
1978	324,840	22,530	15,050	15.05	15.00
Total			$98,050	$98.05	$73.95
Average			19,610	19.61	14.79

The examining estate tax attorney recommended a value of $247.97 per share for the 172 shares included in the estate. The returned value was $127.35 per share. To arrive at the recommended value the agent used a variation of the formula which appeared in A.R.M. 34. The computation used in this case to support a value of $247.97 per share for the Marigold Bookstore, Inc. common stock was as follows:

275

(1) Average net tangible assets and average net income were computed for the five-year period ended December 31, 1978:

Year Ended 12/31	Net Tangible Assets	Net Income	Net Worth
1974	$152,207.24	$39,266.73	
1975	167,718.05	21,295.00	
1976	155,951.21	18,215.87	
1977	148,962.50	16,203.49	
1978	147,361.10	15,045.90	$127,345.05
Total	$772,200.10	$110,026.99	
Average	$154,440.02	$22,005.40	

(2) Application of formula:

Average annual net income	$ 22,005.40
Less: 8% of average net tangible assets of $154,440.52 or	12,355.20
Net income attributable to intangible assets	$ 9,650.20
Value of intangibles – $9,650.20 capitalized at 8%	$120,627.50
Add: Net worth per balance sheet	127,345.05
Total	$247,972.55
Value per share for 1,000 shares	$247.97

Incidental to the primary error of relying on a formula to determine fair market value, incorrect amounts were used in the computation. The figures shown under net tangible assets are in reality total assets for each year. The income indicated for 1974 is considerably greater than that appearing in the financial data supplied by the taxpayer and no reason was given for using the higher figure. Finally the December 31, 1978, net worth should have been $119,857.25, or $119.85 per share, which figure included $1.16 per share for goodwill on the books. Even if these inaccuracies had been corrected, the formula approach to valuation questions such as that involved here is entirely erroneous.

What has been the effect of the examiner's reliance on a formula to evaluate this stock?

(1) By using an average earnings per year he has overlooked completely the vital fact of the company's declining earnings in the latest years. Because of the clearly defined trend, the 1978 income figure of $15,045.90 is far more representative of the future earnings potential of the business than is the average. Latest year's earnings are the most indicative of future prospects. On the basis of the

returned value of $127.35 per share, 1978 earnings reflect a return of 11.8%. Such percentage does not appear unreasonable in this case.

(2) Application of arbitrary capitalization rates reflecting an 8% return on tangibles and the capitalization of remaining earnings at 8% to obtain intangible value amounts merely to the making of two guesses of questionable nature without factual evidence to sustain either of them. If we assume that a fair rate of return for this type of business is 8%, the better procedure is to capitalize a representative earnings figure (in this instance 1978 income) at that rate. To attempt to segregate value based on so-called normal earnings and those produced by whatever goodwill or other intangible assets the business may possess requires a degree of clairvoyance unobtainable by any appraiser.

(3) The examiner's value indicates that this business was worth almost $248,000 as of the basic date. In essence, this valuation attributes approximately 100% of intangible value to this small college retail bookstore. (Net tangible asset value was $118,700.) On the basis of 1978 earnings the suggested value represents an overall capitalization rate of 6.1%. When it is recognized that the capital stock of some of the largest and most progressive corporations in the country were selling on the market at rates of capitalization many times higher than this as of the basic date, or stated another way at lower price/earnings ratios, the unrealistic aspects of this valuation become apparent.

(4) The facts show that earnings are declining. Current 1978 income was only $15.05 per share and the December 31, 1978, book value was $119.86 per share. By resorting to a formula valuation the examiner ignored the significance of these facts and gave no weight to the size or type of business or its economic environment. Unrealistic methods reflecting a fictitious value have been substituted for the exercise of common sense and judgment weighing the factual evidence and arriving at an opinion in accordance with accepted methods and normal practice.

Comparing Stock Market Evaluation to the Formula Approach

One final comment on the unreasonableness of a formula approach to security valuation may be worthwhile. This concerns the practical question of how and on what basis transactions on the public security exchanges evaluate corporate intangibles.

In a study conducted in the Appeals Division several years ago we found evidence of an interesting correlation between market value and intangible value in the corporate stocks traded on the New York Stock Exchange. What is particularly significant is the fact that the conclusion suggested by this study was diametrically opposed to the goodwill theory outlined in A.R.M. 34.

The main purpose of the study was to ascertain what, if any, relationship existed between the size of a merchandising or manufacturing corporation, its type of capital structure and its price/earnings ratios, reflected by the market price of the stock in the New York Stock Exchange. One of the byproducts of the study was a schedule showing the market value apparently being ascribed to corporate intangibles by the investing public. To illustrate, it was found, as a general rule, that as the price/asset value ratios increased, corresponding price/earnings ratios did likewise although at a considerably lesser rate. The table below summarizes the statistics underlying this conclusion:

No. of Companies	Price/Asset Value Ratio	Price/Earnings Ratio
10	0 – 40%	19.37
54	40 – 60%	9.98
129	60 – 80%	9.10
144	80 – 100%	9.69
108	100 – 120%	11.40
58	120 – 140%	10.70
61	140 – 160%	11.68
32	160 – 180%	12.90
31	180 – 200%	13.80
37	200 – 250%	13.55
43	250 – 400%	19.51
8	400% – & over	23.50

One notable exception was found with respect to those companies which were selling for less than 40% of their tangible asset value, for in such cases price/earnings ratios averaged at the high level of 19.37. On the other hand companies which were selling between 80% and 100% of their tangible asset value recorded an average price/earnings ratio of 9.69. As the price/asset ratios moved upward from the 100% level, however, price/earnings ratios tended to increase.

If we set up a hypothetical example based on the data above and work an A.R.M. 34 computation starting with market value instead of working toward it, the following result is obtained:

Assume we have to value one of the 108 corporation securities falling in the 100% to 120% group above (all amounts are on a per share basis)-

Tangible asset value – $10
Market value   – $11
Earnings ($11   11.40) $.97
Indicated capitalization rate
   ($.97 $11) = 8.9%(or about 11 times)
Return on tangibles 8.9% x $10 =   –.89
"Excess earnings" $.08
Indicated return on intangibles
   (.08 x $1) = 8.0%(or about 12 times)

As we know the formula prescribes a dual capitalization rate, one attributable to the tangible assets and a second higher rate attributable to intangibles. The computation above seems to show that the investing public will pay more per dollar of earnings attributable to intangible assets than it will pay for the earnings from the tangible assets. Or stated another way, the capitalization rate which may be said to reflect the earning power of the intangibles drops as the overall value increases. Presumably, therefore in lieu of an 8% (or 10%) return on net tangibles and a 15% (or 20%) capitalization of "excess earnings" to find intangible value, the rates should be reversed. In any case, according to the market study, the rate of return on intangibles would in many instances be the lower of the two, and under no circumstances can a realistic correlation between stock value, price/earnings or price/asset value ratios and intangible values be obtained through application of a formula approach.

Lesson 11

COMMON ERRORS IN VALUATION - DISCOUNTS; SUBSEQUENT EVENTS

CONTENTS

OBJECTIVES

At the end of this lesson you will be able to:

1. List key characteristics of the four types of discounts considered.

2. Explain when and why such discounts are invalid in corporate security valuations.

3. Describe the major reason why the use of subsequent events by an appraiser is erroneous.

APPLYING ARBITRARY DISCOUNTS

This lesson describes four typical situations where discounts of closely-held stock values or other business interest values are outwardly or secretly used by taxpayers or their representatives. Naturally, the attempts to discount heavily are made in the valuations accompanying Federal estate tax or gift tax returns. The less value reported, the less tax to be paid. The premise of this lesson is not that discounting is always to be avoided, but rather that the proper use of the process is permissable only when justified.

Lack of Marketability

By far the most frequent claim for substantial discounts in value of closely-held securities is made on the basis that the stock lacks marketability. It is axiomatic that the value of a stock is reduced by anything which tends to reduce its marketability. The Court of Claims stated this principle most concisely in the case of Central Trust Co. v. U.S., 305 F.2d 393 (Ct. Cl., 1962) as follows:

> "It seems clear. . ., that an unlisted closely-held stock of a corporation . . ., in which trading is infrequent and which therefore lacks marketability, is less attractive than a similar stock which is listed on an exchange and has ready access to the investing public."

The extent, however, to which any restriction or limitation on market-ability will reduce the value of a specific stock as of a certain date is entirely a matter of opinion. Appraisers can, therefore, let their conscience be their guide in reducing values for the all encompassing factors of marketability.

If the owners of closely-held stocks should try to list a block of such securities on a stock exchange for sale to the public, they would probably have to make the offerings through underwriters or syndicates. We expect that the price at which these stocks will be offered to the investing public will be lower than the market prices for reasonably comparable stocks which were already listed and being traded publicly. There will be costs for registering nonpublicly traded stocks with the Securities and Exchange Commission involving, among other fees, the expense of preparing a prospectus. In addition, the underwriters themselves will have to receive commissions. The actual costs of such an offering might be as high as 10% to 25% of the selling price to the public. Instead of free shares of the stock, voting trust certificates might be marketed, and with the restriction on voting rights these certificates might be appraised at a reduced value. The appraiser should not lose sight of one very significant fact, however. Most stocks which are closely-held are so held because there have <u>never been willing sellers--not because there have never been any willing buyers</u>.

If a stock is held by a family group and the company is headed by one member of the family, whose estate holds a substantial number of shares of the stock of the company, it is claimed by many taxpayers that the death of the decedent would adversely affect the value of the company's stock. The tragic effect of the loss of the "guiding light" of the business, is often advanced despite the contradictory evidence of subsequent earnings and progress far better than those reported during the decedent's term of office. Another claim to reduce the so-called marketability of the stock is that the controlling stock-holders mismanage the company and cannot be ousted, or that the controlling stockholders paid themselves overgenerous salaries for their services to the corporation. Such arguments will have to be appraised in the light of the facts in each case. It is true that the death of a capable manager may work adversely as far as the corporation is concerned. However, as we indicated in Lesson 4, in many instances the corporation has foreseen this and has provided adequate insurance to enable it to hire competent management personnel upon the death of a corporate founder.

As in other factors which are used as a basis for claiming a discount, the marketability factor must be considered but by no means must it be thought to be controlling or all important in these types of valuations. The most effective way to deal with the arguments that market-ability reduces the value of the stock is to indicate that you have taken it into consideration in your overall appraisal of the stock and for that reason you have applied a conservative capitalization rate, or weighted certain of the other factors from a conservative standpoint to give effect to this marketability factor. In no case should arbitrary percentage discounts be resorted to as an answer to the claim of lack of marketability. Rev. Rul. 77-287, included as Handout 15-1 of this course is relevant to this subject.

The strong prohibition against specific "rules of thumb" or flat percentages as a lack of marketability discount arises from our essential understanding of the valuation process. There are an infinite variety of pertinent factors affecting a stock's fair market value and its marketability is only one of these. We face an impossible task if we approach the problem of valuation from the standpoint of assigning specific numerical or percentage weights to each factor. By far the most rational and defensible approach is to state that the value is less than that which would be assigned a fully marketable equity. The dollar or percentage amount of reduction is better left unstated if at all possible.

Sometimes, however, an appraiser will be requested to be very specific and to quantify the amount of discount for lack of marketability (as well as for other factors). This is frequently the case during cross examination at trial. In such an instance the testimony may lack credibility and may be disregarded if the witness is unable to speak to this point. For that reason it is advisable to examine the new issue market of companies whose stock is going public for the first time. It may be possible to select a few new issues, around the valuation date, of companies of comparable quality, size or earnings history. By reference to the underwriting discounts and miscellaneous expenses experienced by these new issues, it is possible to develop a reasonable judgment of the cost of creating a public market for the stock being valued, expressed as a percentage of gross proceeds. This may be useful as objective evidence of the marketability factor's valuation.

Minority Interest

We would probably get fairly unanimous agreement that the contention for a discount because of a minority interest is the second most frequent argument proposed by taxpayer's representatives. The statement is usually made that a share of stock of a minority block is worth considerably less than a similar share in a controlling block of stock. Of course, where there are actually controlling blocks sold, they will usually bring a larger price than small minority interests in the same or similar organization. However, you can very easily overcome the arguments for a minority interest discount by referring to and relying upon the comparable corporation analysis. In the first place, listed stocks are traded in minority blocks only. Therefore, the price/earnings ratios and price/assets ratios which are derived from the analysis of comparable corporations reflect the investor's reaction to the various factors of valuation in buying and selling minority interests. It is entirely proper that these ratios have relevance in the valuation of a minority block of a closely-held corporation.

282

Another point is that we have to assume that the controlling stock-holders and officers of a company will live up to the fiduciary responsibility with which they are entrusted. By law they are not to take unfair advantage of the minority stockholders and they can be subject to legal action brought against them by the minority stock-holders if they conduct themselves improperly. Theoretically, unless we assume that the controlling stockholders are taking unfair advantage of the minority stockholders, there is no reason to appraise their stock at different values per share.

It is unrealistic to expect that the position concerning discounts for minority interests will always prevail in settlement negotiations. The United States Tax Court and other courts have on occasion sanctioned specific discounts for this factor. The principle of minority interest discounts has been accepted by the courts and we should note the two following landmark decisions on the issue:

1. <u>Cravens v. Welch</u> 10 F. Supp. 94 (D.C. Cal., 1935). This was an income tax valuation case and the Government was contending for a minority interest discount. The court found for the Government stating ". . . minority stock interests in a 'closed' corporation are usually worth much less than the proportionate share of the assets to which they attach."

2. <u>Mathilde B. Hooper</u> 41 B.T.A. 114 (1940), acq. and nonacq. 1942-1 C.B. 9, 24. This decision applied the reasoning in <u>Cravens</u> to the estate tax valuation area.

On the other hand the denial of any so-called minority discount in valuing shares of a family-owned investment holding corporation was promulgated in <u>Richardson v. Commissioner</u> 2 T.C.M. 1039 (1943), aff'd 151 F.2d 102 (2nd Cir., 1945), cert. denied 326 U.S. 796 (1946). In this case the Tax Court judge ruled that because the taxpayer and his family owned all of the stock no minority interest discount should be permitted.

Hidden Discounts

And finally we come to the most difficult kind of unwarranted discount to detect--so-called hidden discounts. Frequently arbitrary discounts are not taken directly but are hidden beneath other factors as they are applied during the appraisal. For instance, if the appraiser premises his or her valuation upon an average annual earnings figure of $25,000 per year for the past 15 years when current earnings for the most recent year are $100,000, and such current earnings can be reasonably expected to continue, the appraiser has in effect used a hidden discount of 75%. Similarly, if a 20% rate of capitalization is used when 10% is the going rate for publicly-held stocks of comparable companies, there is a 50% hidden discount in this appraisal. It is not difficult to select so-called comparatives which are not comparable or which distort the overall ratio for one reason or another and thus obtain rates of capitalization which reflect these hidden discounts. This is an especially favored device of appraisers with easy consciences who can use the system to produce desired results rather than an impartial objective appraisal.

In summary, we might refer to hidden discounts as a distortion of the underlying facts which pertain to each appraisal. If the appraiser exercises common sense and sound judgment in selecting and analyzing the facts, hidden discounts will not be injected into the valuation. Appeals Officers should be constantly alert to this type of deviation from sound valuation principles.

SUBSEQUENT EVENTS

In general, all courts of law in the United States adhere to the rules excluding subsequent events from evidence in cases requiring appraisals at specific dates. As to the inadmissibility of subsequent events in the forming of an opinion as of an earlier date we can cite Boyd v. Wyly, 124 U.S. 105, 107 (1887) and the Conqueror, 166 U.S. 110 (1897) another early decision.

The United States Tax Court has in the past accepted evidence as to subsequent events not as evidence of value or as the foundation upon which the value is made, but merely as confirmation of the reasonableness or accuracy of estimates of the future, allegedly made by the appraiser on the basis of facts known at the date of appraisal. Of course, from a realistic standpoint this Tax Court practice permits appraisers to make remarkably accurate prophecies of the future. It is quite possible to be 100% right in their so-called estimates if they choose to be. In this connection see Couzens v. Commissioner, 11 BTA 1040, 1165 (1928) Gilbert Butler 4 BTA 756(1926); and Dwight and Lloyd Sintering Co., Inc, 1 BTA 179(1924).

A particularly interesting and probably noteworthy opinion on the use of subsequent events is found in the decision in Ithaca Trust Co. v. U.S. 279 U.S. 151, 155 (1929) handed down by Justice Holmes. An excerpt from this opinion follows:

"The question is whether the amount of the dimunition is to be determined by the event as it turned out of the widow's death within six months or by mortality tables showing the probabilities as they stood on the day when testator died. The first impression is that it is absurd to resort to statistical probabilities when you know the fact. But this is due to inaccurate thinking."

"Tempting as it is to correct uncertain probabilities by the now certain fact we are of the opinion that it cannot be done but that the wife's interest must be estimated from mortality tables".

284

"Like all values as the word is used in the law it depends largely on more or less certain prophecies of the future; and the value is not less real at the time if later the prophecy turns out false than when it comes true* * *."

The Service itself has a history of ruling out consideration of subsequent events in valuation problems. In this respect we refer to CB I-1, A.R.R. 747, page 353; CB I-2, A.R.R. 1086, page 122; and 3 CB A.R.R. 161, page 345.

In Sinclair Refining Co. v. Jenkins, 289 U.S. 689(1933), there was a period of patent infringement rather than an appraisal at a fixed date to be decided upon. For purposes of assessing damages the Court accepted evidence as to earnings from the patents after the cessation of the infringement to show what earnings might have been realized during the infringement. That would seem to be a device to which the Court resorted to be sure that the infringer did not escape just punishment through the use of legal technicalities. But in American Chemical Paint Co. v. Comm. 66 F. 2d 381, (3rd Cir. 1933) overruling and reversing 25 BTA 1208, (1932) the Third Circuit cited the Sinclair case in support of its ruling that subsequent events were admissible in evidence as to value at a fixed earlier date. A very few other Court decisions are premised on subsequent events. In Guggenhiem v. Helvering, 117 F. 2d 469 (2nd Cir. 1941) cert. denied, 314 U.S. 621 (1941) it was held that the American Chemical Paint Co. decision was due to a misinterpretation of the opinion in Sinclair Refining Co. v. Jenkins.

Foresight rather than hindsight is the basis which must be used for valuation. This is certainly reasonable in view of the fact that the appraiser must put himself or herself in the position of a willing buyer and a willing seller who, of course, as of the valuation date would have no knowledge of subsequent events.

Lesson 12

COMMON ERRORS IN VALUATION – CARELESS USE
OF COMPARATIVES

CONTENTS

OBJECTIVES

At the end of this lesson you will be able to:

1. Identify at least seven factors of similarity to look for in selecting corporations for use in a comparative analysis.

2. Explain how dissimilarity of rate of growth or capital structure can invalidate a publicly held corporation as a useful comparative company.

CARELESS SELECTION OF COMPARATIVES

As noted in our disucssion of Revenue Ruling 59-60, in Lesson 6, the use of comparatives is one of the most useful techniques available to the appraiser for determining the fair market value of closely-held stock. In using the comparative analysis, however, it is essential to select valid comparatives in order for the study to be meaningful.

Some points to consider in selecting corporations that are comparable are listed below:

(a) Is the company engaged in the same or a similar type of business?

(b) Is the position of the company in the competitive field similar to that of the company to be valued? On this point we would consider such factors as the size of the company, its reputation, the quality of its management, etc.

(c) Does the company have a fairly similar rate of growth as measured by gross income?

(d) Are the percentages of net income to gross income and net income to sales and similar analyses in line?

(e) Are the type and adequacy of plant facilities and working capital comparable?

286

(f) Is diversity or lack thereof of the company's products or services comparable to the corporation to be valued?

(g) Is capital structure of the corporation which we are using as a comparative as similar as possible to that of the company we are valuing? If not, some adjustment for this difference should be made.

Most of the above points are self-explanatory, however, a few words may be appropriate on some of them. In ascertaining if the corporations which we are using as comparatives are engaged in the same or a similar type of business as the company to be valued, we will have to make allowances for the inevitable, unique characteristics that every business enterprise possesses. It may be impossible to find corporations whose financial information is published and whose stocks are traded either on an exchange or over-the-counter, engaged in a reasonably similar type of business. The rule of reason will have to apply. Although the type of product may not be exactly the same as between two given companies, the market and the economic history governing the manufacturing of such products may be so identical, that the listed corporation can quite validly be used as a comparative.

Additional factors such as the competitive position of a company, its size, business reputation, quality of management, should be checked and the appraiser should be aware of the relative status of the comparative corporations in these respects. By no means, however, should companies be discarded as comparatives solely because of a distinction in these matters. In the usual case, we will find reliable and helpful comparatives to be in short supply and therefore the appraiser should adopt a liberal attitude in selecting those to use for his or her analysis. On the growth and income trends, as well as the relation of net income to gross income or to sales, it is important that these factors be weighed and commented upon in selection of comparatives. Here again, judgment has to come into the picture, always with the thought in mind that an expert witness testifying to a valuation will have to support the selection of comparatives with convincing reasons, showing why they are comparable and why whatever differences that exist were not thought to be disqualifying. The magnitude of a company's investment in plant and equipment, its working capital, net current asset value, liquid ratio, and diversity of products are elements which require consideration but should be accorded less weight as far as influencing the appraiser's decision to reject a given comparable company. In summary, we might say that if any of the foregoing items differ to a substantial degree from the same factor in the corporation to be valued, serious consideration should be given to omitting that listed or publicly-traded corporation from the comparative analysis.

One of the most essential factors which must be recognized in a comparison of this type is the difference in capital structure which invariably exists between one corporation and another. The unlisted, closely-held corporation will, in most cases, have a common stock issue, little or no funded debt, and no senior securities. On the other hand, many listed corporations (and in any given selection of comparatives an appraiser is bound to find some) have one or more preferred stock issues, and funded debt in the form of corporate bonds, debentures, or even long term bank loans. With a more complex capital structure a company invariably shows a different common stock price/earnings ratio from that of an enterprise with a simple capital structure. This point will be discussed in more detail later in the lesson.

In the paragraphs to follow, some of the pitfalls which must be guarded against in selecting and analyzing comparatives are discussed in detail.

Lack of Comparability in the Rate of Growth as Measured by Net Income

For purposes of illustrating this point we will set up a hypothetical problem. First, we will assume the following income pattern with respect to two imaginary corporations:

Income for the Year	Company A	Company B
1975	$100,000.00	$500,000.00
1976	200,000.00	400,000.00
1977	300,000.00	300,000.00
1978	400,000.00	200,000.00
1979	500,000.00	100,000.00
Average for 5 years	$300,000.00	$300,000.00

Using the above five-year income figures, (which approach for apprai- sal purposes has wide acceptance although there is nothing sacred in the five-year period,) and giving attention to only the average earn- ings figure, the valuation of Companies A and B would be identical. However, it is evident that prudent investors would not pay the same price for the stock of Company B as they would for that of Company A in view of the income history of the two corporations. This would be so even were all other factors equal.

On the basis of the income histories shown above, it is unreasonable to expect a valuation derived from an analysis of Company A to furnish a meaningful indication of the value of Company B, or vice versa. With such dissimilarity in past rates of growth, that is, earnings trend, a capitalization rate based only upon latest year's income of either company could be used to determine the value of the business with more accuracy than a capitalization rate based on average yearly income for any prior period of years. For example, if Company B's stock was selling for only three times its five-year average earnings this would represent, in effect, nine times its latest year's earn- ings. Using the same basis for Company A, we would apply the nine times factor to 1979 earnings of $500,000 which would result in a valuation of $4.5 million for the company. This, in turn, represents a fifteen times capitalization of five-year average earnings. In view of the increasing earnings trend in Company A, it is quite logical to expect its fair market value in relation to its average earnings to be considerably higher thus reflecting a more improved rate of capitalization than would be true with respect to Company B with its declining trend in earnings.

Noncomparable Capital Structure

Effect of Capital Structure on Capitalization Rates

The usual method of selecting comparable corporations and preparing an analysis of such companies in order to value a closely-held corporation is made on the basis of the common stock price/earnings and price/asset ratios and on the dividend yields. The ordinary appraisal will reflect a study of the corporation's earnings and market price in terms of the per share value of common stock only. When we are comparing two corporations of different capital structure there is a very vital need to give cognizance to this difference, and in many cases an adjustment of the price/earnings or price/assets ratios must be made. To illustrate this, we will set forth a hypothetical example.

Assume two practically identical businesses, each earning $200,000 from operations before taxes, interest on bonded indebtedness and dividends. All of Company C's securities are actively traded on the public market. Company D is closely-held. With all other factors of value being equal, we assume further that Company C has outstanding bonds, preferred stock and common stock, and that the other, Company D, has no securities senior to its common stock. We will assume that Company C has a capital structure as follows:

(a) 3% debentures in the amount of $500,000 selling at face value;

(b) 5% cumulative preferred stock selling at par of $100 per share, in the amount of $250,000; and

(c) Common stock selling on the public market at $100 per share in the amount of 2,500 shares.

Assume a 50% rate of tax applicable to these corporations and on this basis the following computation of the rates of capitalization and values can be made:

	Company C	Company D
Operating profits available for interest	$200,000.00	$200,000.00
Less: Debenture interest	15,000.00	....
Taxable income	$185,000.00	$200,000.00
Less 50% tax on income	92,500.00	100,000.00
Income available for dividends	$ 92,500.00	$100,000.00
Less: Preferred stock dividend	12,500.00	....
Income available for common stock	$80,000.00	$100,000.00
Value of common stocks	$250,000.00	Closely held
Common stock price/ earnings ratio($250,000/$80,000)	3.125	....
Income available for interest and dividends	$107,500.00	....
Value of total securities – Stocks and debentures	$1,000,000.00	....
Price/earnings ratio for total securities ($1,000,000 $107,500)	9.302	....

Applying the above price/earnings ratios to appraise the closely-held stock of Company D the following amounts result:

(1) Price/Earnings ratio for common stock alone
    (3.125 x $100,000.00 earnings) $312,500.00

(2) Price/earnings ratio for total securities
    (9.302 x $100,000.00 earnings) $930,200.00

The effects of diverse capital structures upon a valuation by comparison is evident from the above widely different indicated values for Company D. The computation of a capitalization rate for Company C based upon total securities and total earnings available for such securities produces a much more reasonable valuation for the unlisted corporation than that obtained using the common stock capitalization rate. The reverse procedure, that is, appraising the common stock of Company C, using the ratio of market value of Company D's stock to its earnings, further supports this theory as will now be shown.

With no change in the income figures or capital structures, or the market values of the preferred stock and debentures, we will assume the common stock of Company D is worth $1,000,000 at quoted market prices or ten times earnings, while the common stock of C is closely-held. At ten times its earnings of $80,000 that stock is appraised at $800,000 and $1,550,000 is the value attributed to total securities. But, if the income of $107,500 available for interest and dividends is

290

appraised at ten times earnings, or $1,075,000, and the face or par value of $750,000 for senior securities is deducted from such figure, $325,000 would be the appraised value of the common stock. As we are assuming the corporations are identical in all respects except capital structure, the latter appraisal of the business of Company C is clearly more reasonable of the two.

To further illustrate this point on a simplified basis, we will leave out the element of interest on funded debt in our comparison between the two hypothetical companies. The following example indicates that identical amounts can be obtained providing the senior securities of one of the companies are taken into consideration in making the comparison:

	Company E	Company F
Income subject to taxes	$200,000.00	$200,000.00
Less: 50% tax on income	100,000.00	100,000.00
Income available for dividends	$100,000.00	$100,000.00

In this problem we have assumed that Company E has a 5% cumulative preferred stock issue of $100 par value having a total market value of $500,000.00.

Dividends on preferred stock	$25,000.00	-0-
Income available for dividends on common stock	$75,000.00	$100,000.00
Market value of common stock at quoted prices	$500,000.00	Closely- held
Price/earnings ratio common stock only	6.67	....
Price/earnings ratio total stocks	10.00	....

Using the price/earnings ratios computed above, the following appraised values for Company F are obtained:

	Company F
Based on the price/earnings ratio for common stock only (6.67 x 100,000)	$667,000.00
Based on the price/earnings ratio for total stock (10.00 x 100,000)	$1,000,000.00

Now assume the common stock of Company E is closely held while that of Company F is worth $1,000,000, or 10 times earnings at its quoted market price. To appraise Company E the following computation could be made:

	Company E	Company F
Price/earnings ratio applied to earnings available for common stock alone (10.0 x $75,000)	$750,000.00	
Add: Market value of preferred stock	500,000.00	
Value of total securities	$1,250,000.00	

But if we apply the derived price/earnings ratio pertaining to Company F (of 10.0), to Company E's total earnings available for all securities (of $100,000) we find a total value of: $1,000,000.00

Less: Preferred stock at market price   500,000.00

Value of the common stock $500,000.00

Since we have assumed all other variables are identical we should expect the market values of companies E and F to be identical. As we can see from the computations the only way identical values for the two businesses can be obtained is by using the total capital and total earnings approach.

The foregoing illustrations indicate rather graphically the need for giving differences in capital structure more than just cursory attention when we use the comparative analysis to appraise closely-held stock. It is true that even with the above adjustments other differences which we have not gone into, in this oversimplified hypothetical example, will cause companies of different capital structures to produce incorrect answers to some degree. It is up to the appraiser to select the best method and the least erroneous conclusion based on all the elements of value and facts of record.

Capital Structure and Corporate Size--Effects Upon Price/Earnings Ratios

We have spent considerable time in the foregoing paragraphs to show from hypothetical examples how capital structure differences affect capitalization rates in the use of a comparative analysis for appraisal purposes. We are able, based on certain research material, to go further and show how different capital structures as well as other factors have a direct relationship to the going market prices of publiclytraded corporate securities. In the discussion which follows we will describe the procedure and the results of a project conducted within the Internal Revenue Service; examining the effects which different capital structures and different corporate sizes have had on the price/earnings ratios disclosed by listed stocks on the New York Stock Exchange. Although this study was made several years ago the conclusions are still important and worthy of our attention today as we consider contemporary stock valuation issues.

It is axiomatic that a third mortgage on a parcel of real estate carries with it more risk than a second mortgage, which in turn is more risky than a first mortgage on the same parcel of real estate. A corollary to this premise is that investors expect rates of return in proportion to the risk which they are incurring.

The common stock of a corporation which also has outstanding substantial amounts of preferred stock and funded debt is analogous to the third mortgage on real property. The rights of the common stockholders to the income and the value of the corporate business, are similar to the rights of the holder of the third mortgage who must take an unfavorable position with respect to the holders of the second and first trusts, as far as return on investment and the proceeds to be obtained if the property is sold under a foreclosure procedure.

Stock Market Study Results

In the forementioned study which comprehended all manufacturing and merchandising corporations having their common stocks traded or quoted on the New York Stock Exchange as of February 28, 1957, an analysis was made of the relationship between price/earnings ratios, the type of securities which the corporations had outstanding and the size of the corporation as measured by its total value. This study, although based on facts existing as of a certain date, is believed to be informative because it relates to those stocks which are traded on one market and concerns a period in time when tax rates were comparable to those existing currently. Companies which had no earnings available for their common stocks were eliminated from the analysis.

The companies used in this study were grouped first according to the percentage of the common stock value to the value of the total outstanding stocks and funded debts based upon prices on or about February 28, 1957. A division was made for every 10% with the exception of the first group which covered a 20% spread. Thus, for example, corporations having common stock of value not exceeding 20% of the total value of all its outstanding securities would be included in the 0 to 20% group. Actually none of the companies exhibited a capital structure this extreme. Similarly in the 100% group those corporations having only common stock outstanding were listed. The values of the outstanding common stocks and the earnings available for the common stocks of the companies of each group were totaled and the price/earnings ratios were derived from these figures. Chart A indicates the average ratio of price to latest year's earnings for each group with the point plotted at the midpoint, that is at the 25, 35, 45, etc., mark. These points are connected by a solid line to illustrate the basic trend. The dotted line on this chart connects similarly derived points showing the price-five-year average earnings ratios. Both graphs show a definite upward trend and indicate, among other things, that the price/earnings ratios disclosed by listed common stocks have a definite variation relative to the percentage of capitalization which is devoted to common stocks. Of course, like any other generalization, we would have to state that as regards particular corporations the qualification that all other things being reasonably equal would have to be met before these conclusions could be applied. Since the price/earnings ratios shown on the chart are whole figures, we would have to clarify that capitalization rates (that is, the percentages which are reciprocals to the ratios used) tend to decrease as the percentage of common stock increases.

Chart B displays an identical analysis of the price-latest year's earnings and price-five year average earnings relationships on a total security basis. Relating this graph to Chart A we arrive at a most interesting conclusion; that after a corporation's common stock amounts to approximately 85% of the total value of the company, there is relatively little variation in price/earnings ratios up to the 100% common stock companies.

Since the corporations come from a common market place and are confined to manufacturing and merchandising companies only, it is believed that the number of corporations in each percentile grouping are sufficient to make them homogeneous groupings. For this reason, it would appear that valuations and resultant price/earnings ratios for each homogeneous group should be fairly comparable regardless of the breakdown of the capital structure.

As evidence of the validity of the total capital approach we note the relatively slight variation in price/earnings ratios on Chart B. The line connecting the computed midpoints on Chart B, shows readily that the price/earnings ratios, disclosed by relating the valuation of entire businesses to the total earnings available for all securities fall for the most part within a four-point spread, that is, between 11 and 15 times. The narrow confines of price/earnings ratios for all groups tends to confirm our premise stated in the prior paragraph, namely, that regardless of individual price/earnings ratios as disclosed for the common stocks within each group, the overall price/earnings ratios will show little variation if each group is compared on a total capital basis and assuming they consist of homogeneous units.

Corporations pay no taxes on interest paid on their funded debt, so in order to derive a precise answer the above analysis should reflect an adjustment for the taxes which were not paid on the income available for interest. In years when tax rates are more substantial and excess profits taxes may be enforced, some variation of the capital structure adjustment and earnings adjustment which we have used will be necessary. One method would be to use the price/earnings ratio computed on the basis of total earnings prior to income taxes. Such a method, of course, would lend itself also to valuations of sole proprietorships and partnerships.

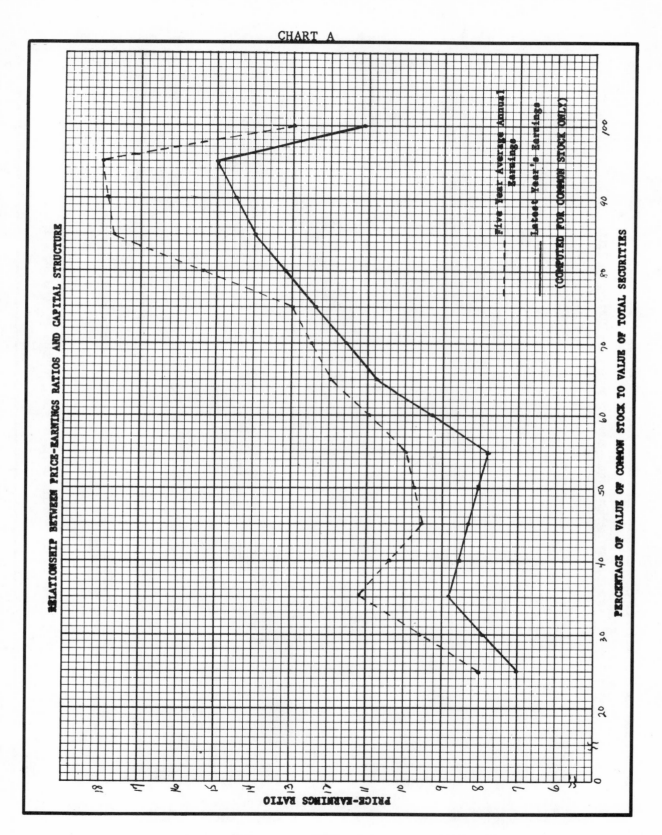

CHART A

RELATIONSHIP BETWEEN PRICE-EARNINGS RATIOS AND CAPITAL STRUCTURE

Five Year Average Annual Earnings

Latest Year's Earnings

(COMPUTED FOR COMMON STOCK ONLY)

PERCENTAGE OF VALUE OF COMMON STOCK TO VALUE OF TOTAL SECURITIES

PRICE-EARNINGS RATIO

295

CHART B

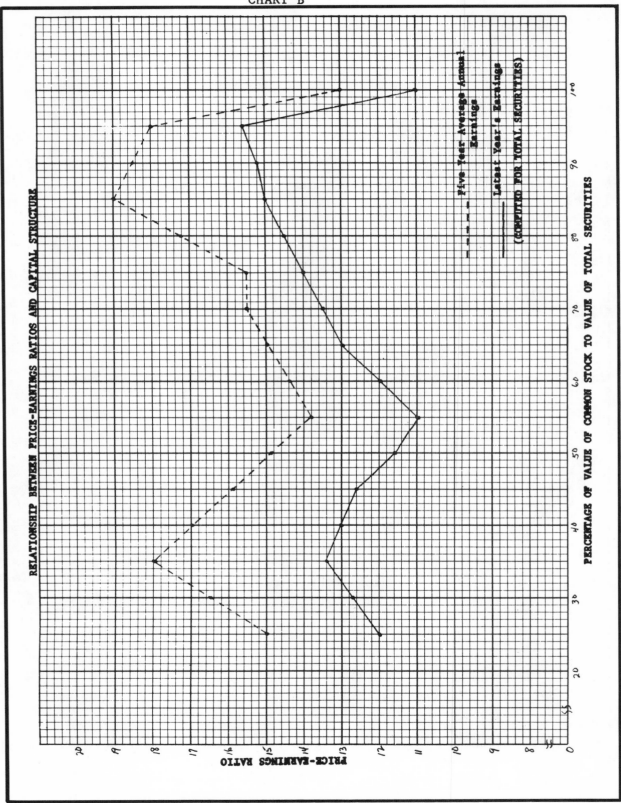

RELATIONSHIP BETWEEN PRICE-EARNINGS RATIOS AND CAPITAL STRUCTURE

PERCENTAGE OF VALUE OF COMMON STOCK TO VALUE OF TOTAL SECURITIES

PRICE-EARNINGS RATIO

----- Five Year Average Annual Earnings

——— Latest Year's Earnings

(COMPUTED FOR TOTAL SECURITIES)

296

It is fairly common for the ordinary appraisal to be made by using market price per share of common stock and earnings per share of common stock. These data are published in such financial or statistical services as Moody's Investment Manuals, and Standard and Poor's Investment Service. In comparing a closely-held corporation with corporations having senior securities not in excess of 15% of the total value of the business an error from a common-stock-only approach would, in most cases, be small enough to overlook. But if the companies have radically different capital structures, and many of them have large preferred stock or funded debt issues outstanding, substantial errors will result unless the capital structure differences are taken into full account in working up a comparative analysis. A comparison on the basis of a common-stock-is-a-common-stock theory requires less work and takes less time than does a more exact method. As may be noted, however, when the common-stock-only approach is used, and a complex capital structure exists in the comparable corporations, much lower appraisals result. Most of the closely-held family corporations have common stocks only. Therefore, the low values which can be attributed to these stocks based on an inexact comparison with listed corporations is frequently adopted since the appraiser is certain that the ultraconsevative result will find favor with the taxpayers who quite naturally are seeking to avoid as much tax as possible.

Size Differentials Between Comparatives

A corollary to the analysis on the effects of capital structure upon price/earnings ratios was a study of the effects of the size of corporations upon such ratios. We have mentioned the size of the corporations as one element to consider in choosing your comparatives. Consequently, it is relevant to explore what effects dissimilar sizes might have upon the all important price/earnings ratios.

There are numerous ways to measure size. For instance, we can use volume of sales, total assets, or total net worth. The one which is used herein is the total value of the business as disclosed by the market price of all outstanding corporate securities.

The same companies and the same date are used in this analysis as were used in the capital structure study. Charts C and D, and the following schedule summarize the results of this study.

297

Schedule 1

Manufacturing and Merchandising Companies With
Common Stocks Listed on the New York Stock Exchange

Effect of Size Upon Rates of Capitalization

Market Price Of Outstanding Stocks and Long-Term Debts:			Price/earning Ratios on basis of:		
Minimum Value	Maximum Value	No. of Companies of This Size	Price/ Assets Ratios	Latest Years Earnings	5- Year Average Earnings
1,000,000	4,999,99	17	0.62	11.51*	12.26*
5,000,000	9,999,999	36	0.79	8.95	10.10
10,000,000	24,999,999	131	0.87	9.78	11.35
25,000,000	49,999,999	118	0.93	10.40	11.76
50,000,000	99,999,999	119	1.17	11.18	13.74
100,000,000	499,999,999	156	1.37	12.84	15.91
500,000,000	or more	51	2.02	16.13	18.56

Total value-126,717,378,081	628	1.63	14.28	16.87

*These are the only figures which are not consistent with the conclusions to be drawn from this summary.

A brief glance at the schedule discloses that in general the market value per dollar of earnings and per dollar of asset value increases rather consistently and somewhat in proportion to the percentage of the increase in size. The single exception is the $1 million to $5 million group which disclosed disproportionately high price/earnings ratios. Only consistent income-producing companies were used in this analysis.

There may be some question as to why the value of a company per dollar of earnings should increase in proportion to increases in corporate size. This tendency seems to be quite logical, however, in view of the practical considerations which most investors follow when making their buy or sell decisions. For one thing, the most successful companies gradually become the largest companies and in many cases become the leaders in their particular industries. Their very success and consequent size is ample evidence to the investing public that each of these enterprises has the ability to meet and survive competition and also has the ability to develop and grow either from internal expansion of its plant and products or by means of mergers. High quality management is ordinarily a prime requisite in such firms and with such the investing public is likely to place greater confidence in these corporations. Certainly, the securities of such corporations are better known to the public and become by that same fact more marketable. Any of these reasons could account for the greater interest, popularity and consequent higher ratio of price to earnings. Regardless of the underlying causes, however, it is apparent that a genuine and easily discernible trend exists with respect to the size of the corporate enterprise and the price/earnings ratios which it displays.

Chart C sets forth a simple bar graph of the average size of corporations falling in the various capital structure classifications. Of interest is the gradual upward trend after common equity equals 50% and the sharp rise when size of company and percent of common hit their peak. However, the drop in size displayed by the 100% common stock companies points up the fact that the larger the company the greater the tendency, and probably the necessity, for finding other sources of capital. And a corollary conclusion is that with complexity of capital structure and increased size, profitability and investor appeal also increases.

Chart D shows the interrelationship of price/earnings ratios and price/tangible asset value ratios of all corporations studied. The analysis was made for all companies on the basis of their total security value, i.e., their long-term debt, senior securities, and common stocks as well as on a common-stock-only basis.

CHART C

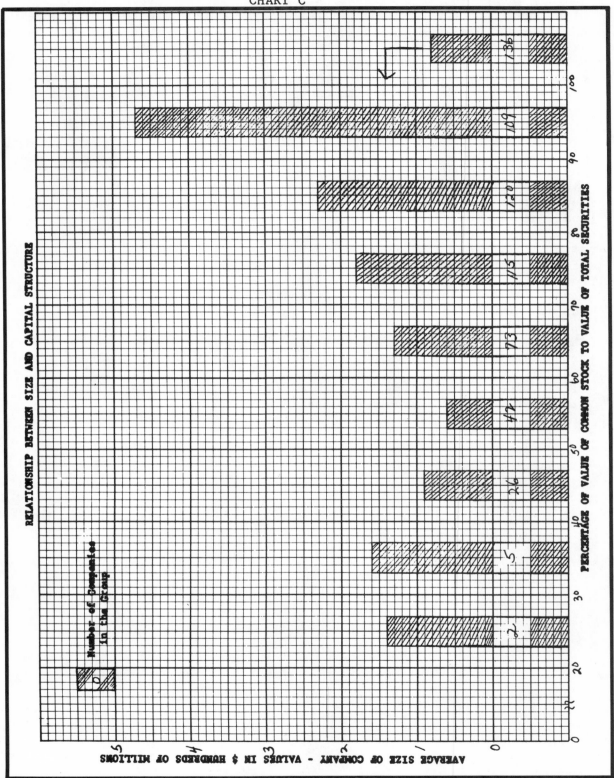

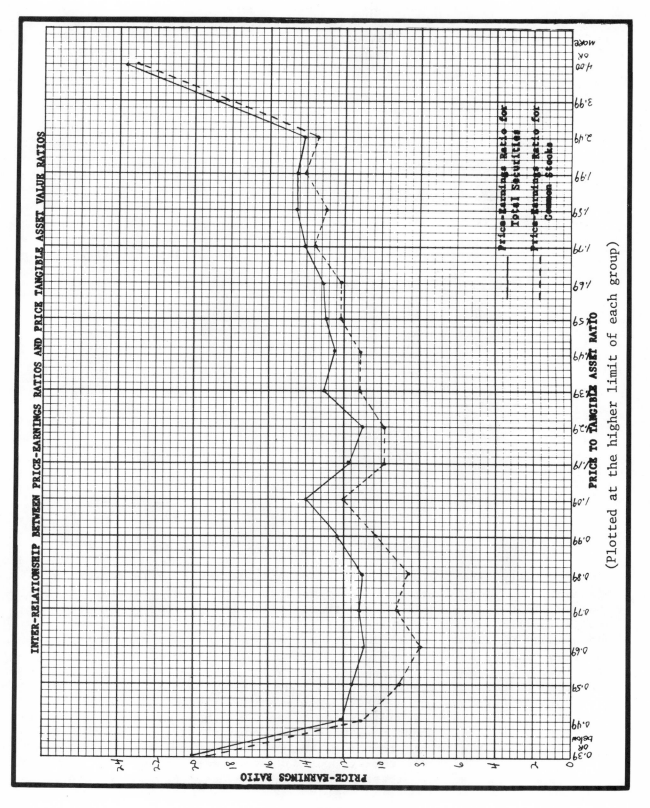

INTER-RELATIONSHIP BETWEEN PRICE-EARNINGS RATIOS AND PRICE TANGIBLE ASSET VALUE RATIOS

PRICE TO TANGIBLE ASSET RATIO

PRICE-EARNINGS RATIO

Price-Earnings Ratio for Total Securities

Price-Earnings Ratio for Common Stocks

(Plotted at the higher limit of each group)

The following schedule contains the statistical data in greater detail from which Chart D was derived. Of interest on this table is the greater consistency of the price/earnings ratio upward trend as we reflect more of the capital structure in the computation and the fact that the last analysis encompassing the total securities outstanding exhibits the most constant price/earnings ratio pattern.

Schedule 2

Price Net/Tangible Assets Ratio and Price/Earnings Ratio

Number of Companies	Price/Assets Ratio		Price/Earnings Ratios		
	Min.	Max.	Common Stocks	Total Stocks	Total Securities
10	0.00	0.39	19.37	19.37	20.56
14	0.40	0.49	11.71	11.71	12.13
40	0.50	0.59	9.16	9.38	11.76
52	0.60	0.69	8.14	8.46	10.91
77	0.70	0.79	9.07	9.53	11.09
85	0.80	0.89	8.58	9.12	10.58
59	0.90	0.99	10.54	10.52	12.36
56	1.00	1.09	12.14	12.60	14.18
52	1.10	1.19	9.95	10.10	11.65
40	1.20	1.29	9.83	10.34	11.09
18	1.30	1.39	11.10	11.49	13.14
36	1.40	1.49	11.01	11.35	12.51
25	1.50	1.59	12.06	12.16	12.86
17	1.60	1.69	12.17	12.23	12.98
15	1.70	1.79	13.60	13.65	14.11
14	1.80	1.89	13.01	13.34	14.46
17	1.90	1.99	14.07	14.17	14.47
37	2.00	2.49	13.36	13.55	14.03
43	2.50	3.99	19.47	19.51	19.77
8	4.00 and Over		23.50	23.50	23.79

Price/earnings ratios are based on latest year's earnings.

Theoretically, the risk to common stock holders would be increased by issuance of long term debt as opposed to issuance of a senior stock issue. This will be so because there will be greater precautions taken on the part of the corporation to insure to bond holders the continuity of income and return of capital to which they have a right. While a similar assurance is given to the holders of preferred stock, it is by no means as strong as that which is held by bond holders. The bond holders who are creditors of the company have first call upon the company's income and assets in the event of liquidation, prior to the equity owners. We would expect, based on this and assuming that there will be a relationship between size, capital structure, and the relationship of earnings to the market price, that the price/earnings ratios would be highest for companies with most stock to total ratio, and successively lower for each of the other classes in order.

302

As a matter of fact, this assumption is substantially borne out by the facts as disclosed by the above schedule as far as most of the groups are concerned. However, those corporations which had common stocks and funded debts in two lower size groups did not conform to the general pattern.

As a final phase of this study a comparison was made by industry combining all of the factors in order that any correlation, if such existed between corporate size, type of industry, and price/earnings or price/asset value ratios could be ascertained. For purposes of this study, of which the following schedule is a summation, the corporations are ranked by price-latest year's earnings ratios with a breakdown by 10 broad industry categories.

Schedule 3

Manufacturing and Merchandising Companies with Common Stocks Listed on N.Y. Stock Exchange. Capitalization Rates by Industrial Groups

No. of Co.	Type of capitalization rate — Industry	Price-earnings ratios for common stocks — Latest year's earnings	Last 5 years average earnings	Price-earnings ratios for total securities — Latest[3] year's earnings	Last 5 years average earnings	Average size of Co. as measured by value of total securities (000 omitted)	Price-assets ratios for total securities
82	Machinery of all types	18.10	20.97	18.93	12.04	[2]228,654	1.68
123	Heavy industry (Steel, chemicals, paper, etc.)	14.33	18.30	15.20	18.87	353,805	[2]1.78
7	Containers other than glass	12.38	14.93	14.13	16.97	[2]231,320	[2]1.33
83	Transportation equipment (Aircraft, autos, RR's, etc.)	12.28	[2]13.04	12.97	[2]13.84	310,433	1.68
52	Building materials and equip.	11.79	14.73	12.96	16.19	131,907	1.49
74	Food processing	11.60	[2]13.25	[2]12.98	[2]14.80	111,543	[2]1.15
106	Household and personal goods	11.56	14.09	12.90	15.53	108,903	1.39
9	Graphic arts and publishing	10.64	13.13	11.28	13.91	37,952	1.36
6	Miscellaneous manufacturing	8.79	10.53	9.93	11.59	33,310	1.15
1	Leather and leather goods other than shoes	6.42	9.14	6.42	9.14	5,422	0.64
541[1]	Total manufacturing industries	13.53	15.99	14.49	16.98	216,002	1.61
108	Total merchandising industries	11.42	13.13	12.43	14.28	120,318	1.25
649	All manufacturing and Mds. Cos.	13.29	15.65	14.25	16.67	200,079	1.56

[1] There are some duplications with companies included in more than one industry.

[2] This rate departs from the numerical sequence from highest to lowest of the first column for price-to-latest years' earnings ratios for common stocks.

[3] Long-term debts are included and interest on such debts has been included in earnings.

There are several interesting observations that can be made from the analysis as depicted on the attached schedule. One apparent conclusion is that the three ratios which have been computed for each of the industry groups have only slight correlation as between industries. By this we mean that the industry which reports the higher price-latest year's earnings ratio does not show similarly high ratios of price to asset value or price to average earnings. To illustrate, referring to the detailed data of which this schedule is a summary, it was noted that Electrical Machinery ranked first in price-latest year's earnings, third in price-average earnings and fourth in price/asset value ratio. Similarly Optical and Photographic Manufacturers ranked seventh as far as price-latest year's earnings, fifth on the average earnings relationship to price, and third on the price/asset value relationship.

By far the most significant conclusion that we draw from the foregoing study, however, is the fact that the rule is not correlation but divergence. An illustration of this is the Shoe Merchandising industry which ranked eighth in price to latest year's earnings, 32nd in price to five-year average earnings and 36th in price to asset value. As we go down the list we see many examples of wide variation in these particular ratios within a single industry. One other example is the Drugs, Toiletries and Cosmetic industry which ranked 28th in price-latest year's earnings ratio and at the same time it was 12th in price-five years' average ratio and seventh in price to asset value ratio.

How can we explain these variations? Why should corporate equities in the Lumber and Plywood industry, for example, be 22nd in ranking as far as price to latest-year's earnings ratio is concerned, seventh in price to average earnings relationship, and 47th as far as price/asset value? There seems to be relatively little basis for an explanation of these dissimilar indications.

It must be recognized, however, that at the upper and lower extremes of the ranking there seems to be a greater amount of similarity than in the center portion. Thus we find that in the lowest ranking industires many companies make an equally poor showing as far as average earnings and asset values are concerned.

One result of the study of the relationship of market price of listed securities to their earnings and tangible asset values is evident from the schedule summarizing Chart D. It seems fairly conclusive that the stated relationships which certain authorities in the security analysis field contend exist between price/asset value ratios and price/earnings ratios cannot be substantiated to any degree. The table is self-explanatory, however, we should note the pronounced fluctuation in price/earnings ratios vis-a-vis price asset value ratios. We might say in summary that there is some general increase in the price/earnings ratio as there is a general increase in the price/asset value ratio. But as a definite, provable conclusion this study is proof that such a generality lacks reality.

Generalized conclusions as we have made based upon the research study discussed in the foregoing paragraphs are of a qualitative rather than a quantitative nature. It is believed that similar trends or deviations could be found by studies made of other markets and as of other times although the amounts of such variations would assuredly change in answer to the optimism or pessimism of the investing public. The consistency of the results obtained would be proportionate to the number of companies which are being considered in each class or grouping. The sample should be sufficiently large to insure a homogeneous group and avoid distortion.

Throughout this study of the rates of capitalization, the preferred stocks and the funded debts have been included under corporate capital; and income available for interest and for dividends has been used to measure the value per dollar of earnings. No other basis of computation will recognize the important changes in capital structure over a period of time.

It has been mentioned that such financial publications as Barron's Weekly, Moody's Investment Manuals, and Standard and Poor's Investment Service all compute price-latest year's earnings ratios on a common stock alone basis. We should not lose sight, however, of the primary purpose for which these published ratios are prepared. They are held out to the readers of these services as barometers of the investing public's opinion as to the fair market value of the securities which are being quoted. Common stocks with senior securities taking preference over them, are referred to in the investment field as "leverage" stocks. Such stocks fluctuate more violently in price than do nonleverage common stocks; that is, they are more speculative than the nonleverage stocks. Thus, as an aid to appraising market fluctuations and the reaction of the market to various economic, political and financial events, the ratios computed by the published sources can benefit from having such leverage stocks reflected in their statistics and thereby imparting to their indices more fluidity and greater reliability as current public opinion gauges.

SUMMARY

There seems to be adequate justification that in the interest of more accuracy generally we should make comparisons on the basis of total capital structure and total income available for all stocks and bonds. As in any other phase of valuation, this technique is not an exact science and we cannot expect to arrive at a definite and incontrovertible value for closely-held stock merely by the use of the comparative analysis. After we have made a comparison with all available corporations which in our judgment seem to be comparable, the most that we have achieved is to create one additional factor which should be given weight and relected in the appraisal which we are to make.

It would not be logical or consistent with public policy to devote to each and every appraisal of closely-held stock the same amount of time, effort and study regardless of other considerations. We should give due regard both to the time available and to the importance of the issue and arrive at an estimate of the justifiable time which we as Appeals Officers should devote to this particular problem. If we can arrive at a substantially correct result that is reasonable for all normal standards without a detailed and time-consuming analysis, and such result is conducive to a settlement of the issue to the mutual satisfaction of both parties, the taxpayer and the Government, there would seem to be no reason for a refinement of the general comparison approach. But if there are substantial amounts of tax involved and a court proceeding appears likely, the more exact and comprehensive analysis is essential.

It is undoubtedly a difficult task to attempt to ascertain from a possibly brief review of the case file, prior Revenue Agents' reports, tax returns, taxpayers' protests and appraisals whether a complex and complete valuation is necessary. As in all matters coming before the Appeals Division the element of judgment cannot be eliminated. Amount of tax is no reliable criteria in deciding whether a given valuation issue should be pursued to the ultimate. Frequently, a significant issue may be brought to trial when only small amounts of tax are involved but the case is one which will serve as a precedent for much larger and more important cases to follow. A very helpful guide to Appeals Officers in determining the amount of time and effort to be expended on a given valuation is to attempt early in consideration of the case to decide whether trial is likely and expert testimony will be needed in order for the Government to put on an effective case. If this condition exists you should lose no time in pursuing a line of attack as outlined above and in the foregoing pages of this material. There is no excuse for delaying development of a case for eventual trial until the last moment. We know from experience that Government trial attorneys are often at a disadvantage because of the pressures of a heavy workload. The least that can be done is to supply them with competent and well- prepared opinion testimony so that the Government's case can be tried before the court as effectively as possible.

Lesson 13

COMMON ERRORS IN VALUATION - CAPITALIZATION
RATES, PAST EVENTS, IMPROVISING

CONTENTS

OBJECTIVES

At the end of this lesson you will be able to:

1. Demonstrate how the use of a latest year's price/earnings ratio produces invalid results when applied to an average earnings figure.

2. Explain how the use of nonrepresentative past events distort predictions of future earning capacity.

3. Describe a typical improvisation to use in making a comparative analysis when truly comparable corporations are lacking.

CAPITALIZATION RATES

As indicated earlier one of the major goals of an appraisal of a business entity is the determining of a valid capitalization rate at which to project a value for the expected future income stream of the company. While an industry oriented comparative analysis is one highly successful way of ascertaining a valid price/earnings ratio, we must exercise care in the application of such a multiplier. A common error encountered in this respect be it accidental or intentional is the misapplication of current capitalization rates to average earnings.

Applying Single Year Rates of Capitalization
to Average Income for Long Periods

In applying price/earnings ratios it is important that the ratio is applied to a comparable income figure reflecting an income period identical with that upon which the price/earnings ratio is based. To illustrate we have included below a tabulation of hypothetical price/earnings ratios computed from a source such as Moody's Manual of Investments for the 10-year period 1970 through 1979. Such ratios are published in Moody's Manual for 200 common stocks and are used by security analysts to get a general indication of overall capitalization rates. The second column of the tabulation contains the amounts of assumed income realized by a hypothetical corporation whose stock we are trying to value.

Year	Price/Earnings Ratio	Income to be Appraised
1970	12.50	$10.00
1971	14.11	20.00
1972	13.79	30.00
1973	16.95	40.00
1974	18.00	50.00
1975	17.41	60.00
1976	20.91	70.00
1977	17.44	80.00
1978	18.08	90.00
1979	18.50	100.00
Average	16.77	$ 55.00

Each of the rates shown in the above schedule applies to the latest single year's income for the year indicated. Ordinarily the average price/earnings ratio of 16.77 will be rounded off to a ratio of 16 1/2.

The average ratio is the average rate according to the computation at which the investing public appraised latest year's income in each year throughout the 10-year period ending in 1979. It would not be acceptable to capitalize 1979 income of the unlisted corporation of $100, at 6% (16.5 x 100) or $1,650 of value per share for the capital stock. It is equally wrong to apply the 6% capitalization rate to the average income of $55 arriving at a value of $900 per share for the stock. This error is commonly encountered and should be guarded against. Of course the preferable method is to apply the latest year's ratio (18.5) to the latest year's earnings to obtain an indicated value of $1,850 per share.

If we have available the price to average earnings ratios of a set of comparable corporate stocks, it will also be correct to apply the average of such ratios to the average earnings of the closely-held company. Thus, if the industry disclosed an average price to ten-year average earnings ratio of 22 times we would be justified in applying such a ratio to the average earnings of $55.00 per share to obtain another indication of fair market value for the closely-held corporate stock. The primary point here is to compare like things.

PAST EVENTS

Another error not infrequently met in the appraisal of closely-held stocks is the reliance by the appraiser upon past events in the corporate history which have no place in the current appraisal of future expectancy of the business. A case in point involved the valuation of

X Corporation in which case drastic changes in the basic business of the company caused the past results not to be representative of the future. Although somewhat dated in content the case provides a useful illustration of the error.

Using Nonrepresentative Past Events

The company was engaged in shipbuilding and ship repair work. Prior to the Second World War this company operated on a very small scale and had a plant investment of less than $100,000. During that war and the subsequent Korean conflict its operations increased many times over, although most of the facilities which it used were Government-owned. Understandably, the corporation recorded sales in this period at the highest rate in its history either before or since. In the late 1950's operations dropped back to a new normal level far above the pre-1940 level but substantially lower than those realized during either war period.

The foregoing facts indicate that undoubtedly the war years' earnings of X Corporation would bear little or no relation to the current and future expected profits as of the valuation date in 1961. In addition, the X Corporation had been using facilities up to 1958 which it did not own and which it leased from the United States Government. The company also operated a farm equipment distributor's franchise obtained from the Caterpillar Tractor Company. An additional complication revolved around the fact that the company had attempted to diversify its business in the years 1956 through 1958 and these attempts had all ended in costly failures. Naturally the company's operating results up to 1959 reflected these conditions.

In 1959, X Corporation leased a large 18,000 ton drydock from the U.S. Navy. Also in 1959 all Government-owned facilities at the shipyard were purchased by the corporation. In 1960, the company bought a 3,500 ton drydock which it used for various repair operations. Since 1959 substantial business originated from the reactivation of merchant ships. The equipment distributing phase of the operations was not productive of much revenue and in most of the years since its inception the costs and profits of this department were about equal.

As of the valuation date, therefore, we have a business to appraise which is significantly different both in scope of operation and certainly in future prospects than that which had existed up to 1958. X Corporation is no longer a small, one-person operation of the prewar years, nor is it a booming wartime shipyard flooded with national defense work. Furthermore, it has evolved out of the uncertainty of reconversion and has abandoned such impulsive investments as characterized its immediate postwar period. From 1959 up to the basic date (and certainly from an investor's standpoint, this would be for the forseeable future also), X Corporation was in the business primarily of repairing small ships in its own 3,500 ton drydock, repairing large ships in an 18,000 ton drydock which was leased from the Navy, and distributing and selling Caterpillar farm equipment. Essentially, therefore, X Corporation is engaged now in a type of business and magnitude of business which had developed after World War II and the Korean War. In view of all of the foregoing it seems entirely justifiable that any earnings figures prior to 1959 will have little significance as an index for future expectations of this corporation in 1961.

A related point to the one discussed here is a fact that the further away from the basic date in point of time that the information is, the less weight and the less significance it has for valuation purposes. By this we mean that earnings ten years earlier can by no means be as important to a potential buyer of a security as the earnings in the immediately preceding year would be. As we have stated the current year's earnings are the nearest thing we have to the future and as such they constitute the best and primary indication of what the future holds. Thus, it is not only in those cases such as we have described in this lesson where the company has in effect become almost a completely new enterprise, that past events are carefully scrutinized and accorded lesser weight as they become removed from the basic date, but in every case this interval in time is an element which must be kept in mind.

In the actual situation described primary attention was given to the operating results of the company for the three latest years. These data were much more representative of the company's future than any other period.

IMPROVISING

At times the search for comparatives will be fruitless. There will just be no similar or any remotely similar listed corporation which can be utilized as a means of comparing the market price, earnings, asset value and dividend rate to the closely-held stock to be valued. In such instances, the other factors of valuation which have been enumerated previously will come into full play and final decision will rest exclusively upon them. Sometimes, however, there may be available information on listed stocks not in the same industry or the same type of business but of a similar type of competitive position, for example, or a similar type of general security, which can be used for comparison purposes.

One Approach to Improvisation

To illustrate, if the closely-held corporation had an issue of 7% noncumulative preferred stock which had to be valued it will be extremely interesting and pertinent to find out what such issues, if there are any, are bringing on the nation's market places. A tabulation of such 7% noncumulative preferred issues on which information can be ascertained would be extremely helpful to the appraiser and could be made the basis of an expert opinion in the event of trial.

311

Another possibility is to compare the closely-held stock with listed companies occupying the same competitive position. For instance, a case was referred for consideration involving a claimed discount below market value of the Coca-Cola Company stock prior to the time the company had any real competitors. It was apparent in view of Coca-Cola's undisputed position in its own industry that if the comparative approach was to be used there would have to be some improvization or variation upon it. The valuation date was at a time when Coca-Cola had no true competitors and even though its stock was actively traded on the New York Stock Exchange it seemed that some additional basis for sustaining the market value would be needed to counteract the taxpayer's arguments. The line was taken by the Service that the market value of Coca-Cola stock on that date was in line with other "blue chip" securities. That is, the stocks of other top grade listed corporations who were the undisputed leaders in their own fields were selling on a basis comparable to that upon which Coca-Cola common was selling. The summary sheet, Schedule 4, which follows, illustrates the procedure which was used in this analysis.

As indicated by the schedule Coca-Cola stock was selling at a ratio of $15.96 per dollar of earnings while the various industry leaders which were used for comparison purposes were selling on the average for $15.20 per dollar of earnings. There was a wide range of price/earnings ratios; however, the bulk of these ratios fell between 13 and 17 times earnings. This analysis served to support the Government's contention that the Coca-Cola Company stock was not selling at any unusual premium over its actual fair market value and was in fact in line with most of the other blue chip high grade leading corporations whose stocks were being publicly traded.

Comparatives for the Coca-Cola Company

Industrial Companies With Incomes Greater Than $10,000,000
(Excluding Metallurgical and Aircraft Companies)

Name of company	Total market quotational value of stocks and bonds*	Latest year earnings available for interest and dividends*	Dollars of value per dollar of earnings*
Companies With No Years of Loss For Ten Years			
Allied Chemical and Dye Corp.	$ 359.8	$ 20.9	$17.23
American Can Co.	306.6	17.7	17.31
American Tobacco Co.	411.3	28.9	14.25
duPont (E.I.) de Nemours and Co. ..	2,017.6	86.9	23.21
Eastman Kodak Co.	354.9	20.1	17.68
General Electric Co.	974.3	56.2	17.32
General Foods Corp.	218.4	15.2	14.32
General Motors Corp.	2,253.9	195.6	11.52
Great Atlantic and Pacific Tea Co..	238.3	18.7	12.77
Kresge (S.S.) Company..............	141.0	10.1	14.00
Liggett and Myers Tobacco Co.	372.7	21.6	17.23
National Biscuit Co.	152.3	10.7	14.17
National Dairy Products Corp.	154.9	13.2	11.74
Penney (J.C.) Company..............	238.7	16.2	14.71
Proctor and Gamble Co.	381.7	28.6	13.33
Reynolds (R.J.) Tobacco Co.	362.2	25.5	14.18
Union Carbide and Carbon Corp.	673.9	42.2	15.95
United Fruit Co.	204.7	14.9	13.72
Woolworth (F.W.) Co.	336.8	24.5	13.72
Total for 19 companies............	$10,154.2	$ 668.0	------
Average for 19 companies.........	534.4	35.2	15.20
The Coca-Cola Company..............	461.1	28.9	15.96

* ($ in millions)

SUMMARY

Each of the variations or modifications of the comparative analysis discussed in this lesson are justified by sound judgement and logic. It is just as easy to derive inaccurate valuations by using accepted techniques incorrectly as by using incorrect methods. It should be apparent to you by now that the overriding requirements in security appraisals are the application of common sense, accounting know-how and integrity. These attributes will assure professional results.

Lesson 14

COMMON ERRORS IN VALUATION - ADJUSTING FOR NONRECURRENT ITEMS AND NONOPERATING ASSETS OR INCOME

CONTENTS

OBJECTIVES

At the end of this lesson you will be able to:

1. Describe methods used to adjust projected corporate earning power to reflect accurate past earnings and elimination of extraordinary nonrecurring items.

2. Explain the principle of segregating nonoperating assets and nonoperating income for separate valuation.

3. State the basis on which we can expect the courts to adopt the segregated approach.

FAILING TO ELIMINATE NONRECURRENT ITEMS

A reasonable estimate of the future earning capacity of a business must rely to a great extent upon the historic operating and financial results of the company up to the date of valuation. Past earnings are our chief evidence of future earning power. As the earnings data recede in time from the current period they become less and less dependable as indications of the company's potential. In the final analysis current earnings are usually the best available indication of future operating results.

The importance of earnings in the appraisal of a business enterprise makes it essential that appraisers make certain that the earnings data which are used are accurate and present a true picture of the company's earning capacity. It is necessary, therefore, that all nonrecurring items of income or loss reflected in past years' earnings be eliminated in order that only those earnings from sources which can reasonably be expected to continue are reflected in the estimate of future earning capacity. A hypothetical case in point follows:

315

Laurel Corporation came out of the Vietnam war period faced with the necessity of reconversion and finding a substitute for the war business which it had handled. The management attempted various ventures in diverse fields in which the corporation had never had any prior experience. As a result of these experiments Laurel Corporation sustained sharply reduced earnings or losses in the years 1973, 1974, and 1975.

The stock of this corporation had to be valued as of June 1, 1978. The financial data disclosed in brief the following net income and earnings per share of common stock:

Year	Net Income After Taxes	Earned Per Share of Common Stock
1973	$ 31,473.00	$ 62.95
1974	(506,685.00)	(1,013.37)
1975	20,750.00	41.50
1976	178,849.00	357.70
1977	400,189.00	800.38
1/1–5/27/78	188,327.00	376.65
Total	$312,903.00	$625.81
Average	$ 57,767.00	$115.55

The examining Revenue Agent had appraised the stock of the corporation at $2,500 per share. The taxpayers submitted an appraisal which contended for a value or from $800 to $1,000 per share for this stock. The above schedule of earnings would indicate on an average earnings basis that the agent's determination could not be supported. On the other hand, the latest year's earnings appear to be more than adequate relative to the $2,500 proposed valuation. Investigation disclosed that losses totaling $848,000 had been deducted in the years 1973, 1974 and 1975 and such losses were attributable directly to various ill-advised sidelines in which the company had invested during that period. All of these ventures had failed and had been abandoned by the end of 1975. There was no reasonable expectation that such activities would ever be attempted again by the corporation.

When earnings were adjusted to eliminate the nonrecurring losses and the consequent tax adjustment, a different picture of the earning capacity of this corporation was obtained.

Year	Net Income After Taxes	Earned Per Share of Common Stock
1973	$ 74,701.00	$ 149.40
1974	69,660.00	139.32
1975	104,994.00	209.99
1976	126,434.00	252.87
1977	400,189.00	800.38
1/1–5/27/78	188,327.00	376.65
Total	$964,305.00	$1,928.61
Average	$178,026.00	$ 356.05

It is apparent from the revised earnings figures above that a substantial understatement of the corporation's true earning capacity results if unadjusted profits are relied upon. Instead of using average earnings of $115.55 as a factor in making the appraisal, the revised average of $356.05 or almost 4 times the reported figure, is the proper amount to use. It is significant that in this particular case the taxpayers' appraisal made no adjustment for the substantial nonrecurrent losses which were sustained by the corporation in the years 1973 through 1975.

To illustrate the effect of an understatement such as the foregoing a comparative analysis of listed stocks of similar corporations indicated a price-average earnings ratio of 11.22. Applying this ratio to the reported average earnings figures of $115.55 per share, indicates a fair market value for Laurel Corporation stock of $1,296.47. By contrast, if we used the revised average earnings figure of $356.05 per share which constitutes a more correct estimate of the future earning capacity of this business, a value of $3,994.88 per share is indicated. The latter figure is more in line with the agent's appraisal since he used revised earnings also, and incidentally it did not conflict nearly as much with any of the other valuation factors which we will not go into at this point.

The preceding example deals with the elimination of nonrecurring loss items, however, it should be borne in mind that any nonrecurrent item, either loss or profit, should be removed from past earnings in order that the most valid index of the corporation's earning capacity in the past can be obtained. The result an appraiser gets in weighing the various factors of valuation is only as reliable as the elements which are used. If the very important earnings factor is not correct or is distorted in any fashion the end result in the appraisal will be far removed from a representative fair market value.

SEPARATING INVESTMENT AND OPERATING ASSETS OR INCOME

The Segregated Approach

An appraiser will consider many factors in making an evaluation of the capital stock of a closely-held corporation. One element which needs attention is the fair market value of the nonoperating investments of the company and more particularly its holdings of marketable securities. The reasoning underlying the following discussion will ordinarily be applicable as well to investments in nonoperating real estate.

When valuing a going concern of the manufacturing, merchandising, or services categories the earnings trend and record play a most important part. We give considerable weight to the rate of earnings, or return as it is referred to, realized on the invested capital of the business. The security analyst is also interested in the price/earnings ratios which are considered acceptable by investors in the specific industry.

The profits of an operating company are produced by all of the operating assets, tangible and intangible, owned by the business. Such intangible factors as trade name, goodwill, customer lists, management skill, credit rating, competitive position, etc., contribute their share to the realized earnings. It is the cumulative effect of all of the assets of the business which produces the net income. The analyst has to recognize, however, that there may exist certain corporate assets which play no part in the operating profits realized. If these assets are in turn productive of income such earnings are incidental to the operation of the business and should be segregated from net operating income.

In most instances nonoperating assets will produce income at a different rate than the operating segment of the business. For example if the firm holds $1 million in U.S. Government bonds carrying an 8 1/2% interest rate we cannot logically capitalize the total earnings from the operation of the business plus the interest earned on the investments at the same rate. The industry in which the corporation operates may disclose a range of 15% to 20% in capitalization rates for the year preceding the valuation date. It would make no sense to apply such a capitalization rate to total earnings when we know that $85,000 of such earnings (after appropriate income taxes) came from lower, fixed return investments. Recognition of this concept underlies the segregated approach.

It is essential that when investment assets are of a large amount they be accorded separate treatment in the overall appraisal of the business. The example to follow illustrates one method for giving effect to this factor.

Assume the following hypothetical situation. The following figures reflect various amounts pertaining to the financial position of Zinnia Corporation in the year 1979:

318

	Total	Per Share
Working capital	$ 100,000	$ 1.00
Net fixed assets at depreciated cost	400,000	4.00
Assets used in the business	$ 500,000	$ 5.00
Investments in securities at market price	500,000	5.00
Net total assets	$1,000,000	$10.00

The corporation has 100,000 shares of common stock outstanding.

Computation of income after charges including taxes:

	Total	Per Share
From operations	$50,000	$ .50
From investments in marketable securities	25,000	.25
Total Net Income	$75,000	$ .75

We will assume now that the stocks of other companies which are comparable to Zinnia Corporation except that they hold no marketable securities are selling on the market at approximately 7 times earnings. We will further assume for simplicity that the investment securities owned by the corporation are tax free bonds which are readily marketable at the quoted market price.

The operating and investment branches of this business should be appraised separately as follows:

Operating earnings capitalized at 14.3% (or a price/earnings ratio of 7)	$ 350,000
Investments at current market value	$ 500,000*
Total value of 100,000 shares	$ 850,000

---

*(The same result would be obtained if investment income should be capitalized at 5%, the proper rate indicated by its return rate).

It would be in error to capitalize the entire corporate income of $75,000 at 14.3%, that is, to appraise the entire capital stock of this business at $525,000. The marketable securities which are returning a rate of around 5% to the company are certainly worth no less than their market price. By the same token, the income attributable to these securities should not be capitalized at a rate having no relation to the return which the investments are producing.

The Courts' Acceptance

It is fine to theorize upon proper and logical valuation approaches, but we must inject realism into our appraisals. Many supposed reasonable theories have been ignored or destroyed by legal decision. We are fortunate in this instance to have some rather clear-cut dictum from courts of law on the validity of the segregated approach.

Schlegel v. U.S.
71 F. Supp. 495 (1947)

The issue in this case was the fair market value of two gifts of the Class B stock of Schlegel Manufacturing Co. These were minority blocks. The company made narrow weave fabrics for the automotive industry. The company was family owned and closely-held. As of the valuation dates it owned marketable securities having a fair market value of $1.6 million, or the equivalent of more than $230 per share. The taxpayers' witnesses testified to values for Schlegel stock of $171 to $202 per share. The Government's witnesses testified to values ranging from $400 to $449 per share. The major difference in approach was the segregation of the investment assets by the Government's witnesses with a corresponding increase in the per share value of Schlegel Class B stock. The Court determined a value of $360 per share for the gifts.

Pertinent excerpts from the decision follow:

"It can hardly be denied that the market value of the readily saleable securities owned by the two (operating) companies was a relevant fact bearing upon the value of the capital stock.

"The method of valuation adopted by the plaintiff's witnesses treated the investment activities of the parent company as a part of the manufacturing business, although the surplus invested in securities was neither required nor used in the company's manufacturing business. The balance sheets for the ten preceding fiscal years show that it always maintained a favorable position of liquidity apart from its investments. The evidence demonstrated no need for the large reserve represented by investments, either for anticipated conversion costs or possible changes in its business. The same is true of the Canadian subsidiary. The indefiniteness of the plan of the Canadian company to construct a new building for its manufacturing operations was not sufficient justification of a reserve for that purpose. In view of all the circumstances the defendant's valuation witnesses were warranted in viewing the investment activities of both the parent company and its Canadian subsidiary as ventures independent of the manufacturing business and in basing their valuations in part on the consolidated balance sheets and income accounts of the parent company and its subsidiary, and in considering the manufacturing operations of both companies separate and apart from the investment activities." (Parenthetical portions and underlining supplied.)

Worthen v. U.S.
192 F. Supp. 727 (1961)

At first glance this decision might be interpreted as a refutation of the segregated approach. Closer study discloses however, that the decision merely emphasizes that the rationality of the approach must be demonstrated in each case before the Court will accept it. Such reasonableness was evident in Schlegel. Here, however, the approach, though admitted by the Court to be a valid one, was not held applicable because of certain factors. The excerpts explain the Court's thinking.

This case involved the fair market value of the common stock of a closely-held corporation which was engaged in the manufacture of folding paper boxes. The company owned government securities of approximately $400,000 amounting to about $60 per share. Taxpayers' expert valued the stock at $104 per share and Government's witness testified to a value of $163 per share. Again the major difference in approach was the segregation of investments for separate appraisal by the Government's expert.

The Court found a value of $104. The excerpts following show why this conclusion was justified: (Underlining and parenthetical expressions supplied)

"It is the contention of government that since the corporation had about 25 per cent of its total tangible assets invested in government securities, while the average investment in such securities by the companies chosen by the government as comparable was only 7 per cent, this allegedly excess investment should be valued separately. There are cases in which such a procedure is justified.

"Thus the value of a share of stock is really composed of two elements, a share in the value of the company as an operating business, and a share in the value of the investment in securities. Hence it is proper to find that the value of a share is the total of these two values separately determined. Schlegel v. United States, D.C., 71 F. Supp. 495 (1947).

"More important, (however) it cannot be found that the corporation did have an investment fund here in excess of its operation needs and separable from them. Government's expert assumed that because (the company) had an investment in government securities much larger than that of the companies selected for comparison, that this represented funds not needed in the business and simply held as an investment. Such an assumption is unjustified on several counts.

"In the first place, it involves a misinterpretation of the nature and purpose of the corporation's holdings of government securities.

"What actually occurred was that the corporation temporarily converted as much of its cash as possible into government securities at the end of its fiscal year because this resulted in a state tax saving because such securities were tax exempt under the Massachusetts statute then in force, Mass. G.L. Ch. 63 S 30. subd. 3(b). Hence a large part of the corporation's holdings of government securities at the close of its fiscal year is clearly not a permanent investment of excess funds, but merely a temporary conversion of cash reasonably needed as working capital for the business.

"In order to determine whether (the company) did have assets not needed for its business operations which could properly be evaluated separately by the method used by the government's expert, a proper comparison would be between the relative amounts of working capital, that is, the excess of total current assets including cash and its equivalent in readily marketable securities over current liabilities. As shown by the calculations in plaintiffs' Exhibit 4, (the company's) 1953 total working capital amounted to 19 cents per dollar in 1953 sales. The comparable figure for the companies used by government's expert was 21 cents per dollar of sales and for the companies used by plaintiffs' expert was 20 cents per dollar of sales. Certainly this does not indicate that (the company's) total cash and holdings in government securities was excessive.

"Moreover, government's expert seems to have worked solely from the figures shown in financial statements without making any inquiry as to particular factors which might affect the amount of working capital needed by the corporation. In fact, the corporation had been following the policy of setting aside earnings in excess of its usual dividend for the purpose of financing a program of expansion and rehabilitation.

"These plans were in fact carried out, utilizing accumulated earnings. There clearly was no accumulation by the corporation of assets in excess of business needs which would require separate evaluation."

Conclusion

From the foregoing, we can conclude that the segregated approach to the valuation of the stock of closely-held corporations owning large investments in marketable securities has validity and is so recognized by the courts. The approach, however, cannot be applied indiscriminately. The court will expect any appraiser who uses the separate appraisal technique to be able to clearly indicate that the so-called nonoperating investments were in fact excess working capital not needed in the operation of the business. The appraiser will also have to demonstrate that the working capital ratio of the closely-held corporation computed without the marketable securities was comparable to other operating companies in the industry, and that the corporation's future plans for possible expansion, modernization, etc., could not reasonably require accumulation of extra funds.

There is good reason to believe that if we can show that the corporation's working capital position was satisfactory, exclusive of any investments, and that other aspects of the company's operation and its industry do not justify the maintenance of excess working capital, a court will listen with some degree of receptiveness to an opinion premised upon the segregated approach. Of course, such an approach will be merely one of the factors considered by the appraiser and the impression cannot be left with the court that exclusive consideration was given to this approach.

FAILURE TO CONSIDER ALL EVIDENCE OF VALUE

In the absence of an established market for a particular type of property, whether it be capital stock or any other property, there is many times little evidence of value other than expert opinion. But opinions are of little weight as evidence if they are not reasonable and susceptible to coherent and logical exposition. Opinions to be worthy of serious consideration must be based upon all of the facts and the conclusions arrived at must indicate that logical reasoning has been applied. It is not necessary or advisable for valuation witnesses to exhaust all possible methods for computing value and then to average the answers which they have obtained in order to get the final result. In fact, there is no logic behind such a procedure. Witnesses must, however, be able to state that they have considered all of the pertinent factors and they must enumerate those which are of primary concern; such as assets, past and present earnings, dividend-paying capacity, future earning capacity, the prospects for growth or decline in the business, and the adequacy or inadequacy of existing plant facilities, to name a few. Also, witnesses should be prepared to show why they considered one factor or more to have greater weight than others or to have predominant weight for the particular appraisal they are making, and the process of reasoning employed in selecting or rejecting factors when making estimates of value. There are many court decisions which refer to one or more of the items just briefly mentioned above. There are cited below a select group of such decisions.

All factors bearing on value must be given consideration. (Julian Ann Schroth, 5 BTA 326 (1926), and Laird, et al. v. Commissioner, 85 F. 2d 598(3rd Cir. 1936). Also Minnesota Rate Cases, 230 U.S. 352; 434 (1912).) It is a legal question as to whether or not correct theories and principles have been applied in determining value (C.B. & Q. Railway Co. v. Babcock, 204 U.S. 585, 596 (1907); also International Harvester Co. v. Kentucky, 234 U.S. 216 (1913)).

"* * * Estimates of value made by friendly witnesses, with no practical illustration to support them are *** too unsafe, as a rule, to be made the basis of a judicial award." (<u>The Conqueror</u>, 166 U.S. 110, 134 (1897)).

The weight to be accorded to the opinions of experts depends on their approach to the question and the criteria which governs their estimates. (<u>Dayton Power and Light Co. v. Commissioner</u>, 292 U.S. 290 (1934), and <u>St. Joseph Stockyards Co. v. U.S., et al</u>, 298 U.S. 38 (1936)).

Valuation for tax purposes should conform to standard business practices insofar as possible (<u>Guggenhiem v. Rasquin</u> 312 U.S. 254 (1940)). Values should not be premised upon improbable future estimates (<u>Olson v. U.S.</u> 292 U.S. 246,257 (1934)).

Earning capacity under efficient management should be considered rather than past earnings under an incompetent management, for example. (<u>Harris Trust and Savings Bank v. Earl</u>, 26 F. 2d 617, (8th Cir. 1928)).

The courts have been more or less uniform in holding that all pertinent evidence of value must be considered by an opinion witness. It is the appraiser's duty to insure that all relevant material is assembled and in such form as to be presentable as evidence before the Court in the event testimony as an expert is necessary. On this latter point we might mention that an early preparation of schedules and supporting statements in final form is of inestimable assistance to the valuation expert when the case is finally being prepared for trial.

SUMMARY OF COMMON ERRORS

This concludes the last of five lessons in this course devoted to the subject of common errors in valuation. It might seem like overkill on the subject; the proportion of material and time is relatively high. The primary purpose of this course, however, justifies our giving intensified attention to the typical errors of business interest appraisals.

The course is not aimed at creating security or other property valuation experts among Appeals Officers. In addition to describing proper valuation approaches to valuing various kinds of property improper methods and techniques must be pointed out. This approach is supportive of the Appeals mission. These common errors lessons provide Appeals Officers who encounter valuation issues in tax settlement negotiations, with in depth analysis of some of the most prevalent errors in appraisal practice. Whether the use of these questionable approaches is for deception or wholly unpremeditated, Appeals Officers are bound to be more effective in settling such issues on an equitable basis if they are fully informed of what to look for. Presumably, if we can identify the erroneous methods early in the negotiation process, and at the same time introduce more valid accepted approaches, settlements of these troublesome issues should be more frequent and satisfactory.

Lesson 16

THE EXPERT WITNESS

CONTENTS

OBJECTIVES

At the end of this lesson you will be able to:

1. State the so called "ten commandments" for experts to follow in order to be effective.

2. Describe the way expert witnesses should participate at an Appeals conference so that Appeals Officers will be able to use them effectively in securing settlements of valuation issues.

INTRODUCTION

This lesson is for the purpose of acquainting Appeals Officers with the characteristics and attitude which make up an effective expert witness. These comments should make us better able to weigh the trial hazards of a given issue by providing guidelines which will enable us to accord full and proper consideration to the expert's potential testimony. You should bear in mind that while much of the information relates to the <u>trial</u> of a valuation issue, it is equally applicable to the expert's performance at settlement conferences. An evaluation of any appraisals in the file when the case is first considered may be made easier by this information. The material presented has been gathered from the following sources: (a) personal experience of members of the National Office Appeals Division in observing government and outside experts in action; (b) material written by others; and (c) admonitions of the U.S. Tax Court's Judge Pierce in a discussion of the subject at an Engineering Institute held in Washington, D.C.

THE EXPERT'S " TEN COMMANDMENTS"

Perhaps the best starting point for this discussion is Judge Pierce's "Code for Experts" which follows.

The effective expert witness will:

First, be prepared by:

a. Knowing the concepts - knowing the definition of "fair market value,"
b. Knowing the specifics - the facts in the case,
c. Outlining and organizing his or her testimony in full, and
d. Preparing necessary basic exhibits in a format suitable for introduction into evidence.

Second, testify effectively by:

a. Speaking clearly and slowly,
b. Stating his or her qualifications fully but without bragging,
c. Stating his or her opinion and explaining how it was arrived at,
d. Being concise, but complete - holding to the essentials,
e. Not being a partisan,
f. Recognizing those facts which are unfavorable,
g. Being courteous, frank, calm - not losing control, and
h. Being unafraid to say "I don't know."

It would seem that the admonition "Be Prepared" would be well enough understood to require no further comment. However, we have found many experts who were not prepared in one or more areas of a given valuation issue. Many experts, otherwise qualified to express an opinion of value, do not even know the definition of fair market value as that term is used for tax purposes. For example, a prominent appraiser of literary works stated that his appraisal for Federal income tax purposes would have been different if it had been made for Federal estate tax purposes. The appraiser explained that the estate would be faced with liquidating the property immediately while another type of owner could market it normally. It was necessary to point out to him that the concept of fair market value in the Federal tax field is consistent regardless of the type of tax being imposed, and that a forced sale such as he was presupposing in the estate tax situation does not meet the definition.

In another case a written appraisal of the value of mounted animal trophies valued the items at their replacement cost. Our investigation revealed that these trophies had only slight value under the "willing buyer - willing seller" concept. However, the taxpayer's appraisers failed to mention that their values were based on the replacement cost approach. The moral, of course, is to be sure that appraisals have been made with the proper concept of fair market value clearly understood by the expert.

QUALIFYING THE WITNESS

Preparation and knowledge of the facts are basic to any case, yet often the expert (or the attorney) has taken neither the time nor the effort to make sure that the testimony is organized and susceptible to being presented in a logical and complete manner. Lack of good organization of the material can lead to omission of important facts. We suggest that the potential expert prepare a list of questions for the attorney which will provide the means of getting the full story in the record logically, fully and effectively.

In going over the printed transcript of the testimony of a government expert in the recent trial of a valuation issue, we were appalled to find that he launched right into his appraisal without stating his qualifications. This brought a quick objection from the petitioner's attorney. When the expert's excellent qualifications were revealed, the judge quickly overruled the objection and caustically suggested that the respondent's attorney should have qualified his witness first. This is an example of the lack of preparation where both the expert and the attorney were remiss.

When qualifying an expert, whether in court or in a conference, the particular education and experience of the expert should be carefully stated so that all may be able to judge the expert's qualifications to express an opinion. Occasionally, petitioner's counsel will offer to stipulate that the expert is qualified to testify. This flattering offer should be refused and the court told of the expert's background so that the court can objectively judge the qualifications, and, more important, so that the trial record can include this essential information. Similarly, when an expert appears at an Appeals conference his or her qualifications should be furnished to both parties at the table.

This leads us to the actual presentation of the expert's opinion testimony. Writing for the August 1964 American Bar Association Journal is Mortimer H. Nickerson, a chemist who had sage advice for would-be expert witnesses.

In essence he stated that to get an intelligent answer, you have to ask an intelligent question. If the answer is to be highly technical, the question must be technical in content and must be clear enough so that the desired answer can be elicited. With all due respect to the skill of lawyers it is asking too much that they feel at home with the highly specialized language of another field. It is distressing for an expert witness to be subjected to a barrage of questions from a supposedly friendly attorney which really don't mean what the attorney thinks they mean. In fact, they may be technologically unintelligible, while at the same time sounding like the best English.

The witness has to respond to questions of the attorneys, but has little or no opportunity to discuss, rephrase or correct from the witness chair. Witnesses can, of course, refuse to answer and then perhaps be permitted to explain why. But these alternatives do nothing good for the case. The lawyer should consult with the experts beforehand on the wording of questions and these questions should be thoroughly understood.

The technical valuation field places the same responsibility on an attorney, or for that matter, on an Appeals Officer when eliciting opinion testimony at a conference.

Up to this point we can say that the prospective expert should know the definition of the term, "fair market value," should be thoroughly familiar with all of the facts in the case, should prepare or assist the attorney to prepare the proper questions to qualify the witness and to enable him or her to present a logical and coherent story to the court. The expert should assist the attorney in understanding the technical aspects of the case. And, finally, the expert and attorney should rehearse to present a smooth, clear and concise case.

PERILS AND PITFALLS

Now for the second part of Judge Pierce's Code, the actual presentation by the expert on the witness stand. What is the image that the expert is supposed to project in court and how can the attorney enhance it? What can the attorney do to keep from inadvertently destroying it? Strictly speaking, experts are supposed to be completely objective and nonpartisan. They present either factual data or well-considered opinions which, presumably, are shared by a majority of the appraisal community to which they belong. Theoretically, the expert's testimony will not be in conflict with any other expert of equal skill. Nevertheless, experts are in court only because one side or the other has retained them and this could be interpreted as establishing a partisan bond. Most experts like to get paid for their work, and this could conceivably be an influencing factor in their testimony.

Beyond these inevitable facts, however, experts are independent professional people. They are retained by an attorney or client, but are not employed by them. There is no employer-employee relationship. Experts' testimony are theirs alone, and they are not, or should not be, "instructed" by the attorney as to the technical content of the testimony. This does not preclude pretrial collaboration and mutual agreement as to what evidence to present and how, but it must be clearly evident from the manner in which the evidence is presented under direct examination that the facts and opinions are those of the expert and not mere rubber-stamped approvals of the attorney's or the taxpayer's views.

In the act of testifying, the expert should speak loudly enough, clearly enough, and slowly enough. Remember, unless the judge and court reporter can hear what is said, little good is accomplished. Moreover, unclear speech inevitably leads to mistakes in the transcript of the testimony. Figures can be particularly puzzling to the court reporter if not properly identified. Often the reporter will not know whether, for example, three, one, thirteen means dollars, percentages, or a date. Technical jargon should be kept to a minimum, and where it must be used, an explanation in everyday English should be included.

In telling his or her story the expert witness should be concise, but complete. In direct testimony the expert must exercise discipline to use words carefully and sparingly. Experts should focus on those points and facts which are unassailable or easily defended and refrain from offering unnecessary comments where the pertinence of the views can be questioned. The more loquacious they are the more vulnerable they become.

To no small degree, the expert's desired air of self-assurance and convincing manner is based on ego, and that in itself can be the expert's most vulnerable point. The opposing attorney may ask technical questions of the expert in some unrelated field, or on some detail so trivial that the expert does not know the answer. Under these circumstances the expert should admit frankly that he or she doesn't know. This honest answer is by far the best course, and actually may even add to the stature of the witness as an expert. It is certainly the safest course, because the expert who claims knowledge that really isn't possessed is well on the way to being proved to be either incompetent or a liar. In interviewing a prospective expert prior to employment, the trial attorney should ask many questions, and should become suspicious if there isn't a proper sprinkling of "I don't know's" and a certain amount of resistance to a few harebrained technological ideas which should be thrown out deliberately.

What is wanted in an expert is an aggressive devil's advocate, not an amiable, agreeable soul anxious to please. Experts should be extremely interested in devising ways of attacking their own testimony and their attorney's strategy. In that way they can most effectively test their own conclusions and guard against any surprises which might be sprung by the opposing side.

In the final analysis the business of testifying as an expert at a formal hearing or in a court trial has three fundamental requirements to be successfully carried off. These are:

  (a) Be honest.
  (b) Use common sense.
  (c) Have the courage of your convictions.

The expert must remember that nothing is absolute in the technical areas where expertise is needed for evidence. No expert can know all there is about any one field. If experts' manner and deportment are proper and if they demonstrate their know-how convincingly, they will be listened to and their testimony will be accorded the full share of its deserved attention.

THE EXPERT AT THE APPEALS CONFERENCE

There is little practical use or benefit to be derived at the Appeals level from expert opinion which carries a restriction on disclosure. By this we mean that the opinion of value by an otherwise qualified appraiser is not worth much as a negotiating tool if the Appeals

Officer is not free to disclose the name and qualifications of the expert. Many times we have had to discard off-the-cuff opinions by knowledgable specialists because they were reluctant to lift the cloak of confidentiality from their opinions. All that an experienced tax practitioner has to do to completely nullify such opinions is to say "Here's my expert; where's yours?" It is because of this fact of life that the Appeals Division will insist on the freedom to mention the expert's name if necessary in settlement conferences before undertaking to employ an outside appraiser.

The question of unauthorized disclosure is sometimes raised by Appeals Officers when we are contemplating engaging an outside expert on a particular valuation matter. In a memorandum dated June 15,1964, the then Chief Counsel, Sheldon S. Cohen, took the following position on this point:

"Divulging Tax Return Information to Contract Appraisers

This is in reply to (a) memorandum of March 27, 1964 asking for an opinion as to 'whether or not tax return information may be divulged to contract or fee appraisers to the extent necessary for the appraisers to determine the fair market value of properties they are hired to appraise for the Service.' It is understood that the appraiser would be 'employed on a contract (or fee) basis to determine the fair market value of property appearing in specific tax returns,' but that 'aside from the name of the taxpayer, the only tax return information normally necessary to disclose to contract or fee appraisers concerns the property to be appraised.'***

"Our initial concern is whether or not the subject disclosures are restricted by provisions of Sections 6103 or 7213 of the Code or 18 U.S.C. 1905.***

"Section 6103 of the Code was enacted to protect the privacy of the taxpayer and to encourage compliance with our voluntary self-assessment tax system. It was believed that taxpayers would be less hesitant in reporting their full tax affairs if they could do so without fear of this information being made available to their competitiors in business or their friends or enemies. Thus in determining whether or not Section 6103 should be construed as restricting necessary disclosures to contract or fee appraisers, one of the factors to be considered is whether such disclosures would operate in derogation of the legislative intent underlying Section 6103. With this design in mind, we are of the opinion that Section 6103 does not restrict necessary disclosures to such appraisers, who are disinterested in the taxpayer's affairs and who are only doing a job to assist the Service in determining tax liability.

"The authority to disclose information for investigative purposes is specifically provided by Reg. 301.6103(a)-1(i) with respect to estate and gift taxes. There is every reason why the same authority should apply to other classes of taxes administered and enforced by the Commissioner.***

"In summary, it is the opinion of this office that tax return information may be furnished to contract or fee appraisers to the extent necessary for the appraisers to assist the Service in determining the fair market value of properties. We would not expect this to entail the actual inspection of tax returns."

Other pertinent references concerning disclosure are Section 7217 of the Code which relates to penalties, and the Disclosure of Official Information Handbook, Chapter (21)00 of IRM 1272.

Disclosures of confidential tax information to contract appraisers are made under the authority found in Code 6103(k)(6) and temporary regulation 404.6103(k)(6)-1(b)(5). This section of the Code and its corresponding regulation permits investigative disclosures necessary to obtain information which would assist the Service in its efforts in respect to examinations, collection activity, civil or criminal tax investigation, etc. Disclosures may occur only if it is determined that the information to be obtained is not otherwise reasonably available.

CONCLUSION

In conclusion, it is the objective of Appeals Officers to make judicious use of whatever documentary or oral expert opinion evidence available to them in an effort to equitably dispose of valuation issues. Such questions are peculiarly susceptible to settlement, since a single correct answer does not apply. If the Appeals Officer and the taxpayers' representative, together with their respective experts' opinions can deal objectively, candidly and with an honest desire to find a reasonable answer, the result will be far more satisfactory than we could ever hope to achieve in a court of law. Of course, if the taxpayers' representative offers no tangible evidence in support of the original valuation then the Appeals Officer has no alternative but to keep the nature of any expert opinion evidence possesed by the Government undisclosed. In the usual case, however, where there is a free exchange of views, there is no reason for Appeals Officers not to place their cards on the table in seeking an acceptable dispostion of the issue.

Lesson 17

UNIQUE VALUATION QUESTIONS

CONTENTS

OBJECTIVES

At the conclusion of this lesson you will be able to:

1. Determine the correct basis for the valuation of a closely-held preferred stock.

2. Explain the position that the Appeals Division should take when the value of a corporate stock as of an earlier date has been determined in accordance with a U.S. Tax Court decision.

UNIQUE VALUATION QUESTIONS

Approach to Valuing Closely-Held Senior Securities

Although the great majority of corporate stock valuation issues coming before the Service involve common stocks, there may be occasion to appraise preferred stocks or corporate bonded indebtedness of a family-owned corporation. The first part of this short lesson will cover the basic principles to use in evaluating such senior securities.

Corporate bonds are valued as debt instruments of a company rather than as part of the corporate equity. Since such long term bonds are normally negotiable there is a considerable market for such issues of publicly-traded corporations. It is feasible therefore to find comparable bond issues that are quoted on the New York Bond Exchange or other exchange to use in developing a market value indication for the closely-held bonds.

Major criteria for appraising corporate bonds are: a) the degree of security of the bonds - in other words how well the company can meet its obligations, and b) the extent to which the corporation's earnings exceed the annual interest requirements. When the investment marketplace appraises corporate bonds additional key considerations are the stated interest rate in comparison with the rate demanded by the market and the current yield of the bond issue. Yield is the relationship of annual interest to current market price. For example, a bond selling at 88 1/2 and carrying a 9% interest rate will be said to

332

have a current yield of 10.17%. If the bond sold at face value (normally bonds are in $1,000 units) the yield would be 9%. Bond quotations are in reality percentage figures. Thus the example hypothesized a market price of $885.00 — 88.5% of $1,000.

An added factor entering into corporate bond evaluation is the yield to maturity (YTM). This concept tells us the percentage yield we will realize if we hold a bond until it matures. Take this example for illustrative purposes. Assume we have bought one 6% XYZ Corporate Bond, face $1,000, at 90. Assume also that there are ten years to maturity of the bond. The yield to maturity is calculated by relating the annual increment in value (interest plus discount) to the average investment. Computation is as follows:

$$YTM = \frac{\$60(\text{annual interest}) + \$10(\$100 \text{ discount} \div \text{number of years to maturity})}{\$1,000(\text{maturity value}) + \$900(\text{purchase price}) \div 2}$$

$$YTM = \frac{\$70}{\$950} = 7.37\%$$

Publishers of financial and market information will show bond prices, interest rates, current yields and YTM's. The investing public will consider these facts as well as many others in making its buying and selling decisions.

Preferred stocks are also subject to substantial public investor interest. As in bond values, preferred stocks derive their market value from the basic financial strength of the corporation to pay the dividends required. The stated dividend rate, either a percentage or a dollar amount, is a major consideration in appraising these stocks. Such factors as convertibility, participating potential, callability, and preference as to assets in the event of liquidation are all critical to the market price of preferred stocks.

In the instance of closely-held bonds or preferred stocks the comparative approach is just as important as in the case of common stock valuations. The approach, however, should be varied somewhat. Since the yields are almost all important in the market's appraisal of fixed income securities we should direct the comparative analysis to specific publicly-traded bonds or preferred stocks which have comparable interest or dividend rates, yields and other similar rights. Thus an analysis of comparable preferred stocks might be concentrated on those carrying similar interest rates, convertibility and participation privileges, for comparison purposes. Indicated yields of a representative crosssection of preferred stocks in the same or similar industry will be most persuasive in leading the appraiser to a fair market value range for the closely-held security. A case in point is described in the first related handout for this lesson.

Weighing a Prior Court Valuation

This unique situation is patterned on an actual Appeals Division case. The crucial question raised by the case file deals with the weight to give a prior judicial determination of fair market value of the same stock. The second handout for this lesson describes the situation and will provide a basis for in depth discussion of the issue. The importance of this question to the Appeals Division should be apparent.

CONCLUSION

The unique areas of valuation described in this lesson are of particular interest to the Appeals Division. Frequently valuation issues involving senior securities are given little attention by taxpayers and the IRS examining officers while the usually more significant common stock valuation issues are debated and argued. It is only when the case is nearing potential trial, often after the issuance of the statutory notice that the senior security valuation receives attention. Similarly, Appeals Officers will be the recipients of situations like the Juniper Corporation case file. Both areas are typical of the complex and nonprecedential problems which come before the Appeals Division.

Lesson 18

SUMMARY

OBJECTIVES

At the end of this lesson you will be able to:

1. Restate the objectives of the course.

2. Describe several source materials each Appeals Office should have available for reference purposes.

3. Identify the kinds of data you will need in order to evaluate closely-held securities or to test the validity of appraisals in the file.

SUMMARY

This training course has been presented not so much with the view that Appeals Officers should become professional valuation experts, but rather that they should, before reaching a conclusion on valuation issues:

1. Be aware of the essential elements necessary to a satisfactory development of valuation issues,

2. Be able to recognize the omissions or errors in the taxpayers' or Government's case,

3. Know how and when to remedy such defects in the case development by referring the issue back to the examining officer or enlisting the services of the National Office valuation staff if the need exists, and

4. Be reasonably certain when recommending trial of valuation issues that the Government's position will be supported by the facts and by opinion evidence.

If these objectives are accomplished, this course will have served its purpose.

Procedures for requesting the Services of the Engineering and Valuation Branch of the National Office are set forth in IRM 8(14)51.

VALUATION DATA CHECKLIST

As an aid for you to use when confronted with a closely-held security valuation issue in settlement negotiations the following checklist of minimal needs for information is offered:

a) Detailed balance sheets of the corporation for a period preceding the valuation date of at least five years.

335

b) Detailed income statements of the corporation showing product and departmental breakdowns for the latest five preceding years.

   Note: Corporate audit reports are preferable in supplying these two needs.

c) A complete schedule of the dividend record of the company and any of its subsidiaries for the last five years preceding the valuation date.

d) Statements of rights and preferences of all senior securities of the corporations and data as to any preferred dividend arrearages.

e) A complete description of the type of business involved and a brief history of the company, including all available data pertaining to the quality of management.

f) Financial data as described in (a) and (b) pertaining to all subsidiary companies.

g) A list of the stockholders - their interests and family relationships (only the major stockholders are necessary if there are over 50 stockholders).

h) A statement and description of the sales of any shares of the stock if they occurred within a ten-year period prior to the valuation date.

i) A detailed description of the terms of any stock option or restrictive sales agreement applicable to the shares of stock to be valued.

j) An indication of the fair market value of all investments of the company in such nonoperating properties as marketable securities, real estate, etc.

FINANCIAL REFERENCES

A further aid you may find useful is the following partial list of reference works and source materials. The first list includes those publications which can justifiably be placed in Appeals Office libraries. The second list is a more complete bibliography on the subject of valuation.

I   Group A - Information comparable to that found in the following reference publications is essential in considering closely-held corporate stock valuation questions. These sources will provide financial data and market quotations.

    (a) Moody's Manual of Investments - Industrial

(b) Wall Street Journal

(c) Standard and Poor's Industry Surveys

(d) Value Line Investment Survey

Group B - Publications comparable to the following are suggested
for inclusion in the libraries of the larger Appeals
Offices.

(a) Standard and Poor's Corporation Records (6 vols.)

(b) Commercial and Financial Chronicle

(c) National Stock Summary

(d) Value Line Investment Service

(e) Wall Street Journal

(f) Bureau of National Affairs Tax Management Portfo-
lios:
Chalmers, 132-2nd. T.M., Aaluation of Assets.
Henderer, 221 T.M., Valuation of Shares of Closely
Held Corporations.
Hocky, 248 T.M., Blockage
Chalmers, 299 T.M., Valuation of Real Estate

The publishers of the foregoing are as follows:

1(a)   Moody's Investors Service, Inc.
       99 Church Street, New York, New York, 10004

1(b),2(e)   Wall Street Journal
            30 Broad Street, New York, New York, 10004

1(c),2(a)   Standard & Poor's Corporation
            345 Hudson Street, New York, New York, 10014

1(d),2(d)   Arnold Bernhard & Co., Inc.
            5 East 44th Street, New York , New York

2(b)   William B. Dana Company
       25 Park Place, New York , New York

2(c)   National Quotation Bureau, Inc.
       46 Front Street, New York , New York,

Note: Needed publications should be requisitioned through normal
       channels and will be supplied subject to availability of
       funds. Also refer to "Tax Reference Material Standards"
       (Exhibit 1 - IRM 1(14)20).

II Source Materials and Text Books on Valuation

Financial Source and Reference Materials:

1. Barron's Magazine
2. Business Week Magazine
3. Commercial and Financial Chronicle
4. Federal Tax Valuation Digest
5. Journal of Accountancy, The
6. Journal of Taxation
7. Institutional Investor Study, Report of the SEC, H.P. Doc. No. 92-64, 92nd Cong. 1st Sess. XXIX (1971).
8. Investment Companies by Wiesenberger
9. Magazine of Wall Street
10. Moody's Manual Investments
    a) Banks and Insurance Companies
    b) Government and Municipals
    c) Industrials
    d) Public Utilities
    e) Transportation
11. National Bond Summary
12. National Stock Summary and Monthly Stock Summary
13. Standard and Poor's Corporation Records
14. Standard and Poor's Industry Surveys
15. Standard and Poor's Unlisted Stock Reports
16. Value Line Survey
17. Wall Street Journal

Text Books

1. American Society of Appraisers (annual manuals - volumes 1 through 8)

2. The Evaluation of Common Stocks by Arnold Bernhard

3. Financial Statements, Form Analysis and Interpretation by Kennedy & McMullen

4. Rev. Rul. 59-60, IRS 1959-1 CB, 237 (Included as Appendix A)

5. Security Analysis by Graham and Dodd, 4th Edition

6. Valuation of Property by Bonbright (2 volumes)

7. When Corporations Go Public, edited by Carlos L. Isreals and George M. Duff, Jr.

8. Valuation Theories and Decisions of the S.E.C., Chelcie Bosland, 1964

Appendix

B

Internal Revenue Service Rulings

1. Rev. Rul. 59–60, 1959-1 C.B. 237.
2. Rev. Rul. 65–192, 1965-2 C.B. 259.
3. Rev. Rul. 65–193, 1965-2 C.B. 370.
4. Rev. Rul. 68–609, 1968-2 C.B. 327.
5. Rev. Rul. 77–287, 1977-2 C.B. 319.
6. Rev. Rul. 78–367, 1978-2 C.B. 249.
7. Rev. Rul. 79–7, 1979-1 C.B. 294.
8. Ltr. Rul. 7953001.
9. Ltr. Rul. 8010017.

REV. RUL. 59–60

In valuing the stock of closely held corporations, or the stock of corporations where market quotations are not available, all other available financial data, as well as all relevant factors affecting the fair market value must be considered for estate tax and gift tax purposes. No general formula may be given that is applicable to the many different valuation situations arising in the valuation of such stock. However, the general approach, methods, and factors which must be considered in valuing such securities are outlined.
Revenue Ruling 54–77, C.B. 1954-1, 187, superseded.

Section 1. Purpose.

The purpose of this Revenue Ruling is to outline and review in general the approach, methods and factors to be considered in valuing shares of the capital stock of closely held corporations for estate tax and gift tax purposes. The methods discussed herein will apply likewise to the valuation of corporate stocks on which market quotations are either unavailable or are of such scarcity that they do not reflect the fair market value.

Sec. 2. Background and Definitions.

.01 All valuations must be made in accordance with the applicable provisions of the Internal Revenue Code of 1954 and the Federal Estate Tax and Gift Tax Regulations. Sections 2031(a), 2032 and 2512(a) of the 1954 Code (sections 811 and 1005 of the 1939 Code) require that the property to be included in the gross estate, or made the subject of a gift, shall be taxed on the basis of the value of the property at the time of death of the decedent, the alternate date if so elected, or the date of gift.

.02 Section 20.2031-1(b) of the Estate Tax Regulations (Section 81.10 of the Estate Tax Regulations 105) and Section 25.2512-1 of the Gift Tax Regulations (Section 86.19 of Gift Tax Regulations 108) define fair market value, in effect, as the price at which the property would change hands between a willing buyer and a willing seller when the former is not under any compulsion to buy and the latter is not under any compulsion to sell, both parties having reasonable knowledge of relevant facts. Court decisions frequently state in addition that the hypothetical buyer and seller are assumed to be able, as well as willing, to trade and to be well-informed about the property and concerning the market for such property.

.03 Closely held corporations are those corporations the shares of which are owned by a relatively limited number of stockholders. Often the entire stock issue is held by one family. The result of this situation is that little, if any, trading in the shares takes place. There is, therefore, no established market for the stock and such sales as occur at irregular intervals seldom reflect all of the elements of a representative transaction as defined by the term "fair market value."

Sec. 3. Approach to Valuation.

.01 A determination of fair market value, being a question of fact, will depend upon the circumstances in each case. No formula can be devised that will be generally applicable to the multitude of different valuation issues arising in estate and gift tax cases. Often, an appraiser will find wide differences of opinion as to the fair market value of a particular stock. In resolving such differences, he should maintain a reasonable attitude in recognition of the fact that valuation is not an exact science. A sound valuation will be based upon all the relevant facts, but the elements of common sense, informed judgment and reasonableness must enter into the process of weighing those facts and determining their aggregate significance.

.02 The fair market value of specific shares of stock will vary as general economic conditions change from "normal" to "boom" or "depression," that is, according to the degree of optimism or pessimism with which the investing public regards the future at the required date of appraisal. Uncertainty as to the stability or continuity of the future income from a property decreases its value by increasing the risk of loss of earnings and value in the future. The value of shares of stock of a company with very uncertain future prospects is highly speculative. The appraiser must exercise his judgment as to the degree of risk attaching to the business of the corporation which issued the stock, but that judgment must be related to all of the other factors affecting value.

.03 Valuation of securities is, in essence, a prophesy as to the future and must be based on facts available at the required date of appraisal. As a generalization, the prices of stocks which are traded in volume in a free and active market by informed persons best reflect the consensus of the investing public as to what the future holds for the corporations and industries represented. When a stock is closely held, is traded infrequently, or is traded in an erratic market, some other measure of value must be used. In many instances, the next best measure may be found in the prices at which the stocks of companies engaged in the same or a similar line of business are selling in a free and open market.

Sec. 4. Factors to Consider.

.01 It is advisable to emphasize that in the valuation of the stock of closely held corporations or the stock of corporations where market quotations are either lacking or too scarce to be recognized, all available financial data, as well as all relevant factors affecting the fair market value, should be considered. The following factors, although not all-inclusive, are fundamental and require careful analysis in each case:

(a) The nature of the business and the history of the enterprise from its inception.

(b) The economic outlook in general and the condition and outlook of the specific industry in particular.

(c) The book value of the stock and the financial condition of the business.

(d) The earning capacity of the company.

(e) The dividend-paying capacity.

(f) Whether or not the enterprise has goodwill or other intangible value.

(g) Sales of the stock and the size of the block of stock to be valued.

(h) The market price of stocks of corporations engaged in the same or a similar line of business having their stocks actively traded in a free and open market, either on an exchange or over-the-counter.

.02 The following is a brief discussion of each of the foregoing factors:

(a) The history of a corporate enterprise will show its past stability or instability, its growth or lack of growth, the diversity or lack of diversity of its operations, and other facts needed to form an opinion of the degree of risk involved in the business. For an enterprise which changed its form of organization but carried on the same or closely similar operations of its predecessor, the history of the former enterprise should be considered. The detail to be considered should increase with approach to the required date of appraisal, since recent events are of greatest help in predicting the future; but a study of gross and net income, and of dividends covering a long prior period, is highly desirable. The history to be studied should include, but need not be limited to, the nature of the business, its products or services, its operating and investment assets, capital structure, plant facilities, sales records and management, all of which should be considered as of the date of the appraisal, with due regard for recent significant changes. Events of the past that are unlikely to recur in the future should be discounted, since value has a close relation to future expectancy.

(b) A sound appraisal of a closely held stock must consider current and prospective economic conditions as of the date of appraisal, both in the national economy and in the industry or industries with which the corporation is allied. It is important to know that the company is more or less successful than its competitors in the same industry, or that it is maintaining a stable position with respect to competitors. Equal or even greater significance may attach to the ability of the industry with which the company is allied to compete with other industries. Prospective competition which has not been a factor in prior years should be given careful attention. For example, high profits due to the novelty of its product and the lack of competition often lead to increasing competition. The public's appraisal of the future prospects of competitive industries or of competitors within an industry may be indicated by price trends in the markets for commodities and for securities. The loss of the manager of a so-called "one-man" business may have a depressing effect upon the value of the stock of such business, particularly if there is a lack of trained personnel capable of succeeding to the management of the enterprise. In valuing the stock of this type of business, therefore, the effect of the loss of the manager on the future expectancy of the business, and the absence of management-succession potentialities are pertinent factors to be taken into consideration. On the other hand, there may be factors which offset, in whole or in part, the loss of the manager's services. For instance, the nature of the business and of its assets may be such that they will not be impaired by the loss of the manager. Furthermore, the loss may be adequately covered by life insurance, or competent management might be employed on the basis of the consideration paid for the former manager's services. These, or other offsetting factors, if found to exist, should be carefully weighed against the loss of the manager's services in valuing the stock of the enterprise.

(c) Balance sheets should be obtained, preferably in the form of comparative annual statements for two or more years immediately preceding the date of appraisal, together with a balance sheet at the end of the month preceding that date, if corporate accounting will permit. Any balance sheet descriptions that are not self-explanatory, and balance sheet items comprehending diverse assets or liabilities, should be clarified in essential detail by supporting supplemental schedules. These statements usually will disclose to the appraiser (1) liquid position (ratio of current assets to current liabilities); (2) gross and net book value of principal classes of fixed assets; (3) working capital; (4) long-term indebtedness; (5) capital structure; and (6) net worth. Consideration also should be given to any assets not essential to the operation of the business, such as investments in securities, real estate, etc. In general, such nonoperating assets will command a lower rate of return than do the operating assets, although in exceptional cases the reverse may be true. In computing the book value per share of stock, assets of the investment type should be revalued on the basis of their market price and the book value adjusted accordingly. Comparison of the company's balance sheets over several years may reveal, among other facts, such developments as the acquisition of additional production facilities or subsidiary companies, improvement in financial position, and details as to recapitalizations and other changes in the capital structure of the corporation. If the corporation has more than one class of stock outstanding, the charter or certificate of incorporation should be examined to ascertain the explicit rights and privileges of the various stock issues including: (1) voting powers, (2) preference as to dividends, and (3) preference as to assets in the event of liquidation.

(d) Detailed profit and loss statements should be obtained and considered for a representative period immediately prior to the required date of appraisal, preferably five or more years. Such statements should show (1) gross income by principal items; (2) principal deductions from gross income including major prior items of operating expenses, interest and other expense on each item of long-term debt, depreciation and depletion if such deductions are made, officers' salaries, in total if they appear to be reasonable or in detail if they seem to be excessive, contributions (whether or not deductible for tax purposes) that the nature of its business and its community position require the corporation to make, and taxes by principal items, including income and excess profits taxes; (3) net income available for dividends; (4) rates and amounts of dividends paid on each class of stock; (5) remaining amount carried to surplus; and (6) adjustments to, and reconciliation with, surplus as stated on the balance sheet. With profit and loss statements of this character available, the appraiser should be able to separate recurrent from nonrecurrent items of income and expense, to distinguish between operating income and investment income, and to ascertain whether or not any line of business in which the company is engaged is operated consistently at a loss and might be abandoned with benefit to the company. The percentage of earnings retained for business expansion should be noted when dividend-paying capacity is considered. Potential future income is a major factor in many valuations of closely held stocks, and all information concerning past income which will be helpful in predicting the future should be secured. Prior earnings records usually are the most reliable guide as to the future expectancy, but resort to arbitrary five-or-ten-year averages without regard to current trends or future prospects will not produce a realistic valuation. If, for instance, a record of progressively increasing or decreasing net income is found, then greater weight may be accorded the most recent years' profits in estimating earning power. It will be helpful, in judging risk and the extent to which a business is a marginal operator, to consider deductions from income and net income in terms of percentage of sales. Major categories of cost and expense to be so analyzed include the consumption of raw materials and supplies in the case of manufacturers, processors and fabricators; the cost of purchased merchandise in the case of merchants; utility services; insurance; taxes; depletion or depreciation; and interest.

(e) Primary consideration should be given to the dividend-paying capacity of the company rather than to dividends actually paid in the past. Recognition must be given to the necessity of retaining a reasonable portion of profits in a company to meet competition. Dividend-paying capacity is a factor that must be considered in an appraisal, but dividends actually paid in the past may not have any relation to dividend-paying capacity. Specifically, the dividends paid by a closely held family company may be measured by the income needs of the stockholders or by their desire to avoid taxes on dividend receipts, instead of by the ability of the company to pay dividends. Where an actual or effective controlling interest in a corporation is to be valued, the dividend factor is not a material element, since the payment of such dividends is discretionary with the controlling stockholders. The individual or group in control can substitute salaries and bonuses for dividends, thus reducing net income and understating the dividend-paying capacity of the company. It follows, therefore, that dividends are less reliable criteria of fair market value than other applicable factors.

(f) In the final analysis, goodwill is based upon earning capacity. The presence of goodwill and its value, therefore, rests upon the excess of net earnings over and above a fair return on the net tangible assets. While the element of goodwill may be based primarily on earnings, such factors as the prestige and renown of the business, the ownership of a trade or brand name, and a record of successful operation over a prolonged period in a particular locality, also may furnish support for the inclusion of intangible value. In some instances it may not be possible to make a separate appraisal of the tangible and intangible assets of the business. The enterprise has a value as an entity. Whatever intangible value there is, which is supportable by the facts, may be measured by the amount by which the appraised value of the tangible assets exceeds the net book value of such assets.

(g) Sales of stock of a closely held corporation should be carefully investigated to determine whether they represent transactions at arm's length. Forced or distress sales do not ordinarily reflect fair market value nor do isolated sales in small amounts necessarily control as the measure of value. This is especially true in the valuation of a controlling interest in a corporation. Since, in the case of closely held stocks, no prevailing market prices are available, there is no basis for making an adjustment for blockage. It follows, therefore, that such stocks should be valued upon a consideration of all the evidence affecting the fair market value. The size of the block of stock itself is a relevant factor to be considered. Although it is true that a minority interest in an unlisted corporation's stock is more difficult to sell than a similar block of listed stock, it is equally true that control of a corporation, either actual or in effect, representing as it does an added element of value, may justify a higher value for a specific block of stock.

(h) Section 2031(b) of the Code states, in effect, that in valuing unlisted securities the value of stock or securities of corporations engaged in the same or a similar line of business which are listed on an exchange should be taken into consideration along with all other factors. An important consideration is that the corporations to be used for comparisons have capital stocks which are actively traded by the public. In accordance with Section 2031(b) of the Code, stocks listed on an exchange are to be considered first. However, if sufficient comparable companies whose stocks are listed on an exchange cannot be found, other comparable companies which have stocks actively traded in on the over-the-counter market also may be used. The essential factor is that whether the stocks are sold on an exchange or over-the-counter there is evidence of an active, free public market for the stock as of the valuation date. In selecting corporations for comparative purposes, care should be taken to use only comparable companies. Although the only restrictive requirement as to comparable corporations specified in the statute is that their lines of business be the same or similar, yet it is obvious that consideration must be given to other relevant factors in order that the most valid comparison possible will be obtained. For illustration, a corporation having one or more issues of preferred stock, bonds or debentures in addition to its common stock should not be considered to be directly comparable to one having only common stock outstanding. In like manner, a company with a declining business and decreasing markets is not comparable to one with a record of current progress and market expansion.

Sec. 5. Weight to Be Accorded Various Factors.

The valuation of closely held corporate stock entails the consideration of all relevant factors as stated in Section 4. Depending upon the circumstances in each case, certain factors may carry more weight than others because of the nature of the company's business. To illustrate:

(a) Earnings may be the most important criterion of value in some cases whereas asset value will receive primary consideration in others. In general, the appraiser will accord primary consideration to earnings when valuing stocks of companies which sell products or services to the public; conversely, in the investment or holding type of company, the appraiser may accord the greatest weight to the assets underlying the security to be valued.

(b) The value of the stock of a closely held investment or real estate holding company, whether or not family owned, is closely related to the value of the assets underlying the stock. For companies of this type the appraiser should determine the fair market values of the assets of the company. Operating expenses of such a company and the cost of liquidating it, if any, merit consideration when appraising the relative values of the stock and the underlying assets. The market values of the underlying assets give due weight to potential earnings and dividends of the particular items of property underlying the stock, capitalized at rates deemed proper by the investing public at the date of appraisal. A current appraisal by the investing public should be superior to the retrospective opinion of an individual. For these reasons, adjusted net worth should be accorded greater weight in valuing the stock of a closely held investment or real estate holding company, whether or not family owned, than any of the other customary yardsticks of appraisal, such as earnings and dividend-paying capacity.

Sec. 6. Capitalization Rates.

In the application of certain fundamental valuation factors, such as earnings and dividends, it is necessary to capitalize the average or current results at some appropriate rate. A determination of the proper capitalization rate presents one of the most difficult problems in valuation. That there is no ready or simple solution will become apparent by a cursory check of the rates of return and dividend yields in terms of the selling prices of corporate shares listed on the major exchanges of the country. Wide variations will be found even for companies in the same industry. Moreover, the ratio will fluctuate from year to year depending upon economic conditions. Thus, no standard tables of capitalization rates applicable to closely held corporations can be formulated. Among the more important factors to be taken into consideration in deciding upon a capitalization rate in a particular case are: (1) the nature of the business; (2) the risk involved; and (3) the stability or irregularity of earnings.

Sec. 7. Average of Factors.

Because valuations cannot be made on the basis of a prescribed formula, there is no means whereby the various applicable factors in a particular case can be assigned mathematical weights in deriving the fair market value. For this reason, no useful purpose is served by taking an average of several factors (for example, book value, capitalized earnings and capitalized dividends) and basing the valuation on the result. Such a process excludes active consideration of other pertinent factors, and the end result cannot be supported by a realistic application of the significant facts in the case except by mere chance.

Sec. 8. Restrictive Agreements.

Frequently, in the valuation of closely held stock for estate and gift tax purposes, it will be found that the stock is subject to an agreement restricting its sale or transfer. Where shares of stock were acquired by a decedent subject to an option reserved by the issuing corporation to repurchase at a certain price, the option price is usually accepted as the fair market value for estate tax purposes. See Rev. Rul. 54–76, C.B. 1954-1, 194. However, in such a case the option price is not determinative of fair market value for gift tax purposes. Where the option, or buy and sell agreement, is the result of voluntary action by the stockholders and is binding during the life as well as at the death of the stockholders, such agreement may or may not, depending upon the circumstances of each case, fix the value for estate tax purposes. However, such agreement is a factor to be considered, with other relevant factors, in determining fair market value. Where the stockholder is free to dispose of his shares during life and the option is to become effective only upon his death, the fair market value is not limited to the option price. It is always necessary to consider the relationship of the parties, the relative number of shares held by the decedent, and other material facts, to determine whether the agreement represents a bona fide business arrangement or is a device to pass the decedent's shares to the natural objects of his bounty for less than an adequate and full consideration in money or money's worth. In this connection see Rev. Rul. 157 C.B. 1953-2, 255, and Rev. Rul. 189, C.B. 1953-2, 294.

Sec. 9. Effect on Other Documents.

Revenue Ruling 54–77, C.B. 1954-1, 187, is hereby superseded.

REV. RUL. 65–192

The general approach, methods and factors outlined in Revenue Ruling 59–60, C.B. 1959-1, 237, for use in valuing closely held corporate stocks for estate and gift tax purposes are equally applicable to valuations thereof for income and other tax purposes and also in determinations of the fair market values of business interests of any type and of intangible assets for all tax purposes.

The formula approach set forth in A.R.M. 34, C.B. 2, 31 (1920), and A.R.M. 68, C.B. 3, 43 (1920), has no valid application in determinations of the fair market values of corporate stocks or of business interests, unless it is necessary to value the intangible assets of the corporation or the intangible assets included in the business interest. The formula approach may be used in determining the fair market values of intangible assets only if there is no better basis therefor available. In applying the formula, the average earnings period and the capitalization rates are dependent upon the facts and circumstances pertinent thereto in such case.

Section 1. Purpose.

The purpose of this Revenue Ruling is to furnish information and guidance as to the usage to be made of suggested methods for determining the value as of March 1, 1913, or of any other date, of intangible assets and to identify those areas where a valuation formula set forth in A.R.M. 34, C.B. 2, 31 (1920), as modified by A.R.M. 68, C.B. 3, 43 (1920), both quoted in full below should and should not be applied. Since it appears that such formula has been applied to many valuation issues for which it was never intended, the Internal Revenue Service reindicates its limited application.

Sec. 2. Background.

A.R.M. 34 was issued in 1920 for the purpose of providing suggested formulas for determining the amount of March 1, 1913, intangible asset value lost by breweries and other businesses connected with the distilling industry, as a result of the passage of the 18th Amendment to the Constitution of the United States. A.R.M. 68 was issued later in the same year and contained a minor revision of the original ruling so that its third formula would be applied in accordance with its purpose and intent.

Sec. 3. Statement of Position.

.01 Although the formulas and approach contained in A.R.M. 34 were specifically aimed at the valuation of intangible assets of distilling and related companies as of March 1, 1913, the last two paragraphs of the ruling seemingly broaden it to make its third formula applicable to almost any kind of enterprise. The final sentences, however, limit the purpose of such formula by stating that "In * * * all of the cases the effort should be to determine what net earnings a purchaser of a business on March 1, 1913, might reasonably have expected to receive from it, * * *," and by providing certain checks and alternatives. Also, both A.R.M. 34 and A.R.M. 68 expressly stated that such formula was merely a rule for guidance and not controlling in the presence of "better evidence" in determining the value of intangible assets. Furthermore, T.B.R. 57, C.B. 1, 40 (1919), relating to the meaning of "fair market value" of property received in exchange for other property, which was published before A.R.M. 34 and A.R.M. 68 and has not been revoked, set forth general principles of valuation that are consistent with Revenue Ruling 59–60, C.B. 1959-1, 237. Moreover, in S.M. 1609, C.B. III-1, 48 (1924) it was stated that "the method suggested in A.R.M. 34 for determining the value of intangibles is * * * controlling only in the absence of better evidence." As said in *North American Service Co., Inc.* v. *Commissioner,* 33 T.C. 677, 694 (1960), acquiescence, C.B. 1960-2, 6, "an A.R.M. 34 computation would not be conclusive of the existence and value of goodwill if better evidence were available * * *."

.02 Revenue Ruling 59–60 sets forth the proper approach to use in the valuation of closely held corporate stocks for estate and gift tax purposes. That ruling contains the statement that no formula can be devised that will be generally applicable to the multitude of different valuation issues. It also contains a discussion of intangible value in closely held corporations and some of the elements which may support such value in a given business.

Sec. 4. Delineation of Areas in Which Suggested Methods Will Be Effective.

.01 The general approach, methods, and factors outlined in Revenue Ruling 59–60 are equally applicable to valuations of corporate stocks for income and other tax purposes as well as for estate and gift tax purposes. They apply also to problems involving the determination of the fair market value of business interests of any type, including partnerships, proprietorships, etc., and of intangible assets for all tax purposes.

.02 Valuation, especially where earning power is an important factor, is in essence a process requiring the exercise of informed judgment and common sense. Thus, the suggested formula approach set forth in A.R.M. 34 has no valid application in determinations of the fair market value of corporate stocks or of business interests unless it is necessary to value the intangible assets of the corporation or the intangible assets included in the business interest. The formula approach may be used in determining the fair market values of intangible assets only if there is no better basis therefor available. In applying the formula, the average earnings period and the capitalization rates are dependent upon the facts and circumstances pertinent thereto in each case. See *John Q. Shunk et al.* v. *Commissioner,* 10 T.C. 293, 304-5 (1948), acquiescence, C.B. 1948-1, 3, affirmed 173 Fed. (2d) 747 (1949); *Ushco Manufacturing Co., Inc.* v. *Commissioner,* Tax Court Memorandum Opinion entered March 10, 1945, affirmed 175 Fed. (2d) 821 (1945); and *White & Wells Co.* v. *Commissioner,* 19 B.T.A. 416, nonacquiescence C.B. IX-2, 87 (1930), reversed and remanded 50 Fed. (2d) 120 (1931).

Sec. 5. Quotation of A.R.M. 34.

For convenience, A.R.M. 34 reads as follows:

> *The Committee has considered the question of providing some practical formula for determining value as of March 1, 1913, or of any other date, which might be considered as applying to intangible*

assets, but finds itself unable to lay down any specific rule of guidance for determining the value of intangibles which would be applicable in all cases and under all circumstances. Where there is no established market to serve as a guide the question of value, even of tangible assets, is one largely of judgment and opinion, and the same thing is even more true of intangible assets such as good will, trade-marks, trade brands, etc. However, there are several methods of reaching a conclusion as to the value of intangibles which the Committee suggests may be utilized broadly in passing upon questions of valuation, not to be regarded as controlling, however, if better evidence is presented in any specific case.

Where deduction is claimed for obsolescence or loss of good will or trade-marks, the burden of proof is primarily upon the taxpayer to show the value of such good will or trade-marks on March 1, 1913. Of course, if good will or trade-marks have been acquired for cash or other valuable considerations subsequent to March 1, 1913, the measure of loss will be determined by the amount of cash or value of other considerations paid therefor, and no deduction will be allowed for the value of good will or trade-marks built up by the taxpayer since March 1, 1913. The following suggestions are made, therefore, merely as suggestions for checks upon the soundness and validity of the taxpayers' claims. No obsolescence or loss with respect to good will should be allowed except in cases of actual disposition of the asset or abandonment of the business.

In the first place, it is recognized that in numerous instances it has been the practice of distillers and wholesale liquor dealers to put out under well-known and popular brands only so much goods as could be marketed without affecting the established market price therefor and to sell other goods of the same identical manufacture, age, and character under other brands, or under no brand at all, at figures very much below those which the well-known brands commanded. In such cases the difference between the price at which whisky was sold under a given brand name and also under another brand name, or under no brand, multiplied by the number of units sold during a given year gives an accurate determination of the amount of profit attributable to that brand during that year, and where this practice is continued for a long enough period to show that this amount was fairly constant and regular and might be expected to yield annually that average profit, by capitalizing this earning at the rate, say, of 20 per cent, the value of the brand is fairly well established.

Another method is to compare the volume of business done under the trade-mark or brand under consideration and profits made, or by the business whose good will is under consideration, with the similar volume of business and profit made in other cases where good will or trade-marks have been actually sold for cash, recognizing as the value of the first the same proportion of the selling price of the second, as the profits of the first attributable to brands or good will, is of the similar profits of the second.

The third method and possibly the one which will most frequently have to be applied as a check in the absence of data necessary for the application of the preceding ones, is to allow out of average earnings over a period of years prior to March 1, 1913, preferably not less than five years, a return of 10 per cent upon the average tangible assets for the period. The surplus earnings will then be the average amount available for return upon the value of the intangible assets, and it is the opinion of the Committee that this return should be capitalized upon the basis of not more than five years' purchase—that is to say, five times the amount available as return from intangibles should be the value of the intangibles.

In view of the hazards of the business, the changes in popular tastes, and the difficulties in preventing imitation or counterfeiting of popular brands affecting the sales of the genuine goods, the Committee is of the opinion that the figure given of 20 per cent return on intangibles is not unreasonable, and it recommends that no higher figure than that be attached in any case to intangibles without a very clear and adequate showing that the value of the intangibles was in fact greater than would be reached by applying this formula.

The foregoing is intended to apply particularly to businesses put out of existence by the prohibition law, but will be equally applicable so far as the third formula is concerned, to other businesses of a more or less hazardous nature. In the case, however, of valuation of good will of a business which consists of the manufacture or sale of standard articles of every-day necessity not subject to violent fluctuations and where the hazard is not so great, the Committee is of the opinion that the figure for determination of the return on tangible assets might be reduced from 10 to 8 or 9 per cent, and that the percentage for capitalization of the return upon intangibles might be reduced from 20 to 15 per cent.

In any or all of the cases the effort should be to determine what net earnings a purchaser of a business on March 1, 1913, might reasonably have expected to receive from it, and therefore a representative period should be used for averaging actual earnings, eliminating any year in which there were extraordinary factors affecting earnings either way. Also, in the case of the sale of good will of a going business the percentage rate of capitalization of earnings applicable to good will shown by the amount actually paid for the business should be used as a check against the determination of good will value as of March 1, 1913, and if the good will is sold upon the basis of capitalization of earnings less than the figures above indicated as the ones ordinarily to be adopted, the same percentage should be used in figuring value as of March 1, 1913.

Sec. 6. Quotation of A.R.M. 68.

Also for convenience, A.R.M. 68 reads as follows:

The Committee is in receipt of a request for advice as to whether under A.R.M. 34 the 10 per cent upon tangible assets is to be applied only to the net tangible assets or to all tangible assets on the books of the corporation, regardless of any outstanding obligations.

The Committee, in the memorandum in question, undertook to lay down a rule for guidance in the absence of better evidence in determining the value as of March 1, 1913, of good will, and held that in determining such value, income over an average period in excess of an amount sufficient to return 10 per cent upon tangible assets should be capitalized at 20 per cent. Manifestly, since the effort is to determine the value of the good will, and therefore the true net worth of the taxpayer as of March 1, 1913, the 10 per cent should be applied only to the tangible assets entering into net worth, including accounts and bills receivable in excess of accounts and bills payable.

In other words, the purpose and intent are to provide for a return to the taxpayer of 10 per cent upon so much of his investment as is represented by tangible assets and to capitalize the excess of earnings over the amount necessary to provide such return, at 20 per cent.

Sec. 7. Effect on Other Documents.

Although the limited application of A.R.M. 34 and A.R.M. 68 is reindicated in this Revenue Ruling, the principles enunciated in those rulings are not thereby affected.

REV. RUL. 65–193

Revenue Ruling 59–60, C.B. 1959-1, 237, is hereby modified to delete the statements, contained therein at Section 4.02(f), that "in some instances it may not be possible to make a separate appraisal of the tangible and intangible assets of the business. The enterprise has a value as an entity. Whatever intangible value there is, which is supportable by the facts, may be measured by the amount by which the appraised value of the tangible assets exceeds the net book value of such assets."

The instances where it is not possible to make a separate appraisal of the tangible and intangible assets of a business are rare and each case varies from the other. No rule can be devised which will be generally applicable to such cases.

Other than this modification, Revenue Ruling 59–60 continues in full force and effect. See Rev. Rul. 65–192.

REV. RUL. 68–609

The purpose of this Revenue Ruling is to update and restate, under the current statute and regulations, the currently outstanding portions of A.R.M. 34, C.B. 2, 31 (1920), A.R.M. 68, C.B. 3, 43 (1920), and O.D. 937, C.B. 4, 43 (1921).

The question presented is whether the "formula" approach, the capitalization of earnings in excess of a fair rate of return on net tangible assets, may be used to determine the fair market value of the intangible assets of a business.

The "formula" approach may be stated as follows:

> *A percentage return on the average annual value of the tangible assets used in a business is determined, using a period of years (preferably not less than five) immediately prior to the valuation date. The amount of the percentage return on tangible assets, thus determined, is deducted from the average earnings of the business for such period and the remainder, if any, is considered to be the amount of the average annual earnings from the intangible assets of the business for the period. This amount (considered as the average annual earnings from intangibles), capitalized at a percentage of, say, 15 to 20 percent, is the value of the intangible assets of the business determined under the "formula" approach.*

The percentage of return on the average annual value of the tangible assets used should be the percentage prevailing in the industry involved at the date of valuation, or (when the industry percentage is not available) a percentage of 8 to 10 percent may be used.

The 8 percent rate of return and the 15 percent rate of capitalization are applied to tangibles and intangibles, respectively, of businesses with a small risk factor and stable and regular earnings; the 10 percent rate of return and 20 percent rate of capitalization are applied to businesses in which the hazards of business are relatively high.

The above rates are used as examples and are not appropriate in all cases. In applying the "formula" approach, the average earnings period and the capitalization rates are dependent upon the facts pertinent thereto in each case.

The past earnings to which the formula is applied should fairly reflect the probable future earnings. Ordinarily, the period should not be less than five years, and abnormal years, whether above or below the average, should be eliminated. If the business is a sole proprietorship or partnership, there should be deducted from the earnings of the business a reasonable amount for services performed by the owner or partners engaged in the business. See *Lloyd B. Sanderson Estate* v. *Commissioner*, 42 F.2d 160 (1930). Further, only the tangible assets entering into net worth, including accounts and bills receivable in excess of accounts and bills payable, are used for determining earnings on the tangible assets. Factors that influence the capitalization rate include (1) the nature of the business, (2) the risk involved, and (3) the stability or irregularity of earnings.

The "formula" approach should not be used if there is better evidence available from which the value of intangibles can be determined. If the assets of a going business are sold upon the basis of a rate of capitalization that can be substantiated as being realistic, though it is not within the range of figures indicated here as the ones ordinarily to be adopted, the same rate of capitalization should be used in determining the value of intangibles.

Accordingly, the "formula" approach may be used for determining the fair market value of intangible assets of a business only if there is no better basis therefor available.

See also Revenue Ruling 59–60, C.B. 1959-1, 237, as modified by Revenue Ruling 65–193, C.B. 1965-2, 370, which sets forth the proper approach to use in the valuation of closely held corporate stocks for estate and gift tax purposes. The general approach, methods, and factors, outlined in Revenue Ruling 59–60, as modified, are equally applicable to valuations of corporate stocks for income and other tax purposes as well as for estate and gift tax purposes. They apply also to problems involving the determination of the fair market value of business interests of any type, including partnerships and proprietorships, and of intangible assets for all tax purposes.

A.R.M. 34, A.R.M. 68, and O.D. 937 are superseded, since the positions set forth therein are restated to the extent applicable under current law in this Revenue Ruling. Revenue Ruling 65–192, C.B. 1965-2, 259, which contained restatements of A.R.M. 34 and A.R.M. 68, is also superseded.

REV. RUL. 77–287

Valuation of securities restricted from immediate resale. Guidelines are set forth for the valuation, for federal tax purpoes, of securities that cannot be immediately resold because they are restricted from resale pursuant to federal securities laws; Rev. Rul. 59–60 amplified.

Section 1. Purpose.

The purpose of this Revenue Ruling is to amplify Rev. Rul. 59–60, 1959-1 C.B. 237, as modified by Rev. Rul. 65–193, 1965-2 C.B. 370, and to provide information and guidance to taxpayers, Internal Revenue Service personnel, and others concerned with the valuation, for federal tax purposes, of securities that cannot be immediately resold because they are restricted from resale pursuant to federal securities laws. This guidance is applicable only in cases where it is not inconsistent with valuation requirements of the Internal Revenue Code of 1954 or the Regulations thereunder. Further, this Ruling does not establish the time at which property shall be valued.

Sec. 2. Nature of the Problem.

It frequently becomes necessary to establish the fair market value of stock that has not been registered for public trading when the issuing company has stock of the same class that is actively traded in one or more securities markets. The problem is to determine the difference in fair market value between the registered shares that are actively traded and the unregistered shares. This problem is often encountered in estate and gift tax cases. However, it is sometimes encountered when unregistered shares are issued in exchange for assets or the stock of an acquired company.

Sec. 3. Background and Definitions.

.01 The Service outlined and reviewed in general the approach, methods, and factors to be considered in valuing shares of closely held corporate stock for estate and gift tax purposes in Rev. Rul. 59–60, as modified by Rev. Rul. 65–193. The provisions of Rev. Rul. 59–60, as modified, were extended to the valuation of corporate securities for income and other tax purposes by Rev. Rul. 68–609, 1968-2 C.B. 327.

.02 There are several terms currently in use in the securities industry that denote restrictions imposed on the resale and transfer of certain securities. The term frequently used to describe these securities is "restricted securities," but they are sometimes referred to as "unregistered securities," "investment letter stock," "control stock," or "private placement stock." Frequently these terms are used interchangeably. They all indicate that these particular securities cannot lawfully be distributed to the general public until a registration statement relating to the corporation underlying the securities has been filed, and has also become effective under the rules promulgated and enforced by the United States Securities & Exchange Commission (SEC) pursuant to the federal securities laws. The following represents a more refined definition of each of the following terms along with two other terms—"exempted securities" and "exempted transactions."

(a) The term "restricted securities" is defined in Rule 144 adopted by the SEC as "securities acquired directly or indirectly from the issuer thereof, or from an affiliate of such issuer, in a transaction or chain of transactions not involving any public offering."

(b) The term "unregistered securities" refers to those securities with respect to which a registration statement, providing full disclosure by the issuing corporation, has not been filed with the SEC pursuant to the Securities Act of 1933. The registration statement is a condition precedent to a public distribution of securities in interstate commerce and is aimed at providing the prospective investor with a factual basis for sound judgment in making investment decisions.

(c) The terms "investment letter stock" and "letter stock" denote shares of stock that have been issued by a corporation without the benefit of filing a registration statement with the SEC. Such stock is subject to resale and transfer restrictions set forth in a letter agreement requested by the issuer and signed by the buyer of the stock when the stock is delivered. Such stock may be found in the hands of either individual investors or institutional investors.

(d) The term "control stock" indicates that the shares of stock have been held or are being held by an officer, director, or other person close to the management of the corporation. These persons are subject to certain requirements pursuant to SEC rules upon resale of shares they own in such corporations.

(e) The term "private placement stock" indicates that the stock has been placed with an institution or other investor who will presumably hold it for a long period and ultimately arrange to have the stock registered if it is to be offered to the general public. Such stock may or may not be subject to a letter agreement. Private placements of stock are exempted from the registration and prospectus provisions of the Securities Act of 1933.

(f) The term "exempted securities" refers to those classes of securities that are expressly excluded from the registration provisions of the Securities Act of 1933 and the distribution provisions of the Securities Exchange Act of 1934.

(g) The term "exempted transactions" refers to certain sales or distributions of securities that do not involve a public offering and are excluded from the registration and prospectus provisions of the Securities Act of 1933 and distribution provisions of the Securities Exchange Act of 1934. The exempted status makes it unnecessary for issuers of securities to go through the registration process.

Sec. 4. Securities Industry Practice in Valuing Restricted Securities.

.01 *Investment Company Valuation Practices.* The Investment Company Act of 1940 requires open-end investment companies to publish the valuation of their portfolio securities daily. Some of these companies have portfolios containing restricted securities, but also have unrestricted securities of the same class traded on a securities exchange. In recent years the number of restricted securities in such portfolios has increased. The following methods have been used by investment companies in the valuation of such restricted securities:

(a) Current market price of the unrestricted stock less a constant percentage discount based on purchase discount;

(b) Current market price of unrestricted stock less a constant percentage discount different from purchase discount;

(c) Current market price of the unrestricted stock less a discount amortized over a fixed period;

(d) Current market price of the unrestricted stock; and

(e) Cost of the restricted stock until it is registered.

The SEC ruled in its Investment Company Act Release No. 5847, dated October 21, 1969, that there can be no automatic formula by which an investment company can value the restricted securities in its portfolios. Rather, the SEC has determined that it is the responsibility of the board of directors of the particular investment company to determine the "fair value" of each issue of restricted securities in good faith.

.02 *Institutional Investors Study.* Pursuant to Congressional direction, the SEC undertook an analysis of the purchases, sales, and holding of securities by financial institutions, in order to determine the effect of institutional activity upon the securities market. The study report was published in eight volumes in March 1971. The fifth volume provides an analysis of restricted securities and deals with such items as the characteristics of the restricted securities purchasers and issuers, the size of transactions (dollars and shares), the marketability discounts on different trading markets, and the resale provisions. This research project provides some guidance for measuring the discount in that it contains information, based on the actual experience of the marketplace, showing that, during the period surveyed (January 1, 1966, through June 30, 1969), the amount of discount allowed for restricted securities from the trading price of the unrestricted securities was generally related to the following four factors.

(a) *Earnings.* Earnings and sales consistently have a significant influence on the size of restricted securities discounts according to the study. Earnings played the major part in establishing the ultimate discounts at which these stocks were sold from the current market price. Apparently earnings patterns, rather than sales patterns, determine the degree of risk of an investment.

(b) *Sales.* The dollar amount of sales of issuers' securities also has a major influence on the amount of discount at which restricted securities sell from the current market price. The results of the study generally indicate that the companies with the lowest dollar amount of sales during the test period accounted for most of the transactions involving the highest discount rates, while they accounted for only a small portion of all transactions involving the lowest discount rates.

(c) *Trading Market.* The market in which publicly held securities are traded also reflects variances in the amount of discount that is applied to restricted securities purchases. According to the study, discount rates were greatest on restricted stocks with unrestricted counterparts traded over-the-counter, followed by those with unrestricted counterparts listed on the American Stock Exchange, while the discount rates for those stocks with unrestricted counterparts listed on the New York Stock Exchange were the smallest.

(d) *Resale Agreement Provisions.* Resale agreement provisions often affect the size of the discount. The discount from the market price provides the main incentive for a potential buyer to acquire restricted securities. In judging the opportunity cost of freezing funds, the purchaser is analyzing two separate factors. The first factor is the risk that underlying value of the stock will change in a way that, absent the restrictive provisions, would have prompted a decision to sell. The second factor is the risk that the contemplated means of legally disposing of the stock may not materialize. From the seller's point of view, a discount is justified where the seller is relieved of the expenses of registration and public distribution, as well as of the risk that the market will adversely change before the offering is completed. The ultimate agreement between buyer and seller is a reflection of these and other considerations. Relative bargaining strengths of the parties to the agreement are major considerations that influence the resale terms and consequently the size of discounts in restricted securities transactions. Certain provisions are often found in agreements between buyers and sellers that affect the size of discounts at which restricted stocks are sold. Several such provisions follow, all of which, other than number (3), would tend to reduce the size of the discount:

(1) A provision giving the buyer an option to "piggyback," that is, to register restricted stock with the next registration statement, if any, filed by the issuer with the SEC;

(2) A provision giving the buyer an option to require registration at the seller's expense;

(3) A provision giving the buyer an option to require registration, but only at the buyer's own expense;

(4) A provision giving the buyer a right to receive continuous disclosure of information about the issuer from the seller;

(5) A provision giving the buyer a right to select one or more directors of the issuer;

(6) A provision giving the buyer an option to purchase additional shares of the issuer's stock; and

(7) A provision giving the buyer the right to have a greater voice in operations of the issuer, if the issuer does not meet previously agreed upon operating standards.

Institutional buyers can and often do obtain many of these rights and options from the sellers of restricted securities, and naturally, the more rights the buyer can acquire, the lower the buyer's risk is going to be, thereby reducing the buyer's discount as well. Smaller buyers may not be able to negotiate the large discounts or the rights and options that volume buyers are able to negotiate.

.03 *Summary.* A variety of methods have been used by the securities industry to value restricted securities. The SEC rejects all automatic or mechanical solutions to the valuation of restricted securities, and prefers, in the case of the valuation of investment company portfolio stocks, to rely upon good faith valuations by the board of directors of each company. The study made by the SEC found that restricted securities *generally* are issued at a discount from the market value of freely tradable securities.

Sec. 5. Facts and Circumstances Material to Valuation of Restricted Securities.

.01 Frequently, a company has a class of stock that cannot be traded publicly. The reason such stock cannot be traded may arise from the securities statutes, as in the case of an "investment letter" restriction; it may arise from a corporate charter restriction, or perhaps from a trust agreement restriction. In such cases, certain documents and facts should be obtained for analysis.

.02 The following documents and facts, when used in conjunction with those discussed in Section 4 of Rev. Rul. 59–60, will be useful in the valuation of restricted securities:

(a) A copy of any declaration of trust, trust agreement, and any other agreements relating to the shares of restricted stock;

(b) A copy of any document showing any offers to buy or sell or indications of interest in buying or selling the restricted shares;

(c) The latest prospectus of the company;

(d) Annual reports of the company for 3 to 5 years preceding the valuation date;

(e) The trading prices and trading volume of the related class of traded securities 1 month preceding the valuation date, if they are traded on a stock exchange (if traded over-the-counter, prices may be obtained from the National Quotations Bureau, the National Association of Securities Dealers Automated Quotations (NASDAQ), or sometimes from broker-dealers making markets in the shares);

(f) The relationship of the parties to the agreements concerning the restricted stock, such as whether they are members of the immediate family or perhaps whether they are officers or directors of the company; and

(g) Whether the interest being valued represents a majority or minority ownership.

Sec. 6. Weighing Facts and Circumstances Material to Restricted Stock Valuation.

All relevant facts and circumstances that bear upon the worth of restricted stock, including those set forth above in the preceding Sections 4 and 5, and those set forth in Section 4 of Rev. Rul. 59–60, must be taken into account in arriving at the fair market value of such securities. Depending on the circumstances of each case, certain factors may carry more weight than others. To illustrate:

.01 Earnings, net assets, and net sales must be given primary consideration in arriving at an appropriate discount for restricted securities from the freely traded shares. These are the elements of value that are always used by investors in making investment decisions. In some cases, one element may be more important than in other cases. In the case of manufacturing, producing, or distributing companies, primary weight must be accorded earnings and net sales; but in the case of investment or holding companies, primary weight must be given to the net assets of the company underlying the stock. In the former type of companies, value is more closely linked to past, present, and future earnings while in the latter type of companies, value is more closely linked to the existing net assets of the company. See the discussion in Section 5 of Rev. Rul. 59–60.

.02 Resale provisions found in the restriction agreements must be scrutinized and weighed to determine the amount of discount to apply to the preliminary fair market value of the company. The two elements of time and expense bear upon this discount; the longer the buyer of the shares must wait to liquidate the shares, the greater the discount. Moreover, if the provisions make it necessary for the buyer to bear the expense of registration, the greater the discount. However, if the provisions of the restricted stock agreement make it possible for the buyer to "piggyback" shares at the next offering, the discount would be smaller.

.03 The relative negotiation strengths of the buyer and seller of restricted stock may have a profound effect on the amount of discount. For example, a tight money situation may cause the buyer to have the greater balance of negotiation strength in a transaction. However, in some cases the relative strengths may tend to cancel each other out.

.04 The market experience of freely tradable securities of the same class as the restricted securities is also significant in determining the amount of discount. Whether the shares are privately held or publicly traded affects the worth of the shares to the holder. Securities traded on a public market generally are worth more to investors than those that are not traded on a public market. Moreover, the type of public market in which the unrestricted securities are traded is to be given consideration.

Sec. 7. Effect on Other Documents.

Rev. Rul. 59–60, as modified by Rev. Rul. 65–193, is amplified.

REV. RUL. 78–367

Valuation; closely held securities. The valuation, for purposes of Section 2512 of the Code, of stock in a closely held company should take into account a proposed merger of the company with a publicly owned corporation.

Advice has been requested concerning the value of corporate stock for purposes of Section 2512 of the Internal Revenue Code of 1954, under the circumstances described below.

Three shareholders, *A*, *B*, and *C*, each owned a one-third interest in *X* corporation. These same individuals each owned a 20 percent interest in *Y* corporation, a publicly owned company. Their shares in *Y* corporation, taken together, were a majority interest.

In January 1975, the two companies publicly announced an intention to merge *X* corporation with *Y* corporation. The merger was subject to the formulation of a detailed agreement regarding the consideration to be exchanged, and subject to the approval of the stockholders of both corporations.

Two months after the announcement, *A* made a gift of some of the *X* corporation stock to *D*. In March 1976, all details concerning the merger were finally completed and the merger effected shortly thereafter. The shareholders of *X* corporation received one share of *Y* corporation stock in exchange for each share in *X* that they held. Prior to the merger, there had been no sales of *X* corporation stock.

The question presented is whether the proposed merger should be considered in the valuation of the gift of the *X* stock.

Section 2512 of the Code provides that a gift shall be taxed on the basis of the value of the property on the date of the transfer. Section 25.2512-1 of the Gift Tax Regulations states the following general rules:

> ** * * The value of the property is the price at which such property would change hands between a willing buyer and a willing seller, neither being under any compulsion to buy or to sell, and both having reasonable knowledge of relevant facts. . . . All relevant facts and elements of value as of the time of the gift shall be considered. * * **

Section 25.2512-2(f) of the regulations provides the following guidelines for valuation of corporate securities for which actual sales are lacking:

> *(f) Where selling prices or bid and asked prices are unavailable. If the provisions of paragraphs (b), (c), and (d) of this section are inapplicable because actual sale prices and bona fide bid and asked prices are lacking, then the fair market value is to be determined by taking the following factors into consideration:*
>
> *(1) In the case of corporate or other bonds, the soundness of the security, the interest yield, the date of maturity, and other relevant factors; and*
>
> *(2) In the case of shares of stock, the company's net worth, prospective earning power and dividend-paying capacity, and other relevant factors.*
>
> *Some of the "other relevant factors" referred to in subparagraphs (1) and (2) of this paragraph are: the good will of the business; the economic outlook in the particular industry; the company's position in the industry and its management; the degree of control of the business represented by the block of stock to be valued; and the values of securities of corporations engaged in the same or similar lines of business which are listed on a stock exchange. However, the weight to be accorded such comparisons or any other evidentiary factors considered in the determination of a value depends upon the facts of each case. * * **

Rev. Rul. 59–60, 1959-1 C.B. 237, as modified by Rev. Rul. 65–193, 1965-2 C.B. 370, and as amplified by Rev. Rul. 77–287, 1977-2 C.B. 319, outlines some methods and factors to be considered when valuing shares of stock on which market quotations are unavailable. Although nine representative factors are discussed, the ruling advises that *all* relevant factors affecting fair market value should be considered.

In the present case, no share of *X* corporation stock had been sold prior to the date of the gift. The announcement of the merger two months before, as well as the preliminary decision to merge, did not attempt to fix the consideration to be exchanged. The value of the stock, for purposes of the merger, was not finally agreed upon until one year after the gift.

The concept of "fair market value" is premised on a hypothetical sale in which both the prospective buyer and seller have reasonable knowledge of the facts. See *Estate of Reynolds* v. *Commissioner*, 55 T.C. 172, 195 (1970), acq., 1971-2 C.B. 2.

The standards set by the Regulations and Rev. Rul. 59–60, as modified and amplified, reflect the reality of the marketplace. A prospective seller would inform a prospective buyer of all favorable facts in an effort to obtain the best possible price, and a prospective buyer would elicit all the negative information in order to obtain the lowest possible price. In this arm's length negotiation, all relevant factors available to either buyer or seller, known to both, provide a basis on which the buyer and seller make a decision to buy or sell and come to an agreement on the price.

Accordingly, the valuation of the stock of *X* as of the date of the gift should take into account the effects of the public announcement of the merger and all information covering the status of the merger negotiations available to the buyer and seller.

REV. RUL. 79–7

Valuation; transfer in contemplation of death; stock of closely held corporation. An individual who owned a controlling stock interest in a closely held corporation transferred a minority stock interest that was included in the individual's gross estate as a transfer in contemplation of death. The minority interest transferred and the stock retained by the individual until death are treated as one block of shares in determining the value of the stock interest includible in the gross estate.

Issue

Whether the interest in a closely held corporation that is includible in the decedent's gross estate under Section 2035 of the Code should be valued as a minority interest in the corporation, under the circumstances described below.

Facts

The decedent, *A*, owned 600 shares of the common stock of *X* corporation, a closely held corporation. The 600 shares represented sixty percent of the outstanding stock of *X* corporation. In 1974, two years prior to death, *A* transferred 300 shares to *B, A*'s child, in a transfer that was determined to have been made in contemplation of death. The stock transferred by *A* was therefore includible in *A*'s gross estate under Section 2035 of the Code. In addition, the 300 shares *A* owned outright at the time of death were included in the gross estate under Section 2033 of the Code.

Law and Analysis

Section 20.2031-2(f) of the Regulations provides that in determining the value of a decedent's stock interest in a closely held corporation for purposes of the federal estate tax, consideration should be given to the degree of control of the corporation represented by the block of stock to be valued. The question presented in the instant case is whether the 300 shares of *X* corporation stock included in the decedent's gross estate under Section 2035 of the Code is to be valued as a minority interest in the corporation, without reference to the stock interest included in the decedent's gross estate under Section 2033.

Rev. Rul. 59–60, 1959-1 C.B. 237, sets forth guidelines for the valuation of shares of capital stock of a closely held corporation. Both Section 20.2031-2(f) of the Regulations and Rev. Rul. 59–60, state that the determination of value of such closely held stock is to be made with reference to a range of factors in the absence of an established "market" in the shares. It is assumed that there is no established "market" for closely held corporate stocks. See Rev. Rul. 59–60, cited above.

At the time of *A*'s death, Section 2035(a) of the Code provided that the gross estate shall include the value of any interest in property transferred by the decedent (except in the case of a bona fide sale for an adequate and full consideration in money or money's worth) in contemplation of death. Section 20.2035-1(e) of the Estate Tax Regulations provides that the value of an interest in transferred property includible in a decedent's gross estate under Section 2035 is the value of the interest as of the applicable valuation date, determined in accordance with Section 2031 of the Code and the Regulations thereunder.

Underlying the provisions of Section 2035 of the Code is the intent to prevent the avoidance of the estate tax by taxing inter vivos gifts made as substitutes for testamentary transfers as if they were testamentary transfers. *Milliken* v. *United States,* 283 U.S. 15 (1931). Consequently, the value of property included in the decedent's gross estate under Section 2035 should be treated, for purposes of the estate tax, in the same manner as it would have been if the transfer had not been made and the property had been owned by the decedent at the time of death. *Humphrey's Estate* v. *Commissioner,* 162 F.2d 1 (5th Cir. 1947). *Ingleheart* v. *Commissioner,* 77 F.2d 704 (5th Cir. 1935); Rev. Rul. 76–235, 1976-1 C.B. 277.

In the situation presented here, the stock interest in *X* corporation transferred by *A* to *B* represented a minority interest in the corporation. However, pursuant to the court's decisions in *Humphrey's Estate* and *Ingleheart,* the value of the stock included in the gross estate under Section 2035 of the Code should be taxed as if the decedent had retained the stock until death. If *A* had not transferred the 300 shares, then a total of 600 shares of stock would have been included in *A*'s gross estate under Section 2033. That block of shares would represent a controlling interest in *X* corporation and would be valued, in accordance with Rev. Rul. 59–60, cited above, taking into account the controlling interest the shares represent.

Holding

The 300 shares of *X* corporation stock includible in *A*'s gross estate under Section 2033 of the Code, and the 300 shares includible under Section 2035, are to be treated as 1 block of 600 shares of stock for purposes of determining whether the stock includible in *A*'s gross estate represents a minority or majority interest in *X* corporation. Under these circumstances, the inclusion of the 300 shares of stock under Section 2035 of the Code will have the same tax effect as if the decedent had retained the 300 shares until death.

The conclusion of this ruling would be the same under Section 2035 of the Code as amended by the Tax Reform Act of 1976 for that amendment merely eliminated the requirement that the transfer be in contemplation of death. The purpose of the statute, as amended, remains the same as it was prior to modification.

NATIONAL OFFICE TECHNICAL ADVICE MEMORANDUM
[Code Sec. 2031]

Gross estate; Included v. not included; Valuation of large block of listed securities; Controlling interest; Liquidating value; Discount for lack of marketability and discount applied to corporate held insurance proceeds as factual questions.—CCH.

Issue

1. Whether it is appropriate to give primary consideration to earnings as an indicator of value in the valuation of a 100 percent interest in an operating company.

2. What authority there is for a large discount for lack of marketability where a majority or 100 percent interest is involved.

3. Whether the life insurance proceeds of policies can be ignored or discounted in determining the value of a 100 percent interest in the operating company holding the proceeds.

Facts

H and W died simultaneously in an accident ***** each owning one-half community property interest in 100 percent ownership of a closely held corporation, which was engaged in the construction business. On the one decedent's life the corporation had an insurance policy, that at the moment of death became an account receivable of the corporation.

Applicable Law

Section 20.2031-1(b) of the Regulations provides the fair market value is the price at which the property would change hands between a willing buyer and a willing seller, neither under any compulsion to buy or to sell and both having reasonable knowledge of relevant facts. All relevant facts and elements of value as of the applicable valuation date shall be considered in every case.

In *U.S.* v. *Cartwright*, 411 U.S. 546, at 551 the Supreme Court affirmed the willing buyer-willing seller concept of Regulation Section 20.2031-1(b) as the appropriate measure of fair market value for estate tax purposes.

Section 2031(b) of the Internal Revenue Code provides that the value of unlisted stocks shall be determined by comparison with the value of publicly traded stock in the same, or similar line of business and also by the consideration of other factors.

Section 20.2031-2(f)(2) of the Regulations provides that in determining value of a closely held corporation's stock the company's net worth, prospective earning power and dividend-paying capacity, and other relevant factors should be considered.

Rev. Rul. 59–60, 1959-1 C.B. 237 indicates that the determination of fair market value, being a question of fact, will depend upon the circumstances in each case. No formula can be devised to account for the multitude of valuation issues that arise in estate and gift cases. A sound valuation will be based upon all the relevant facts, but the elements of common sense, informed judgment and reasonableness must enter into the process of weighing those facts and determining their aggregate significance.

Rev. Rul. 59–60, 1959-1 C.B. 237 also provides that earnings may be the most important criterion of value in some cases whereas asset value will receive primary consideration in others. In general, the appraiser will accord primary consideration to earnings when valuing stocks of companies which sell products or services to public; conversely, in the investment or holding type of company, the appraiser may accord the greatest weight to the assets underlying the security to be valued.

Section 20.2042.1(c)(6) of the Regulations provides that the corporate ownership of life insurance proceeds from a policy on the decedent's life payable to a corporation wholly-owned by the decedent will not be attributed to the decedent through his stock ownership. However, the proceeds of certain life insurance policies shall be considered in determining the value of the decedent's stock.

Section 20.2031-2(f) of the Regulations provides that among other relevant factors in valuing the shares of a closely held corporation, consideration should be given to life insurance policies payable to the corporation as a nonoperating asset of the corporation. The weight assigned to life insurance proceeds should be to the extent that the proceeds were not taken into account in the determination of net worth, prospective earning power and dividend-paying capacity of the company.

In the *Estate of John L. Huntsman* v. *the Commissioner* 66 T.C. 861 (1976) the tax court determined that the proceeds of "key man" life insurance policies payable to two related corporations on the life of their president and sole shareholder should be taken into consideration as assets of the corporation, but such proceeds are not to be added to the value of the stocks of the corporation determined. The court determined the value of the corporation based on comparative analysis with companies in the same, or similar line of business, and increased the values to give consideration to the strong cash position of the two corporations, due in part to the insurance proceeds.

Rationale

Issue I. For estate tax purposes, fair market value is determined by Regulations Section 20.2031-1(b)'s willing buyer-willing seller concept. The concept has been accepted by courts as the basis for estate tax as it was in *Cartwright.* As indicated in Rev. Rul. 59–60 the valuation process must weigh all relevant factors with the use of common sense.

Section 2031(b) of the Code indicates that the value of unlisted stock should be determined by comparative analysis of the publicly traded stock of similar companies and other relevant factors. Rev. Rul. 59–60 states that earnings are generally the primary consideration in the valuation of an operating company. However, relevant factors, such as a 100 percent interest with a liquidating value in excess of the earnings based value, may override other valuation factors. The reasonable willing buyer-willing seller concept would require such a conclusion.

Issue II. The willing buyer-willing seller concept of Section 20.2031(b) is a factual matter. Section 20.2031(b) and Revenue Ruling 59–60 indicate that value of unlisted or closely held stock should be determined by comparison to publicly traded stocks and consideration of all other valuation factors.

One factor to consider is the lack of a public market for the closely held stock. To compensate for the lack of marketability of a closely held stock company a discount factor may be applied to the value of the company derived from analysis of publicly traded companies.

The size of the discount (if any) is a factual determination. However, a premium is generally given when the interest to be valued is a controlling interest and conveys either the power to operate or liquidate the corporation.

Issue III. In light of Regulation Sections 20.2031-2(f) and 20.2042-1(C)(b), and the *Huntsman* case the treatment of insurance proceeds, paid to a corporation on the death of its sole shareholder, must be considered in valuing the stock of the corporation and should not be merely added to the value of the corporation without the proceeds. If there is an apparent business purpose for the proceeds due to the shareholder's death, then the proceeds may be discounted. Conversely, if the shareholder's death will have a negligible effect on the company's operations, the proceeds will be discounted only for the fact that they are an account receivable.

Conclusion

Issue 1. Although earnings are generally given primary consideration in the valuation of an operating company, the willing buyer-willing seller test may require that liquidating value be given primary consideration to an operating company if its liquidated value is considerably greater than its earning-based value.

Issue 2. There is no statutory or regulatory authority for a discount for lack of marketability where a majority or 100 percent interest is involved. Discounts for lack of marketability is a factual question, which courts determined on a case-by-case basis to compensate for the lack of a market for the stock, whose value is determined by comparison with publicly traded companies in the same or similar line of business. A premium is generally given for a majority block of stock which involves control of management and operations.

Issue 3. Corporate held insurance proceeds should be treated as a nonoperating asset in valuing the corporation. The discount, if any, applied to the proceeds in valuing the company is a factual question.

NATIONAL OFFICE TECHNICAL ADVICE MEMORANDUM
[Code Sec. 2512]

Valuation of gift; Closely held stock; Discounts to reflect minority interests.— CCH.

Issue

Whether discounts reflecting minority interests should be employed in determining the fair market values of simultaneous gifts of 33 1/3 percent of the stock in a closely held corporation to three separate trusts for the benefit of each of the donor's children.

Facts

Donor, *A*, owned all of the outstanding shares of stock in company *X*, the sole asset of which is a parcel of real estate. On December 30, 1976, *A* made simultaneous gifts of 33 1/3 percent of the stock in *X* to three trusts, one for the benefit of each of his three children. The trustees of each trust are a bank and *A*'s wife. The trustees have the power to sell and liquidate.

At the time of the gifts, there were no agreements among the trustees with respect to the voting or disposition of the corporate shares. There were no corporate by-laws or other instruments restricting the voting or disposition of corporate shares by any shareholder. There were no negotiations under way for the disposition of the corporation's assets or the disposition of the shares in question before or subsequent to the date of the gifts. The corporation still owns the assets in question and the trust still own the corporate shares.

Law

Section 2501(a)(1) of the Internal Revenue Code of 1954 provides that a tax is imposed for each calendar quarter on the transfer of property by gift during such calendar quarter by any resident or nonresident. Section 2512(a) provides that the value of the property at the date of the gift shall be considered the amount of the gift.

Section 25.2512-1 of the Gift Tax Regulations defines the value of property as the price at which such property would change hands between a willing buyer and willing seller, neither being under compulsion to buy or sell, and both having reasonable knowledge of relevant facts (the well-established definition of fair market value). The Regulations provide that the value of a particular kind of property is not the price that a forced sale of the property would produce. Nor is the fair market value of an item of property the sale price in a market other than that in which such item is most commonly sold to the public, taking into account the location of the item wherever appropriate, and that all relevant facts and elements of value as of the time of the gift shall be considered.

Section 25.2512-2(a) of the Gift Tax Regulations provides that the value of stocks and bonds is the fair market value per share or bond on the date of the gift. Section 25.2512-2(e) of the Regulations provides that where the donor can show that the block of stock to be valued, with reference to each separate gift, is so large in relation to the actual sales on the existing market that it could not be liquidated in a reasonable time without depressing the market, the price at which the block would be sold outside the usual market, as through an underwriter, may be a more accurate indication of value than market quotations. Section 25.2512(f) of the Regulations provides that the degree of control of the business represented by the block of stock to be valued and the values of securities of corporations engaged in the same or similar lines of business which are listed on a stock exchange are among the factors to be considered in valuing stock where there are no sales prices or bona fide bid and ask prices.

In *Estate of Sanford* v. *Commissioner,* 308 U.S. 39 (1939), the court stated that an important, if not the main purpose of the gift tax was to prevent or compensate for avoidance of death taxes by taxing the gifts of property inter vivos which but for gifts would be subject in its original or converted form to the tax laid upon transfers at death; that one purpose of the gift tax was to prevent or compensate for the loss of surtax income where large estates are split up by gifts to numerous donees; and that the gift tax was supplementary to the estate tax and that the two are pari materia and must be construed together.

In *Helvering* v. *Hutchings,* 312 U.S. 393 (1941), the court held that where a donor conveyed property in trust for the benefit of numerous beneficiaries he was entitled to separate exemptions or exclusions of $5,000 for each beneficiary.

In *Richardson* v. *Commissioner,* 2 T.C.M. 1039 (1943), *aff'd.* 151 F. 2nd 102 (2 cir. 1945) *cert denied* 326 US 796 (1946), the issue was the value of five gifts of stock totalling 5,100 shares (5.1 percent of the 100,000 shares issued and outstanding) to the donor's children. Stock in the corporation was owned by petitioner, his brother, and their families. Petitioner contended for a minority discount and argued that no one except a bargain hunter would want to buy a minority stock interest in a family holding corporation, and then only for the purpose of realizing its assets upon liquidation, which would have entailed heavy taxes.

The response of the Tax Court to the petitioner's contention was as follows:

> *If the arguments of petitioner were to prevail any cohesive family owning securities having a market value readily ascertainable from trading on the open public market could organize a family holding corporation, transfer to such a corporation the securities which it owns, and then deal with the stock of the family corporation on the basis that it has by reason of petitioner's arguments a market value of only approximately half of the market value of the securities owned by such a corporation, thus cutting in two gift taxes and estate taxes which would otherwise be payable on the transfer of the securities themselves. We cannot agree. Closely held stock of a family holding company which was never sold on the open market and was never intended by the organizers of the corporation to be sold, but was intended to be held by members of the family to evidence their respective beneficial interests in securities which were bought and sold by the corporation and which were dealt in on the open market, can only be valued in any real or practiced way by primarily considering the value of the securities owned by the corporation. Any other approach would, in our opinion, be futile.*

The court determined the value of the corporate stock to be $98.08 per share, a pro rata share of the market value of the corporation's assets on the date of the gifts. The value of the gifted stock was found to be not less than $95.509 per share, the value contended by the respondent.

In affirming the Tax Court decision, the Second Circuit's rationale offered by Judge Hincks was as follows:

> *To me, at least, the findings and opinion when read together strongly suggest that the valuation adopted was based upon some*

such theory as was enunciated by the respondent's experts whereby the controlling criterion of value for stock such as this was taken to be not its fair market value as provided in the applicable regulations of the Treasury Department but rather some notion of "intrinsic value." If so, the holding was erroneous. . . .

Feeling that there is substantial doubt as to whether the conclusion is based upon proper standards, I should favor a remand so that the Tax Court might have opportunity to correct the error if one was made or to remove the doubt which exists as to the standard which was actually applied. . . . My brothers, however, feel that the finding that the "fair market value" was not less than $95.509 per share sufficiently attests the use of proper standard and this court should affirm the valuation as made.

In *Whittemore* v. *Fitzpatrick*, 127 F. Supp. 710 (D.C. Conn. 1954) the issue was the value of 600 shares of stock of a family owned corporation transferred in trust for the benefit of the donor's three sons. Prior to the transfer of 600 shares, 200 for the benefit of each son, the donor owned the 820 shares of stock of the corporation issued and outstanding. The court relied on *Hutchings* to find that three gifts were made. Section 1005 of the Internal Revenue Code of 1939 was interpreted to mean that each gift was to be valued separately. The court then found the value of each block of 200 shares of stock on the basis of prices unrelated investors would pay for minority interests in the company. The court found irrelevant the defendant's argument that plaintiff would not be a willing seller at a price such an unrelated buyer would be willing to pay for the stock. The court noted that if the test for fair market value is to be used, it is necessary to assume a willing seller at a price a willing buyer would pay. This conclusion seems to differ with that of the Tax Court in *Mundy* v. *Commissioner*, T.C.M. 1976-395 in which the court noted that the willing seller-willing buyer concept is not satisfied by establishing only one-half of the equation.

In *Hamm* v. *Commissioner*, T.C.M. 1961-347, *aff'd* 325 F. 2d 934 (8 Cir. 1963), the issue was the valuation of stock in a closely held corporation. The court found the fair market value of underlying net assets attributable to the 1,000 shares of common stock issued and outstanding to be $11,684.96 per share, and the value of 263⅓ shares of gifted stock to be not less than $8,506.40 per share, the value contended by the Commissioner.

In affirming the Tax Court decision, the 8th Circuit stated that "the Tax Court's determination here, as a practical matter, certainly equates with a finding that the value of the stock was the stated figure and not ungently hints that the taxpayers might well consider themselves fortunate that it was not higher." The court also noted that an identical finding was upheld in *Richardson*, although one judge expressed doubt about the actual standard employed in the case.

In addressing the minority interest issue, the court commented as follows:

> *Here the taxpayers assert that if the Tax Court made any finding of market value of United Common it was one which related only to the value of all the common and was not a determination as to the minority interests involved. There is no merit in this contention. The court's ultimate finding was as to the fair market value of 263⅓ shares of common capital stock of United Properties, Inc. . . . If, in view of the overall complete ownership of the common by the Hamm family, this minority interest point has any real validity, the foregoing convincingly demonstrates the minority interest aspect was considered by the court and that its determination was made as to that specific interest.*

In *Blanchard* v. *Commissioner*, 291 F. Supp. 348, (S.D. Iowa 1968) the issue was the value of six gifts of 76⅓ shares of stock in a closely held company. The Blanchard family owned 1,048 shares or 52.4 percent of the 2,000 shares outstanding. The gifted stock and other stock owned by the Blanchard family was sold within three weeks after the date of the gifts for more than double the per share price subsequently paid the minority stockholders for their stock by the acquiring entity. Negotiations for sale of the Blanchard stock were conducted prior to the date of the gifts. The court found the value of the gifted stock to be the value for which the Blanchard family sold their stock.

In responding to the taxpayer's contention that each gift of 76⅓ shares of stock be valued as a minority interest, the court considered *Whittemore* but found its reasoning not sufficient for the *Blanchard* case. The court further stated that application of the rule that minority interests are worth less per share would be quite strained in this case because it would ignore the realities of the situation, and that so long as the gifted stock was controlled by the family, it has to be valued as a majority interest. The court cited *Hamm* and noted the appeals court's expression of doubt as to the validity of valuing a portion of family stock as a minority interest when the controlling interest was owned by the family.

In *Driver* v. *United States*, 76-2 U.S.T.C. 13155, the issue was the value of gifts totalling 5,712 shares of stock in a closely held company on December 31, 1968, at which time there were 13,600 shares issued and outstanding. The values of identical gifts of 5,712 shares of stock by the same donee on January 2, 1969, were not at issue. The court distinguished *Whittemore* and *Blanchard* and looked to form over substance to find that the gifts made on December 31, 1968, and those made on January 2, 1969, effected transfer of a majority interest. The court denied a minority interest discount on the basis that it would simply transcend form over substance. The distribution of corporate stock upon completion of gifts in 1968 and 1969 was as follows:

Donor	2,180*
Donor's sister	1,834
Donor's nephew	3,262
Donor's nephew's wife	408
Donor's nephew's 3 children	5,508
Employee of company	204
Employee's wife	204

*The court noted that 5,712 shares were gifted on both dates, however, the breakdown by donee totals 5,710 shares.

In *Rufus F. Turner* v. *Commissioner*, T.C. Memo. 1964-161, *aff'd* 343 F. 2d 150 (4th Cir. 1965) the issue was the fair market value for income tax purposes of 200 shares of stock in a closely held company. In responding to the argument that the stock be valued as a minority interest the Tax Court commented as follows:

> *A minority interest in a family owned business may be entitled to some discount in evaluation. . . In the present case, however, an outsider is not acquiring a minority interest in a family corporation, rather the owner of the largest block of shares is increasing his holding and diluting the value of other interests. Surely he cannot complain that this block is worthless to him, when if anything, it would seem to be worth more.*

In affirming the Tax Court, the 4th Circuit concluded as follows:

> *Our review of the record and a consideration of the briefs and oral arguments convince us that the determination is well supported and should not be disturbed for we are far from being prepared to say that it is clearly erroneous.*

The Tax Reform Act of 1976, P. L. 94-455, 1976-3 C.B. (Vol. 1) made substantial revisions to the estate and gift tax law. The House Report, H.R. Rep. No. 94-1380, 94th Cong. 2d Sess. 11 (1976), 1976-3 C.B. (Vol. 3) 745, discusses the reasons for the change as follows:

> *Under present law, there is a substantial disparity of treatment between the taxation of transfers during life and transfers at death. In general there are three factors which provide a decided preference for lifetime transfers. First, the gift tax rates are set at three-fourths of the estate tax rates at each corresponding rate bracket. Second, lifetime transfers are not taken into account for estate tax purposes and the estate remaining at death is subject to tax under a separate rate schedule starting at the lowest rates. Thus even if the rates were identical, separate rate schedules would provide a preference for making*

both lifetime and deathtime transfers rather than having the total transfer subject to one tax. Third, the gift taxes are not generally taken into account for either transfer tax base. In the case of a gift, the tax base does not include the gift tax but the payment of the tax results in a decrease in the value of the estate retained by the donor. However, if the property were retained until death, the tax base includes the full value of the property, even though a portion is likely to be required to satisfy estate taxes. Thus, even if the applicable transfer rates were the same, the net amount transferred to a beneficiary from a given pre-tax amount of property would be greater for a lifetime transfer solely because of the difference in the tax bases.

As a matter of equity, your committee believes the tax burden imposed on transfers of the same amount of wealth should be substantially the same whether the transfers are made both during life and at death, or are made only upon death. . . .

Your committee believes that it is desirable to reduce the disparity of treatment between lifetime and deathtime transfers through the adoption of a single unified estate and gift tax rate schedule providing progressive rates based on cumulative lifetime and deathtime transfers. However, your committee is retaining part of the incentives for lifetime transfers. Thus, the provisions of present law under which the amount of the gift tax is not included or "grossed up" in the transfer tax base are continued except in the case of gifts made within three years of date of death. In addition, the annual gift tax exclusion of $3,000 per donee is continued. The advantage of avoiding a transfer tax on the appreciation which might accrue between the time of a gift and the donor's death represents a further incentive for lifetime transfers.

Rationale

Interests in family owned corporations, and joint family interests in property in general represent a substantial portion of inter vivos and testamentary transfers. The issue of whether transfer by gift of fractional interests in such property between family members should be valued independent of the family relationship has been a continuous source of controversy since enactment of gift tax laws. A basic question is whether Congress intended that transfer of a given amount of wealth during lifetime, at death, or both should result in a materially different tax base. Where intra-family transfers of fractional interests in property are discounted to reflect minority interests, the tax base is substantially less than would be the case if similar distributions of the same property were made at death.

In *Sanford,* the court concluded that the gift tax was supplementary to the estate tax and that the two must be construed together. The court further noted that one purpose of the gift was to prevent the loss of income where large estates are split up by gifts to numerous donees.

In enacting the unified transfer tax provisions of Section 2001 of the Code, Congress codified the requirement that the gift tax and estate tax provisions be construed together. The committee report (H.R. 94-1380) set forth the reasons for changes in the estate and gift tax laws enacted as part of the Tax Reform Act of 1976, and compared the advantages of lifetime transfers over deathtime transfers before and after the revisions were made.

The committee stated, that as a matter of equity, the tax burden imposed on transfers of the same amount of wealth should be substantially the same whether the transfers are made during lifetime, at death, or both. The committee identified the lower gift tax rates, the fact that lifetime gifts were not taken into account for estate tax base purposes, and the exclusion of gift taxes paid from both the lifetime and deathtime transfer base as the three general factors providing a decided preference for lifetime giving under existing law.

The committee identified the incentives for lifetime transfers retained in revised gift tax law as: the exclusion of gift taxes paid from the transfer tax base, the annual exclusion of $3,000 per donee, and the appreciation in value that may accrue between the date of a gift and the donor's death. The committee did not recognize the diminution in wealth resulting from fractional interest transfers among family members during lifetime as a factor creating a preference for lifetime transfers under law existing before or after the Tax Reform Act of 1976. Discounting intra-family transfers of interests in family controlled businesses to reflect minority interests will not permit achievement of the committee's objective of equal tax bases for lifetime or deathtime transfers of the same amounts of wealth.

Section 2512(a) of the Code provides the value of property on the date of the gift shall be considered the amount of the gift.

Section 25.2512-1 of the Regulations defines fair market value in terms of well-established willing seller-willing buyer concepts, provides that the value of property is determined in the market in which it is most commonly sold, and provides that all relevant facts and elements of value at the time of the gift be considered in valuing the gift. Section 25.2512-2(e) provides for blockage adjustments for publicly traded stocks. Section 25.2512-2(f) provides that the degree of control represented by the block of stock to be valued is a factor to be considered in valuing the stock.

The market in which stock in family controlled corporations is normally sold consists of other family members, and unrelated parties seeking control. Valuation concepts based on blockage theories apply to minority stock interests in corporations whose stock is publicly traded, and are not applicable to stock in closely held family controlled corporations. Family control is a significant element of value to family stockholders as evidenced in *Blanchard*. Family members normally benefit in a similar manner when a closely held family controlled corporation goes public.

The requirement that gift and estate tax laws be construed together (*Sanford*), the expression of legislative intent in the House Committee Report, and the regulatory provisions relating to valuation factors to be considered and the market in which sales transactions are assumed to occur seem to require consideration of intra-family relationships when valuing intra-family transfers of property by gift. Valuation of property transferred by gift among family members on the basis of transfers of similar property between unrelated parties under competitive market conditions does not conform to these requirements.

In most cases, family shareholders in closely held family controlled corporations realize a control element of value from their interests when control of the corporation is sold to unrelated parties, even though their interests may not be sufficient to significantly influence the operation, sale, or liquidation of the company. When such interests are transferred to other family members, the control element of value is also transferred.

When an interest in family controlled property is transferred from a family member to an unrelated party, the control element of value attaches to the interests retained by other family members unless the interest transferred to the unrelated party is itself a controlling interest. In this case, the interest would be valued on the basis of assumed competitive market conditions.

The courts have not been consistent in resolving valuation issues involving intra-family transfers. In *Whittemore,* the court interpreted the law and Regulations to mean that an intra-family transfer of less than a controlling interest in a closely held corporation was to be valued independent of the family relationship. The court assumed a sale in a competitive market between unrelated buyer and seller.

Richardson, Hamm, Turner, Blanchard, and *Driver* reflect a broader interpretation of the law and Regulations in that the reality of family relationships and other special circumstances affecting property fair market values are explicitly or implicitly recognized. This broader interpretation is consistent with the holding in *Sanford* that gift and estate tax laws must be construed together, and with the House Committee's indication that the law provides equal tax bases for lifetime or deathtime transfers of the same amount of wealth.

Conclusion

In determining the fair market values of gifts of $33^{1/3}$ percent of the stock in corporation X by A to each of his three children on December 30, 1976, no discounts should be employed to reflect minority interests in the corporation.

Appendix

C

Table of Significant Ratios

Ratio	Formula	Significance
I. *Liquidity Ratios*		
1. Current ratio	$\dfrac{\text{current assets}}{\text{current liabilities}}$	The extent that short-term debt is covered by assets converted within the same time period.
2. Quick or acid test ratio	$\dfrac{\text{current assets} - \text{inventory}}{\text{current liabilities}}$	The extent that short-term debt is covered by liquid assets.
3. Basic defensive interval	$\dfrac{\text{cash} + \text{marketable securities} + \text{accounts receivable}}{\left(\dfrac{\text{cost of goods sold} + \text{selling \& administrative expenses}}{360}\right)}$	Number of days a firm can operate without having to resort to revenue from sales.

Ratio	Formula	Significance
II. *Leverage Ratios*		
1. Debt ratio	$\dfrac{\text{total debt}}{\text{total assets}}$	Percentage of funds provided for by creditors.
2. Times interest earned (common stock)	$\dfrac{\text{earnings before interest and taxes}}{\text{interest expense}}$	The capability of a firm to pay its interest obligations.
3. Times interest earned (preferred stock)	$\dfrac{\text{earnings before interest and taxes}}{\text{interest expense} + \left(\dfrac{\text{preferred dividends}}{1\text{-tax rate}}\right)}$	The capability of a firm to pay its interest obligation and dividends to preferred shareholders.

Ratio	Formula	Significance
III. *Activity Ratios*		
1. Inventory turnover	$\dfrac{\text{net sales}}{\text{year-end inventory}}$	The number of times inventory is replenished during the period.
2. Average collection period	$\dfrac{\text{accounts receivable}}{\left(\dfrac{\text{net sales}}{360}\right)}$	The period of time between a sale and collection of cash.
3. Accounts receivable turnover	$\dfrac{\text{net sales}}{\text{accounts receivable}}$	The number of times receivables are being paid in relation to sales.
4. Fixed asset turnover	$\dfrac{\text{net sales}}{\text{net fixed assets}}$	Gross revenue rate of return on the fixed assets.
5. Total asset turnover	$\dfrac{\text{net sales}}{\text{total assets}}$	Gross revenue rate of return on all assets held by a firm.

Ratio	Formula	Significance
IV. *Profitability Ratios*		
1. Income from sales	$\dfrac{\text{net sales} - \text{costs of goods sold}}{\text{net sales}}$	Percentage of revenue contributed toward satisfaction of firm expenditures.
2. Profit margin on sales	$\dfrac{\text{net profits after taxes}}{\text{net sales}}$	Percentage of net income from sales.
3. Return on total assets	$\dfrac{\text{net profits after taxes}}{\text{total assets}}$	Rate of return on total firm investment.
4. Return on common equity	$\dfrac{\text{earnings available for common stockholders}}{\text{common shareholder equity} + \text{unrestricted retained earnings}}$	Rate of return on shareholder investment.

Ratio	Formula	Significance
V. Market-Oriented Ratios		
1. Book value per share (common)	$\dfrac{\text{total assets} - (\text{short-term and long-term debt} + \text{preferred equity})}{\text{number of common shares outstanding}}$	Total liquidated value of a firm based on historical cost.
2. Earnings per share (common)	$\dfrac{\text{earnings available for common shareholder}}{\text{number of common shares outstanding}}$	Earnings of a firm for each share of common stock.
3. Earnings per share (preferred)	$\dfrac{\text{earnings available for preferred shareholders}}{\text{number of preferred shares outstanding}}$	Earnings of a firm for each share of preferred stock.
4. Dividend payout	$\dfrac{\text{cash dividend paid per share}}{\text{earning per share}}$	The amount of dividends paid in relation to how much each share earned.

Appendix

D

Cases Using
Comparative Corporate Analysis

Case	Citation	Court	Year	Comparable Attributes and/or Ratios Used or Considered
Staley v. Commissioner	41 B.T.A. 752	Tax Court	1940	1. Price : net worth 2. Price : average yearly earnings
Richardson v. Commissioner	151 F.2d 102 (45-2 USTC 10,225)	Court of Appeals	1945	1. Actual price that could be obtained for stock v. price based on asset value (used in lower court)
Daily v. Commissioner	1947 P-H TC Memo ¶47,025	Tax Court	1947	1. Average yearly earnings 2. Price : average share earnings Court: Book values and dividend record should have been considered.
Spitzer v. Commissioner	6 TCM 332	Tax Court	1947	1. Price : book value 2. Price : earnings 3. Price : dividends
Cochran v. Commissioner	1948 P-H TC Memo ¶48,094	Tax Court	1948	Per share and total values for: 1. Sales 2. Earnings 3. Net worth 4. Dividends Court: Considered comparable approach sound, especially since the companies chosen were so closely comparable.

Case	Citation	Court	Year	Comparable Attributes and/or Ratios Used or Considered
Miller v. Commissioner	1953 P-H TC Memo ¶53,155	Tax Court	1953	1. Sales : invested capital 2. Net income before taxes: sales 3. Earnings on invested capital 4. Earnings : price 5. Dividend : yield Court: Considered only the market value of competing and comparable companies along with many other factors.
Metcalf v. Commissioner	1954 P-H TC Memo ¶54,003	Tax Court	1953	Not given, although comparative company analysis was used by petitioner's witnesses.
Harrison v. Commissioner	1958 P-H TC Memo ¶58,157	Tax Court	1958	Court: Did not accept comparable company approach as set forth by witnesses for the petitioner. Evidence is not stated in the record.
Levenson v. Commissioner	282 F.2d 581 6 AFTR 2d 6153	Court of Appeals	1960	Comparable company was not comparable.
Worthen v. United States	192- F.Supp 727 7 AFTR 2d 1801	District Court	1961	1. Percentage return on invested capital 2. Price : earnings ratio 3. Dividend yield 4. Amount of investments in United States securities 5. Price : book value

Case	Citation	Court	Year	Comparable Attributes and/or Ratios Used or Considered
Central Trust Co. v. U.S.	305 F.2d 393 (10 AFTR 2nd. 6203)	Court of Claims	1962	Court: Said 3 ratios should be considered as most significant. 1. Price : earnings 2. Price : dividends 3. Price : book value Court: Significant weight given to comparative corporate technique. 4. Market price : earnings paid out 5. Market price : return on invested capital 6. Profits : net worth 7. Dividends : net worth 8. Market value : net worth
Louis v. United States aff'd. by:	17 AFTR 2d 1433 369 F.2d 263 18 AFTR 2d 6318	District Court Seventh Cricuit	1965 1966	1. Market price 2. Testimony is not presented 3. There was a representative sale
Bardahl v. Commissioner	1965 P-H TC Memo ¶65,200	Tax Court	1965	1. Price : earnings
Jungbluth v. United States aff'd by:	253 F.Supp 338 17 AFTR 2d 1371 371 F.2d 416 18 AFTR 2d 6321	District Court Seventh Circuit	1966 1966	1. Price : book value 2. Dividend yield 3. Price : earnings ratio Court: Validity of comparison is diminished when only one com-

Case	Citation	Court	Year	Comparable Attributes and/or Ratios Used or Considered
				pany is used for comparison (as was done by one of the witnesses for plaintiff).
Russell v. United States	260 F.Supp 493 18 AFTR 2d 6278	District Court	1966	1. Plaintiff witness's testimony with respect to comparable companies was deemed meaningless by the court, as witness chose "giants" of the industry to be comparable. 2. Government expert also used comparative method — and Court agreed with his testimony. Factors used not set forth.
Yeazel v. Coyle	21 AFTR 2d 1681	District Court	1968	1. Market price
Righter v. United States	439 F.2d 1204 27 AFTR 2d 71-1691	Court of Claims	1971	1. Price : earnings 2. Dividend yield 3. Price : book value Court: Did not find that there were any comparable companies, thus little weight accorded.
Blass v. United States	344 F.Supp 669 29 AFTR 2d 72-1252	District Court	1972	Court found no justification for the government's relying solely on the comparable company approach. 1. Earnings : book value

Case	Citation	Court	Year	Comparable Attributes and/or Ratios Used or Considered
Korslin v. United States	31 AFTR 2d 73-1390	District Court	1973	2. Price : book value Price : earnings ratio Both parties used same approach.
Pinkerton v. Commissioner	1974 P-H TC Memo ¶74,071	Tax Court	1974	1. Price : earnings ratio 2. 110 percent of gross income 3. Dividend yield 4. Price : net tangible asset
Thalheimer v. Commissioner	1974 P-H TC Memo ¶74,203 Remanded 76-1 USTC 13,139 cert. denied 79 S. CO. 317 (1076).	Tax Court	1974	1. Price : earnings ratio 2. Price : cash flow 3. Price : book value
Tallichet v. Commissioner	1974 P-H TC Memo ¶74,255	Tax Court	1974	1. Price : earnings ratio Companies chosen were not comparable.
Hetson v. United States	36 AFTR 2d 75-6505	Court of Claims	1975	1. Price : earnings ratio
Hall v. Commissioner	1975 P-H TC Memo ¶75,141	Tax Court	1975	1. Price : earnings ratio 2. Dividend yield 3. Dividend payout ratio 4. Relationship of percentage earned on average com-

Case	Citation	Court	Year	Comparable Attributes and/or Ratios Used or Considered
				mon stock equity and ratio of market price to book value 5. Price : cash flow
Salsbury v. Commissioner	1975 P-H TC Memo ¶75,333	Tax Court	1975	1. Price : earnings ratio Court: Companies were not truly comparable.
Stoddard v. Commissioner	1975 P-H TC Memo ¶75,207	Tax Court	1975	1. Price : earnings ratio 2. Dividend yield 3. Price : book value 4. Several specialized formulas were used—since stock of a newspaper was at issue.
Huntsman v. Commissioner	66 TC 861	Tax Court	1976	1. Price : earnings ratio
Clarke v. Commissioner	1976 P-H TC Memo ¶76,328	Tax Court	1976	1. Price : book value 2. Earnings : book value Court: Petitioner's witnesses found no comparable companies. Respondent's witness used comparable companies method not comparable.
White v. Commissioner	1976 P-H TC Memo ¶76,382	Tax Court	1976	1. Price : earnings ratio 2. Price : net worth

Case	Citation	Court	Year	Comparable Attributes and/or Ratios Used or Considered
Jenner v. Commissioner	1977 P-H TC Memo ¶77,054 Reversed on other issue 577 F.2d 1100 (1978) (78-2 USTC 13,251)	Tax Court	1977	Court: Comparative approach not useful in this case since the companies were substantially larger.
Tully v. United States	41 AFTR 2d 78-1477	Court of Claims	1978	1. Dividend yield 2. Price as a percentage discount from net asset value. Court: Petitioner's second witness, only one who used comparable approach, was most persuasive and convincing. 1. Price : earnings ratio 2. Price : book value 3. Dividend yield
Newcomer v. United States	447 F.Supp 1368 (42 AFTR 2d 78-6403)	District Court	1978	1. Price : earnings ratio 2. Earnings per share 3. Dividend per share 4. Price : book value 5. Earnings : book value
Koffler v. Commissioner	1978 P-H TC Memo ¶78,159	Tax Court	1978	Common stock: 1. Price : earnings ratio 2. Price : cash flow 3. Market value : book value 4. Total invested capital "technique" : relationship

Case	Citation	Court	Year	Comparable Attributes and/or Ratios Used or Considered
				of total market value of all long-term debt, preferred stock and common stocks to: 1) book value, 2) total adjusted earnings, 3) total earnings paid out. With respect to preferred stock, yield was considered.
Goodrich v. Commissioner	1978 P-H TC Memo ¶78,248	Tax Court	1978	1. Yields of high-grade industrial bonds 2. Price : earnings 3. Price : book value 4. Price : dividends paid Note: This case considered 5 separate stocks. Comparable approach not used for all of them.
Meijer v. Commissioner	1979 P-H TC Memo ¶79,344	Tax Court	1979	1. Comparable company's stocks were in declining trend 2. Leveraging ratio 3. Working capital : book value Comparable approach gives little weight.

Appendix

E

Transfer Tax Table

	(A)	(B)	(C)
			Tax rate
			on excess
Amount subject to tax		Tax on	above amont
	but not	amount in	in Column A
exceeding	exceeding	Column A	(Percent)
$	10,000		18
10,000	20,000	1,800	20
20,000	40,000	3,800	22
40,000	60,000	8,200	24
60,000	80,000	13,000	26
80,000	100,000	18,200	28
100,000	150,000	23,800	30
150,000	250,000	38,800	32
250,000	500,000	70,800	34
500,000	750,000	155,800	37
750,000	1,000,000	248,300	39
1,000,000	1,250,000	345,800	41
1,250,000	1,500,000	448,300	43
1,500,000	2,000,000	555,800	45
2,000,000	2,500,000	780,800	49
2,500,000	3,000,000	1,025,800	53
3,000,000	3,500,000	1,290,800	57
3,500,000	4,000,000	1,575,800	61
4,000,000	4,500,000	1,880,800	65
4,500,000	5,000,000	2,205,800	69
5,000,000		2,550,800	70

Appendix

F

Valuation Information Checklist*

---

*Reprinted with permission from Peat, Marwick, Mitchell & Co. Adapted from Herbert S. Adler, "So You Want to Acquire a Company," *Management Focus,* Vol. 27, No. 3, May/June 1980, p. 36. Copyright ©️ 1980.

MISCELLANEOUS INFORMATION

- Exact business name
- Address
- Date and state of incorporation (if applicable)
- States in which the company is qualified or registered to do business
- Location of minute books, by-laws, certificate of incorporation (if applicable), and other company records
- Brief history of company
- Description of products and/or services
- Fiscal year
- Capitalization—owners' equity composition
- Rights of each class of stock and other securities or other specific ownership rights
- Owners' agreements and term thereof
- Names of owners and holdings (percentages, totals, etc.)
- Bank balances (including averages)
- Bank references
- Credit rating
- Names, addresses, and reputations of accountants
- Names, addresses, and reputations of attorneys
- Special permits, licenses, and agreements involving the company

PERSONNEL

- Directors and their affiliations
- Officer: For each position—duties, age, health, salary, service, experience, personal plans for the future, other interests (including time devoted thereto), and holdings
- Organization chart
- Employee contracts: Terms, expiration date(s)

- Number of employees in production, sales, administration, etc.
- Union contracts: Terms, expiration dates
- Strike record, labor morale, handling of labor relations
- Labor market
- Pension, profit sharing, insurance, stock bonus, deferred compensation, and severance plans
- Comparison with industry as to number of employees, hours per week, and wages rates for the past five years and for the past twelve months

OPERATIONS

- Description, including significant changes in past years:
  1. Capacity and percentage of utilization
  2. Production controls (scheduling and inventories)
  3. Shipping and receiving controls
  4. Accounting controls
- Principal suppliers and terms
- Distribution methods and terms (also, brokers or agents and compensation arrangements)
- Branch offices and their operations
- Subsidiaries, their operations and intercompany dealings
- Government contracts and subcontracts
- Seasonal factors
- Public and owner relations

SALES

- Description of market
- Number of customers and names of principal customers
- Gross and net sales for the past five years and for the past twelve months
  1. Penetration of market by product
  2. Possibilities of increase through existing lines and by diversification
- Sales comparison with the industry for the past five years and for the past twelve months
- Sales history, accounts receivable activity, customer continuity
- Sales correspondence
- Sales policies and method of compensation of sales personnel
- Pricing policies and fluctuations in the past five years

- Principal competitors
- Relative size in the industry
- Comparative advantages and disadvantages
- Significant lines produced in past years
- Nonrelated activities
- Advertising and other sales promotion programs
- Research program
- New developments
- Industry trends
- Current and future prospects
- Copies or summaries of significant supply and/or marketing contracts

EARNINGS AND DIVIDENDS

- Earnings record and budget for the past five years and the last twelve months, break-even point, gross profit margins, and reasons for variations, nonrecurring income, and expenses
- Earnings comparison with the industry for the past five years
- Dividend and earnings record for the past five years in total and per share
- Potential economics
- Current and future prospects
- Analysis of selling, general, and administrative expenses

PLANT FACILITIES

- Location
- Shipping facilities
- Real estate taxes
- Land
  1. Acreage
  2. Cost
  3. Assessed value
  4. Fair market value
- Buildings
  1. Description, including pictures, if available
  2. Age and condition
  3. Area
  4. Depreciation: Reserves, methods, rates, policies
  5. Assessed value

6. Fair market values (recent appraisals)
7. Fire insurance
- Title to realty and title policy
- Machinery and equipment
  1. Description
  2. Age, condition, efficiency, insurance coverage
  3. Depreciation: Reserves, methods, rates, policies
  4. Total acquisitions during the past five years
  5. Analysis of most recent additions
- Future plant, machinery, and equipment requirements
- Capitalization versus repair policies
- Capital expenditures and repairs for the past five years
- Percentage relationship of production costs and comparison with the industry
- Efficiency of operations
- Subcontracting done by others
- Certificates of necessity
- Facility contracts or leases
- Surplus or idle buildings or equipment

ASSETS

- Relationship of cash to current liabilities
- Age and number of accounts receivable (latest accounts receivable aging)
- Provision for bad debts
- Inventories for the past five years
  1. Relationship of inventories to current assets
  2. Location
  3. By-products
  4. Pricing methods
  5. Accounting procedures and practices
- Analysis of notes receivable
- Analysis of investments
- Subsidiaries
  1. Treatment on parent company's balance sheet
  2. Analysis (per checklist) of significant items
- Analysis of other assets
- Patents held

LIABILITIES

- Current federal and state tax status and tax payments for the past three years
- Commitments for new buildings, machinery, inventories
- Long-term loans outstanding and terms
- Debentures outstanding and terms
- Dividend and interest arrearages
- Leases: Location, areas, terms
- Insurance coverage, fidelity bonds, and amounts
- Pensions, profit sharing plans, and other employee related activities
- Contingent liabilities: Warranties, patent, etc.; infringements and loss contracts
- Litigation, claim, and assessment record and present status

FINANCIAL DATA

- Annual statements and audit reports for the past five years
- Tax returns for the past five years
- Reports to Securities and Exchange Commission (if applicable)
- Explanation of how consolidations, if any, were effected and separate statement for each company involved
- Chart of accounts
- Book, net quick, liquidating, and market values for the past five years
- Working capital for the past five years and normal requirements based on trade practices, credit terms to customers, consignments, finished inventory, and raw inventory
- Net working capital ratios for the past five years
- Net quick position for the past five years
- Annual depreciation compared with capital additions for the past five years
- Inventory turnover for the past five years
- Cash, inventory, and working capital requirements for the past five years
- Interest charges for the past five years
- Exchange, if any, on which the company's stock is traded
- Recent stock sales and prices paid

COMPARISON WITH COMPARABLE COMPANIES

The following ratios for the subject company should be compared with those of comparable companies for the past five years and, if data are available, by quarters for the current year:

- Price to earnings
- Price to book value
- Sales to accounts receivable
- Sales to inventories
- Sales to fixed assets
- Earnings to book value

PROJECTED FINANCIAL DATA

- Pro forma balance sheet
- Earnings forecast

Appendix

G

List of Sources to Consult

BOOKS

Bishop, John A. and Rosenbloom, Arthur H. *Federal Tax Valuation Digest.* Warren, Gorham & Lamont, New York, 1979.

Bittker, Boris I. and Eustice, James S. *Federal Income Taxation of Corporations and Shareholders.* Warren, Gorham & Lamont, New York, 1979.

Campbell, Ian R. *The Principles and Practice of Business Valuation.* Richard De Boo Ltd., Toronto, 1975.

Cooper, George. *A Voluntary Tax? New Perspectives on Sophisticated Estate Tax Avoidance.* Brookings Institution, Washington, D.C., 1979.

McCarthy, George D. and Healey, Robert E. *Valuing a Company.* Ronald Press Company, New York, 1971.

O'Neal, F. Hodge. *Close Corporations: Law and Practice,* 2nd ed. Callaghan & Company, Wilmette, Illinois, 1971.

Owens, George and Beach, Donald I. *Business and Securities Valuation.* Methuen Publications, Agincourt, Ontario, 1972.

Weston, J. Fred and Brigham, Eugene F. *Managerial Finance,* 5th ed. Dryden Press, Hinsdale, Illinois, 1975.

Willis, Arthur B. *Partnership Taxation,* 2nd ed. McGraw-Hill Book Company, New York, 1976.

ARTICLES

Abbin, "Gift, Estate and Income Tax Exposure from Recapitalizing Closely Held Companies," 10 *University of Miami Institute on Estate Planning* 120 (1976).

Abbin, "The Partnership Capital Freeze—An Alternative to Corporate Recapitalization," 13 *University of Miami Institute on Estate Planning* 1800 (1979).

Abrams, "Tax Planning for Agreements Disposing of a Shareholder's Closely Held Stock at Death," 57 *Georgetown L. J.* 1211 (1969).

Banks, "Legal Issues in Securities Valuation," 25 *Tax Executive* (1973).

Bell and Earls, "How to Reduce the Potential Estate Tax Bite on Stock in a Closely Held Corporation," 11 *Tax. for Accts.* 272 (1973).

Berall, "Recapitalizing Close Corporation May Be Planning Solution for Major Stockholder," 3 *Estate Planning* 96 (1976).

Braitman, "The Eye of the Beholder: A Fresh Look at Fair Market Value," 52 *Taxes* 269 (1974).

Brody and Berger, "Formulas May Be Used to Value Closely Held Businesses in Light of IRS Opposition," 4 *Estate Planning* 394 (1977).

Castleman, "The Use of Restrictive Agreements in Estate Tax Valuation of Farmlands and Other Properties," 64 *Kentucky Law Journal* 785 (1976).

Curtis and Moore, "Tax-Free Redemption of Stock Should Be Considered in Estate Plan of Owner of Close Corporation," 2 *Estate Planning* 32 (1974).

Dan, "An Updated Analysis of Tax Planning for Closely Held Corporations and Their Shareholders," 56 *Taxes* 897 (1978).

Dant, "Courts Increasing Amount of Discount for a Minority Interest in a Business," 43 *Journal of Taxation* 104 (1975).

Eber, "How to Establish Value for Close Corporation Stock That Will Withstand an IRS Audit," 4 *Estate Planning* 28 (1976).

Eder, "The CPA's Role in Appraising Closely Held Corporate Stock," 2 *Review of Tax. of Individuals* 25 (1978).

Englebrecht, "A Statistical Look at Tax Court Compromises in Estate and Gift Tax Valuation of Closely Held Stock," 55 *Taxes* 395 (1977).

Englebrecht, "Valuation of Closely Held Oil and Gas Corporations for Estate and Gift Tax Purposes," 25 *Oil and Gas Tax Quarterly* 273 (1977).

Englebrecht and Davison, "A Statistical Look at Tax Court Compromise in Estate and Gift Tax Valuation of Closely Held Stock," 55 *Taxes* 395 (1977).

Englebrecht and Lesson, "Valuation of Closely Held Stock," 31 *Tax Executive* 57 (1978).

Feld, "Current Techniques to Valuing Minority Stock Interests or Stock with Restrictions," 3 *Taxation for Lawyers* 244 (1975).

Feld, "The Implication of Minority Interest and Stock Restrictions in Valuing Closely Held Shares," 122 *Univ. Penn. Law Rev.* 934 (1974).

Fellows and Painter, "Valuing Close Corporations for Federal Wealth Transfer Taxes: A Statutory Solution to the Disappearing Wealth Syndrome," 30 *Stanford Law Review* 895 (1978).

Fitzgerald, "Estate Tax Implications of Close Corporate Stock Redemptions," 117 *Trusts of Estates* 245 (1978).

Gelman, "An Economist-Financial Analyst's Approach to Valuing Stock of a Closely-Held Company," 36 *J. Taxation* 353 (1972).

Graham, "Valuation of Stock on Closely Held Corporations: An Estate Planner's Dilemma," 30 *Chartered Life Underwriters Journal* No. 3, 36 (1976).

Greene, "Valuation Inclusion of Community Property in the Gross Estate: A New Approach," 15 *Houston Law Review* 93 (1977).

Greenwald, "Pricing the Stock of a Closely Held Corporation for Federal Estate Taxation," Part I—46 *New York State Bar Journal* 421; Part II—46 *New York State Bar Journal* 535 (1974).

Hartwig, "Valuing an Interest in a Closely Held Business for the Purpose of Buy-Sell Agreements and for Death Tax Purposes," 26 *Univ. of Southern Calif. Inst. on Fed. Tax.* 215 (1974).

Heath, "Valuation Factors and Techniques in Mergers and Acquisitions," *Financial Executive*, April 1972, p. 34.

Houston and Mounger, "Valuation of Shares in a Closely Held Corporation," 47 *Mississippi Law Journal* 715 (1976).

Jensen, "Stock Valuation Formulas for Estate and Gift Taxes," 117 *Trust & Estates* 238 (1978).

Johnson, "Buy-Out Agreements in Planning the Estate of a Stockholder-Employee of a Closely Held Corporation," 15th *Idaho State Tax Inst. Proceedings* 66 (1973).

Kahn, "Mandatory Buy-Out Agreements for Stock of Closely Held Corporations," 68 *Mich. L. Rev.* 1 (Nov. 1969).

Katten, "Valuing Securities Subject to Buy-Sell Agreements," 17 *National Public Acct.* 32 (1972).

Koehn, "Internal Revenue Code Section 2032A," 19 *South Texas Law Journal* 315 (1978).

Horner, "Issues and Problems in Valuing Closely Held Business Interests for Estate Tax Purposes, Especially Partnership Interests," 30 *N.Y.U. Inst. Fed. Tax.* 185 (1972).

Lamerson, "Factors That Will Substantiate the Valuation of a Closely Held Corporation," 34 *J. of Taxation* 226 (1971).

Lawinger, "Current Techniques for Reliably Valuing Close Corporation Stock for Estate and ESOT Purposes," 3 *Estate Planning* 32 (1975).

Lee, "Valuing Closely Held Stock for ESOP Purposes Is No Simple Matter," 1 *Pension & Profit-Sharing Tax Journal* 29 (Part 1); 1 *Pension & Profit-Sharing Tax Journal* 31 (Part 2) (1975).

Leimberg, "What to Look Out for in Setting a Value on Assets for Estate Tax Purposes," 9 *Tax. for Accountants* 108 (1972).

Liles, "A New Look at Personal Holding Company Problems: The New Rule of the 1964 Act," 24 *N.Y.U. Inst. on Fed. Tax* 863 (1966).

Litman, "Buy-Sell Agreements for a Closely-Held Corporation," 50 *Florida Bar Journal* 555 (1976).

Maher, "Application of Key Man Discount in the Valuation of Closely Held Businesses," 55 *Taxes* 377 (1977).

Maher, "Discounts for Lack of Marketability for Closely Held Business Interests," 54 *Taxes* 562 (1976).

Martin, "Factors the IRS and Courts Are Using Today in Valuing Closely-Held Shares," 36 *J. Taxation* 118 (1977).

Martin and Sandford, "Applying Fair Market Appraisal Techniques to Closely Held Preferred Stock," 56 *Taxes* 108 (1978).

Martin and Votta, "Accounting and Nonaccounting Factors in Valuing Stock of Closed Corporations," 42 *CPA Journal* 901 (1972).

Matsen, "Establishing the Price for Closely Held Business Buy-Sell Agreements," 5 *Journal of Corp. Tax.* 134 (1978).

Moroney, "Most Courts Overvalue Closely Held Stocks," 51 *Taxes* 144 (1973).

Moroney, "Why 25 Percent Discount for Nonmarketability in One Valuation, 100 Percent in Another?" 55 *Taxes* 316 (1977).

Morton, "Factors Used in Valuation of Closely Held Stock," 20 *National Public Accountant* No. 5, 12 (1975).

Moyer, "Analyzing the Factors that Control the Value of Shares of a Closely Held Corporation," 21 *Taxation for Accountants* 48 (1978).

O'Neal, "Restrictions on Transfer of Stock in Closely Held Corporations: Planning and Drafting," 65 *Harv. L. Rev.* 772 (1952).

Oshins and Lowther, "Stock of Closely Held Corporation Can Lessen Owners' Potential Tax Burden," 5 *Estate Planning* 156 (1978).

Parker, "Buy-Sell Agreements in a Closely Held Corporation," 23 *Tax Executive* 435 (1971).

Pedrick, "The Family Owned Corporation: Planning for the Good Life," 1973 *Law and the Social Order* 729 (1973).

Penner, "Lifetime Estate Planning for the Operation of a Closely Held Corporation," 34 *New York Inst. on Fed. Tax* 1537 (1976).

Pratt and Hugo, "Pricing a Company by the Discounted Future Earnings Method," *Mergers and Acquisitions,* Spring 1972, p. 8.

Index